Jews in the Notarial Culture

In this letter E, two Jewish merchants sell a gilded goblet to two Christians. A third Jew acts as notary for the transaction, a rare depiction of the *sōfer.* For a contract between persons of differing religio-ethnic backgrounds, the notary or scribe must be of the same religion as the seller or promiser. Detail from *In Excelsis Dei Thesauris (Feudal Customs of Aragon), Called "Vidal Mayor,"* folio 114r, compiled between 1247 and 1252 by Vidal de Canellas for King Jaume the Conquerer, of Aragon. Collection of the J. Paul Getty Museum, Los Angeles, California.

Jews in the Notarial Culture

Latinate Wills in Mediterranean Spain, 1250–1350

Robert I. Burns, S.J.

UNIVERSITY OF CALIFORNIA PRESS

Berkeley / Los Angeles / London

University of California Press
Berkeley and Los Angeles, California

University of California Press
London, England

Library of Congress Cataloging-in-Publication Data

Burns, Robert Ignatius.
Jews in the notarial culture : Latinate wills in Mediterranean Spain, 1250–1350 / Robert I. Burns.
p. cm.
Includes bibliographical references and index.
ISBN 0-520-20393-3 (alk. paper)
1. Wills—Spain—Aragon—History. 2. Jews—Legal status, laws, etc.—Spain—Aragon—History. 3. Law, Medieval. 4. Wills (Jewish law) I. Title.
KKT5341.64.B87 1996
346.46′55054′08992—dc20
[344.6550654089924] 95-49937
CIP

Printed in the United States of America

1 2 3 4 5 6 7 8 9

The paper used in this publication meets the minimum requirements of American National Standard for Information Sciences—Permanence of Paper for Printed Library Materials, ANSI Z39.48-1984 ∞

Contents

PREFACE vii

INTRODUCTION 1

1.
The World of the Wills 11

The Jews of the Realms of Aragon 12
Parallel Societies 17
Wills: Hebrew, Romance, Latinate 22

2.
Mechanisms: Notary and *Sōfer* 32

Muslim Scribes 33
The Notarial Culture 38
Jewish Scribes 43
Crossover: Jews in Christian Wills 49

3.
The Role of Kings and Courts 51

Equivalence for Hebrew Charters 51
Crown Testamentary Intervention 54
Larceny and Fraud 58
Young Mossé b. Samiel: Arbitration 65
A Will in Hebrew and Latin 68

4.
Wills: Palma, Perpignan, and Puigcerdá 73

Palma de Mallorca 74
Perpignan 78
Puigcerdá 95

5.
Women in Wills: Widows and Wives 100

The Widow Regina 101
Salamó Bedós and Wife Cobes 104
Astruga, Wife of Jucef Abraham 106
Gentil, Wife of Jacob Abraham Cohen 108
Reina: Widow in Valls 110
Wills and Women 113

6.
The Search 118

Late Fourteenth-Century Latinate Jewish Wills 119
Cognate Occitania 122
Geniza Wills 126
Total History 131

APPENDIX: UNPUBLISHED DOCUMENTS 141

NOTES 193

GLOSSARY OF LESS FAMILIAR TERMS 235

BIBLIOGRAPHY 243

INDEX 263

Preface

This book began as a hobby while I was researching an unrelated topic, the traces left in notarial registers by an obscure and almost undocumented Mendicant order called the Friars of the Sack. I was at the Arxiu Històric Comarcal of Puigcerdá, today a small town of some 5,000 inhabitants tucked into the Catalan Pyrenees, where many dozens of notarial codices reflect medieval life in the period 1250–1350. (The full collection of hundreds of registers continues into modern times, far beyond the period that held my interest.) The wills and codicils of the town's medieval Jews caught my attention and I began collecting them as occasion offered. This circumstance explains the prominence of Puigcerdá wills in the later chapters of this book and in the documentary appendix.[1] As I moved from archives to archives in the area of the old "Realms of Aragon," on the trail of the elusive Sacks, I kept an eye out for materials on Jewish wills. The central archives for the realms, the Arxiu de la Corona d'Aragó at Barcelona, had no such wills but did offer rich documentation about or around them; this reveals much about royal intrusion into Jewish testamentary affairs and something about the strange practice of drafting Latinate, Roman law wills for members of the various Jewish communities.

I have been guilty of large books all my life, but here I have committed only a small one. The dimensions of the topic itself have nothing to do with that choice. The topic is very big indeed and its implications deserve a large book. The kind of testament under study is hard to come by, and when ferreted out requires careful siting in the local context. A pioneer must travel light and expect a difficult job of clearing as well as a small first harvest. If this work alerts other researchers to the rarity and value of such wills, and if these scholars transcribe and contextualize every one they find, these treasures will accumulate until eventually the appropriate large book can be attempted.

Another factor animated this search, as in my previous work on the Muslim communities of medieval Europe. Jews were not a marginal aspect of medieval history, however marginal their community structure may appear within or parallel to the Christian structure. Jews formed an essential element of the whole, not only in their local autonomous as well as interactive existence but as an intrinsic and ubiquitous component of medieval Europe's *histoire totale*. As any teacher of medieval history knows, this integral role is not at all evident from our textbooks or courses. Even a small contribution such as this recovery of Latinate wills may help redress the balance.

This book is not meant for specialists alone but for medievalists at large; consequently, small points familiar to specialists are fully explained here. The work should also be accessible to the general reader and, as a very human story, it should be entertaining and beneficial. To facilitate the reader's task, a glossary of less familiar terms has been added to the text. Several of my doctoral students are exploring such parallel communities, either Jewish or Muslim, in these same realms of Aragon. One of the very best of these researchers, Dr. (and Rabbi) Leila Berner, has produced a focused reconstruction of one local society, "A Mediterranean Community: Barcelona's Jews under James the Conqueror," based on extensive archival labor. The work of another student, Dr. Larry Simon, incorporating archival research on Majorca's Jews, will be noted in chapter 4. Others among my students are incorporating their findings on the region's Jews into their dissertations. One hopes that the explorations of this small school of medievalists will join the growing body of contributions by other scholars on the Jews of the realms of Aragon (many of which works are cited below) to move steadily into mainstream historiography and curricula.

Though the title of each archives consulted is given in full in the text and in the list of abbreviations at the head of the appendix, the notes, and the bibliography, I have used my own abbreviations for each archives in the notes themselves and in document headings. The standard abbreviations, such as ACA for the crown archives, are familiar mostly to Hispanists, but not even to all of them. More indicative abbreviations, such as Arch. Crown, let a wider audience see immediately the origin of a cited manuscript and distinguish it easily from the more accessible published documents. Personnel at the major archives consulted were uniformly helpful. I owe special thanks to Rafael Conde Delgado de Molina, director of the Arxiu de la Corona d'Aragó, and to Jaume Riera i Sans, head of its chancery section. At the Arxiu Històric Comarcal de Puigcerdà, the archivist Salvador Galceran i Vigué proved supportive during my visits there; in subsequent visits over the years his successor and current archivist Sebastià Bosom i Isern has been even more patient and accommodating. At the Arxiu Capitular de la Catedral de Barcelona, the Reverend Josep Baucells i Reig has been unfailingly helpful, as was the Reverend Rafael Caldentey i Prohens in the Arxiu Capitular de la Catedral de Mallorca. The director Carmen Crespo Nogueira and the staff at the Archivo Histórico Nacional also deserve my thanks, as does the Reverend Josep Marquès i Planagumà at the Arxiu Diocesà de Girona. Since the testamentary project was a by-product of my larger project on the Friars of the Sack and since I did not chance to encounter any Jewish wills in pursuing those friars in notarial collections at places like Balaguer, Morella, and Tarragona, I shall postpone thanking the many archivists who facilitated my searches until, ready for publication, the Sacks come marching in.

Several scholars have kindly read this manuscript and offered valuable comments and encouragement: Professor David Abulafia of Cambridge University and Fellow of its Gonville and Caius College; Professor Robert Chazan, chair of the Skirball Department of Hebrew and Judaic Studies at New York University; Professor David N. Myers, my colleague in the Department of History at the University of California in Los Angeles; Professor Norman Roth of the Department of Hebrew and Semitic Studies at the University of Wisconsin in Madison; and Professor Joseph Shatzmiller, Smart Family Professor of Judaic Studies in the Department of History at Duke University. This does not relieve me of responsibility, of course, for infelicities and errors. I must also thank Frances Thomas for her generous typing, my research assistants Marta VanLandingham, Jennifer Green, and Rebecca Winer for proofing, typing, and other services, and William Fulco, S.J., of the University of Southern California and the University of Judaism for some help with the Hebrew. Above all, I am grateful to Professor Jill Webster, then director of the Medieval Centre at the University of Toronto, for being alert for Jewish wills as we worked together in various Catalan archives on a different project; this is especially true for our labors on sixty of the notarial codices at Puigcerdá.

A shorter preliminary abstract of this book was presented by invitation as a plenary address before the Twenty-Seventh International Congress on Medieval Studies at Western Michigan University on May 7, 1992. The research was supported by Faculty Senate grants from the University of California at Los Angeles.

UCLA
1996

Introduction

Last wills afford a special window on medieval society, a view at ground level and from below. Wills can illuminate whole societies or display the religious conscience, ethical institutions, social mobility, or property dynamics of a group or region. Even a single testament allows a glimpse into the testator's family and into the society that formed the context. Historians of modern Europe, with their documentary riches, have understandably exploited this resource more thoroughly than students of the pre-fifteenth-century Middle Ages. Even for the thirteenth century, however, medievalists have been showing enthusiasm both for studying wills in themselves and for using wills to explore other topics, such as charitable philanthropy, the family, or *mentalités*.[1] Within the wills of a given period or place, their formulas, linguistic choices, witness lists, attitudes and motives (secular and religious), and obiter dicta all repay reflection. The many disparate elements in wills require new methodologies or interpretive strategies, by which to integrate and generalize such particulars, especially since the wills so far recovered represent only chance survivals and a limited range of social classes.

A fertile area for exploring the dynamics of thirteenth- and early fourteenth-century wills is the realms of Aragon: the federated lands of Catalonia, upland Aragon, portions of transpyrenean Occitania, and the recently conquered kingdoms of Majorca (the Balearic Islands) and Valencia. A commercial-maritime society of pluricultural mix, it is rich in wills. Barcelona's cathedral or chapter archives alone hold a trove of thirteenth-century wills, some of them clarifying political and economic history in brief asides. The notarial registers throughout the various realms hold a far larger treasure, though the surviving codices begin mostly from the very end of the thirteenth century and its turn into the fourteenth. This circumstance dictates the time bracket in which most wills by Christians or Jews of the realms survive.

Jews in these regions did make at least some (and probably many) Hebrew wills, as we shall see, but none have survived directly. Any number of Jews there also made wills in Latin, on the Christian model, and a fair number of these have survived. No special models existed in the formulary manuals consulted by notaries when drafting the great variety of charters in every field; the Jewish client desiring a will had to be accommodated by the same legal formulas and rhetoric available for the Christian client. These Jewish wills are a curiosity—done in the idiom of Roman law and entered into a notary's Latin codex, sometimes with a lost Hebrew cognate implied. Scholars have occasionally used such wills as a component of their general documentation or even reproduced an occasional exemplar. Thus Richard Emery in his transcription of a *Liber Iudeorum* (or notarial codex specializing in business involving Jews) of Perpignan included perforce the five Latinate Jewish wills extant in it. From Occitan Marseilles Joseph Shatzmiller transcribed and closely analyzed the 1316 will of Abraham of Draguignan. Yet no one has recognized such wills as a peculiar artifact, a genre inviting separate study. It seems appropriate to designate these testaments here as "Latinate Jewish wills."

Whatever the substance of the legacies, the Latinate format brought the Jewish will itself and all its details under the assumptions, interpretations, and dispositions of the Roman law then infusing every aspect of Christian society. Such technical terms as *universal heir* (the foundation of a Roman law will, without whom no will is valid) and *legitima* (a portion the testator must assign to his other children or specific individuals) had life as controlling dynamics. One testament below, for example, tried to forestall the Falcidian and Trabellianic fourths that otherwise would have prevailed in Roman distribution. Two interpretive traditions met in the Jew who made a Latinate will; each was ancient, comprehensive, complex, and impermeable to the other. The Latinate will entered not only the notary's codex but also the newfangled Roman law courts so beloved of the Catalan sovereigns. Thus these Jewish wills are not merely wills *in* Latin but are an acculturative *Latinate* phenomenon.

A related phenomenon, Romance Jewish wills of the Renaissance period, especially from fifteenth-century Aragon, have received some attention, as chapter 1 will explain. These wills come from a radically different world, both in legal and in human terms, involving a disoriented and dying Spanish Jewry. And the exemplars thus recovered are themselves still very rare. For the Early Modern period David Malkiel of the Ben Gurion University of the Negev has completed an article on the rabbinic debate over Early Modern notarial wills. His current research covers wills from various western Sephardic exile communities, starting with those of Livorno and Pisa from the seventeenth to the nineteenth century. Professor Malkiel has already done extensive work on Jewish wills in the notarial archives of Venice during the sixteenth and seventeenth centuries; after a broad study of the wills of Italian Jews in those centuries, his long-range goal encompasses such wills in Europe at large.

Latinate Jewish wills are valuable in themselves, each a small window on some family grouping. Cumulatively, if an aggregate of such wills can eventually be assembled, they can tell us about interfamilial or kin patterns and about the Jewish communities producing the wills. Incidental detail is also available in wills for money values, cherished belongings, philanthropies, or legalisms. Latinate wills issued from both Christian and Jewish communities, providing a glimpse into the operation of concurrent jurisdictions and into one of the multiple mechanisms binding the two autonomies and bridging their activities.

The study of Catalan medieval Jews is currently enjoying a renaissance, both in Spain and in the United States. Scholars such as Jaume Riera i Sans, Manuel Grau Montserrat, J. R. Magdalena Nom de Déu, Elena Lourie, and Gabriel Secall i Güell are representative of the proliferating bibliography. The journal *Calls* deserves special note in the movement. Drawing on current scholarship, Yom Tov Assis has given us a history of the Jews of the realms of Arago-Catalonia from 1213 to 1327. In the United States similarly representative names include Robert Chazan, Mark Meyerson, David Nirenberg, and Norman Roth. Leila Berner's forthcoming history of Barcelona's Jews in the reign of Jaume the Conqueror shows what can be done by skilled and industrious rummaging in the Catalan archives; even in manuscript form this history has attracted attention. My own *Muslims, Christians, and Jews in the Crusader Kingdom of Valencia* draws on those archives for a regional study. This present exploration of a neglected but potentially important byway is meant as a modest contribution to those collegial efforts.

Names

Catalan toponyms in this book are in Castilian since maps and history books commonly give them so; Catalan Lleida, Osca, and Xàtiva, for example, are not immediately recognizable as the familiar Lérida, Huesca, and Játiva. Catalan Cerdanya is retained throughout to include both modern Catalan Cerdanya (Castilian Cerdaña) and French Cerdagne, since the region was a medieval unity under that Catalan form. When a toponym is part of a personal name in Catalonia, the toponym and anthroponym will appear in the original Romance language, Catalan, accompanied where necessary with a clarifying translation into the recognizable modern form (Besers/Besés as modern Béziers). At times this yields an oddity such as Castilian Puigcerdá appearing alongside Catalan Puigcerdà. Since the testaments studied here are from Catalan or Catalan-dominated areas, the notaries' Latin translations of Christian names must be translated back into Catalan. For the same reason the bilingual rulers of the realms of Aragon will appear in their Catalan forms (Jaume, Pere, Alfons) rather than in their Aragonese or their modern Castilian variants. Some adjustment must be made for names obviously Aragonese. Names of Jews pose a different problem, less of translation (*Podium Viridum* to "Puigvert") than of identification. The Catalan scribes had consecrated forms for various familiar Hebrew names, but they also accepted oral variants or evolved forms or even created forms as they fell on the scribal ear (Rotben for Rubèn in one testament below). Such variants could be grotesquely removed from the original form. Hebrew Yitzhak, Catalan Isaac, can appear as Acahc, Assach, Ça, Çagui, Ixac, Ysague, and Zag as well as in Occitan variants such as Hasac, Isaqus, Jaziquet, Saconet, Acquin, and Nasac (= En Asac) and in compounds such as Bonisac and Boniac.[2]

Though many male Jews in the Catalan regions, and an occasional female, bore biblical or equivalently traditional names, a considerable number operated under Romance names. These Romance or "non-Jewish" names had become so common from the twelfth century onward "that the rabbis decreed that every Jewish boy be given a purely Jewish name at his circumcision."[3] It thus became common for males to have a sacred Hebrew name (*shem ha-qodesh*) for liturgical or religious purposes and a parallel Romance name (*kinnui*) for business and daily life. This Romance name was sometimes used in the Jewish community as well as among gentiles. It frequently translated or approximated a Hebrew or biblical original—Cresques as biblical-messianic Tzemach for "branch," Vidal as Hayyim for "life." A Romance name could also recall the Hebrew sacred name in some merely extrinsic way, by similar sound, for example, or by first letter as mnemonic.

Most Jews here seem not to have had a family name, passed from generation to generation, though well-established family names do come easily to mind for Catalonia, such as Cap, de la Cavalleria, Sa Porta, and Ibn Vives. Shlomo Goitein's conclusion about Jewish family names in Islamic medieval lands as "very common but not general" applies here too. Males identified themselves by their father's given name as their own functional surname, Mossé Vidal thus begetting Vidal Mossé. The eldest son took the given name of his grandfather, living or dead, as his own given name. Women identified themselves as daughters or wives of someone, in lieu of a surname. This traditional pattern circulated a relatively small pool of names among the males. The names call for remark or even translation in the course of this book for several reasons. Curiosity alone stops the reader at names such as Bona Aunís, Goget, Horsa, Mayl, and Sullam. The patterns of names in a family can reveal Judeo-Arabic or Provençal antecedents. The choice of Romance or Romance-modified names can serve as a barometer of assimilation to the surrounding culture and, via percentages in choice of specific names, of prevailing attitudes. Mingled with nontestamentary data the names open a window on intra- and interfamily relationships. Names also say something about the Jewish society of a region as a whole, serving as a common vocabulary useful for a boundary-maintaining mechanism.

Though individual names are rarely "Jewish" by nature and quite a few, such as Astruc, were shared by both Jewish and Christian communities, many names had become a Jewish preserve, or their spelling (as in Jucef) had become ethnically characteristic, or their role as a ready "translation" of a valued traditional Hebrew or Aramaic name had greatly multiplied them, or finally the weight of biblical and traditional names so distinguished the community's profile that a Jewish bloc or pattern or language of names can easily be discerned. By mutual osmosis, likewise, the names supplied by tradition in turn reinforced tradition. To juxtapose the first-name index of Jean Régné's abstracts of some three thousand crown documents about Jews in the realms of Aragon and the period 1213–1327 against the two to three thousand first names in Joaquim Miret i Sans's index for the documents of Jaume I in the years 1217–1276 is to see at a glance how wide an onomastic gap separated the Jewish and Christian communities, even as biblical and other commonalities of names also linked them.[4] This balance—shared assimilationist names as against the very different subsets respectively for Jews and Christians—deserves closer study. Simon Seror's lists of Jewish names in the regions today composing France is a rare effort at compiling the kind of data needed for the Jewish side of such comparisons. He tentatively suggests one defining ingredient of the Jewish pattern as "the abundance of theophoric and augural names."[5] The first category, incorporating God and his blessings, includes such items as Deulocresca and Deulosal (the only two, however, in the documentation for the present book). The second category is predictive and, it is hoped, foreshadowing, including characteristic names resting on *bon* ("good") such as Bofill and Boniac, to be met in future chapters. Seror also feels that culturally "Jewish" names are more balanced by "secular" or common names in Occitan lands than in the Frankish north. He does not address the comparative nature of names as a community language.

Since wills often provide interlinked sets of names, including many names of women found nowhere else, I try to present both the manuscript form and the standard Catalan form (today easier for biblical and common names) as well as a generous sampling of "translations" for the secular *kinnui* names into the probable or plausible Hebrew equivalent. To avoid intrusive digressions, I have tried to present these various forms for each case in ways that seem stylistically appropriate, sometimes grouping the manuscript spelling or the published spelling in notes while standardizing the names for the text, sometimes putting the original in parentheses next to the text's standard, and sometimes discussing the names in a will separately. I stress Catalan name origins rather than Occitan, though the two often yield much the same result as heavy immigration from southern France brought many obviously Occitan names. The notary and the host community heard such names as local and familiar.

Some standard Catalan names with their Hebrew antecedents in parentheses are Aaró (Aharon), Abraham (Avraham), Asser (Asher), Astruc and Bonastruc (Gad or Mazal [Tov]), Daví and Daviu but also David, Isaac (Yitzhak), Jucef (Yosef), Jahudà or Judà (Yehuda, English Judah), Mossé (Moshe, English Moses), Salamó or Salomó (Shlomo, English Solomon), Samiel and Samuel (Shmuel), and Jacob (Yaakov). Common Catalan names such as Benvenist, Bondia, Perfet, or Vidal will be explained in place with their Hebrew-Aramaic connections. For the many names transcribed from Hebrew I shall follow the simple versions given in Alfred Kolatch's dictionary of Jewish given names. This spares the reader the intrusive diacriticals, as the 1993 *Chicago Manual of Style* recommends for Hebrew. Kolatch accompanies his transcriptions with the original Hebrew script for each traditional name. The rare Arabic names can carry their full set of diacriticals without unduly burdening the reader. Connective *ben,* between given name and a father-as-surname element, is either omitted or else implied by the latter's genitive case; occasionally *de* or *filius* serves. A surname in the genitive was similarly common among Christians, so the practice among Jews marked both assimilation and division according to cultural context. In Judeo-Arabic names the Latin *aben* echoes *ibn,* capitalized when it links a true family name as in the hybrid Ibn Vives.

The mildly honorific *En* was sometimes prefixed to Jewish names as to Christian; *Na* was the feminine or could attach to a unisex surname. The feminine article *sa* can replace *de* at times (Sa Porta, but once in our documents "de Sa Porta"). The Catalan and Occitan *En* could also elide into an *N.* As used in documents, that particle seems to indicate deference or respect, as to a person of standing in his community. In literary and chronicle usage of this period *En* was a courtesy title with the range of uses of English *sir.* The more ambiguous *Don* in Castilian and Aragonese was rare in Catalan and more likely to be nobiliary there. Both particles are diminutives of *dominus.* Nina Melechen of Fordham University has extensively studied the documentary use of *Don* in Castile, finding that it applied routinely in thirteenth-century Toledo as a distinguisher for all Jews while also designating nobiliary Christians. By the fifteenth century the usage had apparently narrowed to eminent Christians and Jews. A 1412 prohibition in Castile refused the honorific to Muslims and Jews but seems to have remained without effect. Melechen also traces official efforts from 1313 in Castile to restrict Jews from using "Christian" names. This bizarre development of names and honorifics had no echo in our early realms.

Since women had no "sacred" name, their fancy could be reflected in a great variety of invented names, some of them unique to the individual. Goiten found them so resolutely nonbiblical in his Judeo-Arabic communities as to suggest a taboo, except in Spain, where exceptions were found. A favored feminine name seen in our wills echoes a favored name in those Judeo-Arabic communities—Sitt or "lady," "queen," usually in a combination expressed or implied, as lady or queen of humanity, of Baghdad, of the men, and so on. The equivalent in our wills is Regina (or Reina, since the Latin has one version for both). Another equivalent, Malka, does not turn up in the Catalan documents. A final oddity in the recording of Jewish names is sometimes the use of a male's secular rather than Hebrew name in Hebrew documents. In that case the Hebrew scribe approximates in Hebrew letters the Latin or Romance name; recovering the original Latin or Romance form involves retranslating from the Hebrew approximation while using interpretive conjecture. Seror explores this peculiarity and indexes some four hundred such Hebrew-lettered names from medieval France.

Beyond names, several Hebrew words have been liberated from the italic mode here, such as kabbalah or Bet ha-Midrash, as common to historical discourse or in context self-explanatory.

Moneys

Moneys in testamentary legacies followed the standard medieval pattern of the penny, the sou (or shilling) containing 12 pence, and the pound containing 20 sous or 240 pence. Only the penny and half-penny (òbol) were actually minted and circulated until 1285, the sou and pound being ghost moneys, or moneys of account for reckoning. For serious commerce the crown issued imitation Islamic gold coins, especially the Josephine and pseudo-Josephine mazmodins and the Alfonsine and Almoravid morabatins, as well as silver besants. The common pence-and-sou moneys circulating in the realms of Aragon were the Barcelona, Jaca, Valencia, and Melgueil coinages, the Melgueil or Melgorian prevailing at Catalan Montpellier.[6]

How did these various moneys interrelate in value? King Jaume the Conqueror issued an official exchange rate in 1247 on the occasion of minting his first Valencian money (*reials*). A Valencian sou, or 12 pence, was worth 1½ Barcelona sous, or 18 pence. It was worth 1¼ Jaca sueldos (the Aragonese "sou"), or 15 pence. Both the Melgueil and the Tours rate resembled that of Jaca, respectively 16 and 15 pence. Forty-eight Valencian sous (not 38, erroneously copied at times) made a silver mark. Four sous made a Josephine mazmodin, 3½ sous the pseudo-Josephine. Six sous made an Alfonsine morabatin, 8½ sous the Almoravid, and 3¾ sous made a silver besant. Inflation relentlessly reduced the equivalences, and fiscal vagaries made them fluctuate up as well as down. By 1310 the Valencian sou had fallen to equal only 1¼

Barcelona sous and ⅔ of a Jaca sou, with corresponding shifts throughout the table of exchange. (The 1273 testament in chapter 4 states an equivalence of 8¾ sous per morabatin; if not the Almoravid morabatin, this represents the cheaper Barcelona sous and some inflation.)

In intrinsic value the central Barcelona money had been improved under Jaume the Conqueror in 1221 by issuance of a "double money" (*moneda de doblenc*), with two parts of silver against ten of alloy, and in 1258 by a "triple money" (*moneda de tern*), with three parts silver against nine of alloy. A major change came in 1285 under Jaume's son Pere: an actual sou was finally coined, the famous croat (marked with a cross), worth 11½ pennies of the *moneda de tern*. The croat, also coined as half, third, and quarter croats eventually, was imitated briefly at Roussillon (*sou rossellonés*). The Catalan rulers legislated to exclude from Roussillon all moneys such as the Melgueil sous, in favor of Barcelona money, in 1221, 1253, 1258, 1261, and 1279, but to no avail.

What were such moneys actually worth in purchasing power? A simple knight's fee could be as low as 373 Valencian sous, a solid ecclesiastical benefice 300 sous, a common esquire's ransom after battle with the Moors 150 to 200 sous. An artisan could make up to a sou per day, a sailor a few pence. Ninety-two Muslim bowmen served Prince Pere in 1268 at 4 Barcelona pence each per day; a fifteen-man garrison thrown into a castle in 1276 received 150 sous each per year, while the garrison at another castle were each given 360.[7]

Richard Emery, whose work on the Perpignan Jews is discussed below, reckons that an unskilled worker in 1266 could make 47 Barcelona sous per annum, or a sou each week with holidays excluded. An artisan, he believes, could make 70 sous plus board and a bit for expenses. Emery also feels that a single person could live at Perpignan in the late thirteenth century on some 100 sous a year, "a pretty typical wage for an ordinary workman." In his table of prices annual rental of a house varied from a high of 250 sous to a low of 4 sous and 1 pence, the eight cases examined between 1261 and 1287 yielding a median figure of 35½ sous. Shops in the same period here ran from 100 sous to 12½, the median for all fourteen cases yielding a little over 38 sous. Dowries in the craftsman class at the same time varied from 2,250 sous to 125, all forty cases examined giving a median of 562½ sous. Slaves cost from 375 sous down to 125 sous, the seventeen cases representing a median of 225 sous. The seventeen asses sold in this period and in these records at Perpignan show a high of 75 sous and a low of 7¾ sous, with a median 40 sous. Mules were more expensive, from 250 to 25 sous, the median for twenty-six sales being 93¾ sous. Horses in that period cost 2,400 sous down to 150, the median for nine cases being 500 sous.[8]

Some appreciation of the nature and value of the contemporary regional money will help in interpreting the money-designated legacies in the testaments. Conversely, legacies involving money can add incrementally to the rather exiguous data available now on its use and purchasing value. Since the number of Jewish wills at this stage of their recovery is so very small, the database on money needs to be supplemented with information from the much more numerous Christian wills of the same time and place. As more Jewish wills emerge, their contribution to an understanding of the use and value of these moneys will also increase.

CHAPTER 1

The World of the Wills

The Catalan regions in the thirteenth and early fourteenth centuries formed part of an urban-maritime continuum from Valencia up and around the southern French shores and down the Italian littoral. The Catalan speakers had a tenuous grasp on some areas of their linguistic cousins, the various Occitan groups in southern France over whom they held a traditional claim. The Catalan count was now also king over upland Aragon, and king as well over the recent conquests from Islam, the kingdom of Valencia and the Balearic kingdom. The full dynastic complex was called the Crown or realms (*regnes*) of Aragon. Against Genoa and other rivals, the Catalans struggled to dominate the circle trade with North Africa and Occitania. Though upland Aragon had a significant role in the conquest and settlement of the Balearics and Valencia, Catalan settlers predominated in the new lands and gave them both a Catalan character as an extension of the Catalan homeland.

The realms had recently helped break the power of Spanish Islam, thrusting it into the rump state of Granada, and now stood as inheritor of its Mediterranean role. The count-king was claiming Tunis as his client or "vassal," was dominating the carrying trade of Alexandria in Egypt, was intriguing for succession to the fallen Hohenstaufens in Sicily, and was challenging the Capetians of northern France both as champion of Occitania and as claimant to Sicily. Most of these expansive movements took shape under Jaume the Conqueror (1208–1276), his son Pere the Great (1276–1285), and his grandsons Alfons the Liberal (1285–1291) and Jaume II the Just (1291–1327). During that period Catalan literary and scientific culture crested, producing such figures as the philosopher Ramon Llull, the troubadour Cerverí de Girona, the physician Arnau de Vilanova, the historian-memoirists Bernat Desclot and Ramon Muntaner, and the jurist Ramon de Penyafort. The institutions of the realms also reached maturity during this period, from parliaments to municipal functions to university life. And though Catalan influence over the Occitans waned in southern France, as the northern Franks encroached on and absorbed Occitania ever more effectively, Catalan dynasts still ruled Perpignan and (for a considerable time) Montpellier, commanded vassals like Foix, and shared many cultural and social influences.[1]

The Jews of the Realms of Aragon

The Arago-Catalonian realms were pluricultural. The Catalan and Occitan cultures and languages were cognate, but Aragon proper had its own language, institutions, and folkways. More pertinently, the thirteenth-century conquests had added whole populations of Muslim subjects, both slave and free. Within the new conquests, as well as in the older homelands, a parallel society of Jewish communities flourished. Many Jews had fled north from Almohad Muslim persecution in recent years or were overtaken and incorporated during the crusader advance in Islamic Valencia and the Balearics; the cultural background and frequently the name-forms of this stratum were Judeo-Arabic. Conversely, other Jewish communities and individuals were fleeing south into Catalan lands, away from recurrent Frankish persecutions and expulsions. An even wider immigration movement brought Jews from overseas, for example, from Tlemcen in North Africa, as the crown encouraged Jewish settlement of its new conquests. All this stir and jostle converged on the established native Jewish community, itself older than Christendom or Islam on the peninsula. Though Jews had agricultural interests in the realms and were found in rural towns as well as cities, their urban profile as investors, merchants, and lenders was not in itself alien to the Christian urban profile. The "usurer" of northern Europe became the businessman of these Mediterranean parts. One result was that anti-Semitism, however lively here, would be somewhat differently experienced than in northern Europe.[2]

This convergence of immigrations transformed Jewish society and

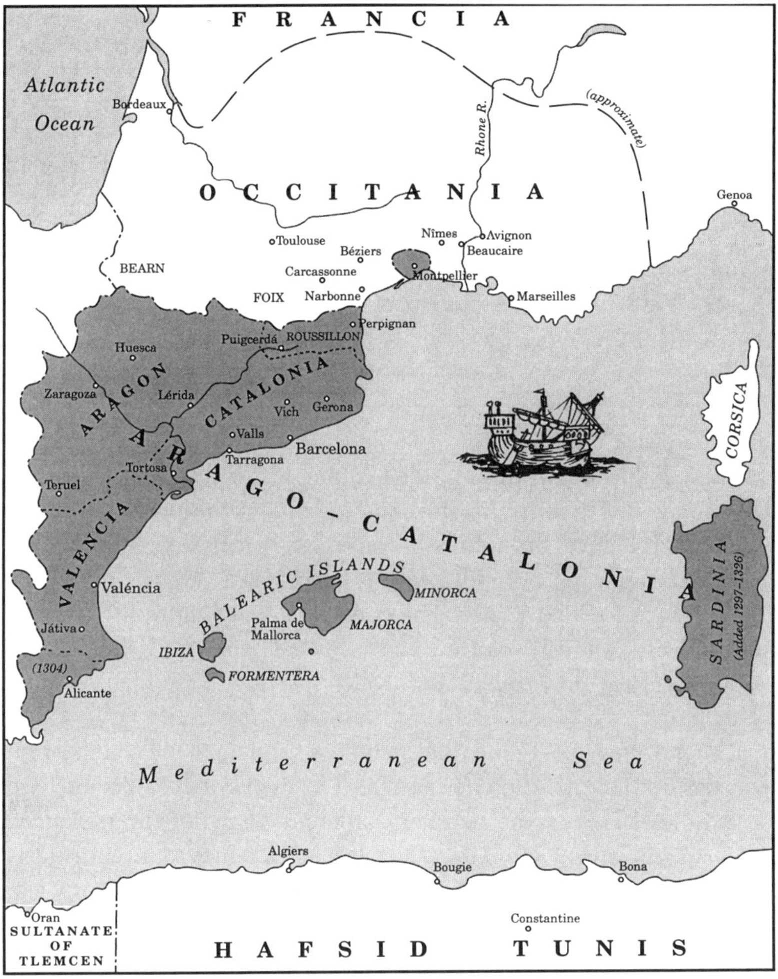

Realms of Arago-Catalonia at Mid-13th Century

culture in the realms. The already interrelated Jewish communities of Occitania would funnel ever more into the realms of Aragon and particularly into Catalan cities like Barcelona, Besalú, Gerona, Lérida, Perpignan, and Valencia. The historian Yom Tov Assis, charting the final great waves of flight from the north, especially in 1291, 1306, and 1322, speaks of the "liquidation" of Occitan Jewry and notes the impact of the newcomers on all aspects of Jewish life—social, religious, cultural, and intellectual—in Catalan areas. Resettlement in Catalan lands did not always bring stability, especially in the overstressed border towns. At Perpignan in 1328 King Alfons IV rebuked Christians who were harassing the exiles because he feared the Jews would go to North Africa or especially to France, to which some wanted to return. The economic loss to the crown would be great, he wrote, "because the Jews are a strongbox and a treasury for kings."

The intellectual and mystical effervescence in Occitan Jewish communities had influenced cognate Catalonia from early in the thirteenth century. As these peoples compressed and ever more intensely experienced each other's presence due to the migrations, that influence became more relentless and disputatious. As Assis remarks: "These influences were completely contradictory to the fundamental principles of Iberian Jewish culture of the Islamic epoch."[3] Yet the rationalist and scientific influences from the Judeo-Arabic sector threatened the Occitans with loss of identity. Meanwhile a series of expulsions from Francia, or northern France, brought Ashkenazic Jewry increasingly south, adding another cultural complex of usages and ideas, a more rigorous and more inward-looking legacy. The convergence was not only of Jewish subcultures, variously evolved and adjusted, but of clashing understandings about how to be a Jew, which intensified the ideological debate.

The movement of Franco-Occitan Jews south into the realms of Aragon was both creative and destructive. The medievalist William Chester Jordan has analyzed the two very different stages of the movement. "The steady stream of voluntary exiles" which moved away from the invading and encroaching Franks from the early thirteenth century onward had a different impact than the mass arrivals of those expelled from all France and French Occitania in 1306. The latter "came in droves" and "with virtually no resources," swelling the Jewish populations all over the Arago-Catalan realms, alarming the Christian population, and challenging the ingenuity of the native Jews to absorb them physically, economically, and psychologically. These displaced persons "never sucessfully integrated in the short time they were given." Invited back to France by a new king in 1315, they were again expelled in 1322, after which, as Jordan notes, "there were virtually no Jews in France." Looking back in 1346 Cresques Elias, a physician and confidant to Pere IV, writing in Hebrew for his Jewish audience, contrasted the contemporary "kingdoms that oppressed the Jews" with "the righteous and merciful kings of Aragon," inspired by God, "who showed mercy on Israel [and] gave refuge to exiles from all corners of the world, [and] treated them with honor."[4] This kaleidoscope of migrating and interacting subcultures, in an affluent commercial society able to cope and reasonably accommodating in its public policy, transformed the native communities.

The flight from the Islamic south was even more significant for Catalan and European Jewish society, a transfer in the nature if not on the scale of the Early Modern expulsion from Spain with its diaspora into Ottoman lands. The historian Bernard Septimus sees the flight from the south as "an important turning point in Jewish history." The Jewish communities of western Islam declined and collapsed, he notes, "while those in Europe, despite an increasingly hostile Christian environment, showed an upsurge of vitality and cultural creativity." This "shift in the center of gravity of Jewish life altered the framework within which Jewish history would unfold," particularly in Spain. Quite simply, Septimus maintains, "Spanish Jewry had just transferred from the Arabic world to Christian Europe, and no aspect of its culture could remain untouched by this shift in historical environment."[5]

A side effect of the increase of Arabic-speaking Jews in the realms was their expanding role throughout the thirteenth century in the crown's fiscal, diplomatic, and chancery structures and their role as courtier savants (the *ḥakīm* phenomenon). So prominent and effective did some Jews become at court that a baronial backlash in 1283 drastically curtailed their roles in governance and fiscality. A little-noticed contribution by the Judeo-Arabic stratum was their preservation and production of Arabic classics in medicine. In 1296, for example, we find Jaume II paying Vidal Benvenist de Porta the serious sum of two sous per day to "write and translate certain medical books from Arabic into Romance [*romana lingua*] which are very necessary to Us." And the same king paid a thousand sous "for translating and rendering from Arabic into Romance [*in romancio*] a certain book of medicine written in Arabic entitled *Halçahahny*"; the translator Astruc de Bonsenyor having died, King Jaume in 1313 was belatedly conveying the sum to his son Jahudà. A more general witness to the widespread Arabic culture of this Jewish stratum is the same king's arrangement in 1302 to have a professor of medicine at his University of Lérida borrow "certain Arabic books of medicine" that "some Jews of Our land have" in order to correct the *pecie*, or excerpt-textbooks, rented to medical students, "restoring" the books when finished to the respective owners.[6]

Among the radical changes ensuing in thirteenth-century Catalan Jewish society, Septimus describes the displacement of the native Jewish aristocratic and courtier class, hitherto apparently unassailable in their wealth and in their secular and rationalist culture. Worldly-wise and pro-Maimonidean, buttressed by royal power, they had made Barcelona Jewish society "a city of princes." Rising to displace them was a Jewish merchant-scholar class emerging into new wealth, more centered on the Torah and mystical religiosity, heavily influenced by Provençal kabbalah and by Franco-German talmudic culture. The religio-intellectual scene was complex, with three competing but interacting dynamics: rationalism, kabbalah, and conservative or geonic-Andalusī traditionalism. Robert Chazan finds Septimus's arguments "for a powerful anti-aristocratic rebellion in Barcelona of the 1230s" to be "not thoroughly convincing," and he argues that "the Jewish aristocracy continued to exert powerful political control in Catalonia all through the thirteenth (and fourteenth) century." Whatever the merits of these opposing views on the revolution in social classes, what stands clear is the wider transformation of Jewish society, the shift out of al-Andalus and France, and the turmoil of converging cultures and visions. An intriguing side effect among all these scholars and courtiers was the appearance of a memorable eccentric whose strange career has points of resemblance to that of his Christian contemporary and Catalan, Ramon Llull. Abraham Abulafia, "founder of Ecstatic kabbalah," was driven by a series of revelations in Barcelona from 1270 to 1280 to go on a mission to Pope Nicholas III (who inconveniently died as Abulafia reached the pope's residence at Soriano, near Viterbo) and to preach from city to city in Italy to both Christians and Jews (with disappointing results).[7]

To what degree these social developments are reflected in the appearance of Latinate Jewish wills, or in their contents, is not easy to say from our present small sampling. The testators do seem to belong more to the class of "new men," however, with its confident generalized affluence and its pieties. The Judeo-Arabic stratum is visible in name-forms, as also and very strongly is the Occitan element. Familial, commercial, and cultural links should eventually emerge from multiplication of such wills and their contextualization from other sources. How the Jewish society both interacted and clashed with the englobing Christian society may also be clarified by examining the role of these alien wills within Jewish society and the complex of legal interference they invited from the crown authorities.

Parallel Societies

Jewish and Christian societies in the realms lived in symbiotic tension, each experiencing within its autonomous self some presence of the other and each invading in small ways the psychological space of the other. As Mediterranean Europe had evolved over the previous two centuries, from a rural backwater to a world-class urban civilization tied into international markets, the ideology of an exclusivist "Christendom" had intensified the immemorial separation of Jews and Christians. Neither people wished to share the public, or much of the private, existence of the other, compromised as that other was by its own religious memory, symbols, values, and traditions. To do so meant to assimilate, to lose to a degree one's own pervasive religious expression or spirit and to be exposed to that of the Other. Christian or Jew "could scarcely penetrate into each other's social sphere," Solomon Katz notes, "for the life of each community was permeated by its own religious symbols and emblems." As Bernard Dov Cooperman puts it, "separation of the two societies" was "integral to *both* their world views." A mutual exclusivity held the two societies apart like a kind of antigravity.[8]

Paradoxically, however, practical considerations and human circumstance threw the members of each society into various kinds of social, commercial, and governmental interaction. Since members of each society might be careless in such necessary mixing, or even seduced in the direction of conversion, the elites in each society were alert to reduce the inevitable dangers and to maintain the psychological defenses. Yet the Jewish patrician classes sent individuals into the Christian administrative or courtier circles; the Jewish community both appreciated their protective influence and suspected their degree of assimilation. In short, a structure of parallel societies existed, pervious to regular mutual interaction and influence. The continuous task of each party in self-identification and self-protection made for a creative tension in this mutual relationship. It also made inevitable a degree of permanent hostility and harassment by the dominant society, which in times of crisis could become brutal.

If the situation itself dictated some status of separation and autonomy for the excluded subject community, validated from the medieval Christian perspective by scriptural authority, the practical form actually accommodating the autonomy was influenced by the *dhimma* model of the neighboring Islamic states. Islam tolerated subject Christians and Jews as "people of the Covenant" (*ahl al-dhimma*) who were allowed to exist in subordinate but semiautonomous parallel societies. Though noncitizens, a *dhimmī* population had rights and duties, enjoyed a circumscribed religious and personal liberty, and connected with the Islamic state through their own religious leaders. Like that Islamic model, the Christian structure conceded to the many communities both of Muslims and Jews in Spain their own internal administrative and judicial system under their respective religio-social leaders, their interior tax support as well as a voice in collecting state taxes, and a range of religious institutions, education, festivities, and personnel, often within a privileged quarter (not the confining "ghetto" invented for the Renaissance and Early Modern times). The status of Muslims and Jews had come to seem sufficiently equivalent that royal charters in the realms sometimes referred to the encompassing religious law of the Jewish communities as their *Sunna,* borrowing the common Christian term for Islam's analogous law.

This Jewish echo of the *dhimma* had not come directly from a Catalan experience of long reconquest. Catalonian contact with Spain's Muslims, unlike that of Aragon or Castile, had been limited until the thirteenth century. Her populations of subject Mudejars had largely been on the far borders at Lérida and Tortosa. The extraordinary conquests of the Balearics and Valencia by Jaume I had transformed that situation, but the Muslims remained more than ever at the periphery of Catalonia proper. A domestic empire had been added, but there was little Muslim impact on the home counties. Thus Islam's *dhimma* status had not given rise to the structure of Christian-Jewish parallelism, nor did it dominate that situation; rather it nuanced it. And despite ecclesiastical perspectives and fulminations, the historian Norman Roth argues, "the laws established full equality for Jews" in civil legalities, a concept "never abandoned throughout the Middle Ages in Spain." However many restrictions and impediments to lateral relationships existed between the parallel societies, the vertical relation of Jews directly to the king meant that they enjoyed in their own way "full and complete" subject status with "the right of representation and appeal in courts of law."[9]

To what extent Spain's Christian countries borrowed their Mudejar *dhimma* model from their Muslim neighbors is a complex problem of diffusion and acculturative adaptation. Despite suggestions that the Byzantine imperial system for harboring Jewish populations underlay the Islamic system itself, that Islamic system seems rather a borrowing in detail from conquered Sassanian Persia, grafted onto a koranic root. From another vantage, the *dhimma* structure reflects the immemorial strategy of empires with indigestible subcommunities. The European West had shared that imperial experience, notably in the Gothic/Germanic peoples of Arian Christianity who managed the proto-European sectors of the Byzantine empire and in the Jewish communities "protected" by Christian scriptural teaching in a providential survival until millennialist mass conversion. However strong such precedents, even as antecedent to Islam, the influence of the full-blown Islamic *dhimma* institution on Western Mediterranean Christian policy must have been more immediate and insistent. From the late eleventh century, as Christian Spain urbanized and grew in wealth and sophistication, populations of Muslims were incorporated on a large scale. Inevitably the situation of the Jews, paired with the Muslims as subordinate autonomies, must have tended to assume in Christian eyes a *dhimma* structure.

Many differences remained, however, both in Christian Spain's application of the *dhimma* concept and in the practical situation of the Jews as against the Muslims. Even a fully borrowed institution is usually distorted and reexpressed by the borrowing culture because of different host institutions, values, and expectations; moreover, such attitudes and institutions reinterpret the subject population even while seeming to keep it in place. Unlike the *dhimmī* communities of subject Muslims, the Jewish communities shared a common language with the dominant population, a long history and a nonmilitary relationship, a much wider base as being present in every corner of Christendom, and a more dynamic interaction with the host country in commerce, tax administration, diplomacy, medical service, and even religious learning. Europe was home to the Jews, immemorially so, whereas subject Muslim autonomies were a recent phenomenon and confined largely to Sicily and Spain. If the Jews, unlike the Muslims, had Christian scriptural "protection," neither Jewish nor Muslim minority enjoyed the solid koranic framework that made persecution rare in Islam. And a rational, Roman law Europe could shift its bases and biases more easily than could a revealed koranic doctrine. The Islamic system might lock its subjects into humiliating subordination and contempt, but it would not betray them further. So even if Jews had a wider and older base, the virus of anti-Semitism could flash along that Europe-wide system, ancient hatreds revivify, and unreasonable expectations suddenly surface.

Unlike the conquered Muslim communities, the Jews had no explicit surrender constitutions or pacts. These were a convenience, however, and not strictly necessary in the borrowed *dhimma* situation; the essential was the implicit acceptance of subject status and duties within the tradition. Thus it is misleading to say that each Jewish community in the realms "had a different degree of autonomy relative to the king."[10] For both Muslim and Jewish communities the king did add to the common autonomy special local or regional privileges, the random accumulation of which could at least mark each such community with a special profile. The king could also spread *en bloc* all such privileges from one locality to another, as when Jaume gave the Jews settling conquered Valencia all the customs and privileges of Barcelona. Nonetheless each community depended directly on the king in all parts of the realms, each an independent small entity jurisdictionally parallel to and outside the municipal system.

The usual form of interior government involved an executive board of "secretaries" or deputies (the *ne'emanim,* or in Aragon the *mukdamim*), plus an assembly or council. The numbers in either group, and their manner of gaining office, varied widely from place to place; smaller places might have a less developed government. A general gathering of the community's adult males might be called to debate and ratify a statute or major decision. Any number of bureaucrats or officials existed for public functions of an economic, juridical, religious, or petty character. Religious leaders included the judge-rabbi (*dayyan*) as well as auxiliary rabbis for special posts; the title was also employed as an honorific, without office. A developed quarter (Catalan *call*) centered around its synagogue (there could sometimes be two or even more), with butchery, market, public oven, tavern, hospice(s), probably the ritual baths, and an exterior cemetery.[11]

The perception of both Muslim and Jewish societies in the realms as a kind of Islamic *dhimma* lent the Jews an adventitious widening of royal protection, because it added to the theological rationale from scripture a practice and tradition long observable among one's Muslim neighbors. By the same token, this perception also helped target the Jews for the conversionary missionary movement promoted here by the crown. More perhaps than the administrative and commercial networks that joined the older Catalan lands to the new conquests, the conversionist movement placed the two minorities in a single perspective. The "Dream of Conversion" that obsessed thirteenth- and early fourteenth-century Christendom ranged from Morocco into China. Its prime domestic targets became the Muslim and Jewish communities of the

Arago-Catalan realms. The new international Mendicant orders—Franciscans but especially Dominicans—put into operation an elite program of Arabic and Hebrew schools and a grassroots program of forced preaching on forays into mosques and synagogues.

The weight of the conversionist movement in the realms fell heavily or mainly on the Jews for a number of reasons: in part on linguistic grounds (Jews spoke Romance as their native tongue), in part from traditional pattterns (Jews had long been an object of conversionary reflection and writing, though not of a systematic program), in part from the friars' new conviction that manipulating the Talmud was the final key to unlocking Jewish solidarity, and in part of course from the relative paucity of Muslims outside Valencia and the growth and vigor of the Jewish communities. So in addition to the burdens of anti-Semitism and stereotyping or the annoying restrictions imposed by ecclesiastical and civil decrees, Arago-Catalan Jews now had to put up with a disorienting invasion of their inmost autonomy and psychological space. A decisive moment in the conversionist invasion came with the Barcelona "Disputation" of 1263, actually a showpiece confrontation in which the king summoned a Jewish champion to refute Mendicant interpretations of a selection of talmudic propositions. The Jews there were not allowed to defend Judaism or attack Christianity. One result was a widely published defense of Judaism disguised as a report on the Disputation, by the great Nahmanides, and a rallying of Jewish resistance and identity.[12]

The world in which the Latinate wills multiplied was a chiaroscuro, therefore, simultaneously light and dark. The reigns of King Jaume the Conqueror and his son Pere the Great, from 1208 to 1285, have often been called the golden age for the realms' Jews. Converging immigration as refugees fled here or followed the magnet of opportunity, remarkable intellectual ferment in the many communities, commercial prosperity and expansion for Jews as for Christians while the new conquests (soon to include Sicily and Sardinia and even Athens) created a maritime imperium, and the extensive presence of Jews at the royal court and at various levels of administration (until baronial opposition from 1283 forced its drastic reduction)—all help explain the golden memories. The encroachments of the friars, alienation from an increasingly Christian public culture, the eventual loss of influence within Christian state structures, proliferating restrictions and humiliations in ecclesiastical legislation, and folkloric indignities—all provided the balancing shadows. A troubled silver age followed the golden; then from mid-fourteenth century came crisis, decline, and with the 1391 massacres, catastrophe. An acculturative interchange between Jews and Christians can be charted between 1250 and 1350, however, revealing a dynamic that did not preclude strong and growing religio-ethnic hostility. This century represented a kind of Indian summer in the relations of the two peoples, with lightning flashes warning of disasters to come. The century of tragedy from the 1391 riots to the expulsion of 1492 lay mercifully in the hidden future.[13]

Wills: Hebrew, Romance, Latinate

Extant wills for Europe's Jewish communities are rare and valuable. One might nonetheless expect to find them in the medieval Spanish kingdoms, with their rooted and prosperous Jewish communities. Spain's Hebrew wills are mentioned in the rabbinic responsa literature, but only when they involved some problem and never with an actual text reproduced. The wills themselves faced many perils to survival. Wills and inheritances were usually family affairs and generally did not require the attention or regulation of the community. Thirteenth-century private charters in any case, whether Christian or Jewish, disappeared on a large scale, save for those in the archives of civil or religious corporations. More to the point, the wave of pogroms which swept over Spain in 1391 wreaked wholesale destruction of early Jewish documentation, while the expulsion of 1492 uprooted communities and records alike. Still, Jews had the same general practice of making wills as did the resident Muslim and Christian communities, a tradition indeed more ancient for Jews.

In his monumental history of early medieval Mediterranean Jews in the Islamic Near East, Shlomo Goitein only reluctantly calls these documents *wills*. "There are no 'testaments' in Islamic and Jewish laws," he notes, and legators rather than "testators" made them. Last dispositions were made by "men and women, rich and poor, learned and plain" in "astounding" numbers as a "general practice," whether on the occasion of serious illness, extreme age, new business arrangements, or risk situations such as a long voyage. Despite the different cultural context for Jewish wills, their different juridical meaning or effect, their somewhat different purpose (they often dealt with one or two issues unsettled by previous gifts and funds), and particularly their freedom from the all-encompassing structures of Roman law, the essential human activity remains analogous to that in other communities and is therefore accepted by Goitein and historians as in general "testamentary." If the Jewish law did not know "the Roman or modern idea of a unilateral testament," it did provide for last dispositions "dealing mainly with the appointment of executors and the distribution of legacies."

In his *Gifts in Contemplation of Death in Jewish and Roman Law* Reuven Yaron traces the evolution of the technical "gift" that served "as a substitute for a testament, which is not known to Jewish law." Such early transfers allowed some "change in the amount of property" as against the standard rules of the divine law of succession. Not to be confused with ordinary gifts, they fell into two classes: an irrevocable grant but the donor retaining usufruct (somewhat corresponding to the Roman law *donatio deductu usufructu*), and another irrevocable grant but only at the endangered donor's consequent death (Roman law had a *donatio mortis causa*). Allied maneuvers such as disherison or disinheriting could complicate the pattern. The operation was bilateral, however, involving the donee or legatee in a ritual or supposition of acquisition. "Jewish law does not know of any unilateral disposition in contemplation of death" but rather this "cooperative liberality," and "the step from bilateral gift to unilateral testament was never taken in Jewish law." Though rising out of similar needs, the Jewish and Roman dispositions had entirely different contexts in this regard and "few, if any," points of influence in their origins.[14]

Properly drafted Jewish last dispositions, however, did not lack form or regulation. Besides the rules of succession, the formalities in the Jewish community offered three categories of "wills." First, a healthy person could give a gift immediately to someone not an heir by those rules, keeping the usufruct for life. Second, a testator whose deathly illness confined him to bed could will away his entire property (less than everything would invalidate his intention "in view of death") in either oral or written form or by an unwitnessed personal note. Third, if facing death but not so debilitated or if facing equivalent danger, such as a long journey or execution, an individual might also prepare a will. A healthy person not in those categories could not make a will. The heirs had a moral duty to carry out the testator's dispositions. Local communities could add regulations as to execution, such as requiring drafting of the will before a scribe or rabbi or public proclamation in the synagogue.[15] It is hard to say whether Latinate wills add a fourth category or rather presume the second or third categories for Jewish testators. It is also not clear whether the Jewish testator in a Latinate will avoided the small complexities, exceptions, qualifications, challenges, court interpretations, and formalities of technical language hedging the properly drafted Jewish will.

The most immediately visible difference in structure between the Roman law and Jewish wills is that witnesses in the latter do not merely validate but actually present the final wishes of the deceased. This difference "reflects a society that trusted living persons more than written documents." A typical Jewish will contains both a date for the visit by the two witnesses and a subsequent date of death. The witnesses recall the physical and mental condition of the testator, a significant and explicit section of the will rather than the routine and formulaic counterpart in a Roman law will. The witnesses then recall the substance of the testament along the lines of "This is what he said . . . ," followed (usually) by a first-person recital by the dying person. The appointment of executors loomed large when business affairs or property were involved; Goitein sees here "a certain aversion to stocktaking and accounting" by the testators, leaving that task to the official postmortem inventory of assets, with a free hand to the executors. The testator also had to clear away debts, which meant for husbands primarily the return of dowry and of the gift promised to the wife in the marriage contract.

Finally, the Jewish will "was bound by God-given laws regulating man's inheritance, not to be tampered with": the firstborn son normally got a double share, a husband received the estate of his wife, a daughter as only child became the sole heir, a wife did not inherit her husband's estate. Goitein's Egyptian Jewish documents sometimes reinforced such provisions explicitly, lest an appeal to Islamic courts upset merely implicit or weak statements. In such an appeal Islamic law might influence the court's decisions. (By Islamic law the testator could dispose freely of only a third of his goods; and besides, the unusually elaborate Islamic inheritance theology might be maneuvered by a malicious Jewish claimant against the will.) Though a few of Goitein's Egyptian wills were detailed and encompassing, usually for a special context, he is convinced that most testators devised their wills "for one main purpose," or at most a few, and that Jewish wills "were partial in nature," merely the final act in the decedent's multiphase disposal of his possessions. An important element of the Egyptian wills, not shared by the Latinate specimens discussed below, is preoccupation with an appropriate funeral and its expenses. Though some wills "were concerned exclusively with charity and burial," testators seem to have arranged their philanthropies before and outside their wills; a tenth to charity "seems to have been regarded as a proper share."[16]

In the realms of Aragon a peculiar Visigothic survival called a *testa-*

ment sacramental, that is, "by oath," echoes something of the Jewish wills' focus on the witnesses. By this device anyone might prepare a last disposition, orally or in writing, on sea or on land, without notary or formalities. The witnesses then had to appear within six months before the altar at the church of Sants Just i Pastor at Barcelona, with a notary, to swear out the provisions before representatives of church and state. The witnesses could range from two to seven but were usually two or three, often relatives. As in the Jewish will, the document itself was redacted after death, on the word of the surviving witnesses. The *testament sacramental,* though not common, was enshrined in Catalan law and received a strong reexpression in the 1283 statute *Recognoverunt proceres.* In any will, Jewish or Christian, there could be two stages of drafting, first by informal notes of notary or scribe and later by a fair copy for the heirs.[17]

The Egyptian evidence raises the question of Islamic intervention in Jewish wills and of the possibility of some practice corresponding to the Latinate will or co-will. Goitein did find Jews applying to Muslim courts, even in family matters. "The great majority of cases," however, involved not litigation but the making of contracts, and "it was common practice to make contracts before Muslim and Jewish authorities concurrently" to reinforce their legality. Conversely, the Muslim courts could interefere in Jewish law, despite the *dhimma* autonomy, especially in inheritance cases. A claimant or heir unsuccessful at the Jewish court, believing the Islamic testamentary regulations more favorable to his point of view, could follow this path, though Jewish authorities "in principle" frowned on such recourse "as a religious offense" when not in some way necessary. There seems to be no evidence, in any case, of a testament made solely or concurrently before Muslim authorities and with Islamic juridical structures.

Information directly from Goitein's earlier wills at Old Cairo will be introduced in chapter 6 for comparison with the Latinate materials from Catalonia. Here his description of the funerary activities that went into operation at a testator's death will afford some idea of the similar activities in Catalan lands. On the day of death a burst of activity brought any number of officials to the house: a judge to oversee, two trustees to take deposit of valuables, two elders to assess worth, a cantor to make funeral arrangements, synagogue beadles to take stock and "do the physical work," a court clerk to record the activity and the inventory, a grave digger to measure the body, and two body washers. The rabbinical court immediately sealed the dead person's possessions and ordered the all-important inventory and assessment. Goitein notes that "it was the policy of the Jewish courts to realize all the assets of the deceased and to sell his inventory immediately after his demise," transferring the proceeds to his executors. Relatives and friends gathered around to help with arranging the burial clothes (on hand or to be purchased), hiring the special mourners, planning the procession, and comforting the bereaved. A schedule of prayers testified to the communal nature of this death and, by extension, of the deceased's last wishes. In Catalonia some Jewish communities had burial confraternities, organized in rotating divisions, to carry out and facilitate the many funerary obligations for the bereaved family; Lérida had seven such groups in 1323 and eight by 1348.[18]

To confuse matters, medieval Spain has also given us notable examples of the Hebrew "ethical wills," of which Goitein finds no trace in his Geniza documentation. These were not real wills, though a rare case does seem to include actual testamentary dispositions. They were instead a literary genre of exhortatory injunctions, a medieval subcategory of Jewish ethical literature. Cast in the form of deathbed advice and instruction, they were short, practical treatises reflecting the ideologies and concerns of the authors and their groups. These ethical statements were very popular and often read by the public as genuine wills. They could include inventories as part of the literary form, or even involve practical commitments.[19]

Of all the wills drafted in Hebrew in the realms of Aragon, only one has thus far surfaced. Unfortunately that document is not a full copy of the original but only a selection of the part relating to the principal heir. Isaac b. Mossé had come of age and wished to manage his own affairs, so he petitioned the Jewish court at Barcelona for his own copy of the will of his father, Mossé b. Isaac of Toulouse (*Tolosa*), "to serve him as title." The three Jewish judges who sign off here explain these circumstances and present as much of the will, "letter for letter, word for word," as pertains to Isaac's own legacies and to those of his deceased younger brother Shealtiel, half of whose legacies also went to Isaac. Two Jewish witnesses "write down, sign, and place [the will] in the hands" of the guardians appointed by the testator, dating it on the twenty-ninth or last day of Iyyar (second month of the Jewish calendar) in the year 5028, which was the Christian date 14 May 1268. The dying man had established five guardians for his daughters, until they married or reached twenty years, and for his two sons until they reached the age of twenty. His wife is not mentioned in this partial copy and may have been dead. The eldest son, Isaac, received the family house, some properties detailed here, one book of each kind from the father's library, and a seat in the synagogue. The younger son received a package of houses and other properties or revenues, again listed in detail. Leila Berner, in her history of thirteenth-century Barcelona's Jewish community, discusses the will, its context and implications, and the family connections of all those involved.[20] This fragment is presumably a representative exemplar of the stream of Hebrew wills which once flowed through the realms of Aragon and whose fugitive traces are visible today only in secondary documentation, Hebrew or Latin, about the legal repercussions of the now-lost originals.

If Hebrew wills were massively destroyed, a fair number at least did remain in Romance versions, hidden away in the registers of Christian notaries or lost in the archives of an obscure convent. Those that do remain in this transcultural garb are almost always post–Black Death and especially fifteenth-century, with late fifteenth-century the norm. For both Christians and Jews, but especially for Jews, those troubled later eras in Spain were in radical contrast to the relative calm of the thirteenth and early fourteenth centuries. The generation of Jews that came after the 1391 universal riots, with their mass forced baptisms, the disappearance or drastic shrinking of communities, the disorientation, the assimilative acculturation, and eventually the Inquisition, inhabited a very different Renaissance world of light and shadow.[21]

The historian José Cabezudo Astrain presented three such very late Romance wills in what has become a standard reference point in approaching medieval Jewish wills in Spain. All three are from Zaragoza in Aragon proper, a highland component of the realms of Aragon as against the Catalan coastal regions. Drawn respectively in 1483, 1484, and 1491, the wills conform to the *Fueros de Aragón,* the Romanized codification of the laws and customs of the upland kingdom of Aragon, promulgated in 1247, and to the attendant practical applications called the *Observancias.* In his four-page introduction Cabezudo conjectures that Jewish testaments were done before Christian notaries only "by exception" and only so that a Christian court might not challenge the bequests. He finds in them "very few" differences from the Christian wills of the region. Christian invocations are lacking, of course. A Jewish cemetery is always chosen, frequently something is left to the synagogue, and the wife receives a return on what funds she brought to the marriage. As in Christian wills, arrangements are made for children's guardians, daughters' marriages, alternate heirs in case of obstacles, a small legacy (usually five sueldos) for each lesser heir, and a division (often very unequal) among the sons.[22] Why or how such domestic dispositions within the Jewish community and legal tradition should be challenged by a Christian court Cabezudo does not explain.

Encarnación Marín Padilla has recently carried forward Cabezudo's work, presenting three late wills made before Christian notaries by, respectively, a Navarro-Aragonese woman in 1467, the wife of an Aragonese physician in 1469, and a Zaragozan man in 1473. From her years in the notarial archives of Aragon in this late period, Marín Padilla argues that Jews took one of four options in disposing of property on the eve of death: sale, gift, testament before a Jewish scribe, and testament before a Christian notary. The sale or sale/buy-back option seems a ploy, "almost always fictitious" in effect, by which not only some Jews but also Christians avoided death duties. The gift option, for any motive, was rare.[23] Wills drawn by Jewish scribes are visible usually only by allusion in later litigation in Christian notaries' records of suits by heirs. Currently M. A. Motis Dolader has examined Jewish wills in the last third of the fifteenth century, again at Zaragoza. He has transcribed two of these and has related the formalities of the *Fueros* code of Aragon to their structure. He conjectures that Jewish recourse to notarial wills is explained by the authentic and formal force of such documents as compared to other kinds of will, to their precise juridical formulation that avoided confusions or deficiencies, and to their function in forestalling force and abuse.[24]

For this upland kingdom of Aragon proper in the fifteenth century, the contributions of Asunción Blasco Martínez have been especially notable. She has published the wills of five Jewish women, respectively, from 1401, 1405, 1415, and 1418 (two wills). Four testators were widows; all had convert or Christian connections. More pertinent to our earlier study are her interpretive conclusions about Jewish wills of the kingdom in the fourteenth and fifteenth centuries. In exhaustively examining the notarial records in the Archivo Histórico de Protocolos in the capital city Zaragoza as well as those in the Archivo Municipal, she has found Jewish notarial testaments "scarce," with none at all for the fourteenth century and "only some few" for the fifteenth, mostly indeed for the late fifteenth. Her impression is that Calatayud and other places of Aragon follow the same pattern. She has encountered "no testament written in Hebrew," though notices show they once existed. Why the imbalance between the fourteenth and fifteenth centuries? Blasco Martínez posits that Zaragozan Jews simply did not usually make notarial wills until the riots of 1391 and especially the Disputation of Tortosa of the antipope Benedict XIII in 1413–1414, with their forced conversions, triggered "sporadic" and then ever-increasing usage. Specifically the wills came "as a consequence of the convert problem at the beginning of the fifteenth century" as it shattered family unity and invited quarrels among heirs. She sees Christian influence in the custom in these late Romance documents of leaving legacies for the poor and in seeking remission of sins, but she notes Jewish particularities in such items as mourning periods, Jewish feasts, and lack of reference to a future life. Our earlier, proper Latinate wills studied below, however, will show a very different context, content, and conclusion.[25] Such very late wills have also been noted from Catalan areas and occasionally transcribed or analyzed: from Gerona (1462 and 1470), Manresa (1391), Majorca (1377, 1388, 1467), Santa Coloma de Queralt (1410), and from the Vives family (1436 to 1514).[26]

Marín Padilla's typology of four options might well accommodate a fifth, as we shall see: Hebrew wills for which a Latin counterpart existed from the start. Such double wills may have been the norm for Latinate Jewish wills—the Latin alone surviving by reason of Christian administrative archives, but even then barely and sporadically. Double or single in format, Jewish Latin wills belonged to a unique earlier world, to a psycho-social "discourse" unusual for both Jews and Christians. They are as much a function of the revival of Roman law as of the contemporary commercial revolution and the peculiarities of Jewish life in the realms at this time. Latinate Jewish wills survive elsewhere than in the Arago-Catalan and cognate Occitan regions, though early exemplars seem even rarer in other lands. Steven Epstein indicates that the will of "Brachamus [Abraham] Ricius de Chalfono" in 1299 at Erice is the earliest extant in Sicily (then under its Arago-Catalan dynasty) in the Latinate category. Epstein adds: "I know of no other place [in Italy] where medieval Jews made formal public testaments" with Christian notaries.[27] As with the upland kingdom of Aragon, practice had changed by the fifteenth century. Ariel Toaff has exhaustively edited the documents by and about Jews in the Umbrian region from 1245 to 1484. For the first century at least, through 1350, there are no notarial wills, though two documents of 1346 concern previous wills and heirs. Toaff does transcribe a number of wills from 1423, 1439, 1445, and later. Occitan wills for the regions not under Arago-Catalan control also exist for these later periods and are noted below.[28]

In the thirteenth century or the opening decade of the fourteenth, both Christian and Latinate Jewish wills are more likely to turn up in the Catalan regions of Spain than in the Aragonese or Castilian. The Catalan areas were intensely commercial-maritime components of the

Mediterranean trade world, multiplying precisely those affluent classes who could most use a will. And as families rose by wealth within the respective Christian and Jewish communities, a corresponding concern to consolidate and maximize a family's wealth should be expected, with public documentation to trace and validate the family's rise. The maritime commercial environment here was also a magnet for immigrating Jews with capital. These regions were also a main focus of the revival of Roman law in Europe. In the newly conquered kingdom of Valencia alone, the compilation of customs for incoming Christian settlers, entitled the *Furs*, was becoming the first Roman code of general application in Europe. Jaume the Conqueror was a major promoter of Roman law, energetically deploying the Bologna graduates who streamed back into his kingdom. His biographer Charles de Tourtoulon praises him as an "apostle" of the new jurisprudence. The legal scholar J. M. Font Rius sees his reign as marking "a stage of high effervescence" in Roman law activity, around whose person the new jurists "swarmed"; laymen "of the highest rank and offices prided themselves on being experts" in Roman law.[29]

An important question needs to be posed explicitly. Why would Jews, established in their own political and juridical semiautonomy, with no Christian legatees or interested parties, submit to the expensive, bureaucratic, and alien forms of the Christian notary, translating their domestic dispositions into Roman law Latin, especially when (as most assert in the opening line) the testators were terminally ill and presumably of limited energies when they summoned the alien notary? First, a personal and commercial overlap joined the two societies so that neither was as alien to the other as might seem. Jews operated easily in the Roman law world of municipal statutes, financial controls, joint ventures, legal procurators, and appeals courts. They entered many business documents in the Christian notary's register, and wills could easily seem another such contract. In any case, rabbinical prohibition of access to non-Jewish courts had never been accepted by Jews in Spain, though such recourse was viewed with disfavor by the other Jews when not patently advantageous in civil cases.[30]

Second, a Latinate version of a Hebrew will was enforceable at law and thus doubly secured the testator. In Jewish law, unless orphans were involved, the role of public authorities was minimal, and the actions of the executors or trustees would normally not be audited. Jewish authorities might see to the testator's property inventory, sign releases of legacies, and turn over charity grants to the proper overseers, but normally they were reluctant to do more. The Jewish scribe in drafting private documents brought prestige and a kind of popular esteem to them, but his work on private charters usually fell short of law and legal enforcement. A Latinate testament could also effect ends not compatible with Jewish law; a male testator could nullify Jewish legal prohibitions, for example, by making his wife his heir. Sometimes for various reasons the king's confirmation was desired for an individual's last disposition, so a Latinate will had to be drawn. Clues as to the kind of problem precluded by the use of Latin testament and authorities can be gathered from actual cases presented on appeal to the king, a number of which will be described.

How did rabbinical authorities view this transfer into gentile forms? Testaments were part of a larger problem involving charters of all kinds, such as debts, deeds, and contracts, entered for Jews in the ubiquitous notarial registers. Abraham Neuman, citing the responsa of the great Ibn Adret who served King Jaume I, concludes that "the rabbinical jurists, while exhibiting a wavering tendency, finally recognized the full validity of these documents of the Christian notaries not only as prima facie evidence but as contractual instrumentalities." One result of this plunge into the notarial culture, claims Neuman, was that "notarial reforms were occasionally introduced in Jewish community practices, emulating the example of the gentile courts."[31] Yom Tov Assis has traced the qualified acceptance of Christian notarial validity by Catalan rabbinic authorities, under various interpretations of the talmudic principle that "the law of the kingdom is law." This "innovation of Nahmanides" (d. 1270) was adopted by another great Catalan, Ibn Adret (d. 1310), and soon became common. Assis also notes that "although Ibn Adret was strongly opposed to the application of non-Jewish law to matters of inheritance, in Catalonia the local laws of inheritance were widely practiced among the Jews who considered the matter purely financial."[32] Latinate wills, beyond their intrinsic value and many uses, thus become part of what Bernard Lewis calls "the delicate and difficult question of influences," where the much studied phenomenon of "Jewish influence on Christianity and Islam" is not yet matched by an exploration of influence or acculturation by those englobing societies on "Jewish religious law" and perceptions, even "in a matter as central as marriage."[33] The notarial culture was insidious and pervasive. Any window on its activities, its acculturative impact on both societies, and its function as a bridge between them merits attention.

CHAPTER 2

Mechanisms: Notary and *Sōfer*

Even in the underdeveloped earlier Middle Ages some Catalan Christians had drawn wills. Antoni Udina i Abelló has been able to find 137 wills in Catalonia for the period 840–1025, and he has studied them for their echoes of Visigothic law.[1] But the ever-ascending trajectory of population, urbanization, and commercial prosperity in the twelfth and thirteenth centuries produced Christian testators in record numbers and caught them up in the sophisticated testamentary procedures and guarantees of Roman law. When Alfonso X the Learned amassed his idealized code of Roman law, the *Siete partidas*, in thirteenth-century Castile, he devoted the entire sixth part, a small book or encyclopedia, to succession and testaments. Under nineteen "titles" it comprises 288 essays or "laws," including each drafting step in model form.[2]

Alfonso's contemporary in the Arago-Catalan realms, Jaume the Conqueror, imposed on conquered Valencia a Romanized law of less detail but more practical effect, covering all the essentials of wills, witnesses, heirs, executors, and every probable convolution of process. His code even set the fee per charter. Drafting a will cost the client a serious 2 sous, whereas other contracts cost only a fourth of that at 6 pence (but 12 pence, a sou, if "sworn"). At Puigcerdá in the Catalan Pyrenees a lifetime later, the crown set an official schedule of fees to control overcharging; this 1304 reform had little effect, even after a stern restoration in 1323, and had to be changed again in 1327. That last schedule presented a complex of many separate fees. Some fifteen categories of document cost 12 pence; declarations of deposit, partnership, and guarantee 3 to 4 pence; an appeal or protest 18 pence (6 more with a response); and a copy of a royal privilege 16 pence. At 12 pence to the sou, here the somewhat less stable Barcelona money rather than the sou of Valencia, such prices were relatively expensive even for artisans. A will, like a nuptial contract, cost 5 sous, with 2 more for any later codicil and 2½ sous for every copy of the will. At Puigcerdá the notary was to pocket a fourth, sending the rest (minus royal taxes) to the city government.[3] These prices were for the "act" as scribbled in an abbreviated way in the notary's codex, which validated and authenticated its content under penalties of law. No copies onto parchment needed to be made, the act itself being an original. If a parchment copy was desired, the original act might be canceled by pen strokes through the text.

Muslim Scribes

In practice, the making of a will lay in the hands of a licensed notary or his Jewish or Muslim scribal counterpart. Each of the religio-ethnic societies in the Arago-Catalan realms, locked away in its own exclusivist administration, contained an official secretariat or scribal component. For Muslims in the subject Mudejar communities, the traditional *ṣāḥib al-wathā'iq* appears under the Christian title *scriba* in his *scribania*.[4] Crown appointments to the office survive from the thirteenth-century realms, and two fine exemplars of their work survive from thirteenth-century Valencia. This was not the *kātib*, or secretary, who served in a ruler's or subgovernor's *kitāba* and corresponded to the notarial scribe of a Christian ruler or other authority. Ibn ʿAbdūn in twelfth-century Seville described the more general *ṣāḥib al-wathā'iq* as requiring some literary talent, beautiful penmanship, and "great" legal knowledge as well as integrity and piety in order to redact marriage and other contracts. Angel Canellas López remarks that this office of general scribe "curiously attained a singular diffusion" in Islamic Spain. Francesc Carreras i Candi, in his study of thirteenth-century Catalonia's notariate, gave his opinion that the notarial-style infrastructure for the conquered Muslims remaining as Mudejar communities was "almost always" in the hands of Jews; this involves a confusion with the special commission to one or another Jew to prepare Arabic documents for Muslims or others trading abroad and with the Arabic department or function of the crown chancery.[5]

The several exemplars surviving to appoint a *ṣāḥib al-wathāʾiq* or "scribe" for a town and district in the realms of Aragon suggest that the office was combined with other high offices, the incumbent presumably farming the actual work to mere professionals. Thus in 1271 King Jaume conferred on Muḥammad, the son of Ismāʿil, lifetime tenure as *faqīh, amīn,* and "scribe" for the Mudejars of Borgia, an arrangement previously set up for his father by the crown. Similarly King Pere in 1278 confirmed to Ḥasān b. Faraj ("Foçan filio de Pharach") the previous appointment by King Jaume to the offices of *qāḍī* and scribe "of the Saracens of Zaragoza and all the districts of Zaragoza," and "for making all Arabic [*sarracenica*] documents."[6] That same year the king ordered his bailiff at Huesca to restore to Ibrāhīm b. ʿAbd Allāh the lifetime scribal office previously held by his father and also by his brother.[7] In 1280 King Pere appointed Muḥammad of Salā "of our household" as *qāʾid* "and scribe of the Saracens of the Moorish quarter of Valencia city" with the same conditions enjoyed by "other incumbents" of such posts. Muḥammad the Moroccan in 1269 got the post of "*amīn* and scribe of the Saracens" at the small town of Chelva in Valencia.[8]

At Calatayud in 1278 the local *faqīh,* or jurist, named simply ʿAlī, who held a court "for adjudicating quarrels and cases that are or will be brought by Christians and Jews against Saracens of your jurisdiction [*alfaquimatus*]," received also the office "of making all Arabic documents [*cartas sarracenicas*]," a monopoly not to be entered by "any other *amīn* or *ṣāḥib al-salāt,* throughout all the land of your alaminate" or *amīn* jurisdiction.[9] King Jaume I issued clarifying legislation for the Muslim community at Lérida in 1274, couched as a privilege and therefore responding to Muslim sensibilities; if a Muslim died "without an heir," the crown was to seize half of the estate and the Lérida Muslim community the other half. This applied to both men and women.[10] At fourteenth-century Huesca in Aragon proper, M. B. Basañez Villaluenga finds that the combined offices of *amīn* (a principal administrative overseer), *ṣāḥib al-ahkām* or *ḥākim* (a secondary judge, the *zabalaquén* to Christians), and scribe all went to the same person, with some exceptions. The recent study by Basañez traces the careers of fifteen Muslims who exercised the triple office at Huesca from 1259 to 1391 as well as a number of other Muslims to whom these luminaries subleased the scribal office. Nearly all, at both levels, were local men, and the holder of all three offices in 1383 complained that qualified scribes were hard to find and keep at lease in that town. Under Jaume II the triple office there was often reassigned on a yearly basis. A typical tax or fee to the crown was 54 Alfonsine gold morabatins, 30 of them for the scribal office itself.

Huesca's scribe, the *ṣāḥib al-wathā'iq*, turns up in a complaint in 1301 by the Muslim community to the king when the Christian officials at Zaragoza passed an ordinance reserving to Christian notaries all contracts or instruments between Muslim and Christian or between Jew and Christian. King Jaume II set up an inquiry. Huesca's scribe becomes visible in the crown registers again in 1340, when a Christian official cut the scribe's salary, provoking a suit by the Muslim community; King Pere the Ceremonious voided the official's act and removed him. In 1361 an individual held the office alone, though the mechanics of distribution make even this case seem to show one original holder for all three functions. Later in the century the crown addressed complaints by Huesca's Muslim community that some of their members avoided making a contract with its fee or else had a document drawn for them by a nonscribe. In either case, the crown decreed in 1370 and 1371, this fee-avoidance was to incur the huge fine each time of a hundred gold morabatins.

For the Valencian kingdom M. C. Barceló Torres has described the stream of official documentation generated by the *qāḍī* office of each region, with Arabic as the "official and public language." For Lérida Josefa Mutgé has transcribed royal charters of 1263 and 1370 appointing Muslims to the conjoined offices of *qāḍī* and scribe. For Navarre Mercedes García Arenal has found that the scribal office tended to be held for life, to run in certain families, and as "a position of extraordinary importance" to be both prestigious and profitable. In contrast, John Boswell felt that he had found evidence of extensive Christian and even Jewish incumbency in Aragon. Though the *Fueros* of Aragon insisted on Muslims holding the office, Boswell argued that the community scribe "was generally not a Muslim before 1360." He cited a Christian notary for Muslims at Calatayud in 1356, at Teruel and Daroca in 1354, and a Jew and then a Christian at Crevillente in 1358. By 1400, he concluded, "most *aljamas* [Mudejar communities] could choose their own *scriptor*" (a development Mutgé denies for Lérida) and "he was always a Muslim." This seems a misreading of the evidence. Such situations were probably neither anomalous nor normal but reflected one of three occasions: a Christian or Jewish scribe licensed for non-*aljama* and especially commercial contracts, analogous to the *Liber Iudeorum* phenomenon; the translator-scribe for crown tax or other extra-*aljama* transference "en chrestianesch"; or the reward or sale of an office to an unqualified holder of the revenues who then subleased to a Muslim, as could happen with any crown revenue source. An abusive intrusion was possible but rare, as in the cases transcribed for southern Valencia by M. T. Ferrer i Mallol with the Muslims protesting.[11]

The researches of Asunción Blasco Martínez are particularly pertinent here. Confining herself to the upland kingdom of Aragon proper and to the fourteenth and fifteenth centuries, she has assiduously gathered archival information. "The results are hardly spectacular," she confesses, with documentation "very scarce," so that "there is hardly any data." Despite this modest disclaimer, she has accumulated a database of eighty-eight notables of the *faqīh* stratum, each with his Aragonese place and chronology within those two centuries. At that time and place the title *faqīh* suffered from imprecision, designating not necessarily a jurist but any Muslim of some learning in rhetoric, theology, jurisprudence, or the like. Even when only a local rich man, pedagogue, or cult leader, however, he enjoyed a relatively elevated status. Blasco Martínez finds that "the majority of scribes, if not all," appointed by the king also held that higher title. Whether most or many of the eighty-eight so titled and surviving in the records, conversely, could function as scribes even in the more backward rural setting of Aragon, is problematic. As for the scribal procedures, she adds, "practically nothing is known." Blasco Martínez transcribes several documents that may contribute toward clarifying the function. And she particularly discusses the reform of 1360, by which the Cortes canceled at least in theory Aragon's law that forced Muslims to use a Muslim rather than a Christian notary; the following year King Pere IV considerably restricted the new freedom by decreeing that "the Saracen *alfaquini* and *scriptores* appointed by Us" in royal places must be used for documents between Muslims. Presumably all such instruments were still redacted in Arabic there.[12]

As with the Jews, Muslims did not know "the Roman and modern idea of a unilateral testament" but did have a common and widespread practice of terminal dispositions. In fact, Islam had a testamentary "science of the shares" so complex, with sophisticated mathematical formulas so predominant, that the great Ibn Khaldūn characterized it as "noble" and "a discipline in its own right." Its theory designated primary heirs who had to receive a minimum of two-thirds of the estate, as against secondary heirs or legatees who shared a maximum of one-third. Compulsory entitlements dictated the fractional shares that could come to each member of the family as well as the inheritance lines for males with priority claims on the residue. A recent juridical analysis of the origins of this theoretical structure began from the study of "intergenerational transmission of property in medieval Islamic Spain and North Africa," which revealed "the wide range of legal fictions to circumvent" the effect of the rules so as to leave property to whomever one wished and in any proportion. That this clash of theory and practice is visible in the genre of the *fatwā,* or authoritative moral decision, rather than in a corpus of Spanish or Andalusī wills suggests that the general testator may have remained more orthodox in actual inheritance strategies. The complexities and local variations of properly Mudejar testaments, precisely in the Catalan lands, can now be examined in *The Book of the Sunna and Sharīʿa of the Moors* just discovered, done in Catalan and Catalan translation from Arabic in 1408, apparently by a Valencian *qāḍī.*[13]

From the moment of conquest, King Jaume I had not hesitated to intrude as a court of appeals for his Muslim subjects. A celebrated trial over water rights between the towns of Eslida and Uxó, which had been adjudicated by Muslim courts under two previous Muslim rulers, found its resolution under Jaume, acting precisely as successor to those rulers. The registers do have cases of Muslim criminal activity against other Muslims finally reaching the king's court. And Muslim officials did appeal to the crown in intractable situations or when they felt aggrieved. No Muslim testamentary records exist in the crown registers, however, and there are no Muslim Latinate wills in notarial codices.

Several reasons converged to block such testamentary activity by the king's Muslims. The traditional populations of Mudejars in the realms had been rural and craft people in the Aragonese highlands or at the Aragonese border (Lérida) or on the Valencian frontier (Tortosa). The highly urban and commercial society of Islamic Valencia was too recently conquered and incorporated, its city notables often gone away to Granada or North Africa, with rebellions echoing through the thirteenth century and into the fourteenth. Islamic and Christian societies faced each other in too raw a state, with no customs yet evolved to soften the outrageous rule by the infidel, a situation seen by Muslims as perhaps transitory. As large an obstacle was Islam's science of inheritance, with its own rigid rules and the need for a skilled mathematical interpreter. In the sophisticated Valencian kingdom too, where Muslim wills might reasonably be expected in quantity, the language barrier was formidable and the cultural divide consequently wider.

The Jewish population in the realms, however, had long been reconciled to gentile sovereignty in both theoretical and practical ways. The Jewish communities constituted full societies with their notables, financiers, and other high strata intact; they lived in mercantile-contractual patterns that mirrored and meshed with the Christian society around them, had immemorial experience in adjusting to that society while conserving their own, and above all spoke and dwelt in the same language with all the subtle acculturation that implied. Particularly in the matter of wills, Jews had more options. Under Islamic rule Jews found Muslim testamentary regulations confining and sought to avoid getting caught in them. On wills "Jewish law was more liberal than Islamic law," Goitein notes, and the Koran "contains a far more detailed legislation on inheritance than the Hebrew Bible," so that "freedom of disposition was limited by a written law to a far higher degree in Islam than in Judaism." In this Islamic context too Goitein repeats his caution that "testator" and "will" are technically incorrect terms, "since there are no 'testaments' in Islamic and Jewish laws." The terms are appropriate only as analogous.[14]

The Notarial Culture

Christians had governmental scribes in their chanceries and bureaucracies (many apparently hired for ad hoc work), general public scribes for the population at large, and scribes with a monopoly on some public utility. Their training, examination, and procedures were strictly regulated by law, and their title of notary was proudly borne. The documents in their registers followed set legal and rhetorical formulas and enjoyed full validity as juridical items "in court and outside," enforceable at law. Though there was no limitation on the number of notaries, their professional guild or college in effect tended to regulate their increase. Each municipality could certify or license its own, as could ecclesiastical corporations, but the crown could license notaries both for local and municipal regions or else for general jurisdiction. Jurisdiction granted might be general, regional, or local; it might attach to some place such as a monastery, to some administrative office such as that of judge or bailiff, or to some official business such as a saltworks or a royal galley. In an earlier period some jurisdictions had been offered by parish and lay or ecclesiastical seigniory. By the reign of Jaume the Conqueror at mid-thirteenth century, there was little or no difference in the realms between notariate and scribeship as licensed and publicly authoritative offices.[15]

In many ways the urban-commercial society of the western Mediterranean world was built around these notaries. They were not university-trained jurists, but their function was not unlike that of many American lawyers, and they were nearly as ubiquitous. Though we still lack statistical studies of the profession for the realms of Aragon, the more complete records for thirteenth-century Italian cities reveal huge notarial populations. Genoa had some 200 in the late thirteenth century, a ratio of 1 to 500 residents. This compares to the current national average in the United States of one lawyer for every 319 citizens, as reported by the Census Bureau and the American Bar Association. Bologna had 2,000 notaries, Milan 1,500, Padua 500, and Pisa 230. So numerous were notaries that many must have also pursued an alternative occupation. They filled the growing municipal and other bureaucracies and helped staff guilds and the many corporations of church and state. In Italy, Daniel Waley notes, notaries held "a quite disproportionate share of offices," had extensive influence in politics, and were among the readiest speakers in public affairs.

Notarial culture transformed Catalan lands at a much slower pace than in Italy, but it was in full flower in the second half of the thirteenth century. Stephen Bensch notes how the number of notaries in Catalonia "multiplied with breathtaking speed" in the reign of Jaume I, so that "by the 1280s more than forty public notaries were active in Barcelona." The population of Barcelona at its maximum pre-plague growth some sixty years later was about 40,000 souls of both sexes and all ages (smaller than many university populations in the United States), and 35,000 might be a fairer conjecture for the 1280s. If one envisions some 10,000 of these, male and often enough female adults, as constituting the regular client pool in commerce, crafts, and corporations, the ratio of active notaries to potential clients would have been 1 to 250, or for the entire population 1 to 875.[16]

The notaries' combination of rhetorical skills and Roman law erudition, while as superficial as the technical knowledge of many modern American lawyers, was quite adequate to their mechanical or formulaic tasks and to their consultative positions. Their services were in demand for the most varied occasions, from marriage and dowry agreements to legal procuration, to partnerships, to contracts of every sort. Commercial transactions required their authoritative instruments—leases, loans, deeds, payments, sales, transfers, authentic copies, bills of lading aboard ship, or bills of exchange. In government notaries functioned at the several layers of tax collection and customs duties, for statutes, records of legal action, inventories, administrative minutiae, army lists, licenses, notices of appointment, treatises, and treaties. Last testaments constituted only one of myriad services, distinguished perhaps by the frequency with which the moribund condition of the testator called the notary away from his public shop to home or hospital. The notarial career and its products consequently constitute an essential element in the history of law, government, rhetoric, finance, urbanism, religion, and that ill-defined but comprehensive field called social history. The notary was omnipresent in this society, not only as one of its active creators but also as its product. He helped shape the merchant society and culture as he represented and mirrored it.

The crown organized and centralized this busy scribbling scene, insisting that only crown-authorized notaries could act validly. A decree to this effect went out on 29 January 1279 from Prince Alfons in separate charters to the royal vicariates of Barcelona, Berga, Cervera, Lérida, Manresa, Montblanch, Ribagorza, Pallars, Tarragona, Vich, and Villafranca del Panadés. The form letter for Barcelona, the model for the others, ordered the vicar "that you cause to be publicly heralded, through the entire vicariate you hold for Us, that no scribe may dare use the office of notary [*tabellio*], except for testaments and dowry charters, besides those who hold authority from the lord king Our father or from Us, under penalty of 100 morabatins." After the public criers had so "heralded" the order abroad, any future documents by unauthorized notaries would automatically be "null and void." The exception for wills and dowries is significant, since these were the least commercial of possible contracts and also may well have touched the lives of more persons than did the larger mass of commercial or real estate documents.[17] In other notices to various communities the crown was careful not to inhibit the limited notarial activities of clerics and others in testamentary and matrimonial charters. As late as 1280 the king wrote that the rector of the church at Cambrils could continue to draft "wills and marriage documents" for those who asked, despite any royal documents seeming to forbid this.[18]

Theoretically neither a cleric nor a Jew could be a notary, and a "testament before a priest" was authentic but non-notarial. Real life proved more variable. A pertinent example of the special notariate was the post awarded in 1264 to "Astruc Azarel, a Jew of Lérida," for life in the *scribania* of Lérida's municipal office of weights.[19] The unusual assignment of a Jew suggests that Arabic/Latin bilingual skills were needed there. A pool of such bilingual Jews supplied the Arabic section of the crown chancery as well as envoys to Muslim powers and translators for the king's surrender negotiations and for rendering Arabic scientific treatises into Latin or Romance. Another example of a Jewish scribe in a general public office was the appointment of "Mossé el Neyto, a Jew of Jaca," in 1272 for life, to "the secretariat of the public granary of the town of Jaca and the office of measuring at the same granary." Mossé's identification here seems to be either as grandchild (Aragonese *net,* Catalan *nét,* Castilian *nieto*) or as clean and pure (Aragonese *neto,* Catalan *net,* Castilian *neto*), the Arago-Castilian suggestions posed because of his identity as from Jaca in Aragon.[20]

A special and very profitable notariate went to Jahudà, the son of the Barcelona patrician and courtier Astruc Bonsenyor. Acknowledging that Jahudà was "suitable and competent at understanding and drafting debt-documents done in Arabic by Saracens, namely, for those who go abroad to Saracen lands, or who obligate themselves to pay certain amounts to some persons in those lands, and that those documents will be better written and understood among the said Saracens if they were written in Arabic rather than in Latin," Jaume II conferred on Jahudà a monopoly "of such debt documents done in Arabic in the city of Barcelona and its territory," documents that thus "gain validity as done by public authority" as long as they are "written by your hand and you have put your signature to them."[21] This last proviso was diametrically opposed to the common permission, or sometimes understanding, that a notarial post could be subfranchised by the holder or that assistants could expand its activity. Doubtless the need for exactness here, and the danger of assistants less able, prevailed.[22]

A common form of special notariate was a local monopoly on Latin charters involving Jews with Christians; these appear in a number of appointments and account for the *Liber Iudeorum* often found in municipal archives.[23] Like all monopolies, this one was resented, challenged, and often forced back into the general competition. In 1257 King Jaume had to reassure the Jews of the Catalan tax collectory of Barcelona-Tarragona that "all your documents made or to be made at the hands of priests or any other ecclesiastical persons licensed for the office of scribe" would have "full validity in every respect whether in law or outside law, as though they were made at the hands of public notaries [*tabelliones*] in our courts of jurates."[24] Eight months later he specifically revoked the monopoly appointment "of a special Jewish notariate to Pere de Colomer." Described elsewhere as "a scribe of the lord king," Pere had apparently won this monopoly as a perquisite of royal service. From now on, as part of its "pristine liberties," the Barcelona "community of Christians and Jews" could "freely draft charters and whatever other writing you want with whatever scriveners or notaries of Barcelona you want, despite any concession of a special notariate made by Us to anyone." The linking of Colomer's revocation with the "pristine liberties" of the wider community marks this document as concerning business between Jews and Christians. The king further revoked "any other grant We made of a special notariate at Barcelona for charters or other writings of Christians or also Jews, firmly decreeing that We or Our successors may never confer or concede to anyone a special notariate in Barcelona."[25]

The privilege was not general in the realms. In mid-1260 King Jaume presented a charter to the Aragonese Pero, son of Poncio Guillermo of Jaca, "that he is the notary public of the Jews of Jaca."[26] At Egea in December 1263 the king gave Simó (Aragonese Simón) Gil of Egea "the notariate of the Jews of Egea all the days of your life, in such wise that you or your delegate may draft and make all instruments of debt and other contracts which will be made or drafted between Christians both of Egea and other places and the Jews of Egea." The monopoly warned that "no one besides you or your delegate may dare from now on to make or draft the said documents, which if drafted have no validity." The crown fee was 20 sous annually, half on the feast of John the Baptist and half at Easter; the fee for his clients was set at "whatever other notaries are accustomed to receive and have." Christians and Jews, present and future, had to respect this monopoly.[27]

The arrangement lasted over ten years. Then in 1275 Jaume granted "to each and every notary of the town of Egea, present and future, that the Jews of Egea present and future can draft their charters of debt, and whatsoever other charters they shall make with any person, with whatever public notary of Egea they wish." This was repeated in negative form: no one could compel these Jews to work "with one notary alone or with whatsoever public notary or notaries of the town," despite any contrary grant. The notaries themselves seem to have sought this antimonopolistic privilege, and as a body they now had to pay the crown annually on the feast of Saint Michael 30 sueldos of Jaca.[28]

Special notariates for Jewish-Christian business continued to function in other towns, however, and it is hard to say which pattern prevailed in Jaume's reign. Barbastro had its own pattern, as small towns probably did. In 1272 the king appointed one man only, Bartolomé Tomàs, to "the notariate of the town of Barbastro, both of Christians and Jews, in such wise that you or whoever you want in your place may draft and write acts, testaments, and any other public instruments that Christians or Jews will have to make in the town of Barbastro." He and he alone is to be accepted as the town's public scribe, paying the crown a fee of 4 gold Alfonsine morabatins every Christmas. As indicated, the notary could hire or train his staff of subnotaries.[29]

Jewish Scribes

Besides this combination of Christian scribes who handled Jewish-Christian business, or indeed any affair between Jews alone that came before them, the Jewish community itself had a special scribal office for documents in Hebrew. This office would also have written documents in Aramaic, then still surviving in legal literature and documents. David Abulafia particularly calls attention to "the use of Hebrew script for Aramaic *ketubot* or marriage contracts." Any language in the Jewish communities of Spain could also be written in Hebrew letters, the phenomenon called *aljamiat,* Castilian *aljamiado.* Arabic, Castilian, and Catalan could appear in this writing system, and in fact a will survives in Hebrew-script Catalan by one Auro (doubtless Judeo-Catalan Aaró) at Monzón near the end of the fifteenth century. Hebrew was the common language for official documents in the Jewish communities of the realms of Aragon at this time, however, and our one surviving but partial will from such a Catalan community is in Hebrew. Christian authorities probably did not bother, and may often have been unable, to distinguish between documents in Hebrew script. Yet Christian authorities did not employ "Hebrew" or "Jewish" as an umbrella term for all writings by or about Jews. Their descriptive terms are linguistic in this context, as with the corresponding Arabic *carta moresca* or *escrites en sarraïnesc.* In my own documents I have not noticed any distinction between *instrumentum iudaicum, hebraicum,* or even *Iudeorum;* all three seem synonyms, usually as rhetorical couplets, for whatever mixture of language and Hebrew script. Whether in the Hebrew or Hebrew-script sense, such "Hebraic" items can justly be translated here as Hebrew and in most cases were probably in that language as well as script.[30]

Goitein has described the Jewish scribal function in the early medieval Mediterranean. Besides the salaried community bureaucrats for official records and correspondence as well as the professional copyists, the *sōfer* was an "all-around Hebrew scribe" able to serve in the first two categories but especially available for a fee to draft marriage, dowry, divorce, commercial, power-of-attorney, testamentary, commercial, promissory, or other documents and contracts. Goitein does not see these men as appointed or even exclusive; the will of al-Wusḥa from Fustat (or Old Cairo) which he describes at length, for example, was written by the cantor and court clerk Hillel b. Eli. Though all male Jews read some Hebrew, not all wrote, particularly in the calligraphy and legalese proper to a witnessed public or semipublic statement. In King Jaume's Arago-Catalonia it is not clear to what degree the average Jew could compose and write in Hebrew or Aramaic. Even in an Islamic world relatively more advanced and affluent, the art of writing in the Jewish community was rather for "future government officials, physicians, scholars, and merchants." As against the "far more widespread" reading, writing "was the distinctive mark of a person belonging to the professional or higher classes." While "women were for the most part illiterate," for men the "cursive used in documents and letters required unusual exertion," for those "capable of mastering it at all." Even those who had mastered the art might prefer to employ the skills of an amanuensis or a clerk.[31]

The scribal function within a Jewish community of Arago-Catalonia was assimilated in Christian records to the notariate (*scribania*) in name and within that local Jewish community theoretically in juridical effect. The office was more stringently organized and official than in Goitein's times and places. The Hebrew scribe for common documents for any local Jewish public in Arago-Catalonia was a salaried bureaucrat in charge of both communal and private legal documents; he was a secretary to the community, presumably able to hire assistant scribes. The responsa[32] of the celebrated Barcelonan rabbi of the thirteenth century, Solomon (Catalan Salomó) Ibn Adret, contain a clear picture of this dignitary. Many places saw the cantor assume the role. Some places had two scribes. At Lérida Jewish communal ordinances had to bear the scribe's signature plus that of a witness. Another community would not recognize any communal or private document as valid unless the scribe had drafted it. Private documents might require both his signature and those of two witnesses actually present. Since Christian authorities at one place accepted the Hebrew document on the scribe's authority alone, the community wished to follow suit and dispense with the usual witnesses; Ibn Adret approved this course, though the Lérida community did not accept the practice.

The Hebrew scribe kept a record book like the Christian notary.[33] He would of course have followed the Jewish calendar.[34] If the general pattern of Jewish scribes elsewhere had an echo in the realms, then each of the Jewish administrative offices in larger communities might have had its scribe (particularly a scribe as court secretary and recording clerk), and an affluent family might have supported one at least as a copyist. Ordinary or private copyists would have filled a function very different from the central public figure the king's registers depict. The three Jews who respectively signed Christian debt instruments at Barcelona as *scriptor* in 1248, 1280, and 1282 may have been private scribes rather than the public functionaries.[35] Conversely, the scribes who wrote up the "books of administration of past" governance, within the community, were probably officials.[36]

We know little of the external testamentary context for Jew or Christian. Josep Pons i Guri tells us that the general custom in Catalan lands was to insert a will in the register only after the testator was defunct.[37] The monumental work on the Spanish notariate by José Bono describes the will *post mortem scribendum* as oral before death, with witnesses, the written document coming later; this procedure of Visigothic origin, however, may have been rather a local behavior, as at Lérida.[38] The Valencian *Furs*, which provides so much testamentary detail, treats both a dying person dictating a will in the presence of a notary and three or four witnesses (not the seven prescribed by Roman law) who can see and hear all the proceedings as well as the case of an oral declaration without a notary but with three male witnesses. In the second case the witnesses were to record the declaration in front of a judge and more witnesses within three months, a version of the *testament sacramental* seen in chapter 1.[39] The testament thus scribbled (and which we have today in the notary's codex) would have been drafted as a charter and presented to the executors and heirs on the third day after death. The most suitable and worthy of heirs received this copy; but co-heirs and legatees could acquire extra copies "when they wish," presumably at the same stiff fee of 2 sous apiece. Sometimes the notary had two books: one for the *nota*, or abbreviated draft, and one for his fuller copy.[40] No one under fifteen could make a will, and no one under twenty could administer his own estate. It is hard to say how many such rules bound a Jewish testator making a Latinate will. Perhaps Jewish law and custom took precedence in substantials, but the mechanics of drafting and all the practical matters must have applied equally to Jew and Christian.

Obviously the Jewish scribe was a "notary" only in a sense analogous to the Christian, since the juridical and social contexts defined the two so differently. Spain's Hebrew scribe, as Abraham Neuman notes, "followed earlier forms of talmudic and geonic origin, but also incorporated changes that grew out of the European background and showed more particularly the influence of Spanish development."[41] Since a Jew was active also in the Christian world, and contracts or acts there fell under the licensed municipal notaries (even under the special notary for Jewish-Christian instruments, as seen above), the king at times restricted the Hebrew private acts to marriage and testamentary documentation, if they were to be recognized as valid beyond the Jewish community. The limited records make it difficult to say how general was the practice. The varying and fluctuating patterns of medieval Christian administration may help explain why a Jew would record both a Latin and a Hebrew contract, especially a will. Such double documents were not bilingual versions, one a translation of the other, but each was rooted in its own juridical tradition and expression. An opposite form of crossover could occur when a Christian voluntarily preferred the Jewish court and records.[42]

The *sōfer* office appears in a crown privilege of 1271 to "all the Jews of Gerona and Besalú and of other places belonging to their [tax] collectory, that in your contracts of marriage or matrimony between any man and woman, you may draft and cause to be drafted Christian [*christianica*] or Hebraic documents" concerning any phase of promise, dowry, gift, or marriage, according to their customs. They could also make any charters of sale, purchase, or rent "both between a Jew and a Christian as well as between a Jew and a Jew." The king orders "scribes who draft documents in Hebrew," as well as all notaries of those places, to respect this arrangement. A waiver attached here suggests that local notaries had resisted this freedom, occasioning a particular statement of a general arrangement.[43]

Crown letters speak of "the rabbis or scribes of the said local community [*aljama*], secretaries, tax collectors, as well as leaders" and "the rabbis or writers [*scriptores*]" who held "the scribal function of the tax collectory or tax chests." The term *rabbi* at that time and region could involve a community function (religious leader, judge, *shoḥet*-butcher, teacher of children) or simply serve as a mildly honorific title; David Nirenberg suggests that *rabbi* corresponded roughly to the wide range of meanings of the Christian term *clericus.*[44] The Jewish communities of Aragon (though not presumably those of Catalonia) received from King Jaume the Conqueror the right of privacy for all their community documents, even against the king: "Never from now forward would he see or cause to be examined the charters or secret documents [*secreta*] of the said Jews." When Jaume II in 1300 sought to examine tax records in a case of suspected tax fraud by Zaragozan Jews, community leaders blocked the move by presenting the original charter of 1271 from his grandfather, and they even got the privilege confirmed.[45]

Another insight into the record-making activities of the communities comes from the city of Valencia. In 1318 Jaume II had given to Jahudà Adarra and his descendants forever the Jewish *scribania* of Valencia city, at a permanent lease of 2 gold Alfonsine morabatins yearly. By this "hereditary lease" (Catalan *enfiteusi*) he was "the only scribe and no other, of the said *aljama;* and you are to write, or cause to be written through a suitable substitute, all the documents and other Hebrew writings of whatsoever kind of contract." He should "not designate or make anyone overlord [proprietarial landlord for the office] except Us and Ours, although it is permitted to you and yours to sell, assign, or alienate the aforesaid notariate [*scribania*] to one of your own condition [*tuo consimili*], thirty days after giving Us or the bailiff-general of the kingdom of Valencia the preemptive option for buying [Catalan *fadiga*]," thus always respecting the crown's ownership, rent, and option to repurchase. The contract is instructive, showing that this was a specially authorized scribe serving the general Jewish public, not to be confused with scribes serving administrators of the community or involved in literary or less authoritative copying. Jahudà has a monopoly ("you alone and no other are to be the scribe of the said *aljama*"). Since the Valencian community was large and busy, the "office" resembled similar grants of public functions in envisioning the establishment of one or more professionals, supervisors over journeymen scribes. The hereditary nature of the office, its odd combination of feudal fief and investment property, and its wholly alienable nature all deserve remark.[46]

As in many grants of public utilities to Christians, Jews, or Muslims in the realms, the beneficiary was expected to employ or subcontract to professionals who would do the actual work. After receiving the contract, Jahudà therefore "established or substituted in the said scribal office two Jews who drew up this kind of document," namely, those done "in Hebrew in the Jewry of the said city, between the Jews of the same community, among themselves or with others." But Jahudà neglected to supervise them properly. During the next decade "these substitutes took excessive fees from those Jews for whom they made the writings." Even worse, payment of the fee did not necessarily secure a document, "but they have to pay again." The irate customers had recourse to the crown. In April 1327 Jaume II commissioned the community to set the fee and to take any necessary steps to forestall "any extortion" or excess, as well as to see that documents were prepared "in a short time and without malicious delay." The community "may vigorously enforce" all this by such penalties as "removal from the said office or from its exercise, and some other added punishment." Then the king added a proviso that tax records, a special category, "are to be made by a Christian notary and not by a Jew, so that anything decreed or ordered about these can be easily found, and that nothing can be added or subtracted or changed about them." If the Catalan and Valencian Jews had the privilege of keeping their documents "secret," as the Aragonese communities did, no record survives of their challenging the king's intrusion here.[47]

The community "notary" turns up in a number of contexts in the realms. Sometimes we have little more than his name, as with "Rabbi Jucef ibn Jacob [Joce Avenjacob], scribe of the said *aljama* of Zaragoza," or another man appointed at Uncastillo to be both "rabbi of the *aljama* and also writer of documents between Jew and Jew." In the case of Lérida, the appointee "can make Jewish charters and writings with legal force within and outside of the *aljama*." In another "the Jewish parishioners of the main synagogue" at Zaragoza raised questions about the salaries of "the notary" and the rabbis.[48] An unusual incident in 1314 involved "Rabbi Azaria, physician [and] writer or notary in the Jewry of the Jews of Zaragoza," who "of necessity had to attend to visiting the sick and therefore could not attend to the exercise of the aforesaid office of notariate." Azaria petitioned the crown to have a substitute named, through whom he could continue to provide the notarial service, such a substitute being in accord with general past custom. The king graciously concurred.[49]

Finding that the *sōfer* in the realms of Arago-Catalonia is "a theme systematically marginalized" by scholars, Asunción Blasco Martínez has gathered some data in an article on that scribe's role in the upland kingdom of Aragon. With information unavailable there for our thirteenth century, she has focused on the very different fourteenth and fifteenth centuries. In general the second half of the fourteenth century saw major changes in the Aragonese *aljamas* or Jewish communities, a trend affecting also the scribal function. Earlier in the century the situation had been more free and irregular. Scribal production at a given community and time did not always enjoy quasi-notarial standing in both Jewish and Christian acceptance, and the communities enjoyed more freedom or input in selecting the scribe. As early as 1301 Jaume II had decreed that documents involving a Christian party must go into a Christian notary's register. (And in 1317 he limited the number of Christian notaries at the capital city of Zaragoza to only forty.) The Cortes of 1360 allowed Jews to choose any Christian notary, however, thus voiding attempts by various cities to confine much Jewish business with Christians to a monopolist Christian notary. A significant change came in 1389 when Joan I limited the doubly recognized *sōfer*-notary to one per community and reserved his designation to the king. The Hebrew title itself appears now also in Latinate form. In 1424, for example, at the petition of the Calatayud *aljama,* the king designated Açach (Isaac) "as *sōfer* [*in çoferium*] or notary" for all testaments, contracts, or other documents, by him or his assistants for anyone, to be fully recognized also among Christians in and out of court.[50]

Were the Christian notary and the *sōfer* rivals for business? Doubtless in some places the two offices went their separate ways, each registering its own Jewish customers. But it was also not uncommon for a Jew to have his testament or sales contract or debt drawn up by both authorities and in both languages, especially in legal transactions between Jews and non-Jews. The double context of such documents had some acculturative effect. Abraham Neuman, citing the celebrated thirteenth-century rabbi Ibn Adret, notes that "it is highly significant that notarial reforms were occasionally introduced in Jewish community practices emulating the example of the gentile courts."[51]

Crossover: Jews in Christian Wills

A form of crossover not related to Jewish wills directly but inviting exploration as part of the wider story of Jews and wills is the appearance of Jews within Christian wills. Jews turn up as legatees, witnesses, creditors recovering sums, agents acting for a will's executor, or simply someone who finds himself enmeshed in the deceased's unfinished business. These several functions may be sampled in the collection of thirteenth-century wills at the cathedral of Barcelona. For example, "I Bonajeua [*Bonyuas* in the manuscript], nurse of the deceased [Christian] Bondia Farner," gave a receipt in August 1273 to Bondia's heir, Guillem de Banyeres canon of Barcelona, acknowledging the eight pounds in Barcelona money Bondia had left her.[52]

In a different situation the Christian Romeu de Sabadell and a Jew named Rúben de Castelldàsens, "public and sworn brokers [*cursores*] of Barcelona city," acting for the executors of the deceased Jaume Gruny in June 1290, had sold "buildings and a farm" in the suburb of Santa Maria del Mar by public auction, claiming for their brokerage fee 80 Barcelonan sous from the price. The three witnesses to their payment included "Isaac Leví a Jew."[53] This sort of intervention must have been common, since Jews as well as Christians were commissioned or licensed as public brokers in purchases and sales. The actual auction and sale apparently took place in 1286, though this receipt for the brokerage fee is dated 1290. An allied operation by the same executors for the same deceased involved a member of an important Barcelona Jewish family. In 1286 this "Abraham Cap, son of the deceased Samuel Cap," acknowledged receipt of 154 Barcelona sous and 5 pence from those executors, through the bank [*tabula campsoris*] of Ramon Fiveller, drawn from that previous sale price, as payment toward retiring a debt the deceased and his wife Sança owed to Cap for both "capital and interest." The Catalan surname Cap stands for Hebrew Rosh.[54]

A different mingling of Jewish and Christian testamentary business was the loan in 1278 by Salomó, son of the deceased Abraham Adret, to a Christian man and wife "out of the money of the heirs of the deceased Isaac Adret," amounting to 78 sous "counting capital and interest."[55] An adventitious curiosity attaches to this document from Barcelona's cathedral archives in that the principal is Salomó d'En Abraham d'En Adret or Ibn Adret, one of the greatest Jewish scholars of his generation in Spain, chief rabbi of Barcelona, and a great power at the king's court. The Christian principals in the 1290 testamentary transaction in the Barcelona suburb, commented on just above, were notable in their own way—the Gruny, or Grony, family were prominent in crown affairs and as wealthy patricians. Such involvements could be multiplied, since there are so many Christian wills surviving as opposed to Jewish.[56] Their relevance here is the widespread Jewish participation in and familiarity with the ubiquitous Christian testaments. This phenomenon must have been a disposing or reinforcing cause for the multiplication of Jewish Latinate wills.

CHAPTER 3

The Role of Kings and Courts

Though the Hebrew scribe's records were generally recognized by Christian courts, particularly for wills and marriage or dowry affairs, there must have been occasional confusion, rejection, or bad experiences with local Christian courts. The crown issued several clarifications (perhaps more, since our records are very incomplete). To the relatively new and growing Jewish community on conquered Majorca island, Jaume in 1252 included among the communal privileges: "that any of you can effect espousals to your wife with a Hebrew [*hebraica*] charter," with the usual financial arrangements. These *instrumenta iudaica* "have the same validity as if they were drawn by Christian public notaries."[1] This is not mere authenticity or practical acceptance within the *dhimma* pattern of subject communities but rather juridical equivalence in the two worlds. The occasion for this privilege was probably not some challenge or denial by local authorities but simply the need to compile statutes suitable for a frontier into which a jumble of Christian and Jewish communities and legal traditions were arriving. The privileges may well have represented practice elsewhere, either general or (to attract settlers by replicating advantages) possibly from one or other advanced locale.

Equivalence for Hebrew Charters

At Zaragoza in 1264 King Jaume I ordered that "the dowry and espousal documents between anyone of the *aljama* of Jews of Zaragoza, drawn or in future made by the hand of any Jewish scribe who is not licensed [*publicus*], are to be observed just as well as though they were made by the hand of a notary public, as long as there are two Jewish witnesses in them according to the custom of the Jews." If any challenge arises, "We desire that [the complainant] accept justice according to the Sunna of the Jews." The term *Sunna*, meaning the practice and deeds of Muḥammad as clarifying the written Koran, was used by the crown to denote the entire Islamic law and custom and sometimes grotesquely the Judaic tradition and law. This odd usage, though not common, was not rare in the crown registers, and a dozen exemplars might easily be cited for the thirteenth century.[2]

In 1278 from his Perpignan palace in the Pyrenees the Conqueror's son, King Jaume II of Majorca, made a similar but wider statute for his parallel kingdom: "All testaments and nuptial documents" drawn by Jews either on the mainland or the islands "can be made and written by a Jewish scribe or scribes in Hebrew script and with Jewish witnesses only, if they wish." Such instruments "are to be held ratified and valid and as public, just as if they were made by Christian notaries public," and had the same effect when presented by men or women "in or out of judicial usage," just like "the wills and documents" of Christian notaries.[3] A particularly valuable witness is the charter of Jaume II of Arago-Catalonia in 1292 to "the whole community of the Jews of Valencia present and future," assuring the equivalence of Hebrew charters with those of Christian notaries, just as in the era of Jaume the Conqueror. "All charters or Hebrew documents drawn or to be drawn about any activities entered or to be entered between any Jews" were to be observed and to have the same effect "just as, in the times of the illustrious lord king Jaume and lord king Pere, those charters or Hebrew documents were accustomed to be observed and used."[4] This rescues for us the pattern of past Valencian practice under Jaume I, while confirming it also at the end of the thirteenth century.

Time is the fatal enemy of documents. Private charters such as wills tend to disappear unless they lodge by chance in some institutional archives. Even the precious public privileges of Jewish communities were at peril from what King Pere the Ceremonious called "the inroads of worms or feeding of insects," which were corrupting even the crown archives.[5] In 1275 Jaume I addressed the Pyrenean Jews in the various towns centered on Perpignan, Prada, and Puigcerdá (which will hold our attention below). He was "aware that damage and danger threaten you in the documents of concessions and privileges you have from us, both because of the breaking of seals and because of water-damage, as well as because of losing [them], and other various hazards that are known to happen daily." He therefore equated "all copies made and taken from these charters, under the control of your own scribe, or the scribe of the court of the place and sealed with the court's seal," as equal in validity to the original.[6] The devastating destructions of 1391 and 1492 brought extensive ruin to the remnants of the even more vulnerable private documentation.

Just as some Jewish wills survived in the Latinate notarial codices (themselves a fraction of their original numbers), so other kinds of Hebrew documents persisted in Latinate notices in the crown registers. The king functioned in Jewish community life as a kind of supreme court for intra-*aljama* legal actions. Some of these cases were appeals from the Jewish Bet Din, but as Abraham Neuman remarks, "in far too many cases the royal personages appear as judges of the first instance" at the request of one or both Jewish parties. Not only did the royal court invoke the Jewish law or sometimes deflect such an issue to Jewish judges but (by decree of Jaume I) it preferred Hebrew documents where available. Norman Roth perceives this appeal to the crown in a sense completely contrary to Neuman's. In Spain Jews frequently used civil as well as criminal royal courts. In such a court the Jew had full standing as a person, unlike his situation in ecclesiastical courts and law. Rulers like Jaume the Conqueror had savant rabbis at hand to advise them in such cases.

Recourse to the ruler was not only by appeal from lower or Jewish courts but was available directly to Jewish subjects and on matters a modern might consider too trivial for the royal ear. Roth notes, for example, an appeal directly to the king about a disagreement over seating in a new synagogue. We need not suspect some reason of state, some eminence in the petitioner, or some financial interest by the crown in prosaic cases that preoccupied kings such as the Conqueror. To Roth this recourse was a form of representation in medieval Spain, "a voice" for the Jew in the general public realm.[7] Living in a permanently parallel society, Jews related directly to king and to crown officials, under crown protection. Paradoxically, this vertical relationship made a more powerful linkage with Christian society, or rather with the pluricultural society called by shorthand Christian, than did the horizontal linkages of shared social and economic connections with their Christian neighbors.

Any number of crown interventions involved documents in Hebrew or Hebrew script. In the 1280s a Valencian Jew had given his son three small towns or villages by a charter in Hebrew. When the kingdom's justiciar confiscated these in connection with a debt, Alfons III ordered the official to respect "the Hebrew documents and also other Hebrew documents drawn between Jews on other contracts."[8] Alfonso also had to give his attention to Hebrew documents of debt, partnership, agreement between *aljamas,* lease of houses, nuptials, and a loan drawn by Rabbi Meir ("Mahir"). Sample cases taken from the king's general registers for 1289 include the purchase in that year by Salamó Baḥya of Murviedro "of the pasturage tax [*erbatge*] of the kingdom of Valencia, as is more fully contained in the Jewish [i.e., Hebrew] charter drawn up for this."[9] Similarly, a lawsuit by four Jews over their inclusion in Lérida's Jewish tax collectory involved "a public Jewish [Hebrew] document drawn up."[10] Salāmah Mālikī ("Malagi") of Barcelona and his son Astruc were involved in a court case over "some buildings and their rental, located in the Barcelona Jewry," put out at lease "with Hebraic documents." To decide the ensuing quarrel the crown ordered an arbitrator appointed from the community to judge "according to Hebraic law and the Sunna of the Jews."[11] In another dispute, between the Lérida Jew Mossé Ibn Zabr ("Cabra") and Chayyim Azarel ("Chaim Azcarel") together with his son David, over the marriage "contracted some time ago" between Mossé and the daughter of Chayyim, the king ordered arbitration by "one Jew, competent and not unacceptable to the parties," using the "Hebrew documents" and proceeding "according to Hebrew law."[12]

Crown Testamentary Intervention

If actual Hebrew wills have rarely survived, considerable documentation *about* Jewish wills and testamentary activity has been preserved in the crown registers. In some cases the king is confirming the will or one of its provisions. In others he addresses fraud that has come to light. In a few he clears the name and clarifies the financial ambiguities of some Jew involved in crown finances just before his death. In yet others the king has to settle disputed wills or an element in such a will, as the heirs squabble over the provisions. A Jew might die intestate or have no direct heirs. Crown officials might have seized his properties or complainants brought claims arising from charges of usury. In more than one case the king intervened to protect or reinforce the widow's right to her dowry, to review the ongoing administration by executors, to establish an administrator for minor children, to sequester property until heirs could be found, or to confer a general crown protection.

In a very early case at Barcelona in 1227 Perfet Vidal Gracià, a Jew and former crown bailiff of Barcelona, left much of his fortune to his seven nephews. The mutual interlacing of crown and personal finances caused the bailiff of Barcelona to sequester Perfet's goods. On appeal King Jaume declared the seven to be proper heirs, released the legacies, and arranged a settlement. The heirs forgave the crown a debt of 11,362½ sous it owed Perfet as well as all other debts owed by King Jaume's father Pere I (II of Aragon) and Jaume's uncle-regent Count Sanç. The crown waived claims on Perfet's property involving business with "butchers, bakers, wine-sellers, clothiers, and all others" and dismissed any other debt. The agreement was to have effect by "each law both Latin and Hebrew." The nephews signed this charter in Hebrew.[13]

In 1268 King Jaume ruled on a will drawn in Hebrew for the deceased Benvenist according to the custom of the Jews. He approved its six executors: Jahudà de la Cavalleria, Astruc Sa Porta, Ismāʿīl Ibn Venist of Morella, Mossé Sullam, Perfet "de Sa" Real, and the widow Jamīla, all "constituted executors according to the custom of the Jews for the aforesaid Benvenist and by him, as manifestly appears in his testament drawn in Hebrew." The text distinguishes between the deceased as "Ben Venist" and his executor as "Ibn [Aben] Venist." The latter's origin so early in recently conquered Valencian Morella supports the conclusion that his immediate antecedents were Judeo-Arabic; his first name is both Arabic Ismāʿīl and Hebrew Yishmael. The Benvenist were a powerful family in the realms and in Occitania as well as in North Africa; in thirteenth-century Catalonia three generations bore the honorific or princely title ha-Nasi. Among the other executors Jahudà de la Cavalleria was particularly distinguished as the treasurer of the highland kingdom of Aragon. In the presence of such notables, King Jaume dispensed all six from having to produce the customary inventory of the decedent's goods.[14]

A related and complex case that same day involved the great Salomó Ibn Adret suing the four Jewish executors of Benvenist de Porta of Villafranca. An earlier decedent, Bonanasc of Besalú, had apparently willed his goods to his children Sara and Belshom (with Ibn Adret as

Belshom's guardian) and to Benvenist de Porta of Villafranca. When Benvenist himself died, leaving his claim to his own son Vidal, the executors for Benvenist (three of whom also served as Bonanasc's executors) assumed control of his goods. Ibn Adret then initiated a suit, arguing that Bonanasc had died intestate, thus obviating the claim of Benvenist/Vidal and returning all of Bonanasc's properties to Belshom, Ibn Adret's own ward. But the executors produced a will naming Bonanasc's daughter Sara as an heir, so King Jaume ruled against his friend and adviser Ibn Adret. The long account of this tangled trial deserves study; it is transcribed below in the appendix, document 6.

The final stage and delivery of sentence took place in the Dominican convent at Barcelona, "in the presence and witness" of a remarkable array of notables, including the bishop and archdeacon of Barcelona, several barons (including two of the Anglesola family), the patrician notable and syndic of Barcelona Jaume Gruny, the king's confessor Arnau de Sagarra (who had studied under Albert the Great at Paris), "and many other witnesses," most notably the greatest canon lawyer in Christendom, Ramon de Penyafort. Penyafort's presence lends an adventitious interest to this charter, but the solemnity and weight of such unusual witnesses shows how seriously King Jaume took this lawsuit between his Jewish subjects. Benvenist de Porta, whose will was in question, was brother to the notable and courtier Astruc de Porta (whom some historians have confused with the towering figure of Nahmanides), from one of the great Jewish families of the realms. Ibn Adret was the king's most prominent Jewish adviser and, of course, a scholar respected then throughout the world of European Jewry and still famous today as RaShBa. The document is not only an example of the crown's role in the testamentary activity of the Jewish communities but also a glimpse into the rarefied world of courtiers, Christian and Jewish, around King Jaume the Conqueror.[15]

Hard on the heels of this elaborate closure came two waivers of prosecution, in the guise of a royal pardon. In the first King Jaume dismissed any possible crown action at law against "Vidal de Porta, the son of the deceased Benvenist de Porta, and the executors of your said father, and your successors in perpetuity" that could be brought "by reason of Benvenist himself and by reason of his deceased son Perfet, and also by reason of the deceased Bonanasc of Besalú or his heirs." The king went on to confirm in perpetuity "all gifts, concessions, establishments or determinations made by Us to the aforesaid Benvenist with Our documents, both concerning the goods of the same Benvenist your father or also concerning the goods of the aforesaid Bonanasc," ratifying and confirming all such documentation.[16] On the same day, the day after that final closure, a similar waiver went "to you the executors of the deceased Benvenist de Porta" and to Vidal, releasing them from responding at law to "the son of the deceased Bonanasc of Besalú or his guardian or also any other persons, about any suits or claims made or to be made against you" in connection with the legacies of Benvenist or Bonanasc. With these final waivers the lawyers forestalled any reopening of this hard-fought case.[17]

A tangled case came before Pere the Ceremonious in 1347 in Valencia. The deceased Astruc de Beers had left behind two sets of children by his two wives. Though divorce or the polygamy sometimes found among Catalan Jews might be suspected here, the phrasing allows for either or both wives to be dead. Neither is named or given any role in the proceedings. The first set of children had a guardian-executor; the second set, presumably younger, had at least a relative as procurator. The quarrel over Astruc's will had gone on "for a long time" (*dudum*) and finally was resolved by a Jew of Tárrega "as arbiter and arbitrator." The son of the first wife got a residence, his father's seat in the Barcelona synagogue, a Bible, and "a volume of Moses of Egypt containing fourteen books" (clearly the *Mishneh Torah* of Maimonides). The son of the second wife was to have had an equivalent share from his father's properties in Villafranca del Panadés, a share his procurator soon rejected. An appeal to the king resulted in a period of calm assessment of the estate by both parties. If they could not reach agreement, the bailiff of Barcelona was then to elect "a third assessor or arbitrator acceptable to the parties," the bailiff enforcing his decision.[18]

An even odder case at Perpignan in 1327 was more easily resolved. The deceased Bonjorn de Barri of Collioure had made his son Daví his universal heir, but only on condition that he stay away from strife-torn Perpignan for ten years and also stay out of the kingdom of Majorca's politics and finances. Should young Daví fail in these conditions, "all his estate would devolve to Us" the king! "Subsequently the aforesaid testator established codicils in which he imposed certain other prohibitory conditions" on his heir and again made the crown his sole heir if Daví did not abide by them. Pleading that the conditions were "very onerous and dangerous" (some false accusations were abroad in the Jewish community), Daví sought and received from the crown release from the conditions.[19]

Certain cases more obviously invited crown intrusion. At Calatayud in 1349 the plague (presumably the Black Death then raging) carried off "a number of Jews among the wealthiest and highest taxpayers," who left behind no heirs. By custom in such cases the community itself took the place of heirs, but this disposition left the other taxpayers overburdened (the estates apparently going to philanthropic and other nontax uses). The crown provided relief by instructing that such estates should go to tax-paying "heirs" who might normally receive some legacy "by testaments, gifts, or otherwise, according to the code or rite of the Jews."[20] In other cases the king seems to have entered with some reluctance, passing the problems on to committees. The physician Master Astruc Bonsenyor of Barcelona petitioned the king in 1349 to take up the case of his friend, the widow Mira (a form of Hebrew Miryam or the popular Catalan feminine Mira for "notable"). The royal register reads: "Recently fallen into grave illness she drew up her testament, which for various reasons or causes proposed in Our presence is said to be null and according to the Hebrew law ought to lack effective validity." As a result, "the dowry of the said Jewess ought to be divided in equal shares among those nearest to her in the family line." King Pere the Ceremonious therefore commissioned Astruc Jahudà des Cortal and Cresques Salamó "to judge whether the aforesaid testament ought to be considered as valid or as null and what ought to be done about the said dowry consequently" according to "the rite of the Jews and [their] law and justice." For their mission the king "by this charter establishes you Our proxies [*vices*]." Thus the king acceded to the role of intervener while distancing himself from the actual complexities of solving the case personally.[21]

Larceny and Fraud

Scandals titillate, so cases of fraud particularly catch the eye. Discovered fraud was also most likely to rouse a demand for justice on the part of other potential legatees and to invite intervention by the crown. A case that preoccupied Pere the Great left a paper trail of nine documents throughout 1285 and 1286, with a final echo in 1287. Jahudà of Limoux (Limós indicating that Languedocian city of origin rather than the Catalan surname Llimós) had died and disputes of an unspecified nature "about the will and about the goods bequeathed to his wife Bonadona" had arisen. King Pere's entry into this fray took the form of an instruction to the bailiff of Lérida "that you do not allow this Bonadona to be unjustly aggravated," so long as she was willing to respond at law to any formal charges.[22] Ten days later the king had been apprised of those charges and had taken them seriously enough to launch a legal investigation: "We have learned that when Jahudà of Limoux, a Jew of Lérida, was dying in his final moments and desired to draw up a will, his wife Bonadona and some Jews among her relatives fraudulently and by force caused him to draft a will beyond what he would have done in sound mind and according to his [real] wishes." The king ordered the bailiff of Lérida "diligently to investigate the truth about this, and to proceed at law against whomever you shall find guilty of the aforesaid."[23]

A half-year later, in receipt of the bailiff's report, Pere expressed his dissatisfaction at its inconclusive nature: "We have learned that you received both oral testimony or depositions of those against whom the investigation was made, and of those witnesses produced on certain points touching that affair, in the business of that investigation that We recall having committed to you against Bonadona, the wife of the deceased Jahudà of Limoux, a citizen of Lérida, and her other accomplices, concerning a fraud committed (it is said) by them in the testament of the said Jahudà." None of this had availed. "We have learned besides," the king continued, "that both those against whom the investigation was made, as well as the aforesaid witnesses, swearing with contempt for religion and vacillating in their depositions, fraudulently varied what they said, suborned, to such a degree that (the truth buried) you cannot appropriately conclude the business of the investigation." The crown's instructions therefore ran: "If from plausible presuppositions or notable arguments you gather that the aforesaid [persons] (against whom the investigation was held, and also against those [witnesses] produced or to be produced) stand as suborned, or in their depositions differing, or otherwise suspect as to speaking the truth: you are to take care to examine them and their words again" and to start a proper lawsuit if that seems reasonable, and "without distractions" to push forward "to a definitive sentence," forwarding it "to Us ourselves, wherever We shall be."[24] Again the king's persistence, intensity, and personal involvement are striking.

The case dragged on. Nearly six months later the new king Alfons wrote to the same bailiff of Lérida. Alfons reviewed the progress of the case under his father, "against Bonadona the wife of the deceased Jahudà of Limoux a Jew of Lérida and her other accomplices, because of fraud said to have been committed by them in the will of the said Jahudà, and also against certain [witnesses] produced in this affair who vacillated in their depositions as suborned." The new king now insisted that "according to the mandate" of King Jaume "you are to proceed in that affair right up to a final sentence, and you are to send that business or trial record to Us immediately, protected by the power of your seal." That was not to be the end: a day would be assigned "suitable to the parties, on which to appear before Us for hearing the sentence on this matter and for proceeding" as shall be necessary.[25] Final resolution of the case does not appear; Bonadona turns up in several more documents that same year, and in late 1287 she claimed and was awarded the return of 500 Jaca sous deposited in the course of her tangled career in court. As in other such cases, Jahudà and Bonadona do not seem special people or court Jews. The situation seems rather one of public scandal, unseemly tumult among the king's more affluent subjects, to be handled for his Jews as he would have done for similar Christians. On the side of the Jews, such cases apparently involved contestants who would not arbitrate or settle within the community but who allowed their dispute to spill over into the royal courts.

In another case in 1286 the new king Alfons required the executors of a Barcelona Jew to present an accounting to his legatees. The king ordered the bailiff of Barcelona and the vicar and the bailiff of Cervera "to compel Biona Shealtiel [*Saltel*] and Isaac Sa Porta, Jews, executors of the testament and goods of the deceased Astrug de Porta, a Jew of Besalú resident at Barcelona, to render an account or reckoning to the children or heirs of the said deceased or even to his guardian or guardians, about that which they administered of the goods of the said deceased." If the executors "perhaps cause delay of the audit," these officials "are to take suitable legal precautions by your authority, in such wise that they cannot dissipate the goods." The officials were also to require the executors (and pledge their property) "to restore to the said heirs or their guardians whatever they are bound to return after the audit." In this episode one must resist the temptation to conflate Astruc de or Sa Porta with Bonastruc de Porta, the great Nahmanides, or with Astruc de Porta de Penadès, both public figures. The deceased here seems an altogether more private figure. This single echo of his postmortem troubles reveals a strong suspicion or near certainty of maladministration by executors, to the detriment of child heirs who required a "guardian."[26]

Yet another fraud "came before" King Pere in 1284. "The Jewess

Boneta" tried "to defraud her daughter," the wife of Bondavid the son of Astruc b. Bonsenyor, concerning "the lawful share that she ought to have from the goods of her mother at the time of her death." Boneta, "forgetful of her blood ties, against the duty of [family] piety and in fraud and injury against the said daughter," transferred all movables to a friend, Shaltiel Astruc, who then "turned them to [her] own ownership, doing business and making contracts and putting out at loan." Because the royal power is obligated to restrain such injury, the culprit must now put all those goods plus the contracts (*cirographa*) before the king's vicar of Barcelona, where the king will make a final decision on this matter.[27]

King Alfons in 1286 had to deal with Sol, the determined widow of Avihu Ibn Rudriq ("Avenrodrich"), a Jew of Teruel. In June the king noted that Sol and her sons "want to flee from here, so as not to pay us the 4,000 gold morabatins" that Avihu had bequeathed to Alfons's predecessor, King Pere the Great. Alfons ordered his official "to arrest without delay" both widow and sons "and to confiscate all their goods" until they would release that sum. At the official rate set by Jaume the Conqueror in 1247, the Alfonsine gold morabatin was worth 6 Valencian sous or 7½ Jaca sous, making the total legacy 24,000 Valencian sous, or 30,000 Jacan. Using an exchange ratio from the early 1280s, David Romano reckons the total at 42,000 Barcelonan sous or 63,000 Jacan. (The disparity in reckoning may reflect the difference between the *maravedí alfonsí* of Alfonso VIII of Castile, current in 1247, and the later coinage of that name by Alfonso X, which had two coins to the earlier *maravedí*'s one.) With such an enormous sum at stake and with the king as beneficiary, royal intervention is understandable. What is not clear is Avihu's motive for such a legacy to the recently deceased king and in effect to the reigning king. A reasonable conjecture might be that Avihu had mingled public and private moneys, after the fashion of the day among tax farmers and financiers, so that the crown's interest was merely in recovering its own. In Avihu's case the context of community taxation, or the need for or gratitude for a privilege, offers alternate possibilities. The explanation may be much more complicated, as in a similar huge gift in a Jewish will to the kings of Majorca and France, to be considered below in chapter 4. Whatever the motive, our own interest is in the attempted fraud and the crown's intervention.

In July the king ordered his official to extract from the prisoner Sol her share of Teruel's current Jewish taxes. An August letter reveals the manner of the fraud: "You hid the testament of your said husband in which, it is said, he bequeathed to the lord king Our father" the 4,000 morabatins. As was common in medieval quarrels, an arbitration was arranged by which Sol surrendered to the crown only 2,500 sous of Jaca—a tenth or less than a fifth of the original sum, depending on the rate of exchange followed. Romano suggests as reasons urgent need for money, legal doubts about one king's legacy going to another king or about the legacy as such (seen in the phrase "it is said"), or just a desire to close the case. King Alfons issued a pardon or waiver, and he ordered his official "that you acquit the said Jewess, and restore and release her movable and property goods which you seized and confiscated from her."

The names in this series of four crown documents are intriguing. The family name Ibn Rudriq suggests an Arabic background, though the names of his brother Jacob and of Jacob's sons Mossé, Samuel, and Isaac carry no such hint. The first document calls him David (*uxor Davidis*), doubtless a scribal confusion of Avihu with Catalan Daviu. The scribes also give him variously as Abayut and (twice) Avayu. Two biblical names are involved: Hebrew Avihud ("majestic father") and Avihu ("he is my father"), the latter seeming best to fit the majority of spellings and the early confusion with Daviu. The Romance first name Sol is declined in the Latin text as masculine, indicating its meaning as "Sun" rather than as derived from Catalan *sòl* for "ground" or the Aragonese adverb for "alone." As Sun it would be a cognate or crossover for Hebrew Shimshona, the feminine for biblical (English) Samson.[28]

Another bit of larceny involved the physician Salamó Ibn Vives, son of Vives Salamó, as executor of Samuel Ibn Vives of Valencia. Salamó Ibn Vives belonged to a major distinguished family of the realms. King Jaume II described his crime and the conclusion of the affair in a wrap-up charter of 1310. The king reviewed "the seizure [*empara*] on Our part, done through Our faithful executive agent [*porter*] Arnau Cortit, of the goods of Samuel Ibn Vives the deceased Jew of Valencia, by reason of the [legal] action Our court was taking against the goods of that deceased because of the security guarantee that he had made to Our court on behalf of the Jew Ayhon Ibn Menax (biblical Hebrew Menashe), because of the Játiva bailiate and its revenues which the said Ayhon had previously purchased at auction." After that action "and against the said attachment, together with Jahudà Ibn Vives, you [Salamó Ibn Vives] laid hold of a certain chest of the said deceased, which was in the house of Na Vives, a Jewess of Valencia, and took away out of it things that were there." To cover up, "you and the said Jahudà, claiming that the said defunct Jew on his deathbed appointed you and the said Jahudà his executors, after his death caused a Hebrew charter to be made" to that effect.

"And when the truth about the foregoing was sought by Jaume de Arters a judge of Our court, Pere de Corell a citizen, and Jahudà Ibn Ḥasan a Jew of Valencia, [all] appointed by Us to the investigation of this, and when they had caused for Our part a communal ban [*alatma*] to be placed on all Jews of the *aljama* of the said city (that on a fixed day they would give testimony concerning what they knew about the goods of the said deceased), against the said ban you omitted saying the truth about what you knew on the aforesaid, within the assigned period of the ban, on account of which you are said to have incurred a penalty of person and goods." Eventually a compromise was worked out by which the physician Salamó Ibn Vives "paid and gave on Our behalf 4,000 Barcelona sous to Our faithful treasurer Pere Martí." The documentary formula does not indicate a criminal fine, however, which doubtless would not have been so huge. It was rather that of a face-saving pardon, an amnesty and restoration of the most sweeping kind.[29] The indignation apparent in this whole account and the rallying of the Jewish community to impose a ban and to force a general mobilizing of Jewish witnesses indicates how seriously both the crown and the Jews viewed such tampering with testaments.

Although accusations that executors had mismanaged a decedent's estate were not uncommon, such charges may have cloaked the impatience of an heir or of other claimants. In 1328 Mossé Cohen, son of the deceased Aaron Cohen of Tortosa, made such a charge in the matter of an important legacy of his uncle Jucef Cohen: "In his last testament he arranged to have a school [of higher learning] organized for the use of poor Jewish students, for which school he willed a certain residence of his located in the Jewry of Tortosa, as well as many books and 1,000 Barcelonan sous to provide for the said school." The uncle's wife Bonadona "consented and approved the will." His heir Aaron, and two other Jews named as executors, held "full power of directing and administering the school and the aforesaid goods." Eventually only one executor survived as director "for sixteen years and more," until his recent death; but "it is said he badly administered the aforesaid school." Now the plaintiff Mossé Cohen asserts "that he as a person connected with the said testator ought to oversee and administer the said school and its properties and fulfill the last will of the said testator" as "the nearest to the said testator." King Alfons ordered a judge of his court to investigate and resolve the case "briefly and simply, all malice put aside," since Mossé was about to sue the "heirs and holders" of the estate of the recently dead administrator.

An oddly similar case came before Pere the Ceremonious thirty years later. Abraham Mayl (a variant of Meir) had left as a pre-gift *inter vivos* to his community at Egea, "out of piety and for his salvation and that of his relatives," a school for young boys. This involved "some houses of his located in front of the synagogue of the Jews of the said town," adjoining other buildings owned by Abraham, "and certain Hebrew books," all on condition that "some master or rabbi of the said community would have to live there and make his residence in those houses and instruct Jewish boys of the said community in their Law, and that the said community could not convert or alienate the said houses to other uses besides those." Some Jews of Egea, however, acting "from hatred of the said Abraham," saw to it that the teacher did not live there or instruct the boys, to the damage both of the community and Abraham. Responding to Abraham's plea, the king ordered the community to respect the conditions of the gift if Abraham's case had been properly presented; otherwise the bailiff's lieutenant would "enforce and compel" this order.[30]

At times the fraud presented before the king does not seem weighty enough to have justified royal recourse. Meir, a Jew of Figueras and son of a deceased physician of the royal household, Master Cresques, deposed that "certain books were left him by his father, among them a book called Avicenna written on delicate calfskin parchments in a round script (otherwise called among Jews 'squared'), and the said book at the time of death was stolen or taken away from his house, and now he has discovered it in the hands of a Jewish surgeon of Barcelona called Master Bonjua Cabrit." King Pere ordered the city's bailiff to sequester the book, investigate the circumstances, and do justice "without any litigation and formal documentation." Though this case involved the disposition of a legacy, it is not clear that an actual will had been prepared, Hebrew or Latin.[31]

The matter of the missing book probably involved more expense than the "certain quantity of oil" left by the dying Hizquia (a Hebrew biblical name) as "legacies to be distributed both as alms and otherwise." Hizquia's father, Master Salamó Bofill of Perelada, another physician of the royal household, complained that Hizquia "had no claims on it" but that it belonged to Salamó "and was being kept in his pharmacy-shop for himself." The Jewish authorities, "invading and opening the shop, took away" the oil. The disposition of this case is illegible but presumably followed the usual course in such minor disputes—investigation by the bailiff and a prudent decision without legalities.[32]

Young Mossé b. Samiel: Arbitration

Twelve documents in Jaume's registers for 1272 detail the case about "the deceased Salamó Samiel, formerly called differently Bonisac Samiel from Carcassonne [and apparently also from Alès above Nîmes], a Jew of Perpignan." Salamó left as his heir Mossé, his boy-child (*impuber*). Mossé and the property were in the hands of his widowed mother, Botina, and two co-executors, Vives Vidal and Astruc of Belcayre (Beaucaire). In his first contact with this situation, the king had confirmed this "will or last testament."[33] Crown confirmation of the will had been appropriate in this instance because the deceased had been involved with public moneys, presumably in farming or collecting taxes. King Jaume therefore received a settlement of 6,000 sous of Melgueil (an Occitan money) from the estate.[34] The king had further concerns, however: "mindful of the industry of the administrators and the amount of the patrimony," he and his advisers feared that the child's "goods might be depleted [*devastari*] or even lost" by inept representation. The previously appointed three may have seemed too amateurish to manage so unusually large a patrimony. The king now "added and associated" as an oversight commission "two residents of Perpignan"—Bonafós Mossé of Narbonne and Samiel, a son of the deceased Cresques of Béziers. They were to audit the actions of the widow and executors each year until the boy was eighteen, "despite the confirmation given by Us to the testament of the said deceased Salamó."[35] Jewish courts intervened regularly in cases of such "orphans," and the king's action probably represented his validation of their action, or else their action as consultants of the crown when he returned the case to the community for adjudication. Such interplay of royal and communal courts was frequent enough; its application to a will allows a glimpse of this Occitan group of relatives and neighbors, part of the migration into Jaume's realms, away from the increasing Frankish control.

At the same time the king extended to all five executors (including the newly appointed reviewers) a formal charter of amnesty or clearance for any "bad or fraudulent or underhanded administration." No civil or criminal action could henceforth be taken under any law, on account of past performance, nor could further accounting be demanded by anyone except the boy heir. To that heir, however, "you are obliged to render an audit and explanation about each and every" such action.[36] A companion document absolved the young heir from any blame or consequence "of any public or private malfeasance" by his deceased father against the crown. It also released "the goods of your said father" from any danger "of being confiscated in whole or in part" by reason of crown claims or rights.[37] A separate charter indicates that malicious gossip and false charges were harassing the family. The king orders that anyone delating or accusing young Mossé or his deceased father must pay court expenses and any damages, unless the accuser can offer solid proof.[38]

Three months later, obviously in response to the executors' intervention, King Jaume again reviewed the facts in licensing all five executors and then specifically gave them "license and authority to buy in Perpignan and the Roussillon region, in the name and for the advantage of the said boy-child Mossé, properties and possessions, together or separately, for 10,000 Valencian sous" and to pay out that sum without interference. Anyone, presumably agents or an individual executor, who "dares to buy" such properties outside those two areas without "the will and consent of all of you" will incur a fine of 1,000 sous for each such action.[39] A companion charter that day made the same point by prohibiting export of Mossé's inheritance outside Perpignan and its region, Roussillon: "For the greater advantage of the boy-child Mossé, and lest his goods be depleted [*dissipari*], We wish and decree by this present charter, that any goods of the said child (namely cash or anything else or funds) not be extracted or exchanged or carried outside Perpignan or the land of Roussillon by a person or persons without the consent" of the five executors, "namely until the said child Mossé has passed the age of eighteen years." Transgressors were to make restitution and also pay the fine of 1,000 sous (here described as of Melgueil) per violation. The investment sum alone reveals the deceased as one of the more affluent Jews of Perpignan. The loan and investment charters of Perpignan studied by Richard Emery confirm this impression and also show some of the loan activity carried on by the executors for young Mossé.[40]

The last three documents of November 1272 put further restrictions on the heir himself. Mossé could not leave "Perpignan or the land of Roussillon for other parts, without the permission of his mother" and other guardians, "until the same Mossé will have attained eighteen years."[41] Another charter blocked his marrying during that time: "Let no one dare or be able to espouse any wife to the aforesaid Mossé, or make or establish a marriage between him and any Jewish woman, until the said Mossé will have reached eighteen years."[42] Finally, during that November King Jaume formally named Mossé's mother Botina as direct guardian. "Noting it to be in harmony with reason and with law, that the mother ought to bring up her boy-children after the father has died," the king made "the said Botina mother and nurturer of the said boy-child Mossé, until he shall attain the age of eighteen years, unless she meanwhile takes a husband."[43]

When Mossé's mother Botina died the following year, King Jaume again entered this testamentary scene. He acceded to the request of the two remaining executors that "another guardian cannot be appointed while you are alive, nor can any administrator or guardian be given to the said ward or adjoined in the said guardianship, unless it shall first be proved against you in Our court that you conducted yourself less than well in that guardianship."[44] Such intense and sustained intervention by the crown in a Jewish testamentary affair may have been unusual, or perhaps it is only better documented than most. The deceased Bonisac does not seem to have been among the highest of Jaume's Jews in wealth or reputation. Neither he nor his little heir Mossé appears elsewhere in the king's registers, and it is difficult to get a sense of his role in crown finances. The episode nevertheless demonstrates how forcefully and minutely the king could intervene in a relatively normal and nonfraudulent case.

At times the crown's role was limited to approving and validating a compromise reached by the contending parties under the legal advice of a local royal judge. In mid-1274 King Jaume "approved, conceded, and confirmed the agreement by Salamó Sullam de Porta and by Vidal Provençal and by Salamó Cohen and Astruc Salamó, Jews, arbitrators appointed with the advice of Pere Rubi, judge for Perpignan and Roussillon, between Astruc Vidal (the son of Vidal Astruc, a deceased Jew of Perpignan) and his brother Abraham on the one side and also Colasana the wife of the said deceased Vidal Astruc, and on the other side Perfet Garcia and Todros [*Toroz*] Garcia [both surnames scribal slips for the noted Jewish family Gracià in Catalonia?] and Vidal, brothers of the said Colasana, in the name and cause of Nina and Petita, the daughters of the deceased Vidal Astruc, concerning the goods namely and the inheritance of the said Nina and Petita, as more fully contained in the charters drawn on the matter."[45]

King Jaume's eldest son Prince Jaume had confirmed a Jewish will as well as an audit of the executor's management and also certain "agreements and arrangements and requests done between the children of the deceased Vidal Astruc of Perpignan and the guardian-executor Bondia of Lunel, appointed in the will." Now in early 1273 the king himself added his confirmation both of the will and of the arrangements.[46] Jaume's son and successor Pere the Great acted traditionally in a 1282 lawsuit "between Astruc Jacob Xixó [Shashon/Sasson] on the one side and his in-law Jucef Cohen on the other, about a matter of marriages and wills." The king instructs the subvicar of Tortosa, before whom the case had come "by delegation of the lord king," to decide it "by the Hebrew Sunna," or law. The casual use of Islamic "Sunna" again shows how acceptable the grotesque usage had become.[47] It appears again in the case of "the deceased Astruc of Gerona formerly of Murviedro," modern Sagunto in the kingdom of Valencia, who had left his estate or a considerable part of it to his daughter Astruga and his nephew Astruguet, both wards "in his testament." King Alfons in early 1286 ordered his bailiff "to uphold and defend" these children in their claim: "You are not to permit these wards to be evicted from ownership of those goods without a legal trial," and "if perchance they have been evicted" from all or part of that legacy, "you are to cause them to be restored in that possession, according as ought to be done by the law and code [*forum*] or Sunna of the Jews."[48]

A Will in Hebrew and Latin

The most fascinating of the royal intrusions into the field of Jewish wills is a charter of Jaume I in mid-1263. In granting his confirmation, conferring royal protection on its child-beneficiary, and summing the major provisions, Jaume supplies a kind of paraphrased will. More to our purpose, he describes the will as existing in two versions, in Latin and in Hebrew. The Jewish wills in Latin examined below may reasonably have had a corresponding Hebrew charter, but we have no survivals by which to test the supposition or to compare two versions. Would the Hebrew have been more detailed and itemized? Was the Latin concerned with the few matters that might enter a Christian court? This 1263 will of Salamó of Tortosa, a Jew of Barcelona, suggests that the two versions were in substance interchangeable and could be treated as one document in two languages.

Salamó had been "some time dead" by the time the case reached the king. Salamó had made "his testament and last will (as is evident) in two charters [*instrumenta*], one of which is written in Latin and validated by Pere de Castellterçol, lieutenant of Guillem de Torrelles Our vicar in Barcelona, and the other is written in Hebraic script [*littera*]." Salamó's executors were Biona Satell, Isaac son of the deceased Bonet of Piera, and Zarc Modec, "our Jews of Barcelona." The universal heir was Bellor, the daughter of Salamó, a minor, "to whom he left all his goods, whatever he had or ought to have anywhere by any title." The executors were explicitly designated also as "guardians and administrators" of Bellor, "just as is contained more amply in the text [*series*] or composition [*forma*] of the said testament." Seeing that the business had been done "correctly and carefully," Jaume confirmed "the entire disposition or text of the aforesaid testament" as to choice of executors, establishment of guardianship, arrangement for Bellor's marriage later ("with the counsel of the said guardians and administrators and also the mother"), and finally "as to each and every [item] contained and likewise expressed in the same testament."

A closing statement allows "that if anyone can show he has a greater claim on the goods of Salamó" than Bellor, in any way or reasoning, this confirmation cannot be cited to the prejudice of such claims, which may be freely brought before the king's bailiff or vicar of Barcelona. Bellor is then put under crown protection in the usual formulas of the safeguard called a *guiatge*. Bailiffs and vicars of Barcelona, present or future, must respect the testament or "incur Our anger and indignation." The document so clearly brings together the themes of bilingual wills and crown intervention that it is presented below in full transcription (see appendix, doc. 2). It does not illuminate the problem of form in such double wills; presumably the Latin notary drafted his text in Roman law forms (as Latin wills themselves show), while the Hebrew text would have displayed the mentality and expressions traditional to Hebrew wills. There would thus have been three texts and "languages"—the megatext of the testator, devised mentally in Romance, the notary's translation into Latin language and legal structure, and the Hebrew scribe's translation of the underlying megatext into his traditional forms and language. The original expression of the testator himself, as will be seen below, was probably informal oral dictation.[49]

Another will of 1263, just five months later, survives because a copy came to rest at Santa Anna, a church of the Canons of the Holy Sepulcher in Barcelona. Probably because the clerics had come into possession of one or more of the will's properties, they had a notarized copy of it drafted in July 1293 and deposited in their archives. The deponent was Astruc "Scandarini," elsewhere "Ascandarini," son of Abraham of Alexandria (Latin *de Alexandria*). Joaquim Miret i Sans and Moïse Schwab, who encountered this single will in compiling their collection of Jewish documents from the eleventh through the thirteenth centuries, were puzzled by the strange surname. Leila Berner found other notices of the family in Barcelona and confirmed the spelling. The name of Astruc's father, Abraham of Alexandria, however, provides a clue to its meaning. Al-Iskandarīya is the Arabic name for the great Egyptian port of Alexandria, where Catalan commercial connections and influence were then dominant and where an ancient Jewish community still flourished under the early Mamluks. The Latin Ascandarinus corresponds to the Arabic *nisba* or epithet-name of origin Iskandarānī (variant al-Iskandarārī). The Latin Scandarini corresponds to an Arabic variant Sikandarānī resulting from confusion of *Is* and *As* with an elided Arabic article *as-*. Thus the son's name reflects an Arabic variant of the father's Latin name.[50]

Astruc Scandarini was very ill when he appointed three relatives or perhaps in-laws (*cognati*) and left most of his wealth to his daughter, Bonasenyora or Bonadona (Latin *Bonadomina*). This legacy included houses in the Jewish quarter, a vineyard in the Mogoria district just southwest of Barcelona, and 800 gold morabatins, or something over 3,200 Barcelona sous. Astruc also left her "twenty-four Hebrew books and the place I have in the synagogue" (such a seat was highly negotiable). If Bonadona should die unmarried, or married and childless, all these properties "are to be converted into alms for the salvation of my soul," distributed at the executors' discretion but with 400 of the gold morabatins going into the executors' pockets. Finally, the executors were to pay Astruc's debts and also to transfer the rents from a special farm called Queralt d'Almoina, in two segments, half in alms for the executors to distribute in the Jewish quarter and half "to the Jew who collects the alms of the Jews of Barcelona." Three Jews signed in Hebrew as executors and three more in Romance as witnesses. Three Christian notaries signed as verifying the copy. Unlike most Latinate wills, this lacks Christian witnesses, while the executors use Hebrew letters. The testament invokes no universal heir or other themes and formulas from Roman law, suggesting that the original 1263 will was not Latinate itself but Hebrew. The notarized copy thirty years later would have corresponded to the will's provision for selling off or "converting" the bulk of the properties if and when the heiress daughter died either unmarried or childless. For that occasion a fully notarized version in Latin would have served as documentation for the religious order purchasing some of that property. Thus Astruc's will may also serve as a model for a type of Hebrew will.

A century ago the prolific English scholar Joseph Jacobs examined a number of crown documents on Jews, including some on wills. From a small sampling he projected a series of general conclusions, all accumulating to make "a lode of Jewish law and custom." He believed, for example, that Jewish wills required the king's confirmation. There is no evidence for this statement, other than the several extant confirmations. Against the argument is the actual rarity of royal confirmations. Even if one argues that entering a will in the Christian notary's codex was reductively a crown confirmation (a very improbable position), there are simply not enough wills to accommodate the presumable number of dying Jews for a given year. The early registers with their many thousands of charters (thousands for Jews alone) display a large number of *guiatges* or documents granting royal protection, in striking contrast to the number of wills confirmed. Indeed it would seem that some reason was needed for such crown intervention. The same skepticism applies to Jacobs's other general conclusions: that property inherited had to be confirmed by the king, that the crown normally appointed guardians for heirs, that "the king settled the alimony of heirs," or that a Jew needed special permission "to transmit farms to his heirs." Jacobs also seems to have confused the ubiquitous *heredad* (estate, farm, property) with an inheritance; such a holding might be inherited, given by the king, bought, or otherwise acquired.[51]

The dynamics of royal intervention, except when invited by some public scandal or uproar or when the crown's finances were entwined with those of the suddenly deceased, would plausibly have followed the pattern of crown intervention in general. Crime and crown business aside, such intrusion was generally invited. A faction, an aggrieved heir, a favored courtier, a procurator for the community, or simply a situation too knotty to be handled at the local level could ask for the attention of the king and the king's courts. As the surviving descriptions of procedure indicate, a large and complicated investigation might ensue, the whole affair tapering off into an arbitration, a waiver/pardon, a fine, or dismissal. The Jewish and Christian communities intersected at this legal level in the case of certain wills; the convergence was even more common at the level of entering a will for a fee into the Christian notary's public record. But most Jews presumably arranged their last dispositions in more traditional manner within their local community.

Testaments were not the only, or even the most usual, legal bridge on which the two peoples interacted. Business and loan contracts between them and before a notary were enforceable at law. Jews and Christians met before the various courts in the realms—municipal, royal, and even episcopal. An amusing example of the last category is the lawsuit transcribed in document 44 below, where Isaac and Abraham Astruc sued before the bishop of Gerona and forced a delinquent creditor to surrender "three copper pots" he had put up as security.[52] Few such occasions involved Jewish law or documentation, however, in the manner in which they intertwined in Latinate testaments. Nor were such occasions invested with the solemnity and the psychological intimacy of actions at law involving a last testament.

CHAPTER 4

Wills: Palma, Perpignan, and Puigcerdá

The wills explored below come from the short-lived Kingdom of Majorca. This double entity comprised the Balearic islands, especially Majorca itself, and on the mainland the Pyrenean and Occitan holdings in the realms of Arago-Catalonia. The mainland holdings included particularly Roussillon with its capital Perpignan, Cerdanya (modern French Cerdagne and Spanish Cerdaña combined) with its capital Puigcerdá, and the great maritime power Montpellier. To these entities were added claims to Sardinia and later even to the Canaries. King Jaume the Conqueror cut away this politically and geographically artificial assemblage to make an appanage kingdom for his second son, also named Jaume. Though the Conqueror arranged this in his testament of 1262, it took effect only at his death in 1276. Before that transition date, these entities evolved and flourished under the Conqueror, their institutions and languages and commerce forming part of the complex pattern of his realms. Culturally and socially the new kingdom remained in the Catalan-Occitan sphere from 1276 until its loss of sovereignty after 1343. Its political status wavered between de facto independence and a semidependence as a vassal kingdom demanded by the crown of Arago-Catalonia, a situation aptly characterized by David Abulafia as "notional independence."[1]

A succession of three kings held the new throne: Jaume II (1276–1311), not to be confused with the contemporary Jaume II of Arago-Catalonia (1291–1327), then Sanç I (1311–1324), and finally Jaume III (1324–1343). Each presided from his double capital, in palaces at Palma de Mallorca (then "Majorca City") and especially Perpignan.

Within three years of the new kingdom's creation, the Conqueror's son and successor Pere the Great had forced his Majorcan brother to declare his new kingdom a fief of Arago-Catalonia and to abide by various limitations on his sovereignty (1279). Before the Conqueror was a decade in his grave, the same Pere had taken back by force both the Pyrenean and the Balearic centers (1285). International diplomatic maneuvers returned the new fief-kingdom to Jaume II of Majorca (1298), bringing some twenty years of cooperation until the Conqueror's grandson Jaume II of Arago-Catalonia began his determined effort to unite both kingdoms under his own rule. The final stage of that project came in 1343 when Pere the Ceremonious of Arago-Catalonia declared Jaume III of Majorca a formal rebel and then conquered and reintegrated both the island elements and the mainland.

This complicated political history masked a remarkable commercial success, the strange kingdom prospering astride trade routes between North Africa, France, and Spain, with Atlantic and Italian connections. Besides its role as distribution center, the kingdom developed a strong textile industry. Exporting to all corners of the surrounding map, from Flanders and Castile to Sicily and North Africa, it became a world commercial power. From 1330 decadence and decline set in, hurried along by the Black Death and ruinous wars.

The kingdom held a considerable Jewish population, both on Majorca and on the mainland. Jewish policies of the several rulers varied greatly, from the benign Jaume the Conqueror to the persecuting King Sanç. Circumstances defining the kingdom's Jewish communities varied more widely, from the immigrant Jewish society mingled with preconquest holdovers at the island's capital Palma, to the transient Jewish community at Perpignan, top-heavy with working capital, to the more settled community at Puigcerdá. Thus the context of any one testament from the kingdom can differ from other testaments there. The ten wills gathered here derive mostly from the era when Jewish society flourished—four from the 1270s, one from the 1280s, four from 1306, and only one from the less advantaged year 1322. All but one were drawn under Jaume the Conqueror or under Jaume II of Majorca.[2]

Palma de Mallorca

Conquered from the Muslims in 1229 and resettled wholesale by Jaume's subjects, Palma and its island of Majorca afforded its Jews a reasonably pleasant existence for nearly a half-century. From about 1285, however, the rulers encouraged "a steady process of dissociation of the Jews from the Christian community in Majorca City," both by restrictions and paradoxically by privileges.[3] By the turn of the century, residence within a newly walled Jewish quarter was being enforced—a situation of housing preference thus changing to a policy of compulsion. The general expulsion from nearby France in 1306 naturally caused fear and consternation among the city's Jews. Then for a decade from 1315 the new king Sanç harassed them, revoking all their privileges, confiscating property including their synagogue, and imposing a massive fine of 95,000 pounds.

These troubles accompanied and may be related to the influx of displaced persons from the 1306 general expulsion from France, which set Jew against Jew. King Sanç reported in 1319 that "roaming alien Jews are flocking here indiscriminately [and] rouse dissension and enmities among Our Jews of the said community."[4] After the king's death in 1324 equilibrium was restored, a calm before the late fourteenth-century storm. At the time of the Majorca City (or Palma) testament about to be analyzed, the Jewish community was still appreciated and prosperous, a mixture of Arabic-familiar natives and immigrant families from the mainland now long rooted: "For the larger part the Jews of the said community live by commerce [*mercantiliter*]," and they were key players in the North Africa to France circle trade.[5]

The long and detailed testament of July 1288 by Zalema, "son of Aaron b. Aarde the Jew" of Palma, had lodged in the archives of the Palma Dominicans.[6] A parchment eleven inches in length, with an elaborated initial, its script is dim and in places illegible or nearly so. In full control of his senses and of "sound memory," though "seized by illness," Zalema appoints his wife Maymona as executor to "receive, distribute, divide, and arrange" all his worldly goods. He chooses "burial in the cemetery of the Jews." Five sous go in alms, presumably on the occasion of the funeral. He leaves his daughter Maazuga, wife of En Horsa the Jew, a legacy of only 10 sous, counting his past financing of her wedding as part of her legacy. An identical bequest and explanation goes to his daughter Axera, widow of Jacob b. Salmó.

Zalema "recognizes" that his son Maymon owns half of "a certain Saracen Negress named Maymona" from Minorca, "whom I bought from Ramon Alber"; the purchase was in Zalema's own name, but half the price had come from Maymon. (The neighboring small island of Minorca had been conquered a year earlier in 1287 and most of its Muslim inhabitants reduced to slavery.) For Maymon's legacy Zalema gives one-half of the half of those buildings which "I and my brother Marçoch b. Aaron" share equally "inside the city of Majorca [Palma] fairly close to the buildings of the synagogue." (Ramon de Trilea, who held these buildings as an allod, had sold them to the brothers.) Zalema also gives his son half of his own half "of some other buildings" which he and his brother Marçoch hold within Palma adjoining the previous set of buildings. For these two complexes an annual rent of 2 morabatins would be owing to Ramon, who continues to hold allodial rights or ownership.

Zalema's "infant children," the boy Abrafim and the girl Carima, are each to get 15,000 pounds of Valencian sous from Maymon's share within three years of Zalema's death. If Maymon "won't or can't" release that sum, his own income from the buildings will be cut to a third of the half until that sum accrues, "to help in the marrying and sustenance" of the two children. Presumably that 30,000 pounds was to give the two their start in life as adults. At 20 sous to the pound (*lliura*) this came to half a million sous. Since a knight's fee could be under 400 sous per annum, the legacy amounted to a substantial fortune. By explicit stipulation Zalema's wife Maymona recovers her *sponsalicium* "just as is contained in her dowry charter." In Roman law terms and local custom this wording should mean her dower, the marital gift promised by a Christian groom at the time of marriage but payable to her only at his death. In fact, however, the Christian phrasing here masks the analogous situation of the Jewish *ketubah* deed given by a groom to his bride, in which he promises a customary sum plus an agreed increment, or *tosefet,* to go to her at his death. The deed would also describe her own dowry and its increment, which the bride could likewise reclaim when widowed.

Everything not covered by the legacies recited above goes to the two children but under the custody and administration of his wife Maymona, who is also to live from this sum. The arrangement is to continue "until Carima has reached the age of fifteen years, and then her mother is bound to arrange a marriage," meeting its expenses from the 15,000 pounds. The boy may have been younger than Carima, but in any case the mother was to continue in control of his inheritance (presumably except for his 15,000 pounds) as long as she lived. After Carima's marriage, and when Abrafim will reach twenty years, he will have the option of taking half of all the goods remaining in Maymona's control, leaving her the other half until her death.

Zalema then notes that his grown son Maymon "holds in commission [*commanda*] by charter from me 21 pounds of Valencian *reials*, give or take a bit [*parum plus vel minus*]." Maymon must give this to his mother Maymona, who will incorporate it into Zalema's other goods. The testator also declares that he had already surrendered to Maymon "the aforesaid half of my said half of the said two building-complexes" being awarded above but by a "charter not yet fully accomplished and not come into effect." He concludes by confirming his intentions, so that if the will "is not valid by right of testament, it may be valid at least by right of codicil or some other right of last will."

The parchment is dated 6 July 1288 and is signed "Zalema son of the deceased Aaron ben Aarde." Witnesses are the Christians Pere de Algaire (the Majorcan town Algaida), Arnau Sureda, Pere Martí, Berenguer Amenller (a form of Ametller), Fèlix Màger (?), Pere Oller, and Pere de Vallbona. A line of Hebrew intervenes, followed by the names of the Jews Maymon "Abennono" (with added abbreviating overstroke) and Omar b. Annum. Both these latter surnames recall the Hebrew Hanun that appears in a Judeo-Arabic family in such variants as Ibn Ohnona, Ouahnon, and Wahnun). Salimah or Salāmah was a popular "secular" name used by Jews in the Arabic world, as somewhat echoing Solomon. The notary Gerald Marí or de Marina and the notary Bernat Sant, both of Majorca, put their signa to the whole. For some reason a formal copy was drawn "from the original testament" again four years later, by the hand and corroboration of the Majorcan notary Arnau Sanmartí on 13 June 1292.

The family structure, without knowing the sequence in which the children appeared, may be represented as:

Aaron b. Aarde

Marçoch b. Aaron — ZALEMA b. Aaron *m.* Maymona

Maazuga *m.* (En) Horsa — Axera *m.* Jacob b. Salmó — Maymon — Abrafim (infant) — Carima (infant)

The names have a Judeo-Arabic flavor as a whole and suggest a family from the massive migration northward under the Almohad rule or a family assimilated after the large Christian conquests over Spanish Islamic lands in this century. The protagonist Zalema was Arabic Salimah, with his brother Marçoch as Marzūq and his father Aaron perhaps with the secular Arabic form Hārūn. His wife Maymona and son Maymon represent Maimūn; two daughters and a slave bear the same name. Maazuga would be a feminine of Marzūq and Axera a feminine of Hebrew Asher; both Arabic Maimūn/feminine Maimuna and Hebrew Asher mean "fortunate." Abrafim is still close to Ibrāhīm and is a usual Judeo-Arabic form. Carima is the popular Arabic name Karīma; Shlomo Goitein notes that it meant "noble" or "distinguished," not "sister" as in modern times.[7] The witnesses are Omar (ʿUmar) and Maymon (Maimūn). The use of *ben* or *aben* in Latinate documents, instead of the genitive or the explicit "son of," usually signals an Arabic background with an *ibn* proudly retained; it appears here for Zalema's father, brother, son-in-law, and both Jewish witnesses, supporting the thesis of a self-consciously "Arabic" circle of family and friends.

Could the Ben Aarde surname be the "Benadi" or Ibn al-Addi Sephardic family? Biblical Hebrew names for Aarde could be Ard and the variants Arda and Ardi, "wild ox." The Catalan honorific En (akin to Castilian Don), though frequent enough, suggests that Maazuga had married someone well established in the Jewish community. His surname Horsa might be Catalan too, as in the prename Ursí (variant Ors), but Hebrew Hoshaya is preferable. The other son-in-law's name, Salmó, is simply Catalan Salamó. All these names would have been pronounced orally to the Catalan notary, some of them falling familiarly on his ear, others perhaps to be approximated as exotic. He then tacked on such Latin suffixes as seemed appropriate. The results, as with Zalema and Abrafim, offer clues to contemporary Catalan pronunciations.

Perpignan

Richard Emery has intensively studied the Jews of Perpignan, exploring seventeen of the earliest notarial registers still surviving there from over a thousand originally in the thirteenth century. He has culled and transcribed 140 documents pertaining to Jews, among which are five testaments from the years 1273 (two testaments), 1277, 1286, and 1322, respectively. Emery's focus was on moneylending and the place of Jews in the local economy, so he had no occasion to analyze the five wills or give them prominence. They repay a close look, however, and help round out my own archival findings at Palma and Puigcerdá in the Majorcan kingdom. Perpignan's Jewish community was unusual in that it was "a new one founded by immigrants who came as moneylenders." Numerous by 1200, it became by 1300 "one of the largest Jewish communities north of the Pyrenees," numbering some hundred families or three to four hundred souls. (In its decline, the town itself could still list 2,675 households in 1355, and 3,346 in 1365.)[8] The Jewish community was prosperous, its affluence widely shared by all its families.

The immigration that created and sustained the Perpignan Jewish community stemmed mostly from Occitania, the part of southern France contested ever more in the thirteenth century by Catalonia and the encroaching Franks. Analyzing surnames, Emery finds that barely a third of this population were Languedocians with northern French origins; thus flight from the Frankish expulsions was not the main factor in its evolution. Instead, opportunity drew native Languedocian Jews with both capital and a moneylending background. The rapid growth of Perpignan, especially in the later thirteenth century with its successful textile industries and world marketing, led to "a relative shortage of capital" with consequent rise of interest on loans, creating a magnet for men with capital and ambition in a "migratory generation." Emery suggests that Perpignan's Jewish immigration "was in large part a movement of capital seeking a higher rate of return."[9] If so (and our evidence is partial and tentative), the immigrants seem to have been mostly petty lenders, dedicated to consumer loans to their immediate Christian neighbors, rather than the Jewish investors and long-distance merchants who formed the crown creditors and aristocratic families of ports like Barcelona (though Emery does not take up this line of inquiry).

As the fourteenth century wore on, Perpignan declined from "one of the major Jewish centers of Western Europe"[10] to a harassed and ever poorer settlement, its moneylenders presumably having shifted south once again, out of troubled Majorca and the now inhospitable Frankish Languedoc. During the prosperous period of most of the wills studied here, the Jewish quarter (newly moved in 1250 as the premier *call* for Roussillon and Cerdanya) was bounded by the modern Rue de l'Anguille, the convent of Saint Dominique behind and below the cathedral, and the Place du Puig.

Of Emery's five wills, the first comes in 1273 and is the briefest and least revealing. It is minimalist in format and substance. Some of the missing formulaic matter, such as a declaration of terminal illness, lies implicit in six "et cetera" conclusions. The will does not formally name executors, however, and except for witnesses it involves only the immediate family. The testator is Bonisac Fagim, about whom we know nothing; the affluence of his will and the Perpignan context suggest a successful career in moneylending. Bonisac's wife Bonafília, also Bonafilla, recovers her dowry "as explained in the Jewish nuptial documents" (the *ketubah* agreements drawn up by the *sōfer*); she receives nothing else. A married daughter Regina, also Reina, receives a token 12½ Barcelona sous, the equivalent perhaps of a laborer's weekly wages. Her inheritance rights had been satisfied by "all that I gave her at the time of her nuptials with her husband."

The unmarried and presumably younger daughter, Bonadona, receives the only other sum explicitly stated, 1,875 Barcelona sous, a workingman's annual wages for nearly twenty years and therefore a considerable sum. Doubtless much of this sum was meant as dowry, since her brothers are told to support her "from my goods" until she has "taken a husband." That Bonadona was also a minor is indicated by the appointment of Jucef de Crassa as her "guardian and administrator." De Crassa or Sagrassa was one of the most active moneylenders in Perpignan, obviously a wealthy man by local standards. This connection, probably familial, underscores the affluent status of Bonisac Fagim's own family. Sagrassa lived just long enough to complete his guardianship, dying a decade later and leaving his wife Regina as guardian of his own sons, Mossé, Vidal, and Vives. His name is an Occitan toponym, either Grasse or Lagrasse.

The bulk of Bonisac's property goes to his two grown sons, Fagim Bonisac and Vidal Bonisac. They are to pay out the legacies and make recompense for any "injuries" (claims or debts) outstanding. The brothers share jointly the status of universal heir. Some Christians but no Jews served as witnesses to Bonisac's testament: Bernat Bellshom the tailor, Guillem Lenger also a tailor, Guillem Joan a silversmith, Bernat Jaume a tilemaker, Pere Saroca, Pere Jaume a farmer (Catalan *hortolà*), and Pere Amorós. Do these artisan categories supply a clue to Bonisac's own social status, or was Bonisac simply their customer or occupational neighbor?[11] The name Fagim, shared by father and son, attracts attention. Obviously it is not a variant of the modern German-Yiddish Fagan or Feigin and probably not a form of Faquim, the Arabo-Catalan title for a savant-physician. (*Ḥakīm* was both a function or title and occasionally a name in Islam, and many Jews bore it proudly in Christian government service—Catalan *alfaquim*, Castilian *alhaquín*.) Irene Garbell argues persuasively that the Sephardic name Fagim involves a Catalan tendency transforming Hayyim, though later she also sees a Provençal pronunciation here on the Catalan-Occitan frontier.

The will as a whole is traditional but minimalist. It does not distribute the testator's goods or leave legacies; presumably Bonisac had taken care of philanthropies and souvenirs or gifts to relatives by earlier arrangements. The will itself simply restores his wife's dowry (as Jewish law required), sets aside a suitable dowry for his minor daughter (again as required), formalizes the arrangement by which his married daughter had already recieved her share of his goods as dowry (sealed by a legalistic token gift here), formalizes the arrangement already made with Jucef Sagrassa as his daughter's guardian, and establishes his two sons as owners of all his property with the duty of supporting their young sister and meeting any unsettled obligations. Since none of this required an accounting of his moneys and properties, we are left with only a general impression of affluence—from the size of the dowry, the status of the guardian, the unusual number of witnesses to lend solemnity, and the marriage of the younger son to a physician's daughter.

This final bit of information derives from a loan document of October 1283 concerning Gaugs or Goigs ("Gaugz," or joys), the widow of Bonisac's son Vidal, herself the daughter of Master Salamó a physician of Narbonne and his wife Regina/Reina.[12] Resolute search through the unpublished sections of Emery's registers might flesh out the family skeleton or turn up new bones, but the present data allow a basic reconstruction:

BONISAC FAGIM *m.* Bonafilla

Fagim Bonisac	Vidal Bonisac *m.* Gaugz	Regina/Reina *m.* X	Bonadona

The second of Perpignan's wills seems more conventional in its verbose length and formulas, but it is not very different in its main concerns. It does afford more details, names and instructs executors, offers options in case of legatees' deaths, and incorporates both philanthropic and cultural activities. The testator was Vidal de Montpeller, son of the deceased Cresques de Marsella. Though Vidal's descriptive "surname" reveals his personal origin as from Catalan Montpellier, as his father's indicates a previous identification with Marseilles, the family was now rooted in Perpignan. Vidal was rather wealthy, as Emery remarks, "worth at least" 6,000 sous or 300 pounds by the evidence in his will. He turns up in the surviving registers only twice before the will itself, however, a "relatively obscure" member of the Jewish community.

Vidal drafted his will in 1273, in the same year as Bonisac, being "of sound mind" and invoking "God's name." He establishes as executors his "in-laws" Astruc Creixent and Perfet ("Profait") Creixent, dispensing them from onerous details of that duty. "They are not obliged to make an inventory of my goods, nor even bound to render an account" to his heirs. They are to incur "no cost or expense" to themselves. Their undertakings will be *in solidum,* so that either man holds full brief in the other's absence. As Vidal's agents they can summon "all my debtors before any tribunal, to recover the said debts," or they can simply arrange payments or even effect compromises through outside arbitrators. In particular, they are to "sell a certain vineyard that I have in the district of Vernet," an extension of the city of Perpignan, across the Tet River. The executors also have special obligations toward two of his daughters, in the guise of custodians or guardians. The executor's surname is the Catalan adjective *creixent,* for growing or growth, from the same verb *créixer* ("to grow") that yields Cresques the testator's father ("may he grow"). The biblical cognate would be the Hebrew Tzemach.

Vidal had four daughters: Regina or Reina, Boneta, Blanca, and Massipa. Blanca becomes the main or universal heir, a circumstance indicating the lack of surviving sons. Boneta is already married, as is Regina; consequently their share of Vidal's goods has already been paid out—"all that I gave her at the time of her nuptials" in each case. Regina also gets "my book" containing "the five books of the law of Moses, which she has and possesses in her control." Boneta receives the rest of Vidal's library: "all my books which I possess and have by me." These bequests may suggest some literacy for women in these communities.

The daughter Massipa gets 75 Barcelonan "crowned" pounds. That amount equaled, in a nonexistent money of account but actually in pennies (*diners de tern*), 1,500 sous of Barcelona, called "coronats" because of the crowned king on their face. The executors, now as guardians, are to invest the sum: "to have and keep and loan it to Christians at interest [*ad usuras*] until my said daughter takes a husband." This outcome is not left to chance; the executors "are obliged to provide a husband for my said daughter," with the advice of Bondia Cohen. Massipa's odd name is not some Hebrew feminine name such as Mizpa ("tower") but simply a common Catalan Christian surname, Macip and Massip (Latin *mancipium,* here as youngster, servant, learner). Massipa is to receive her fortune when she finally marries. Meanwhile the universal heir Blanca "is obliged to provide the said Massipa my daughter with food and drink and clothing and shoes, from my goods, until my said daughter takes a husband." Blanca can use income from the invested legacy to this end.

Vidal's wife Argota recovers "her whole dowry just as contained in the Hebrew [*ebraicum*] nuptial document between me and her," expressed in morabatins, "so that for each gold piece or morabatin of her said dowry, my said wife is to claim back in payment 8 Barcelona sous and 9 pence, and so on until fulfillment of her said dowry." As universal heir, Blanca "is to support my said wife in all her necessities, until she will have been entirely recompensed as to her whole dowry." Argota also receives "all her garments and all my own cloth, and my whole weighing machine that is in my house, except my wine containers and my dying vat that belong to my [universal] heir" Blanca. The "cloth" here seems to be textiles instead of household or personal goods, suggesting in context a mercantile venture. Blanca and Massipa are to have the scales and cloth "until each of them gets a husband." Though both daughters are under the custody of the executors as minors, Blanca as universal heir must "pay all my debts and the aforesaid legacies."

Vidal has a final set of conditions. If Blanca dies before Massipa marries, Massipa is to keep 385 Barcelona sous from Blanca's inheritance, while the rest reverts "to Regina and Boneta in equal shares." If Massipa will have a husband at the time of Blanca's death, Blanca's legacy will revert in equal shares to Massipa, Regina, and Boneta. If Regina should die without a legitimate heir, her share is to go to Boneta and Massipa, "and thus from one to the other survivor in the same way."

The one public philanthropy is a gift of 6¼ sous to the fund of halfpenny alms "for sick Jews."[13] Seven Christians witness the will, some of them the same as in Bonisac's: Bernat Bellshom a tailor, Guillem Lenger, Jaume de Brullà (near Elne), Pere Bernadin, Bernat Just a miller (*moler* for Catalan *moliner*), Pere Amorós, and Guillem Roer as "invited witnesses" (*testes rogati*). This obscure but affluent family yields a small family tree:

Cresques de Marsella
|
VIDAL DE MONTPELLER *m.* Argota

| in-laws
| Astruc Creixent
and
Profait Creixent

Regina/Reina *m.* X — Boneta *m.* X — Blanca — Massipa

The third Perpignan will comes from the hand of Asher de Lunel, a resident (*habitator*) of Perpignan. His given name is Hebrew for fortunate or blessed (here in the Hebrew variant Asser), his surname an Occitan town southwest of Nîmes. He appears "regularly" in Emery's economic documents from 1266 up to his death and last testament in 1277. Ranked by the amount of money he loaned during that time, he is second highest. Asher's will has a number of unusual features. He leaves 12½ sous, out of love for God, "for the construction of the Tet bridge of Perpignan," a secular enterprise not near or connected with the Jewish quarter. Christian wills often had legacies for bridges and that cultural climate may have influenced Asher. But such general philanthropy may well have been a practice within the affluent strata of the Jewish community, its oddity here being its inclusion in a will. "For love of God, in remission of my sins," Asher also leaves the large sum of 625 sous, spread over ten years at 62½ sous per year, to be distributed (presumably to poor Jews) "on the feast that is called, in the Jewish style [*iudayce*] 'the huts' [*cabanes*]"—that is, Sukkot, feast of the Booths or Tabernacles.

Asher's will also has a large cast of characters. Before beginning his division of property, he made a "pre-legacy" to each of his two adult sons. Samiel got 625 Barcelona sous under this rubric, while Mossé kept "whatever he had and acquired from my goods by his own industry or by any other manner or means, and whatever loans are owed him in his own name, with documentation or without." Asher then establishes Samiel and Mossé as "my universal heirs in common, with equal shares in all my goods and in every claim, etc." The brothers cannot divide their common inheritance for ten years, counting "from my death day." Samiel receives a special gift, for as long as the inheritance is held in common: 250 sous plus "suitable" board (*alimenta*) yearly, which would become 625 per annum if he were to marry during that period.

Asher's three daughters each receive as formal legacy 12½ sous "and whatever I gave her at the time of the marriage she entered." Each daughter and spouse is named: Bona Aunís or Bonaunís and her deceased husband Vidal Mossé de Scola (or "of the synagogue"), Bonadona and her husband Mossé Duran de Cabestany (Capestang just southeast of Perpignan), and Druda with her spouse Mossé Davin or Daví de Cabestany. Women's names are more fanciful than men's in the wills; Bona Aunís is a form of Catalan *aunir/unir*, "to unite"; Unís is a Catalan Christian surname. Bona Aunís is also equivalent to the Catalan name Bonajun(c)ta, also used by Christians. Druda, a rare but recognized Jewish name, seems to be the Catalan name Trud ("strong") in the feminine. Bona Aunís's spouse Vidal Mossé had been alive as late as June 1275, according to financial documents in these registers; he had a brother Belan (a variant of the Catalan masculine name Bel?) and three sons named Mossé, Vives, and Bonsenyor. The Cabestany family, which Bonadona and Druda married into, was already prominent in Perpignan. Other documents show that Mossé was a son of Duran de Cabestany and had three sons named Asher, Bondia, and Jacob. Daví's name was taken as a variant for David, though it also has classical antecedents. Duran is a Catalan adjective for "steadfast," used as both a Christian and a Jewish name.

Asher gives his wife Bonafília lifetime possession of "my whole homestead in which I live." His term *mansus* instead of *domus* may carry some pretension to grandeur, an impression strengthened by his description of its site: "on the hill of the town of Perpignan in the quarter of the Jews [*callus* for *call*], and fronting along three sides on streets, and along the fourth side on the residence of the deceased Salves de Bellcaire and on the house of the deceased Vidal Bonet." These last two Jewish neighbors seem to confirm Asher's affluent status. The Catalan name Salves for one of them, used by both Jews and (as a surname) Christians, relates to the concept "saved" or "safe." A Jewish moneylender, Salves may have been from the prominent Occitan town Bellcaire, modern Beaucaire (as his Latinized surname suggests), rather than from Catalan Bellcaire d'Urgell or Bellcaire d'Empordà or Belcaire southeast of Foix, though the latter are distinct possibilities. The deceased neighbor Vidal Bonet may have been related to the moneylender of that name who flourished until around 1280, married to "Mayrona" or Meirona and with two sons Mossé and Bonfill. (Catalan Mairona is a feminine diminutive of Meir, as Perona is of Pere.) Asher's will provides that this corner establishment revert, after Bonafília's death, to the universal heirs Samiel and Mossé and to their progeny.

The brothers must also provide their mother with daily support at any "appropriately elevated" level (*alimenta sua honorifice*). Bonafília also keeps "a certain chest she is accustomed to have," with all its contents, including the 625 sous there. She also gets all his "cloth" (*pannos*), all the household chests as well as "the documents and other things in the said chests," the wine containers or wine cellar, "and the other utensils of my house, so that she may use and enjoy [them] during her life," until they revert at her death to Mossé and Samiel. In a major textile center the *panni* might well have been cloth held for resale, but contemporary documents commonly used the term also for such household items as bedclothes (*pannos lectorum* in a 1300 document by the Majorcan king). Of the two brothers, Samiel seems the more distinguished and probably the elder. Emery characterizes him as "among the most active and probably one of the wealthiest moneylenders in Perpignan, judging from the surviving registers." He had a daughter Aster and a son Mossé Samiel b. Asher; the latter, visible in the registers from 1283 to 1317, became a student of Menahem Meir, the greatest scholar among Perpignan's Jews. The daughter has the Catalan name Aster, technically different from the feminine Hebrew name Ester (English Esther) but etymologically the same.

Asher remembers his two sisters Bonafília and Clara with a lifetime annuity of 25 sous yearly for each, payable on September 1 of every year. If Bonafília survives her husband Salamó de Besers or Besés (modern Béziers, southwest of Montpellier), "and will wish to move to Perpignan to live together with my heirs and to keep residence with them," then these heirs Samiel and Mossé must supply her subsistence. In that last situation, however, the brothers may suspend payment of the cash annuity for as long as the residential arrangement continues. To Bona Aunís or Bonaunís, daughter of his sister Clara, Asher leaves 72½ sous, and to his grandniece Bonfat or Bofet ("Boffata") the daughter "of my nephew [niece?] Sarta a Jew" he leaves 62½ sous. Both of these sums are payable during one year counting from the upcoming Passover or Easter. Neither Christian nor Jewish years began at that time, and the term *pascha* may reflect either the scribe's designation, familiar enough to Asher from his business contacts in Perpignan, or the Jewish feast under that common name.

Sarta as *nepos* would not have been the classical "grandson" (with nephew a possibility) but medieval Latin "nephew" (with grandson a possibility), despite the influence of Catalan *nét* (grandson) versus *nebot* (nephew), as is suggested both by usage and the conjunction with the niece Bona Aunís. When the testator Benvenist Samuel Benvenist wished to use *nepos* as meaning grandson, for example, he added the corresponding Catalan to clarify the Latin word: "nepotum et neptum meorum sive nets e netes." Medieval *nepos* could apply to either gender, and the odd name Sarta could be either Catalan male Sarça or more plausibly a form of Sareta/Sarita as diminutive for Hebrew Sara. "Boffata" is the Catalan name Bonfat (good fate or luck) used by both sexes, though here further feminized by the ending.

A final legacy is for Regina or Reina daughter of the deceased Astruga and deceased Isaac, waiving "whatever she owes me by reason of board [*alimenta*] or in any other way, but without documentation." Was this an orphaned relative or a nonrelative as object of Asher's philanthropy? At this point the testator introduces an unusual condition on the whole will: "I wish and decree and order that neither any of my said daughters nor any other person, except only my said wife, can have or be given a transcript or copy of this present testament of mine, nor are my said [universal] heirs bound to give it to them." Thus Mossé, Samiel, and his wife Bonafília have legal access to the will; but Bona Aunís (or Bonajuncta), Bonadona, and Druda can receive only indirect information from the primary heirs. As befits so solemn a charter, seven "sworn witnesses" sign besides the Jew Vidal Bonfill de Scal: the Christians Guillem Parador the jurist, Guillem Barrau, Joan Martí the shoemaker, Bernat Barrés, Pere Dalmau, Ferran (de) Bonpàs, and Arnau Isarn. The Jewish witness had been a partner with Asher and Samiel in some loan business and with Samiel had been one of the "secretaries" or cogovernors of the local Jewish community.

Taken as a whole, the testament depicts an aristocratic family of means, public-spirited and openhanded, the pious testator firmly in control of business and family. The several bits of information available elsewhere in these registers about the individuals involved confirm this impression.[14] The family emerges from the will as shown in the genealogy on page 88.

A very different kind of will came in 1286 from Sara, widow of Daví or Davin of Cabestany (Capestang), resident of Perpignan. Almost her entire estate goes to the education of Jewish poor children, arranged in detail. Her husband had been a major moneylender together with his sons Mossé and Bonsenyor, unless two men of that same name were prominent then in Perpignan. Since Sara leaves nothing to her immediate family, it is probable that her husband had already funded them, leaving Sara with her dowry and a modest competence. The two sons she chooses to oversee a distribution of dowries to Jewish poor girls seem to add a third brother, Profet Daví de Cabestany, described as brother to Mossé Daví de Cabestany. Her executors are the same Profet plus Duran de Melguelh/Melgor (modern Melgueil), a resident of Béziers.

A peculiarity of Sara's will is that she reckons her legacies in the money of Melgueil, native here until largely displaced by the Barcelona sous under pressure from the king of Aragon. This may reflect her advanced years and attachment to past ways as well as a lack of business adjustments such as her husband might have made. Sara leaves 200 of these sous to her sister Sima, wife of Salamó de Saverdia, and 20 more to Blanca, the daughter of Abraham de Magalas, toward her marriage

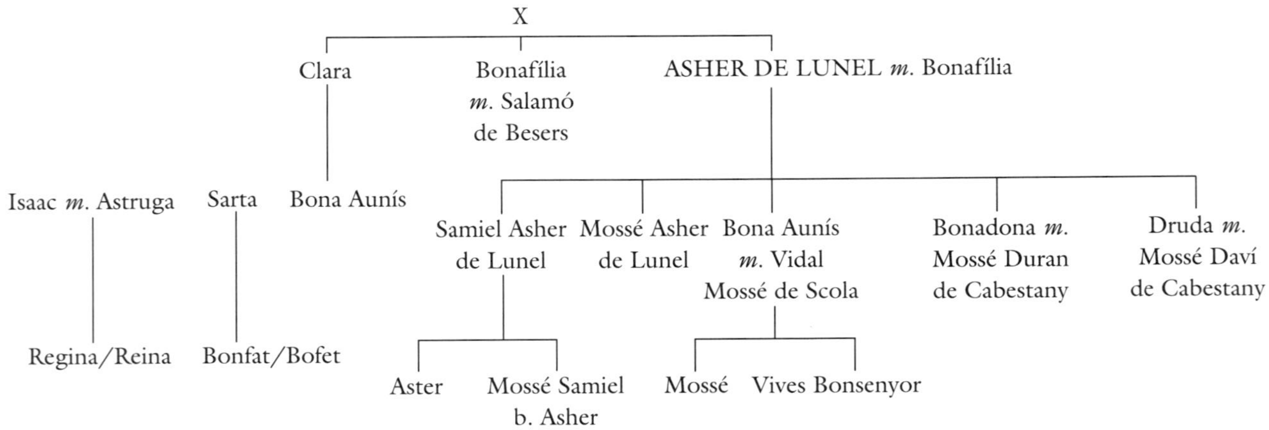
X
Clara
Bonafília
m. Salamó
de Besers
ASHER DE LUNEL m. Bonafília
Isaac m. Astruga
Sarta
Bona Aunís
Samiel Asher
de Lunel
Mossé Asher
de Lunel
Bona Aunís
m. Vidal
Mossé de Scola
Bonadona m.
Mossé Duran
de Cabestany
Druda m.
Mossé Daví
de Cabestany
Regina/Reina
Bonfat/Bofet
Aster
Mossé Samiel
b. Asher
Mossé
Vives Bonsenyor

(*maritamentum*). Sima may be the Judeo-Aramaic name Sima or "treasure" or else the Greco-Latin name Sima/Cyma, "to sprout" or flourish. Sara also leaves 500 sous to the sons of her brother Daví de Melguelh/Melgor, that is, her nephews Jucef, Cresques, and Salamó, divided into equal shares. Her condition for this canny gift is "that my aforesaid executors keep and loan the [sous] at interest during the life of my said brother, and that all interest made with them be given and handed over every year in the life of my brother to my said brother to do with as he will." This stipulation argues that the three nephews were minors and likely to remain so for a while. At the brother's death, the funds were to go to the nephews directly.

No universal heir has so far appeared, but Sara now names him: "I establish as my universal heir my God." Sara spells out the practical terms of this unusual choice. "The remainder of my goods are to be given and distributed, for love of God, to poor Jewish girls for marrying them off [*ad maritandum*]." The administrators of this legacy are to be her two sons, Profet Daví de Cabestany and Mossé Daví de Cabestany. Only Profet is an executor of the will as such, Mossé here supplanting the executor Duran, perhaps because Duran must exercise his general oversight from his residence at Béziers while this specific task requires local contacts and action. The proper executors, however, receive "full agency to ask, demand, and receive all my goods, according to their understanding." They are to pay out all the legacies "within a half year after my death." Seven Christians sign as sworn witnesses: Pere de Òpol a butcher, Guillem Costa a butcher, Pere de Braya a farmhand, Sanç de Vilallonga, Domènec de València (or de Valença, modern Valence on the Rhône), Bernat de Cornellà a glover, and Pere Quer-Rubí (or if the name form is genitive, Querub). The *oppidum,* or fortified area, as toponym of the first butcher, may simply be the new Castell Reial, which included among its many services a butchery.[15]

Sara's testament belongs in the category of those going beyond the domestic sphere to proclaim a public philanthropy on a considerable scale. Concern for dowries or dowry increments was general with both Christians and Jews, but its placement so prominently within a Jewish will does seem unusual. Sara's designation of God himself as universal heir may be unique in Jewish testamentary expression. Does this reflect a scribal scruple to have the element of universal heirhood incorporated, or is this a piety of Sara herself? The formula seems to echo a similar oddity found by my doctoral student Rebecca Winer in some contemporary Christian wills here at Perpignan, with statements such as: "In all my other movable or immovable goods, wherever and however they may be, I establish as my universal heir my lord Jesus Christ, for love of whom let all my goods be given and distributed [to the poor]." The variant in a Jewish will, with God for Christ, may indicate an acculturative influence or perhaps the notary's formula adapted to his Jewish client's sensibilities. The extended family here is seen from Sara's distaff vantage:

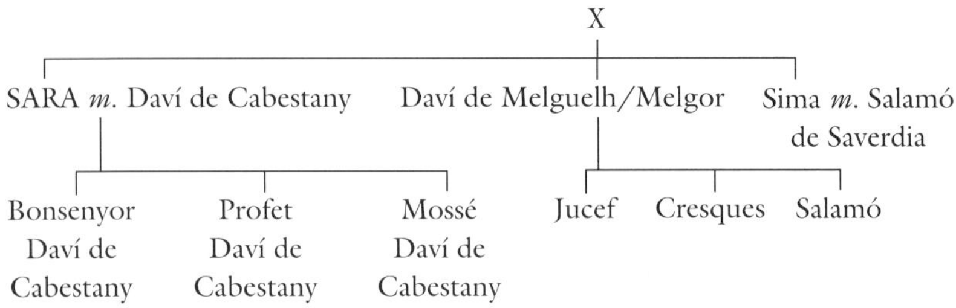

The last of the Perpignan wills is by far the longest and it contains its own surprises. The testator is Asher Mossé Daví, husband of the deceased Bononis and father both of a widowed daughter named Cohen and a minor son Samiel Asher. Lesser players include Astruc, son of Cohen and her deceased husband Bonsenyor Astruc; Asher's aunt (his father's sister) Meirona, with her three daughters; and an unusual panel of Jewish and Christian executor-auditors. There seems to have been a long-standing dispute between Asher and his daughter Cohen in connection with a previous legacy from his wife Bononis.

"Cohen" seems a decidedly odd given name for a woman, with its echo of the priestly function. It cannot be that the Latin notary misheard the Hebrew unisex name Chonen ("gracious") or that Emery's transcription is faulty. The original in the communal archives, kindly supplied for me in photocopy by my student Rebecca Winer, clearly and fully spells out her name no less than eight times. Though Seror lists nearly twenty male uses of the name in Occitania and France in the Middle Ages, always as surname or title, he has found only one other feminine use, as "Choentz." Perhaps "Cohen" is merely the ultimate eccentricity in the individualistic catalog of medieval feminine Jewish names. Feminine Bononis here may be the common name Bona ("good") in diminutive as Bonona, put in the third declension, or perhaps a variant of the Catalan male given name, Bononi.

When Asher had this "settlement of my goods written out and arranged" in November 1322, he was "of sound mind and healthy body, in good sense and full memory." He stipulates that Barcelona money is to be used for all his legacies, thus excluding the older Roussillonaise or Melgorian money as well as the smorgasbord of currencies enjoyed by a frontier town like Perpignan. Asher first sets aside 2,000 sous to be paid to his daughter Cohen "just as soon" as she makes definite plans to remarry. Meanwhile her brother "must provide her with food, clothing, and her other necessities, generously and appropriately, within his house and from his goods." The sum incorporates also a legacy of 25 pounds (500 sous) "which the said Bononis my wife left to her in her last will." Cohen also gets "all her own clothing [*vestes*]" and that of her mother (a considerable gift in a medieval household) as well as all "furnishings, equipment, jewels, and bundles of goods." In case of Cohen's death, all her legacies from father or mother revert to her brother Samiel.

Here the testator introduces a bugaboo: the Falcidian fourth and Trebellianic fourth (*falcidia ac trabelliamea*). The Falcidian proviso was a relic of Roman law guaranteeing any heir at least a fourth of an inheritance, lest the word "heir" have no meaning. The proviso gave an heir the right to diminish the legacies of other heirs in order to secure his minimum fourth of the estate. The Trebellianic fourth allowed an heir to deduct part of the estate before the executors received it. Asher's insistence indicates that such a maneuver was a present danger: "I veto and forbid that Falcidian fourths have any place" in the will. Specifically, neither Cohen nor her son Astruc can "acquire, have or gain anything by reason of the Falcidian waiver of a legal fourth share or in any other way."

The universal heir, of course, is the only son Samiel: "all my books, movable assets [*rauba*], debts owed me, possessions, and all my other goods real and movable, and whatsoever claims and legal actions." Samiel's inheritance must provide restitution for any outstanding debts of the father. If Samiel dies "within the time of his minority [*infra pupillarem etatem*] or at any later time, without legitimate children born of legal marriage, I substitute for him my daughter Cohen if she shall be alive." If Cohen herself dies, then "I substitute for my same daughter and my aforesaid son and heir" any children of Cohen's.

If both Samiel and Cohen die without surviving children, "I wish and order all my aforesaid estate and its goods, wholly and without any diminution, to devolve and revert to the illustrious lord king of Majorca and to his own." This startling proviso calls for explanation. After all, the current king was Sanç, whose behavior toward his Jews was persecutory (a decade of vexations about to end with the king's death). Did

Asher have some close connection to the royal court, an intimacy that might have led to such a gift? Or was the testator so alienated from his extended family (if any), and even from his community, that he cut them off so decisively? Other motives might be conjectured, from simple patriotism to a conciliatory gesture toward the crown. A matching proviso (discussed below) near the end of this long will may supply clues toward clarifying the matter.

Asher instructs his executors "to buy, within the year I am buried, up to a price and value of 20 Barcelona sous, one plot of land." Along with 5 sous in cash, he leaves this "to Astruc, son of the said Cohen my daughter, as the share and inheritance and legacy, and for the whole claim belonging to him in all my goods and those of my deceased wife, as well as in the legacies made by me above and by my said wife to the said Cohen in her last testament," without any possibility of further profit for Astruc. In a similar voiding of potential claims, Asher leaves 10 Barcelona pounds, or 200 sous, to his paternal aunt Meirona (*Mayrona*) and to her three daughters "in satisfaction and recompense for all the legacies and profits and emoluments made by my deceased father in will-form or without a will." This payment is made only on condition that "Meirona herself and her aforesaid daughters, with the agreement and approval of their husbands, must and ought to pay and dismiss all the aforesaid legacies made to them by my father"; and they are to waive any claims on Asher's heir Samiel arising from such legacies. If Meirona and her daughters refuse this condition, Asher's offer to them becomes "worthless and null and void." And if they claim that Asher or Samiel owe them more because of the legacies from Asher's father, then the following conclusion, "for eternal remembrance of the affair," is inserted: "Both the illustrious lord king of Majorca and the illustrious lord king of France shall have and receive" all the legacies and profits made to Meirona and her daughters by that said father; the kings would receive these "in the general indemnities that they want to have from the Jews dwelling in their sovereignties."

This provision sounds less like a charitable shouldering of the community's tax burden than a threat and obstacle to Asher's aunt's insistence on her claims. This expression of ill will about a single legacy would seem to clarify the previous wholesale delivery of Asher's wealth to the king of Majorca in case his nuclear family and their progeny were to cease. Even as a threat, the incorporation of the king of France as a chief beneficiary of a Jewish will in 1322 sounds very odd. The French king had recently contrived to make himself the feudal lord over the

Majorcan king for Montpellier, just as Arago-Catalonia was now feudal lord for the generality of the Majorcan king's holdings. And tension was obvious among the three powers, as each maneuvered for advantage. Was such a legacy designed to placate the French crown? Or to balance the effect of the many French Jews who were making their way back again into France? As for the Majorcan king, he continued to oppress his Balearic Jews with a fine of 95,000 pounds; the will does not direct its legacy here toward helping this communal payment, though oppressive crown demands also affected Perpignan.

Asher seems to view these royal acquisitions as unlikely, since he goes on to set up an elaborate pattern of oversights. As executors and guardians for his widowed daughter Cohen, "as long as she remains without a husband," and separately as executors and guardians for his minor son Samiel, Asher chooses two Christians and two Jews, all residents of Perpignan. The Christians are Guillem Castelló an apothecary and Joan Bonhom a merchant. The Jews are Duran Samiel and Bonjueu Profet ("Bonjuses Profayt"). They all exercise joint "agency and authority" to "rule, direct, and administer" the persons and properties of Cohen and Samiel "as will seem right and just to them." The two Jews, however, "each by himself, can and should legally notarize and loan at interest and for the good of my heir, and should recover the payments from these," reporting on such loans "immediately" within eight days to the two Christian members for approval. All other business, negotiations, payment, and financial administration must be "by the agreement, assent, and approval of all the aforesaid executors together."

A super-executorship monitors the four: "they must render once every year an audit and financial report to Vidal Grimalt, a [Christian] investment financier, and to Vidal Meir ["Mayr"], a Jew of Vilafranca." Emery notes that Grimalt's description as *burgensis* is a technical term in these registers for men who lived on investments in trade, finance, or agriculture, without personal involvement in directing those enterprises either at home or abroad. The Christian must therefore have been a particularly experienced and particularly affluent financier. The Jew was a son of Bonafós de Vilafranca and a resident of Pézénes near Béziers. (The name may refer to Villefranche-de-Conflent or Villefranche-de-Rouergue in Occitania.) Though Vidal Meir appears only fleetingly in the registers, his one purchase is impressive, a house at Perpignan worth 4,000 sous.

Asher makes one final demand: "My son and heir is not able, nor ought he, to sell, pledge, or alienate my residence [*hospicium*] in which

I live, in the Jewish quarter [*callus*] of the town of Perpignan, fronting along one part on the holding of Mossé Bonsenyor and on the other on the holding of Mossé Bonafós, Jews, except by the express assent and approval of my said daughter and the aforesaid executors, guardians and administrators." The first neighbor here was Mossé Bonsenyor de Montpeller (modern Montpellier), son of Bonsenyor Jacob de Montpeller, grandson of Jacob de Montpeller, and brother of Astruc, Cresques, and Samiel—three generations who together stood among the largest moneylending operations in Perpignan. The second neighbor was Mossé Bonafós de Narbona (modern Narbonne), son of Bonafós Mossé de Narbona, husband of Meirona the daughter of Bonsenyor Jacob de Montpeller (just met above), an active moneylender who received from his father in 1284 a block of contiguous houses in Narbonne, valued in 1306 as worth 3,600 sous of Tours. Thus Asher had wealthy neighbors at each side and could call on the service of distinguished Jews and Christians alike.

Besides the notary Ramon Imbert, the text gives as sworn witnesses the Christians Bartolomé Soler, Bernat Gres, Pere Ferran, Guillem Barau [Barravi], Jaume Capdevila, and Jaume Bosc—"all weavers of Perpignan"—another reminder of the city's eminence in textile manufacturing and redistribution.[16] Asher's family emerges from the will as:

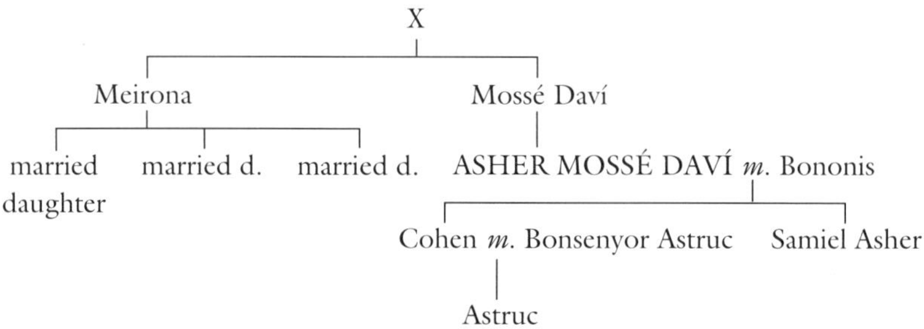

Only these five wills survive for the quarter century covered by Emery's seventeen notarial registers. Since wills elsewhere appear in random patterns in such registers, there is no schema by which the percentage in hand for Perpignan can be projected into the missing codices of the city's early registers. Thus we cannot yet see demographic patterns or know how many or what percentage of Jews here actually made Latin wills. That style of inquiry must await systematic search of richer notarial depositaries, with the subsequent patterns applied to incomplete sets of registers, such as that at Perpignan. A small number of allied documents in these registers points to yet other wills, Hebrew or possibly Latinate. Several are standard exit approvals by minors now grown of age, waiving any legal recourse later against executors.

In 1277, for example, Reina the daughter of Isaac Samiel and Astruga, now over eighteen years old, validates the work of the executors established by her mother's will—Belan Mossé de Scola, Asher de Lunel (mentioned above in Perpignan's third will), and Vidal Bonfill de Scal. Reina has now received all her mother's goods, including loan documents of her debtors and "some other loans that you contracted in my name as contained in the documents of the said debts." This waiver, on the model of similar waivers such as those of the crown to bailiffs at the end of an audit, is one of only a handful surviving at Perpignan from a whole genre. After listing the three Christian witnesses, Reina closes with the promise of yet another document: "Whenever I shall take a husband, I am to make for you a charter of payment and closure with the agreement and approval of that spouse whom I shall take." Thus even a routine will could generate further notarial action, both from the loan procedures of the executors and from multiple waivers such as Reina's. Details about individuals and families from the wills and their contexts can be carefully woven into a wider tapestry.[17]

Puigcerdá

High in the Pyrenees, the Cerdanya region straddled what is now French Cerdagne and Spanish Cerdaña, as part of the mainland holdings of the Kingdom of Majorca. The region had formed part of that kingdom informally even in the lifetime of Jaume I but did so with full effect from 1276 when the Conqueror died. The capital city of the then-unified Catalan Cerdanya was Puigcerdá, a communication and distribution hub connecting Mediterranean Roussillon at Perpignan to Urgell and the markets of Aragon and western Catalonia. Securely walled on its hilltop amid the looming Pyrenean ranges, Puigcerdá in 1300 was well advanced in the ascending curve of commercial development from 1250 to 1350, lively with international merchants and the court of a royal vicar.[18]

The Jewish community, from our surviving evidences, was well established and reasonably prosperous. The even larger community down at coastal Perpignan, capital of the Jewish tax collectory for the Roussillon and Cerdanya regions, held some three to four hundred souls in a hundred families by 1290, nearly half having names suggesting antecedents in southern France. A cursory look through the records for Puigcerdá suggests that at least fifty male adult Jews lived at Puigcerdá, a community therefore half the size of Perpignan's. The growing Jewish community, which constituted 10 percent of Puigcerdá's population by the end of thirteenth century, lived mixed among the Christians here, though a privileged Jewish district was also spreading outside the walls of the original town, north and northwest of the church of Santa Maria. This district, with its synagogue, hospital, and other amenities, centered around the site of the later Franciscan church of Sant Francesc. A Jewish home at Puigcerdá normally held only a nuclear family, the average number of children in a home numbering three to five. Besides the permanent residents, a large number of Jewish businessmen came and went irregularly. Population pressures occasioned a considerable enlargement of the town's walls, encouraging the Jews from the mid-fourteenth century to move their community center farther north within the new walls.

The *Liber Iudeorum* for June 1286 to November 1287 at Puigcerdá, its earliest codex for contracts involving Jews, includes loans by the Puigcerdá Jewish community to Christians in at least 170 towns and villages of Cerdanya. Though focusing on loans, the codex also includes other arrangements, such as dowry notices, marriage agreements, gifts, procuratorships, or receipts. The strong community, explicable in terms of Puigcerdá's international importance, doubtless owed much to the recruitment of Jews by Jaume the Conqueror, with special privileges to those in the Roussillon-Cerdanya district. It must also have benefited from the drift of Jewish population out of Languedoc, away from the increasing French presence, into the Roussillon-Pyrenean refuge.[19]

The *Liber Iudeorum* has some documentation relative to last dispositions, such as a notice about the universal heir of David or Daviu Cohen and an action by which the widow Regina as tutrix named her son Vives to be procurator in receiving buildings at Montpellier. For early wills, however, we must turn to the trove of notarial manuals recording the daily business of the town's Christians. I recently conducted a systematic search through some sixty such codices for the period 1260 to 1335, later extended to random further search. Amid the innumerable wills and codicils, the occasional Jewish will offered a welcome bonus. As a component of the codices they were rare enough, but cumulatively they amounted to more than I had encountered elsewhere for so early a period. I have not attempted to find them all. The next chapter will analyze a representative four, closely clustered in 1306 and 1307, while chapter 6 will provide three more. By way of introduction the present segment will discuss two Puigcerdá testaments: one by Jacob b. Abraham Cohen in 1321 and one by Mossé Eli Bedós in 1348. These wills suffer the usual infirmities of notarial codices, including water damage and wear at top and bottom (obscuring testator and witnesses) and dimming of the paper, which does not survive as sturdily as parchment charters. The spastic hands and careless abbreviations of these hurried notes further deter the researcher, who must often coax the letters or the meaning from bad handwriting.

The first testament in this selection is early enough; it comes from the notary Mateu d'Oliana (active at Puigcerdá from 1277 to 1325) and his colleague Guillem Hualart (active from 1314 to 1329) whose joint *Liber testamentorum* runs from 29 June 1321 to 10 July 1322, roughly a year. The codex contains a single Jewish will, that of Jacob b. Abra(h)am Cohen ("Choen") on 20 November 1321.[20] His Latinized name is clarified from "Jacob Abrae" by a supralinear insert, not "Aven" but "Coen." A resident (*habitator*) of Puigcerdá, having fallen ill, he appoints as executors his sons Abraham Jacob Cohen and Daui (Catalan Daviu) Jacob Cohen. His wife Covallis—Convallis(?)—is deceased, as is his daughter Suora (probably Catalan Sor, for sister.)

One of Suora's daughters, Sança (his *neptis* or granddaughter), comes first among the legatees, with 100 sous. Suora's second daughter Regina gets only 5 sous; a supralinear insert qualifies this as "toward her dowry [*maritagium*]." The third daughter Guoyo also receives 5 sous. The three sisters seem already to enjoy the dowry Jacob had given their deceased mother, and he is not disposed to add to their resources: "and they can request or have nothing else from my goods." A final daughter Judea, married to Felip Maimó, gets 5 sous and the dowry "which I gave." Her son Daviu receives 20 sous. Jacob then recognizes his dead wife's dowry, 1,000 sous. In that sum she had established as universal heirs the sons Daviu and Abraham; he now orders the executors to pay out the thousand. Jacob acknowledges a debt of 100 Barcelonan pounds to his son Abraham, by legal contract (*cum carta*), which he orders paid. After all these items have been taken care of, the two sons inherit "my other remaining goods."

The seven "invited witnesses" are Pere Perats the cobbler, Jaume Brahl, Jaume Borser, Felip Celarer the younger, Guillem of Eina (now in French Cerdagne), Vicent of Eina, Pere Ermengau, and Boniacip [Bo(n)macip?] Leví a Jew. The ambiguous Latin Iacobus may be Jacob rather than Jaume, since only one of the other names is designated as a Jew and two witnesses would be usual. Selar/Celar may be this Felip's name, but a flourish indicates yet another *er* component (Cellerer?). The document would have been dictated in Catalan to the Latin-wielding notary, a common practice; the son's Catalan name Daviu appears at first as Daui, then as Daviu canceled with Davidi substituted, and finally in its correct form Daviu twice. Similarly the last witness is given as Leví, then canceled and the fuller name substituted.

The daughter's name Guoyo or possibly Guoyx has a preceding false start deleted. If Guoyo, it is a variant of the feminine name Goyo seen in the previous will; if Guoyx, it is a version of the better-known Goig. Both versions of Catalan Goig mean "joy." The wife "Covallis" (genitive) has an abbreviatory overstroke promising extra letter(s), and her name remains something of a mystery.[21] Various Cohen and Leví members of the Puigcerdá community appear in the earlier *Liber Iudeorum*. The family members here correspond in part to those of 1306 in Gentil's will in the next chapter. Is the wife here that Gentil, and *Philippus* Fabib? The immediate family may be schematized:

JACOB ABRAHAM COHEN *m.* Covallis (Gentilis)

Abraham Jacob Cohen   Daviu Jacob Cohen   Suora   Judea *m.* Felip Maimó

Sança   Regina   Guoyo   Daviu

Mossé Ali Bedós ("Bedoz") drew up his will on 22 July 1348. Bedós and Bádos are general Catalan surnames. Ali will be examined below. Mossé chooses two men of the Cohen family as his executors and arranges for burial "in the cemetery of the Jews of Puigcerdá," to which he leaves 3 sous. Ten sous apiece go to his brothers Astruc and Salamó, but 7 pounds and 10 sous to his children Salamó, Mossé, and Mirea. The manuscript seems at first to posit two sons, Salamó Mossé and "Mrea." Close reading of texts and tenses shows that Salamó and Mossé are the sons. Mrea is the daughter; the initial letter is blotted (but must be *m:* cf. the preceding Mossé) and no abbreviation is signaled. Her name may be the Catalan feminine Mira, "notable," popular among Jews, or even Hebrew Miryam in the variant Marea.[22]

If any of the three children dies, the freed share reverts to the others. If all die without legitimate issue, the full legacy returns to their mother Regina. The executors are to distribute 5 sous to charity as a *pro anima* legacy as well as "all my clothing." Two sous are for "lamps of the synagogue [*scola*]." Everything else goes to his wife Regina as universal heir. The seven witnesses are all Christians. The family structure is sketchy but can be supplemented from the property inventories drawn on the occasion of the deaths of Ali and of Astruc.

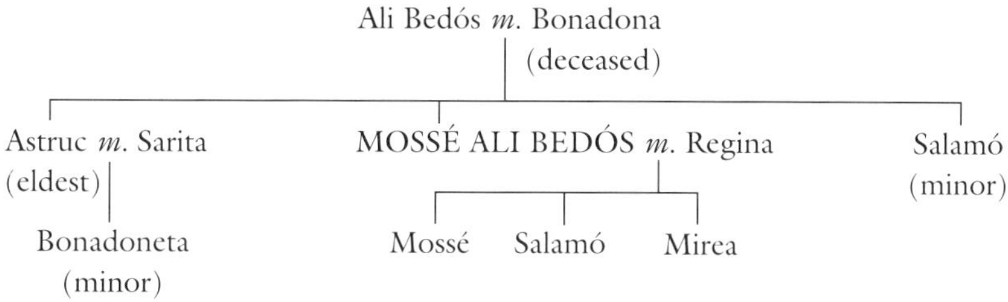

Carme Batlle has published and analyzed the postmortem property inventories both of Mossé Ali in 1348 and of his father Ali in 1344, on deposit at the neighboring cathedral archives of Seo de Urgel. The father's inventory gives him as both Helie (or perhaps nominative Helia) and several times as Ali and En Ali ("N'Ali Badoz"). The son's inventory prefers the form Helie. As with many such inventories, the lists take us into the family's capacious home at Seo de Urgel, reveal the "considerable fortune" involved, and detail the clothing, jewels, and furniture on hand. They also describe at length the Hebrew and other books in a large family library.[23] A Puigcerdá testament from the same family (as first names and surnames strongly argue) will be presented in the next chapter, from 1306. Instead of Ali/Helie, the name Elias appears there. The many appearances of Ali in the 1344 and 1348 inventories and in the 1348 testament tempt one to see here the merger of Arabic ʿAlī with the biblical high priest Eli. The biblical name was not used before the rise of Islam, Goitein informs us, since Eli was considered "ill-fated." Because the name then made a perfect cognate with the secular ʿAlī, however, Eli became "the most common name in the Geniza" community. If Ali/Eli/Helie in the Bedós family has that origin, it may signal antecedents and influence from the Islamic world. Yet the 1306 will describes that (this?) family as from Mazères in southern France. In that migratory age and with general intermarriage, both origins might be accommodated. In his study of French names, Simon Seror subsumes Ali, rare in those parts, under generic Elie for biblical Eliyahu (Greek form Elias).

The next set of Puigcerdá wills deserve a chapter apart. Not only do they form a tight, interrelated group chronologically but they invite extended comment as particularly involving women.

CHAPTER 5

Women in Wills: Widows and Wives

The Puigcerdá notarial collection, unusually numerous and rich, recurrently offers a codex devoted to wills alone, essentially Christian wills. An example is the *Liber testamentorum* by the notaries Mateu d'Alb and Bernat Mauri, for the period 24 June 1306 to 24 June 1307. Among the many testaments recorded during that year, the codex supplies four fine Jewish wills. Since all four were drafted within the same community and within the short span of two months, they offer a group portrait of their society. One will is from a widow, two are by wives with husbands living, while another shows a husband providing for his wife. An extrinsic will, by a widow from Valls in Catalonia, balances this offering—two widows and two wives.

In Jewish law a widow could not inherit from her husband. In practice, however, the husband's assets often came into the widow's hand technically as the delayed gift, or *tosefet* increment, promised in the marriage document, or *ketubah*. A place in the family residence, household articles, and clothing would commonly remain to her. Her dowry also came back to her, often reckoned more highly than the value of goods originally brought to the marriage. Cheryl Tallan has studied the Jewish widows of northern Europe, using both responsa and non-Jewish sources. She has found the more affluent and comfortable among them enjoying, in the private and the economic spheres, "a position of power and authority far greater than that of [their] married sisters." Renée Melammed similarly finds the Spanish Jewish widow of means a free and powerful figure, though her evidence is from the post-expulsion Sephardic diaspora to 1550.[1] The wills analyzed thus far have been mostly by men, though women as frequently seem to have made wills. Here at Puigcerdá, part of the Majorcan kingdom as well as capital of the inland Pyrenean county of Cerdanya, this one codex allows us to confront a series of women contemporaries and neighbors and formally address the theme of women's wills.

The Widow Regina

On 23 October 1306, Regina, the widow of Bondia, dictated a fairly elaborate testament.[2] "First of all I order my body buried," presumably by norms previously conveyed to the family. Regina then provides legacies for six friends; if these are relatives or in-laws, the usual clues are lacking. She leaves 100 sous to Jucef Cohen ("Choen"), 30 to Isaac ("Isach") of Soall, 30 "to the heirs of the deceased Jucef of Soall," 20 "to Mometa the Jewess," 100 to Mancosa the widow of Abraham of La Rochelle ("de la Rotxela"), and 50 "to Aster the sister of the said Mancosa." At this point Regina interrupts the list to assign 100 sous to "some charity, for my soul, on the day of my death."

She then takes up her immediate family, leaving 100 sous "to my daughter Aster, the wife of Fagim Bonet the Jew, for the share and inheritance belonging to her in my goods, in which (and in that dowry she had at the time of her marriage) I constitute her my heiress." The money here is designated as Barcelona sous, which probably should be understood of all the other more general entries. Regina also left "to Gaux, daughter of myself and my aforesaid deceased husband," another 100 sous, characterized by the same dowry and heiress phrases; Gaux's husband is mentioned by name, Astruc Bondia. Finally, "for my soul, I leave as an alms [*elemosina*] for the Jews of Puigcerdá, out of love of God, my bed with all bedclothes and furnishings, which is to stand in the synagogue of the aforesaid Jews." *Elemosina* in the singular here may be a charitable fund (Catalan *almoina*) or even a hospice/almshouse, such as the *espital* that Huesca's Jews maintained from the 1160s.

Though a synonym for synagogue, *scola* may mean here the Bet ha-Midrash synagogue with its yeshiva, since the bed is to stay in the *scola*. Even in that House of Studies, sleeping accommodations were not usual, but an exception was made for scholars in full residence. The term *scola* here invites comment. J. M. Millás Vallicrosa has suggested that the usage derives from the instructional function in Bible and Talmud to youngsters at the synagogue. For Barcelona he distinguishes between the *scola major,* or main synagogue, the *scola menor* of the women, and the *scola dels párvols* (of the little ones) or *hospital de l'almoyna* (almshouse). In reviewing the rights of Majorca's Jews, Jaume III defined the term. "The Jews legitimately have their *scola* or some building whether owned or leased, for prayer according to the Mosaic law, rites, and customs of the Jews, in the aforesaid city, where they have had a synagogue elaborate and exceedingly beautiful, and a building for prayer elsewhere" in the city. The king denied that the Majorcan Jews at the time wanted to build a new synagogue, because legally "new" applied only to the introduction of a synagogue in a locality lacking one; the present *scola* "is instead a repair and rebuilding of the old, which we allow to be called not a synagogue but a *scola* or house of prayer."[3]

The medieval tendency to unite the functions of synagogue (prayer with some study) and house of study of Bet ha-Midrash (religious study with some prayer) may explain the dual terminology here of synagogue/*scola.* Are the two institutions distinguished, but in a single complex, in a rebuke by Jaume II in 1304 to the Jews of Valencia city? "You have gone beyond bounds, for you have constructed and fashioned your synagogue [*sinagoga*] and Bet ha-Midrash [*almidraz*] higher and larger than was allowed or proper. We have ordered and made you reduce this synagogue and Bet ha-Midrash to the original and proper status." The singular possessive pronoun is open to the interpretation that the king sees both institutions as effectively synonymous.[4]

To return to Regina's will. She now names as her executor her son-in-law "Astruc Jucef the Jew to whom I give license, etc." She designates "as universal heirs in all my other goods, wherever and whatever they are, Bondia and Jucef my grandsons, the sons of the deceased Astruc Bondia the Jew." Eight witnesses are listed, four of whom were Jews: Mateu d'Olià, Arnau Payleres, Ramon Rahedor, Astruc de Besalú, Jacob (ben) Abraham Cohen ("Choen"), Bernat Duran, Jucef Abraham, and Vidal "the son of" (ben) Astruc Cre(i)xent. A concluding note shows the executor paying 5 sous as fee to the notary. Three lines drawn from top to bottom through the text indicate that it was vacated or a formal copy was issued to the heirs.

Several aspects of the will invite comment. Regina was doubtless dictating the will in dialogue with the notary; at one point she begins to refer to the community's administrators, in connection with the special charity on her death day, but interrupts herself in order to add a final legacy for her friend Aster, not returning to her expression about the administrators. The deleted phrase "I order that the secretaries" is a glimpse of the *ne'emanim,* officials of the *aljama*'s administrative board, and their role in such charitable actions. The amounts left to charity are small; this commonly meant that more substantial contributions had been separately established beforehand. The legacies are reasonably substantial as pleasant gifts—four of 100 sous, and others of 50, 30, and 20—but they suggest that the bulk of the inheritance passed to the two nephews as universal heirs.

Some of the families whose members appear are also found in the *Liber Iudeorum* a decade or so before: the Bonet, Soall, Choen or Cohen, and Cre(i)xent. In this will the Cohen, Cre(i)xent, and Soall have prominence. Bonet, Cohen, and Cre(i)xent appear also in the Perpignan registers, as might be predicted from the close political and commercial unity of Puigcerdá and Perpignan. (Soall does not turn up, unless the several Scal persons are a variant.) The first names of the will's families, though common enough, also occur in the *Liber* lists: Abraham, Astruc, Bondia, Fagim, Isaac, Jacob, Jucef, Mometa, Regina, and Vidal. The testator's own surname is a puzzle. It seems to be Coras with overstroke (Corans? or Crescas?), but apparently turns up as Comte in Delcor's transcription from the *Liber.* "Regina uxor Bondia Comte" there loans 78 pounds, 1,934 sous, and 97 pence of Barcelona money. Perhaps the name Cresques is meant. Her loan operations indicate property far beyond the total sum of 630 sous in the will, pointing up again the supplementary nature of such wills. A family tree, without attempting to conjecture the order of birth of the children, shows:

REGINA *m.* Bondia Corans (Crescas?)

Aster *m.* Fagim Bonet — Gaux *m.* Astruc Bondia

(children of Gaux and Astruc Bondia:) Bondia — Jucef

Eighteen Jews appear in the will, most of the names reflecting the Catalan environment. The cognate Occitan culture and language may also have been at the root of some or all of the names, of course, and can be seen explicitly in Abraham of La Rochelle. Astruc of Besalú's name announces his or his family's connection to Catalan Besalú. The strong Arabic orientation of the Majorca will of Salema, the son of Aaron B. Aarde, in chapter 4 above, is missing here. Both Christians and Jews in Catalonia used the women's names Aster (star, but also for Ester), Gausax (a variant of Goigs), and Regina or Reina. Bonet, a diminutive of Bo, and Bondia were also common to Christians and Jews there. Soall may be a toponym, since it has a preceding *de;* I can find only one place of that name, a physical feature in the nearby Valle de Aran. Seror suggests Soual l'Etape in the Tarn region. If the *de* functions as *ben,* however, the biblical Hebrew names Shoval (way) and Shual (fox) may apply.[5]

Salamó Bedós and Wife Cobes

A few folios further on, Salamó Bedós ("Bedoz"), formerly of Mazères near Toulouse in Occitania, now ill but of sound mind, entered his will in November 1306.[6] "First of all, I leave Astruc Bedós my father 20 silver pieces of Tours; likewise I order repaid and returned to him on the one hand 7 silver pieces of Tours, and on the other 1 gold florin, which I owe him as a loan." The universal heirs must "provide for my father in food and drink well and properly until the said sums of money shall be fully paid out to him, and the said provision is not to be reckoned in the payment of the said sums of money." Thus the father is to receive a per diem or room and board (implied by the conventional phrase) besides the sums, until those sums are repaid.

Salamó now turns to his sister Baynola, who receives 10 Barcelonan sous, and to his wife: "I testify that I had from my wife Cobes or in her name, at the time of the nuptials, 500 pounds of Tours as her dowry, which I order to be paid and returned to her immediately after my death, when she wishes." Nothing is said of clothing and domestic goods; as seen above, these would usually remain with the widow anyway. Even Christian codes such as the Valencian *Furs* took such prosaic items seriously, at first denying any claim by the Christian widow on the shared bedchamber, on clothing except her daily wear, or on furnishings unless these had survived from possessions brought by her at the time of the wedding. This must have aroused opposition as heartless, for it was soon amended to award the widow bed, bedclothes, and wardrobe.[7]

Salamó appoints Cobes (also Cubes here) administrator-guardian (*domina et potens*) "of my universal heirs listed below and their goods, as long as she shall live." These heirs in turn must "provide her all her life in all her material necessities well and appropriately." Salamó has a daughter, Bonatosa, for whose possible future widowhood he wishes to provide. He orders his universal heirs to give all material care to her, "only and until Vidas of Lunel, a Jew, the husband of the said Bonatosa, will live with her and will make [his] continuous residence with her in one house under one common budget and household." Vidas himself would then receive 10 Barcelonan sous, "which I leave him, in which (and in the dowry I gave Bonatosa with her husband) I made her my heir." If Vidas were already dead or should die "within the space of two years coming up after my death," the other universal heirs below "are bound to marry off the said daughter suitably" and to give her as dowry the 25 pounds of Tours Salamó is putting aside here. Finally, he establishes as universal heirs his sons Elias and Mossé Bedós. "And I substitute, wish, and order that if either of my said sons should die at any time without legitimate offspring," the remnant of his legacy be equally divided between the brother "alive and surviving," Cobes, and Bonatosa.

Salamó's father Astruc Bedós witnessed and approved the provisions. Seven "invited witnesses" (*testes rogati*) follow: Salamó of Valencia, Deulosal of Besalú, Salamó Jucef, Jacob Astruc, and Rubèn Jucef—"all Jews"—with Arnau of Urtx and Ramon Serra, "Christians." This testament essentially leaves Salamó's worldly goods to his sons, but it puts both sons and goods under their mother during her lifetime, while providing a decent living for his own father and for the wife and unmarried daughter. The circumstances of the married daughter seem odd, separated from her husband; the provision here seems designed to mend a broken marriage. The toponymical surnames—Besalú, Lunel (just northeast of Montpellier), and Valencia—suggest something of the mobile commercial society of the Catalan-Occitan lands; Urg, now Urtx, is near Puigcerdá. Among the Jews' first names, the witness Deulosal or "God save him" was perhaps a cross-name for Hebrew Isaiah or Yeshua/Joshua, as the husband Vidal or Vital was a secular name for Hayyim, or "life." Both were also common names for Catalan Christians. None of the friends or witnesses in the widow Regina's will, just three folios back, appear in this group of relatives and friends.

The Catalan notary experienced a moment of confusion with the biblical Rubèn, writing first Rotben (on the analogy of names like Rotland for Roland) but canceling it. Other names offer some difficulty. Bedós and Badós are general Catalan surnames. The wife Cubes/Cobes may relate to the Catalan name Cubí or the Sephardic family Cuby (from Qubbia in Morocco); it is less likely to be a form in diminutive of (Ja)cob. The daughter Baynola recalls Catalan toponyms from late Latin *balneola* for bath (Banyols, Banyoles, Banyolí); as with Cubes, however, these suggestions are merely conjectural. Bonatosa seems an uncommon name, perhaps an augmentative for Bonat; paleographically it is not the more acceptable *Bona cosa*. The male name Vidas among Catalan Jews and Christians was more usually in the singular Vida.[8] Elias is a form of biblical Eliyahu, English Elijah. A family tree shows:

Astruc Bedós *m.* X

SALAMÓ BEDÓS *m.* Cobes/Cubes — Baynola

Bonatosa *m.* Vidas de Lunel — Elias Bedós — Mossé Bedós

Astruga, Wife of Jucef Abraham

The next will in sequence comes on the verso of Salamó's and is dated November 6.[9] Fallen ill, Astruga "with the consent of my husband" Jucef Abraham, a Jew of Puigcerdá, disposes "of my goods." In first place, she gives her mother Fava[10] 600 Barcelonan sous to cover any "share, legitimate inheritance, and claim belonging to her." Astruga's husband can keep this money, however, if he remains unmarried and supports Fava in his home. "I wish and order that, if the said Jucef Abraham my husband shall wish to provide for my mother in his house in all her material needs for all her life, my mother cannot force my husband to pay her the aforesaid moneys, as long as my husband does not take another wife and wishes to remain chaste; if my husband shall take another wife, however, I wish that my mother can immediately compel my husband to pay her the aforesaid moneys." Such conditional provision of funds for spouses who remained unmarried were common enough in male testaments; the novelty here is that the wife sets up the condition and that the money will be only a usufruct that really belongs to his mother-in-law in permanent residence.

That weighty matter extensively clarified, Astruga next presents "to the crown of the scroll of the synagogue [*scola*] of the Jews of Puigcerdá" 50 Barcelonan sous. The "crown" (*'aṭara*) was one form of decoration covering the ends of the rods or staves on which the Torah scroll turned; such decorations were usually gilded or otherwise embellished. The handsome sum here probably covered the cost only partially, since the legacy is "to" the crown.[11] Only now does Astruga take up legacies proper, and these she confines to her children. She has two daughters by Jucef: Aster and Bonafilla or Bonafília. (Both forms appear in the will, corresponding to the two Catalan forms of the feminine of Bonfill.) Astruga leaves these daughters "all my clothing and household furnishings"; clothing was a valuable legacy in medieval wills because of its high market value and because it was passed on from generation to generation.

Astruga then names as universal heirs "in all my remaining goods" the two daughters. Her husband's approval was obviously important. He signs first: "I Jucef, her husband, approve." The "invited witnesses" have more than the usual share of Christians, including a cleric: Pere Salmes, Guillem Comdor, Bernat Colomer, Jaume Orig, Simó de Pinosa the rector of the church of Castellar, Bondia Abraham, and Jucef Cohen. The Christians, reasonably enough, all seem to be local people. Orig is simply an antique variant for the toponym Urg (now Urtx). Castellar of the rector is southwest of Seo de Urgel, near Tost. Salmes may relate to the Catalan family name Salma.[12] The immediate family revealed here is minimal:

X *m.* Fava
|
ASTRUGA *m.* Jucef (b.) Abraham
|
Aster — Bonafília

A notation at the bottom says "Let the husband give 5 sous." Cancellation by three horizontal lines indicates that this sum paid for a copy. Aside from the bequest to the synagogue, the will basically puts everything at the wife's disposition into her daughters' hands. The only other proviso, taking up half the will, ensures that Jucef will take care of his mother-in-law within his household. The sum set aside, 600 sous, must have been adequate as a permanent fund to support an old woman until death. As was customary, Astruga had probably taken care of religious and charitable benefactions and of friends or relatives by timely final gifts. The whole tone of the will suggests a woman of some independent means; she does not appear in Delcor's summaries of money-lenders, but a wife's activities could be masked by her husband's name.

Gentil, Wife of Jacob Abraham Cohen

The fourth will in this Puigcerdá series comes two folios later, dated 21 November 1306, and is again by a woman.[13] "Gentil, wife of the Jew Jacob Abraham Choen" or Cohen, in her illness establishes her husband as her "administrator and executor." Her first arrangement is that Jacob and her universal heirs are to distribute 100 Barcelona sous in charity "for my soul," thoughtfully inserting above the line the ample time frame "within one year." To her daughter Judea, "wife of Fabib Salamó of Barcelona," she leaves a mere 5 sous; with the dowry given at the time of marriage, this is to be Judea's entire inheritance. To her granddaughter ("Regina, daughter of my deceased daughter Goyo"), both in her own right and by "reason of her mother," Gentil leaves another 5 sous; the dowry given at the time of Goyo's marriage to Astruc Deulosal, as stated in the matrimonial documents more fully, is added here. Apparently Deulosal had also married Regina's other daughter Adzero, who had then also died, leaving two daughters Goyo and Adzero. To these granddaughters, for themselves and by reason of their mother's claim, Gentil gives 5 Barcelona sous apiece plus the dowry as described in Adzero's nuptial agreements.

Finally, Gentil established her sons Abraham b. Jacob Cohen and David b. Jacob Cohen as universal heirs; should one of them die without legitimate offspring, the other if living would receive that share too. The "invited witnesses" include the Christians Bernat Pere, Mateu d'En Bord, Joan Bailó, Bernat Collat, Guido de Paretes [*Piritis*], and Arnau Ponç, and the Jews Duran Salamó and Salamó Jucef. The last witness, Salamó Jucef, may be the same man as in the witness list of the Bedós will, but the names and combination are too common to afford certainty. This will has eight instead of the usual seven witnesses, which was permitted. The only candidates for merging two names into one (Joan the bailiff of Bernat Collat) is disqualified by the genitive of the surname Bailó. Gentil's will seems oriented toward retaining the family's resources within the immediate male line. The apparent harshness with which others are treated and the absence of friends and most charities is again surely an illusion. The basic purpose of the will had little to do with pretestamentary dispositions, which had probably taken care of those other concerns. Even the 100 sous for funerary charities reminds us that this would have been a small part of the funeral celebrations, which reflected and maintained social status. The will displays the whole family, which relates to that of Jacob Abraham Cohen, given above:

GENTIL *m.* Jacob b. Abraham Cohen

Abraham b. Jacob | David b. Jacob | Judea *m.* Fabib Salamó | Goyo *m.* Astruc | Deulosal *m.* Adzero

Regina (child of Goyo and Astruc)

Goyo, Adzero (children of Deulosal and Adzero)

The family followed both patronym and surname or title. The father Jacob Abraham (Latin genitive for surname or as ben Abraham) Cohen had as sons Abraham Jacob Cohen and Davit (Catalan David) Jacob Cohen. Gentil in the manuscript follows the now-antiquated Gentill spelling of the Catalan name for "cherished," "gracious," "highborn" (and even "gentile"!). Similarly the Latin Judea reflects the medieval Catalan Judeua (modern Jueva, Hebrew Yehuda feminized). Fabib may be Arabic Ḥabīb or else Hebrew Habib ("beloved"). Catalan Astruc here keeps the antiquated final *h*. The feminine name Goig appears several times in the crown registers; like Joya it is Catalan for "joy". The name Goyo seems a variant either of Goig or of Provençal Goiona. Adzero/Atzero may approximate Hebrew Asher for "blessed". Catalan Duran, a name echoing "endurance," doubtless also had a Hebrew cognate.[14]

These four early wills, all confected in the same year, 1306, indeed within the same two months, reflect independent family groupings. The Jewish community was very small by our contemporary standards. All of Puigcerdá itself held only 660 Christian or other households in 1359, constituting two-thirds of the Cerdanya region's population. This count came in the wake of the ravages of the Black Death and must be adjusted for that context. Still, three wills from the year 1306 offer a ground-level glimpse of family life that must have been a cross section of the small Jewish community (the *aljama*), or of those prosperous enough to make wills. No element within this series of wills as a whole explains why these families, and only these, entered testaments in the Christian notary's book of wills. These were probably not all the deaths in the Jewish community that year; in any case, other codices reserved for testaments at Puigcerdá in other years in the full notarial library do not show the same high percentage of Jewish wills. Nor are the wills homogeneous. Each differs from the other, revealing a unique family problem or situation.

In some respects, of course, these wills echo one another. Each testator is ill; all are concerned to preserve family resources relatively undivided; three of the four have *pro anima* legacies (though presumably all had previously arranged philanthropies); all show strong family feeling; all have some, even many, Christians to bolster the witness lists; all repeat the identification "Jew" for the parties involved, as a legal incantation, though we might not think it necessary for identification. More significant perhaps, three of the four testaments are by women, each in a somewhat different family situation. Regina is a widow who remembers friends, Astruga acts with her husband's consent and has him sign his specific approval, and Gentil acts independently but makes her husband her executor. Even the single male testator establishes his wife Cobes as executor of his will and guardian of his children and property for her lifetime.

Were wills, or wills before Christian notaries, more useful for Jewish women than for men? Were the properties at their disposition, whether as wives or widows, less secure? There is no reason to think so; wills by women had always been usual enough even in Geniza days; and other wills (three of the five from Puigcerdá that we are about to examine briefly) were by men. The balance in the present series simply mirrors the independence and initiative of Mediterranean Jewish women in their domestic sphere. Finally, since there are numerous nontestamentary bits of documentation for Jews scattered unpublished through the Puigcerdá notarial archives, these several family trees and witness lists make a beginning toward reconstruction of that familial community for men and women of all ages.

Reina: Widow in Valls

Far to the south of Pyrenean Puigcerdá and thirty years into the future, a final exemplar can round off this set of women's wills. The testament comes in 1338 from the town of Valls, twenty kilometers inland from Tarragona and a satellite of that grand Catalan city. A bovage tax at the very time of this testament counted 712 households in the town, a figure reduced in the post–Black Death census of 1358 to 587 households and in the census of 1370 to 569. If the Jewish community there held some 30 families at the time of its destruction in the general massacres of 1391, it seems reasonable to enlarge it for the time of the testament to some 45 households. The center of its own district, with a role in the regional network or commune as well, the town boasted its own governance under two consuls plus a division of overlordship by king and archbishop of Tarragona, with a lively commercial, agricultural, and artisanal (especially textile) activity.

Gabriel Secall i Güell has drawn on the surviving local notarial manuals as well as other archival and published materials to re-create the Jewish community in Valls. Four *libri Iudeorum* remain today, for the years 1313–1315, 1313–1324, 1328, and 1342–1344, respectively. The first of these deals with 37 males, including some with their wives; the second has 53 clients. Secall takes these to be families and understands the discrepancy in numbers to indicate the general demographic rise in Catalonia during that decade. A coefficient of three or four persons per family would put between 159 and 212 Jews in Valls around the year 1324.[15]

Secall has found a fascinating testament in this material, drawn in 1338 by Regina or Reina, the widow of Bonjua Cap. Both appear alive and active in the *Liber Iudeorum* of 1323–1324. The Cap family were widely distributed in Catalan lands, an affluent merchant clan; in Valls they were especially involved in marketing cloth. Leila Berner has chronicled their high status and economic activities in thirteenth-century Barcelona. Secall transcribes Reina's will in a footnote, sums its dispositions in his text, and supplies a photograph of one of its folios.[16] A canceling X down the page indicates that a formal parchment copy had been issued. Reina begins by noting her illness as well as her sound "sense, memory, and legal wholeness." She "revokes all my other testaments and last wills drafted or made by me formerly and which I wish to be without validity," a clause suggesting that her children had since died or perhaps that her husband Bonjua had figured in previous dispositions. Without children or husband now, she distributes 2,720 sous to relatives, friends, and charities.

In first place come 500 sous that her executors "are to distribute for marrying off Jewish girls," namely, for dowries. The executors are to invest another 500 sous at interest until the money suffices to buy a Torah for the synagogue. The manuscript has deteriorated in this part, but the verb *lucror* suggests putting the money out at loan, while one fragment seems to indicate doubling the money by that expedient. The result of this financial business, however, is clear: "a Sefer Torah, which Scroll or Sefer Torah [*rotlle sive çafertora*] I wish to give and assign to the school or synagogue of the Jews of the place of Valls." As the five books of Moses used in worship, the Torah was at the center of synagogue life and the most sacred object held by the community. The very large price, something over 500 sous and probably a thousand, was a result not only of the scribal artistry required for any book meant for reading but here especially a product of materials of the highest quality, the services of a *sōfer* skilled in the strict rules guiding every aspect of the sacred task, and the careful reverence that precluded the easy rapidity of a secular bookmaker.

The other large legacy, 1000 sous, goes to Bonafilia, "the wife of En Biona Cap a Jew of Falset," a hill town south of Valls and Tarragona. The mildly honorific En and the husband's surname are our only clues to this in-law whose legacy was larger than those of all other relatives and friends together except for the universal heir. Reina leaves 300 sous to her nephew Astruc Lleó, the son of her sister Asterona (no husband designated). Another 200 sous go to Dolça ("Dulcich," perhaps a form of the related name Dolcenc), the wife of Bonet Isaac. Another 200 go to Abraham "son of the said Cerona." Though Cerona was not previously "said" in the will, its feminine modifier suggests that it is the Hebrew biblical Sharon in its variant Sharona. In the will "Cerona" appears twice and "Asterona" once, raising a suspicion of miscopy of the same name. Assuming they are different, one might follow Seror's name lists, which put both "Esterona" and "Serrona" as variants of Aster/Est(h)er. Though a strong element of conjecture is involved, the Hebrew option Sharona seems more plausible.

The final general legacies are 10 sous apiece to Isaac and Reina, the children of Maymó de Narbona (of Narbonne, but a resident now of Valls). This family may be relatives, since the will insists that the token sum represents "their claim that they have or can have in or on my goods." The executors charged with disbursing all this are the children of her sister Astruga, Isaac Maymó and Abraham Maymó, though "through" the universal heir, Astruga herself. As for nonmonetary legacies, Reina gives to the Sharona just mentioned "a third part of all my cloth, both woolen and linen, both fustian and tow, and also any other kind of cloth" as well as a third part "of my pots and bowls of copper." Astruga is to keep everything else "in the residence [*hospicium*] in which I and she and her [two] children live together." Astruga as heir and the executors are to dismiss all debts by "all poor Jews who are obligated and owe me debts going up to the sum of fifteen sous" in Barcelona silver money (*terna,* Catalan *moneda de tern* of 1258). And Astruga is to restore to these "poor" Jewish debtors the pledges they had given. The witnesses to the will are three Jews: Mossé Barzilai ("Barzelay"), Astruc Lleó, and Isaac ("Isçach") Maymó (Astruc Lleó was her nephew by Asterona and Isaac her nephew by Astruga).[17]

The family tree, though lacking direct heirs from Reina, exhibits a contemporary extended family, in which Maymó de Narbona should be considered a relative.

Asterona — REINA *m.* Bonjua Cap — Astruga *m.* Maymó Abraham

Astruc Lleó (child of Asterona)

Abraham Maymó — Isaac Maymó (children of Astruga *m.* Maymó Abraham)

Legatees:	Witnesses:
Bonafília (*m.* En Biona Cap)	Mossé Barzilai
Dolça (*m.* Bonet Isaac)	Astruc Lleó
Isaac and Reina (children of Maymó de Narbona)	Isaac Maymó
Abraham (son of Cerona/Sharona)	

If Cerona is a variant of Asterona above, Abraham is brother to Astruc Lleó.

Family names merit a glance. The Cap surname was Catalan for Hebrew Rosh as head or chief. Lleó as Latin Leo translates Hebrew Judah/ Yehudah. Astera echoes Catalan and biblical Ester, "star." Barzelay is Aramaic and biblical Barzilai, "man of iron" (cf. Catalan Ferrer). Bonjua is a Catalan variant of Bonjueu and Bonjudá.[18]

Wills and Women

The women's wills done at Puigcerdá within a period of two months invited reflection as a single group phenomenon. Taking all the women's wills at once, each invaluable for its data and implications, some generalities may now be essayed. A preliminary caution should note that a husband's Latinate will was far more important to the average Jewish wife than was the exercise of power or control involved in a widow's or a dying wife's own testament. The complexities of Jewish law might leave the husband's assets in the widow's hands, as was seen above, but the man's heirs and creditors might then move in and throw the whole question into court. A Latinate or notarial will would authoritatively forestall challenge.

The women in our own wills here, notably the widows, belong to relatively affluent strata of their respective communities. Most of them are clearly individuals, not shadows obscured by a notary's formulas. One widow makes God her universal heir, another directs a large sum to be invested in order to commission a Torah for the synagogue, a third extensively and effectively blocks her widower-husband from remarrying. Most arrange for public charities, from children's education to Torah crown to bedclothes for the synagogue. Judith Baskin has suggested that such religious legacies by women represented "female strategies for imprinting their existences on a communal religious life from which they were otherwise barred."[19] But the legacies may also simply extend the primary role of women as keepers of the faith in their domestic sphere.

These wills are not notarial clones, as with so many contemporary Christian wills. They range from a simple family affair (husband as executor, sons as universal heirs, glancing reference to three daughters) to a very complicated remembrance involving eighteen legatees. Each will has at least seven formal witnesses (eight in some cases), but their composition varies from four Jews with four Christians, to seven Christians alone, to two Jews and five Christians, to two Jews and six Christians. The Valls will has three Jews at the beginning of an otherwise illegible line. The artisan character of many of the Christian witnesses in both women's and men's wills may simply indicate the kind of persons with whom the Jews routinely dealt, or this may be the notary's doing. The identity of the Jewish witnesses may become clearer by computer analysis of all the Jewish names in the loan records and other documents at a given place. Witnesses, Jewish or Christian, do not seem to be professionals regularly renting their services.

Women's wills have a strong philanthropic element, at times startlingly generous. And they include other women, relatives or friends, more usually than do the men's wills. The women's wills, perhaps more than the men's, afford glimpses into domestic arrangements. One dying woman makes it clear that she has her husband's consent for the complex dispositions she lists. Since women and women's affairs appear by indirection in the men's wills and since lawsuits and other auxiliary documentation sometimes place women in central roles, the impressions given by women's testaments might be expanded and sharpened by the industrious addition of such fragments. A larger task ahead is to correlate the activities of the women in the wills with the talmudic regulations regarding widows and their husbands' properties and with Jewish tradition and experience generally with inheritances.

Shlomo Goitein has led the way here with regard to Geniza materials on inheritance in an earlier period (ca. 950–1200).[20] He notes how the death of a wife was at worst a difficult situation for the husband, while the death of a husband was a disaster for many wives. Left with only the remnants of the dowry, personal belongings, the delayed marriage gift, and not much else, the widows in the poorer classes were often thrown on public support. Goitein also notes that it was rare for a Geniza husband to make his widow sole heir, since remarriage would shift his property to the new husband. The husband not infrequently made his widow executor, however, showing confidence in her good sense and financial shrewdness; and of course he might declare his widow the guardian of his minor children.

Some elements common in the Geniza inheritance procedures have no echo in the Latinate wills, though they may well have occurred in the widow's Jewish community—for example, the disliked "women's oath" that she held nothing of the dead husband's own property (very strictly interpreted sometimes), or the principle that "heirs have precedence [over widows]." Other elements of traditional inheritance patterns may hide beneath the notarial patterns of expression, such as the husband's statement on his deathbed as to how much he still owed his wife, or the use of an inheritance disposition to cover as much as possible the final debt owed to the wife. If the Geniza fragments have proved so illuminating in such inheritance matters for their own period, the Latinate Jewish wills, as their numbers increase, may be persuaded to reveal as much or more for this later time. The rich responsa literature, in which distinguished experts "responded" to dilemmas of law and life, will illumine the many background details. This source is complicated, however, by the frequent lack of place and time and by the exemplary nature of the genre.

Whatever the prescriptions of custom and Talmud, each community of Jews lived within and interacted with one or another local Christian culture. How the Catalan culture, its perceptions and expression, modified or reexpressed Roman law testamentary experience may have had a strong effect on these Jewish wills and on contemporaries' understanding of them. The current researches of Stephen Bensch on the testamentary data and trends of thirteenth-century Catalan Christians are helpful here. Bensch finds that Christian women made one out of three wills in thirteenth-century Barcelona (up from one in five for the twelfth century); half of these women were wives, not widows. He notes that after 1250 husbands as executors and wives as estate managers become less common in these wills. The wills in general followed the Roman law strategy of a universal heir rather than the previously dominant Visigothic model of equal shares. Demographically, the Christians reveal one or no children in 67 percent of the testaments, which may reflect the advanced age of most testators, whose children were already established elsewhere in this affluent stratum. Bensch also explores the dowry brought by the wife and the dower or promise of a later gift by the husband (*sponsalicium*). The dower, he concludes, had become in fact "a broad grant of rights over all her husband's property"; one consequence was that the wife's name was needed for any property transfer by a husband. A larger result was that the Christian woman in Barcelona had become "a formidable figure with broad discretionary powers over property received from her husband's kin."[21]

Analogous patterns seem to have operated in the Jewish community, where many husbands had promised a delayed marriage gift they could not pay before their death. Such intersections or reinforcements of a Jewish subculture by the host Christian subculture suggest that widowhood and other factors in Jewish women's wills ought to be approached also by reading such wills against the background of law codes of the Catalan peoples, such as the *Furs* of Valencia. Conversely, investigation of some Jewish influence on Christian women's wills, especially in small communities with enough intimacy between Christians and Jews to disconcert the ecclesiastical authorities, also may prove rewarding. Renée Melammed cites a significant case of crossover influence in fourteenth-century Toledo, where the Jews had begun to imitate the Christian division of half the deceased husband's property to the widow, resulting in a debate between the Jewish community's authorities and Asher b. Yehiel, the incumbent of the prestigious Toledo rabbinate.[22]

The role of wives and widows in making testaments and in administering a husband's estate and acting as guardian of children must have resonated differently in the two societies. The use of Roman notarial concepts to supplement the elements of a Jewish will by a Latin will raises intriguing questions about cultural diffusion. Where the activities or rights of women were more or less equivalent in each society, did the Latinate will reinforce the analogous Jewish structure? Where they diverged, did the Latinate will tend to modify Jewish custom? Was the role of the dowry in Jewish society modified, either in attitude or concept, because of the dowry's changing meaning and effects in Latin wills? Women were very strong figures on the Catalan Christian testamentary scene, a context that needs to be related to the parallel Jewish scene.

CHAPTER 6

The Search

Other Jewish wills surely await discovery in the Christian notarial manuals. They are rare and will yield only to serendipity, to researchers alert to their possibility. Professor Jill Webster has called my attention to one such will in the Arxiu Històric de Girona, in the *Testaments* manual of Pere Perrini of Castelló for 1326. Long and complex, this will, the only Jewish testament Professor Webster encountered "in some thirty or forty manuals," details the last dispositions of Jucef Bonastruges of Castelló de Ampurias.[1] A will by Ismael de Oblitis (Olite?) of Navarre was the object of King Pere's attention in 1341 at Barcelona, a reminder that Jean Régné's exhaustive catalog of Jewish documents in the crown registers ends abruptly in 1327, leaving a quarter-century of rich materials unscanned up to 1350.[2]

Besides such archival findings, occasional Latinate Jewish wills continue to turn up in published analyses of Jewish communities in various corners of the realms. Thus Manuel Grau Montserrat, in his doctoral thesis on the Jews of Besalú from the thirteenth to the fifteenth century, gives the will of "Carecausa Mayr" from the Olot archives in the early fourteenth century. (*Cara cauza* in Provençal, as Simon Seror notes, means "beloved person.") And Gabriel Secall i Güell, among the documents in his volume on the Jews of Santa Coloma de Queralt, appends four wills.[3] Considering the many Jewish wills revealed by crown activity up through the first quarter of the fourteenth century, it is logical to expect the same high incidence of extrinsic references to wills by the royal chancery thereafter—even more so, since the volume of general documentation dramatically increases. Crown notices about late fourteenth-century wills, from 1350 to 1390, must also be very numerous.

Another direction for Latinate Jewish testamentary research is to move forward chronologically. If the temper and context of Jewish life in the realms underwent modification in the post–Black Death generation, the communities also enjoyed a strong measure of continuity and strength until the riots of 1391 signaled catastrophic changes. Thus the later fourteenth century may be considered a time of "late" early Latinate wills, valuable for evidence both of acculturative weakening and for continuities.

Three more Puigcerdá wills may be introduced here, ranging from 1370 through 1398 to 1401, along with a will of 1388 from Majorca. Simple analysis, without contextualization, will suffice for the three, letting the pattern of past testaments provide points for reflection.

Late Fourteenth-Century Latinate Jewish Wills

Bonafília or Bonafilla, "wife of Master Jacob Bonet," in her testament of 18 January 1370 at Puigcerdá appoints as her executors Master Boniac Abraham and Yitzhak Astruc ("Itzah Struch"). "Master" here is ambiguous but probably indicates status in the aristocracy of the *ḥakīm* class as savant-physician. Besides burial in the Jewish cemetery, Bonafilla leaves 10 sous for oil for the lamps of the synagogue (*scola*) and "10 in alms for the Jewish quarter [*call*] of Puigcerdá." One son, Master Bernat of Foix, receives 5 sous; the other, Samuel Jacob, gets 5 sous plus an immediate payment of 50 pounds.[4]

The name Bernat in a Catalan-Occitan Jewish family seems unprecedented and suggests an error of some kind. The careful index by Yom Tov Assis for the catalog by Régné, covering nearly 3,500 charters about Jews for over a hundred years (1213–1327) of Arago-Catalan crown registers, does not turn up a single Jew named Bernat; even the short index of converts to Christianity has none. Among Catalan Christians the name was very popular; a first-name index for the documents of Jaume the Conqueror lists over 150 Bernats plus nearly 70 more in abbreviated form. Of Germanic origin, the name has none of the equivalence value of a name such as Benet ("Benedictus"), paralleling Hebrew Baruch or the then popular Berachya. Was this Bernat a convert? It is highly improbable that an apostate son could have appeared in a public Jewish will at this period. Could the scribe have intended the Catalan name Bonat, common to Jews and Christians then?

Paleographically, all letters of this name in the will are clearly present in Romance form, except for the first *e*, which an overstroke indicates: BRNAT. Since Bonat/Bonanat has a deformation or variation as Brunat, Boronat, and Bornat, such readings of the name would solve the puzzle. It is not necessary to fall back on that analysis, however, since Seror has found a Jewish Bernart and a Benaart in Paris and a Bernardus in Marseilles while compiling his lexicon of medieval French Jewish names. The dates of appearance of these names are instructive—respectively 1291, 1292, and 1351—as they are relatively late and therefore suggest the acculturative pressures then increasing. Since Jews of this time and place took various kinds of nonreligious names, including many popular also among their Christian neighbors, perhaps we ought not to cavil at "Bernard." But the name does fall outside almost all contemporary patterns for Jews in the realms and invites in its family context a strong suspicion of undue influence from and deformation by the surrounding Christian culture.[5]

In this testament, 20 sous go to Joia, daughter of Samuel (ben) Abraham Cohen (Joi, like Goig, is Catalan for "joy"). Everything else, movables and real property, goes to Samuel Jacob's daughter Aster, granddaughter of Bonafilla. All seven witnesses are Christians. All money is in Barcelonan sous. All the principals are Jews of Puigcerdá. The family structure is

BONAFILLA *m.* Master Jacob Bonet

Samuel Jacob — Master Bernat of Foix

Aster (daughter of Samuel Jacob)

Ten years later, on 24 March 1388, Regina or Reginona drew up her will at Inca on Majorca island.[6] She was the daughter of Mossé Leví and the wife of a tailor of Inca named Salamó (A)struc. Gravely ill but with faculties intact, she declares her husband both executor and universal heir. Her first concern is that all her debts and obligations be met from the estate "without legal form or fuss." She wishes to be buried in the Jewish cemetery at Inca "before the grave of my said father," with suitable ostentation: "well and elegantly [and] according to Jewish custom." Reginona's sister Goget, wife of Vidal de Montblanc of Majorca, receives 3 pounds "to buy clothing for mourning." Twenty sous each go to Goget's son Bonjudas ("Boniuetes") and her daughter Mayronet, the wife of Bonjuda ("Beniuha Gatbay"). Twenty more apiece go to Reginona's brother Bonet Leví, to another brother Salamó Leví "alias Patit," and to the latter's wife Drison. Reginona also gives 10 sous, "for the love of God," to buy oil to burn "in the lamps of the synagogue." Six witnesses sign, with the notary doubling as a seventh witness; all six seem to be Jews.

Several new names occur. Reginona is simply a diminutive or intensifier of Regina, as Meironet ("Mayronet") is of Hebrew Meir. Beniuha and Boniuetes are variants of Bonjuda(s), *bon* slipping into *ben*. Patit is Catalan Petit, for the Hebrew name Katan ("small"); it is also a Catalan Christian lineage. Three names pose a challenge. Goget seems to be a diminutive of Goig in its variant Gog; Drison may relate to the Occitan name Treysona, cited by Seror only once, at Manosque. The masculine surname Gatbay, despite its intrusive *t* not untypical in Catalan, is the common Jewish surname Gabbai, with an Aramaic etymology as tax collector or as synogogue functionary. The immediate family, in order of appearance, is small:

Mossé Leví

REGINONA *m.* Salamó (A)struc | Goget *m.* Vidal de Montblanc | Bonet Leví | Salamó Leví ("Patit") *m.* Drison

(children of Goget and Vidal de Montblanc:) Mayronet *m.* Bonjuda Gatbay | Bonjudas

Ten years later Jacob Boniac drew up his will at Puigcerdá. Dated April 1398, it leaves a series of small legacies to friends and relatives, including 30 sous for one grandson and 20 to another, 20 sous "to my relative or cousin Ana Goya," 10 to her son, and dowries of 40 sous for each of the daughters of his great grandson Deglossal (Deulosal) Vidal. He returns a dowry of 40 Barcelonan pounds to his wife Marcona and names her universal heir for the bulk of his possessions. For charity he leaves 5½ sous for "the abashed poor," and "all my clothing to my poor relations at the discretion of my executors." Clothing in the Middle Ages was often valuable and cherished, handed down through several generations. Two pieces here are held out for favorite relatives. Twenty sous are set aside as a fund for oil, to be burned "in the synagogue of the Jews of the said town to honor God," at the rate of 5 sous yearly over four years. The seven witnesses include Guillem Gueca taverner and two Jews, Samuel ben Abraham Cohen and Bondit ben Samuel Cohen. In his codicil of 30 February 1401 he selects as executor "Master Meir Bonet physician," a Jew of Perpignan. The witnesses are divided under the rubrics "Christians" and "Jews," the latter comprising the physician Bonet, Deglossal Vidal, and Jacob Cohen. New names here are Catalan Anna from Hebrew Chana/Ana, Marcona as feminine diminutive of Catalan Marc, and Bondit as the past participle of Catalan *dir* in the sense of "well said," unless it is variant here for Bendit ("blessed," for Hebrew Barukh).[7]

Three years later the wills continue. Vidal Bonafos senior (*pater*), for example, a Jew of Perpignan taken ill at Puigcerdá, drew up a long will on 27 February 1401, adding a codicil on August 31.[8] The codicil expands his largesse by giving 2 sous apiece to those assisting him in his last illness. A number of money gifts, some in florins, include: "I leave [money for] a lamp which is to burn in the synagogue or *scola*." But all such post–Black Death wills mirror a different society, both Christian and Jewish. They are not so precious as the early models.

Cognate Occitania

A collateral direction for research on Jewish wills in the realms of Aragon is to turn toward the cognate communities of Occitania, which had been linked culturally and often enough politically with the Catalan regions. Carcassonne was one such entity, its ruling viscounts the Trencavels having been vassals of the count-kings of the realms of Aragon until the Albigensian crusade drove the last viscount into refuge at the court of Barcelona. At least one will from Carcassonne has been discovered and studied, drawn by Isaac Metge in 1305. Ill to death "and desiring eternal life," Isaac drafted it in his own house on August 5. Choosing burial in the Jewish cemetery of Carcassonne, he designates as universal heir and executor his surviving son Vidal Metge. Vidal's own four sons receive two and a half hogsheads (150 gallons) of wine. They also receive as lodgings a room and a kitchen in Isaac's house; if dissatisfied, they can have Vidal rent them a residence of equal value outside the house. Isaac's daughter Regina, wife of Salamó de Lunel, has her choice between 100 sous of Tours or else a ring with a sapphire mounted. The son of Isaac's daughter Dolça (presumably deceased) and the daughter of his son Astruc Metge (also presumably deceased) are to share equally in 100 sous, which are to be invested for them by some undesignated friend of the family. Within six years of Isaac's passing, his heir is to have a crown made, "which is otherwise called in Hebrew *'aṭara,*" for the rod of the Torah, "which I had made for use of the synagogue of the Jews of Carcassonne."

Another gift for the Jewish community is carefully explicated. "In remission for my sins I leave a hogshead of kosher wine [*modium vini iudaicum*] every year," during the heir's lifetime, to be "given and divided in four parts and four festivities, namely, one measure on the feast of the Huts, and another measure of wine on the feast of the Lord's Easter, and another measure of wine on the feast of the Circumcision of the Lord, called in Hebrew Rosh ha-Shana [*Rossana*]." The transcription seems defective here, since only three periods are stated. It is odd to see the notary (surely not the testator) expressing the several times according to the Christian calendar of feasts of Jesus. He also seems to equate the Christian New Year (the Circumcision, or January 1 in the French calendar then used at Carcassonne) with the Jewish New Year in autumn; is he using a calendar metaphor? An alternative explanation might be that the missing fourth distribution belongs after the Circumcision distribution, a suspicion strengthened by a subsequent instruction to begin the whole process on the "feast of Blessed Michael [the Archangel] in the month of September in one year," a feast less inappropriately linked to the time of Rosh ha-Shana. The four distributions may honor the four biblical "new year" divisions of the year, of which only the autumn feast today retains that name. The selection of the feast of the Huts or Tabernacles, the Hebrew Sukkot, recalls a similar testamentary legacy seen above in chapter 4.

Isaac's will yields a small family tree:

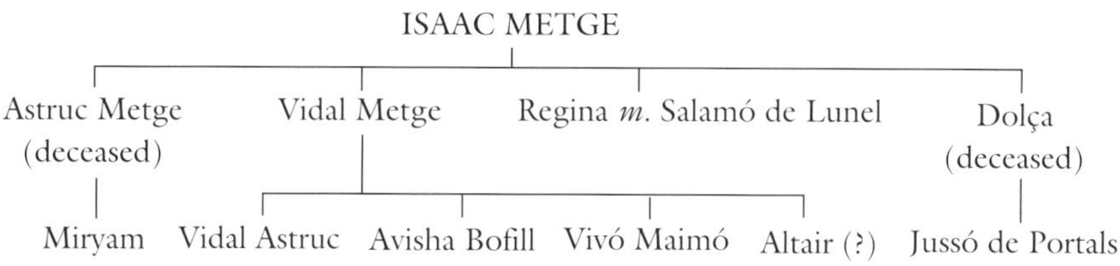

Of the name forms in the manuscript, some are familiar from previous encounters—Latin Astruch, Bonusfilius, Dulcia, Regina, and Salamonis. Others may seem less ordinary—Meriama, the augmentatives Jussonus and Vivonus (respectively, Jucef and Vives), and Jussó. Three forms pose a challenge. Altirenus may echo the Catalan and Castilian prename Altair. Evescha is less likely to be a variant of Evesque/Esveque for Cohen, unusual for these parts, than the more obvious biblical Avishai in its variant Avisha. Mariamona, if not a miscopy, may resolve into either Marimon (from Miremont in France) or Maimó. The witnesses at the end are four Jews and two Christians, the latter respectively a cloth finisher and a weaver.[9]

More elaborate, and with transcription of the full testament, is the last disposition by Abraham of Draguignan on 10 May 1316, discovered by Joseph Shatzmiller and introduced in his *Shylock Reconsidered*. Draguinhan, or modern Draguignan, stood some forty miles northeast of Toulon. It lay in the Marseilles/Provence sovereignty that had been an appanage or affiliate of the realms of Aragon until the 1240s when the French king's brother Charles of Anjou drove out Jaume the Conqueror in a military scuffle for control. Shatzmiller describes the surviving notarial draft, with notes "scribbled at the margins" and the "changes introduced by the testator." The text itself tells how Abraham, "a Jew, citizen of Marseilles," being "of sound mind" ("body" is deleted), makes the following will. To his son Bondaví he leaves 500 Marseilles pounds in money, warning him to be "silent and content with this" since it is all he will get. Abraham's wife Astes he appoints "owner and mistress of each and every possession of mine, and that she is to keep and possess and enjoy the fruit of the said goods." Astes also receives "six silver boxes." To their daughter Bonadona, wife of Profach Deulocresca, go 100 Marseilles pounds (replacing a deleted 500) together with the dowry her husband had already received. Unless Bonadona will sign a formal public document waiving all further shares, she is to lose all but a token 5 Marseilles sous.

Abraham's grandson Abramet, son of Bondaví, receives a vineyard in the Marseilles district, plus two silver belts ("both are worth together 10 pounds") and three rings (a gold ring with a diamond, a gold ring with an emerald, and a ring with a sapphire), together with 20 pounds. As long as Abramet is a minor, his father Bondaví must not himself profit from the vineyard. Abraham's granddaughter Bellanette gets a gilded silver belt worth 14 pounds, as well as 60 pounds for buying more jewelry, 25 pounds in cash, "and a silver box I have worth 4 pounds." For Abraham's brother Mossé Artí there is a cash gift of 10 pounds. To another granddaughter Reginette, also Bondaví's child but married to Salamonet the son of Cresques of Bellcaire (modern Beaucaire), Abraham gives "a silver goblet I drink from and a gold ring with a stone called a diamond worth 6 pounds of the said money (from what I have in my box), and a silver bellholder, and a house located in the

Jewish quarter [*juzateria*] of Marseilles bounded on one side by the southern synagogue." He also leaves 25 pounds "to my niece, Blanquette, daughter of my sister Dolça," and adds in a scribbled note the right of Salamonet to live in and share the house. Finally, for everything else Abraham declares as universal heir his son Bondaví. That concluding stipulation of a universal heir, a requirement in Roman law for wills, seems to be an afterthought, tacked on at the notary's insistence. The testator Abraham had written off his son earlier in the will, explicitly refusing to give him anything beyond a lump-sum gift. Now Abraham has reintroduced the son as heir to everything not expressly given away.

Shatzmiller has fleshed out the portrait of this patriarch and his family, mostly through the records of a lawsuit against the son Bondaví in a loan dispute in 1317. Shatzmiller also carefully analyzes the family's wealth and prominence as well as peculiarities of its structure and the economic situation of Provence at that moment. For the present purposes this early Latinate testament may serve to reinforce the impressions and patterns left by the series of contemporary wills in the realms of Aragon. Valuable keepsakes play a more prominent role in this will, either because Abraham was richer than the other testators we have encountered or because he had no chance to pass out pretestamentary gifts. (He was dead, his will probated, and his legacies released within three months of having recourse to the Christian notary.) Again the force of personality breaks through the ritual formulas, revealing the authoritative father figure, his tender attitude toward his wife, and some family tensions. Ever the businessman, he prices items with care. Yet no philanthropies appear; doubtless the community had secured these or their promise in timely fashion from so distinguished a businessman. Pieties are not expressed—again perhaps the businessman at work. And as in some other wills, only the close family is involved, down to grandchildren and a niece. The family tree is nicely displayed. This seems to have been a warmly close family or at least one given to pet diminutives: Abramet, Bellanette, Blanquette, and Salamonet.[10] A family tree would include:

ABRAHAM DE DRAGUIGNAN *m.* Astes — Mossé Artí — Dolça

Bondaví — Bonadona *m.* Profach Deulocresca — Blanquette

Reginette *m.* Salamonet b. Cresques de Beaucaire — Ballanette — Abramet (minor)

As with the wills of the realms of Aragon, so the Latinate wills from this affiliate or cognate culture can be chronologically extended into the later fourteenth and fifteenth centuries, with due precautions and recontextualization. In this connection the fifteenth-century Jewish notarial wills found by Danièle Iancu-Agou for Aix-en-Provence, Arles, and Marseilles deserve notice, as does the current work of Jacques Chiffoleau at Avignon.[11] The findings at Aix are instructive. Iancu-Agou encountered Jewish wills there only for the late fifteenth century and after; although 106 Jewish marriages turned up between 1460 and 1500, only five wills have joined them. For the early modern period 1501–1525 thirty wills survive at Aix, all, however, all from converted Jews already immersed in an alien context and testamentary tradition.[12]

Monique Wernham has similarly explored the Jewish community of Salon-de-Provence just northwest of Marseilles for the very late period of 1391 to 1435. At one point, drawing from the contents of thirty notarial wills from sixteen families (but transcribing none), she is able to graph eight family trees, to conjecture community wealth, and to analyze the objects of charitable legacies. The larger number of these wills come after 1415.[13] No large body of Jewish wills has thus far surfaced in the Occitan regions for the time period of this book; the few early wills we do have in hand do not encourage comparison in size with the larger amount of testamentary information from Arago-Catalan wills, lawsuits, and notices. Researchers alert to the value of wills and materials connected with wills may one day alter that imbalance.

Geniza Wills

Shlomo Goitein was able to ferret out a number of wills from the hoard of discards and fragments constituting the celebrated Geniza papers. Jumbled over the centuries into a synagogue room in Old Cairo out of reverence for the sacred Hebrew script they bore but lacking any relationship or intrinsic value, the collection constituted a giant wastebasket. Now scattered in archives over Europe and America, these papers total some quarter of a million items; about seven thousand are proper historical documents, as against literary or other materials. "The Arabic language prevails" in that documentary material, though expressed mostly in Hebrew script; Arabic had replaced Aramaic in Jewish courts in Egypt, with Hebrew making some recovery from 1200 on. The chronology of these historical documents stretches from the eleventh into the thirteenth century; business with Sicily, Tunisia, and elsewhere in the West is prominent. "Wills and deathbed declarations are disappointing, insofar as they consist almost exclusively of dispositions about property," though this "often gives a clear idea not only of his possessions but also of his mind."[14]

Chapter 1 above discussed categories, structural characteristics, and some peculiarities of the Geniza testamentary genre. Here a sampling from the wills themselves seems appropriate to suggest continuities and discontinuities and to invite comparison with the Latinate variety. Goitein does not say how many wills or fragments of wills can be found in the Geniza collections or how much of the surviving testamentary information comes from collateral documentation involving the wills, such as lawsuits or inventories. He does transcribe five wills in extenso, describes another in lengthy detail and context, and gives brief résumés or high points from five more.

The wealthy businesswoman Karīma bint ʿAmmār al-Wuḥsha ("the desired") deserves first place in line as the most prominent woman in the Geniza collections; both her piety and notoriety (including expulsion from the synagogue on one occasion) are visible in various documents. Her unusually detailed testament was drafted by the court clerk Hillel b. Eli. A divorced woman with a daughter, she also had an illegitimate son from an illicit union. For the purposes of the will her estate was worth 700 gold dinars (2 dinars might have been an artisan's monthly wage) when she was preparing to die in the early eleventh century. She had already drawn up three Arabic inventories of all of her assets and liabilities, with instructions for acting on each item. She leaves her one surviving brother 100 dinars, her sister 50, a cousin 5, and a stepsister 10. Some personal mementos such as rings and clothing also go to each; the cousin receives, for example, "the bed on which I lie but not the carpets." Al-Wuḥsha sets aside a tenth of her estate for charity, leaving 25 dinars to the Jewish cemetery, 25 more to divide among four synagogues ("for oil, so that they may study at night"), 20 for "the poor of Fustat [old Cairo]," 2 for an orphaned relative, and 10 to Yūsuf's wife and her two brothers.

Al-Wuḥsha plans her funeral carefully, sparing no expense. Her coffin (used rather as a bier) is to cost 6 or 7 gold dinars; her seven items of burial dress are described and individually priced: robe, wrap, skullcap, wimple, kerchief, veil, and cloak, adding up to some 25 dinars. Twenty dinars then cover tombstone, pallbearers, and the cantor "walking behind my coffin." The bulk of her estate "including the rugs and the carpet" go to her illegitimate young son Abū Saʿd. This includes 300 dinars "in gold" at home, 67 more on deposit, and several hundred in loan collaterals. Her daughter, known from other documents to have been alive, receives neither gift nor mention. "Not a penny should be given to the boy's father," though al-Wuḥsha does waive 80 dinars in loans to him and adds a gift of 10 dinars. She names a schoolteacher acquaintance to live in the family house for a weekly pittance to teach the boy a sufficiency of Bible and prayer, but only as much as would be "appropriate." This last provision and her marital history suggest that the boy was a *mamzer,* not merely illegitimate but from a union legally barred, with the consequent liabilities of *mamzerut* status.[15]

In another testament a pious lady of Old Cairo in 1066 wills her house, worth some 170 dinars, in neat shares. A third share ("eight of the twenty-four parts of the house") goes with its rents to two local synagogues. Another third is divided between a brother and a niece. Of the remaining third, half is for a friend's dowry. This left a twelfth of the house, already sold to the daughter of her stepsister, and a final twelfth for funeral expenses. "Two parts of this house shall be sold and the proceeds used for my burial, namely, to carry my body to Jerusalem, the Holy City." She also releases her sister as well as her sister's daughter and grandchildren from any oath or response "before a Jewish or gentile court," presumably in connection with *ante mortem* gifts in lieu of legacies. The beginning and ending of the text are so badly damaged that the testator's name and the witnesses are lost.

A similar concentration on one piece of business is seen in a will of 1090 by a Tunisian merchant who had settled at Alexandria. Ill but of sound mind, he leaves instructions to sell his stocks of sulphur, lichen, and beads. From the proceeds his executor is to give 10 dinars to "the rav" of Egypt, 10 to the synagogue, and all the rest for his funeral expenses. Since the merchandise was both considerable and valuable, the funeral arrangements and especially the "cave" or sepulcher and the "robes" must have been impressive. Again the format is of witnesses reporting a dead man's words and arrangements. In 1143 the wife of a great merchant at Old Cairo made a dying declaration designed to protect the rights of her parents, brother, and a boy by a previous marriage and to guarantee a grand funeral. Sitt al-Ahl, the wife, had received a house from her father, with the stipulation (made with the agreement of her current husband) that her parents and brother could always live on the upper floor. She notes that the slave girl is hers, not her husband's, and that the boy is to stay with her mother. She declares that she has nothing belonging to her husband, and she appoints an executor.

Unsatisfied with her present burial clothes, she gives detailed instructions for a hooded robe of fine material, a mantle, a cloak, and bier furniture, "all to cost about 25 dinars," with a coffin-bier "costing 9 to 10 dinars." Among the mourners, "wailing should be done by Muslims," presumably livelier in that profession. Expenses include "the seven days of mourning." Sitt wishes "to be buried in this house in which I am now"; she is to be carried to the cemetery only when her parents or brother die, apparently so as to lie among her own people in either place.

Yet another will, focusing on a few bits of business and a fine funeral, comes from Sitt al-Ḥusn, wife of a prominent judge around 1150. After some questioning by witnesses to make sure of her coherence and sound mind, Sitt frees two slave girls she had bought and reared as Jews and gives them half of her own half-share in a house as well as "all clothing suitable for women." She gives the same half-house, actually her home, to the community on condition of respecting the slave girls' rights to their fourth of the house for life. The matter of her delayed marriage gift from her husband is discussed but dismissed since it would not now come to her. Her eighth of another house is to be sold to cover funeral costs, including burial garments, coffin-bier, cantors, pallbearers, tomb, and the rest. A usual ceremony of symbolic purchase to convey the husband's approval was deferred, "since it was Saturday." There were four witnesses, two of them unknown to Sitt.

In 1188 a silkweaver of Old Cairo, the sheik Abu ʾl-Faḍl, was interviewed by two witnesses on his deathbed. They tested his mental alertness, as was common in these encounters: "His mind was sound, and he knew what he said and what was said to him; we asked him what time it was and about the identity of the persons present." Abu ʾl-Faḍl testifies that he has "sold" half of his home to his son Abu ʾl-Barakāt and now wills the other half equally to his sons Bayān and Bahā. Bayān receives the family's silk-weaving workshop, but the yarn, silk, house furnishings, "indeed all I possess," will be sold to pay funeral expenses and the 15 gold dinars owed to his wife as marriage gift. Abu ʾl-Faḍl appoints two executors for these transactions, one of them his son Abu ʾl-Barakāt, who will also be guardian for his minor son Bayān. Five dinars go to an absent son. The "residue" of all proceeds goes in equal shares to Bayān and Bahā. To his wife, Sitt al-Rīḍā, he leaves six "copper vessels: a mortar, a pail, a wash-basin, a bucket, an oil jug, and a bowl."[16]

Goitein discusses several other wills in more summary fashion. For example, a huge declaration done around 1100 is unusually full, though only the forty-nine lines of its lower half survive. Goitein sums it under seven headings: assets and liabilities, provision for the wife, choice of his brother as executor and as guardian of the children, charities, division of the bulk of the estate between his children and his brother in equal parts, a note on the firstborn, and a minor postscript. Another will, by Mūsā b. ʿAdayā in 1040, essentially covers dowry and marriage gift to his wife, two dinars to his sister, one to a niece, and a Torah to the synagogue. His son is the exclusive heir, with no need of an executor. This will is in Hebrew.

A similar will was drafted in 1201 at Alexandria for an estate worth 2,550 dinars, an enormous sum. Five executors are named to invest the sum, taking their expenses and half of the profits. The son, then a minor, is sole heir to this fortune. Fifty dinars go to each of two daughters, 10 to each of his sister's (unnumbered) daughters, and a Torah scroll is to be written and given to the community. Finally, the very late will of 1241 by Abu ʾl-Faḍl, a cheese maker, leaves two-thirds of his house to his daughter, just come of age, plus about 2 dinars. A granddaughter gets 2 dinars and his wife 3 dinars (including her marriage gift). The rest goes to his son.[17]

Goitein has observed several times that each Geniza will was more like a final act in a chain of last dispositions. People preferred to make gifts, pay debts, and otherwise round off their lives without the formalities of documentation. Consequently, the wills cannot give us any idea of the decedent's full estate or extended friendships or philanthropic gifts. A few wills did have to go into more detail—for example, when the testator was a transient or the husband was away on business. Commonly a will dealt with one piece of business or two, distributed a few final gifts, and prepared for the funeral. Latinate wills display some continuity with this tradition of Jewish last dispositions. A marked discontinuity is the relatively less attention paid in the Latinate versions to funerary matters.

Since the religious foundations for both formats were identical, other continuities include the regulations controlling dowry, marriage gift, and women as well as the role of the elder son and concern about debts. If some formalities are noticeably different between Geniza and Latinate wills—the "universal heir" in Latinate wills, for example, and the controlling witnesses in the Geniza—the substance or content often coincided. This coincidence was partly a result of shared religious traditions and partly a function of the common situation of any formulation of last dispositions, but perhaps most important was the role of the will within the family and community as reinforcing a continuum of customs and values.

The Geniza wills seem marked by an attempt to avoid an obvious inheritance pattern in order to preclude interference by Islamic authorities and tax collectors in the transference of property. The Latinate wills seem not to exhibit this caution; they appear generally more open and informative. The Latinate wills also seem more individualistic and varied, even idiosyncratic. More reflection is necessary, however, to probe the differences and resemblances. A larger corpus of wills would, of course, facilitate the operation; Goitein calls attention to other unpublished and unanalyzed wills in the Geniza collections, including one excluded from consideration by its very length.[18] The chaotic nature of the Geniza discards makes it far less easy to identify and contextualize its testaments; in contrast, Latinate wills as at Perpignan and Puigcerdá carry a penumbra of other contracts, from which family information might painstakingly be assembled. And where the Geniza experience is closed, a limited group of wills centered on one locale, the Arago-Catalonian and Occitan notarial troves are open-ended for the researcher, both in terms of the many wills yet to be discovered and the many cities and regions that can contribute.

Total History

Each stage in the preceding exploration of Latinate Jewish wills has invited reflection. It would be tedious to repeat here the conclusions and suggestions that emerged. A return to chapter 1, for example, would allow a review of the pluricultural predicament—the paradox of parallel Christian and Jewish societies as semiautonomies, interacting at various levels, notably by their union in the notarial culture, sharing as well as recoiling. The mechanics of that culture, in the analogous activities of the Christian scribe, the Jewish *sōfer*, and the Muslim *ṣāḥīb al-wathā'iq*, and the implications of that culture both as a bridge and as assimilative force were introduced in chapter 2 and carried forward into the king's role in chapter 3. Basic themes running through these discussions are the peculiar character of the last testament and the unique meeting of the Judeo-Arabic and Judeo-Occitan subcultures in the Catalan environment. Actual wills had appeared in the narrative by this point, a large number by indirection in records of crown intervention. Chapters 4 and 5 concentrated on Latinate wills as rescued from the archives of four Arago-Catalonian towns and their Jewish communities. Chapter 5 investigated the role and meaning of women in wills. Finally, chapter 6 presented reinforcing detail from later wills from the fourteenth century and cognate wills from outside the realms but within Occitania.

Some generalizations about the wills themselves remain to be posed. The notarial formalities and tone unify the entire body of Latinate wills here but nonetheless leave the individual wills irreducibly singular, even unique. The testaments range from minimalist, with a few basics on dowry and nuclear family, to expansive. Some testators are wealthy; others show barely enough property to justify the trouble of a Latinate will. A number seek to control the family's future by imposing conditions or arranging for substitute legatees according to marriages, deaths, or childlessness in that future. One man forbids copies of the will to be distributed except to his wife and his universal heir; another requires his two sons to share his estate for ten years before they can divide it and go their separate ways; another forces an heir to waive further claims under penalty of voiding any possible legacy.

Testators often want their debts satisfied, sometimes specifying that repayment be done without legal fuss, but at least one testator specified that creditors supply proper documentation. One orders all legacies paid within a year of his death; some others, especially where a minor was involved, arrange for investments and profits. Almost all the full wills considered are preserved in paper registers, with notarial compression and radical abbreviations; one Latinate will here is on its "original" parchment, though of course the paper draft is an equally true original and legally authoritative. No less than three wills leave large sums to the king; two of these leave everything to him unless the testator's conditions are followed. In none of the dispositions is it obvious that the bulk of the estate is visible; instead, the lack of extended family members and of small mementos to friends or philanthropies argues that the testators had followed a common custom in transferring goods well in advance of death.

One wife notes her husband's approval of the will; one husband notes his wife's approval. As to formalities, one will records the notary's fee as 5 sous; several manuscripts have canceling slashes indicating that a full copy has been delivered; most of the wills meticulously repeat the identifying label "Jew" more than seems necessary (except perhaps to a lawyer). A testator mentions his will's "text" and "form," another revokes previous wills. Most wills have the standard seven witnesses of Roman law, usually Christians but sometimes with one Jew or, more often, two. One will has four Christian witnesses and four Jews, another six Christians and two Jews. Most of these witnesses, when identified, seem to be artisans (tailor, shoemaker, weaver, cobbler, glover, and such)—perhaps accessible neighbors, perhaps paid volunteers, or both.

Institutions and domestic paraphernalia turn up regularly. They include the synagogue, of course, and the Bet ha-Midrash, with oil both for liturgical and study lamps, as well as Torahs and the Torah crown. The wife's dowry (and dowries of daughters both single and married) are commonly discussed, including a reference to the "Jewish nuptial documents" incorporated into the Latinate legal foundations. The Jewish cemetery appears, with a few asides on burial, mourning dress, and funeral arrangements. The inventory of the deceased's goods is mentioned, though not so frequently as one might expect; one testament waives the count altogether, and others probably omitted mention of this post-funerary action as irrelevant. Vineyards are included several times, either because they were so common in the wider Catalan population or because the Jewish community's own wine supply involved such properties. The family residence, with some of its inhabitants, is described sometimes as a *mansus* or *hospicium,* once on a hill and twice as bordered by specific neighbors. Books were obviously cherished, whether single volumes or libraries (twenty-four books in one collection). Household paraphernalia range from weighing scales, dyeing vat, wine containers, and the wooden chests so ubiquitous then in Catalan homes to clothing of many kinds, cloth, utensils, bedclothes, and at least once a fair number of rings and jewelry.

Patterns of piety, less visible where previous *inter vivos* gifts had already gone out, can be seen from time to time. One testament names as universal heir God himself, the actual moneys going to dowries for poor girls and education for poor children. Another sets aside enough cash to have 62½ sous distributed annually for ten years on the Feast of the Tabernacles. A legacy of 6¼ sous goes to the half-penny Jewish alms fund. One woman writes off all loans owed to her below a certain sum. Another leaves her bedclothes and 100 sous to charity. Yet another remembers the "abashed poor," who sought to keep up appearances from their previous state. One man provides that if his daughter as heiress dies childless, his entire estate is to revert to alms, for his "soul's salvation." For God's love, another testator contributes to a bridge over the river Tet. In the end the general impression emerges that these wills were family affairs, especially concerned with obligations to family; formal charity seems to have been managed by other means.

The universal heir was usually the son (or even two sons), or in their absence a brother or preferably the testator's husband, wife, or various in-laws. In one case the executor-guardians were two Christians with two Jews, while in another a super-executor monitored the original executors. One executor, noted in chapter 3 above, worked at his task sixteen years; another group secured a charter of approval for their efforts from the ward when he was finally of age. Some widows were executors for their spouses. Human touches abound. One testator forbade the home to be sold without the family's approval and he left 2,000 sous to be paid to his daughter only when she finalized a hoped-for marriage. Another provided care for a daughter until her wandering husband came back home to live. Guardians sometimes were asked to provide a husband for an unmarried daughter. A condition in another will provided support to a married daughter if, on becoming a widow, she returned to the family home. And in yet another will a wife set up an advantageous situation for her husband as a widower, so long as he did not remarry. Interest (*usura*) is explicitly mentioned in two wills and is implicit in the investments of several. In a society accustomed to widespread slavery in all three communities, only one slave (a half-share of a black woman) turns up. The testator's seat in the synagogue is duly passed on, but only in a few wills here (and once to a daughter, as a negotiable legacy). Here too the arrangement would have been already made and understood without formalities of law.

The king's role becomes clear from court records about such wills. The king can confirm in whole, in part, or in "every item"; he can clarify, settle disputes, or arrange investigation or arbitration. With a pardon he can waive prosecution for testamentary fraud, appoint a super-executor to monitor the others, waive the usual inventory of the decedent's property, sequester the property for a time, compel an accounting, license the executors' investment in real estate, set conditions (the heir cannot travel or marry before the age of eighteen), or settle minute squabbles (a stolen Avicenna from the dead man's library). He could give his protection, under penalty of his displeasure and a severe fine, and he could issue a *guiatge*, or specially formulated charter of protection, covering all the provisos of a will. Closeted with his Jewish savants, the king addressed complex moral issues such as the proper shares for the deceased's two wives and two sets of children. And in one case, where the provisions of two wills by two different decedents collided and where both disputants were wealthy and distinguished, the king mounted a trial before his person in the Dominicans' cloister, a public event resembling the showpiece Disputation of 1263 in its externals. In short, the king could and did do just about anything an appellant could petition, a patriarchal role quite comfortable to medieval sovereigns from count to king. The crown addressed Hebrew wills, to be judged "according to the custom of the Jews," as easily as it took up Latinate Jewish wills that cited Roman law (as in the case of the Falcidian and Trebellianic fourths).

The names in the Latinate testaments hold few surprises, aside from a feminine first name Cohen, one Bernard, and an Ali. Local pronunciations garble even simple names at times and their reconstitution can be difficult or tentative. A few sets of names betray the Judeo-Arabic antecedents of the family, while an *ibn* can do the same for an individual. How immediate such connections were or how linguistically effective is not apparent simply from the names. Judeo-Arabic names do carry an echo of the massive transference of an ancient Judaism from al-Andalus into European or Christian Spain. The Franco-Occitan names are far more numerous, partly because the transference came in later waves, when notarial records of all kinds began multiplying.

The locale for any number of wills examined here was the border areas closest to Occitania—such places as Palma de Mallorca, Perpignan, and Puigcerdá. Again, one cannot be sure whether a name of Occitan flavor or a clear toponym describes the current bearer's origin or that of his father or grandfather, except in cases where a clue is provided. Again, however, the mass immigration can be appreciated from the phenomenon of names as a whole. Of toponyms alone, over a dozen show the bearer's family to have arrived from widely scattered points along the littoral from Narbonne to Marseilles and inland as at Mazères near Toulouse, Alès above Nîmes, Béziers, Beaucaire, Lunel, and even La Rochelle.

A promising field of study would be a comparison of the Latinate Jewish wills and the mass of Christian wills now available. Since fashions and tonalities in Christian wills changed overtly or subtly, such a comparison has to respect the chronological stages in development. Both kinds of will issued from the same notary and from the rigidities and stereotypes of the legalistic notarial culture, but both kinds allowed the testator to express individual and family particularities. Formulaic comparisons should be the easiest; only the notarial version ought to be used in each case, however, since radical compression proper to the notarial codex omits or abbreviates the more routine formulas. The protocol usually disappears or contracts to a few phrases, as do the invocation of God, the preamble of reflections on human destinies, the exposition on motives and present condition, and any extensive titling or rather identification. At the opposite terminal of the notarial draft, the escatocol similarly contracts or collapses—all the end matter, dateline, witnesses, and validation. Fortunately, almost all the Latinate wills keep their witness lists. In the body or text of the will, the disposition in brief form remains, mostly in the appointment of executors and guardians. Here come the place or manner of burial, satisfaction for debts and restitution, and legacies for relatives, friends, or philanthropies (favoring in sequence one's spouse, children, grandchildren, cousins, and then others). A repetitious corroboration and an enforcing sanction to close the text do not usually appear in the Latinate wills.[19]

Subtle and informal differences, however, will differentiate the Christian from the Latinate Jewish will. Beyond the obvious elements—such as synagogue, Jewish cemetery, names falling within a recognizable range of "Jewish" choices, the removal of pious legacies so often from the testament to previous gifts *inter vivos,* and the pattern of Jewish law or custom on dowry recovery—perhaps the resolute concentration on immediate family makes an emphasis more common to the Latinate Jewish wills. Reflection should focus on the will as a whole, its tone and mood, and the revelation of the individual beneath the formulas in order to propose points of contrast, of assimilation, or of common culture.

As a historical source, wills are many genres at once. They are legal documents, the aspect under which they were first and for long studied. They are literary products, quite self-consciously so in rhetorical form and inevitably so in their individual substance. They are economic records, strictly tied to the history of money, property, classes, and costs. They are cultural artifacts, revealing mentalities and shaping them, proclaiming and reinforcing family structures, showing occupations, libraries, household goods, attitudes, and values. In that context, as widely acknowledged, they are religious statements, both implicitly and often enough explicitly, fashioning a continuity in piety and practice between the generations and into the next life. Wills are above all human documents—a last farewell, a reaching out, a final time to order one's domestic world, a solemn last statement, sometimes a cry for help.

Jacques Chiffoleau, in his study on Provençal wills, would have us go beyond an appreciation of all these threads of life to weave them into a unified tapestry, respecting the testament's unity and meaning in its totality. He sees a dialogue between society, the individual, custom, and law, a union of the sacred and profane worlds the testators inhabited, in effect a *histoire totale* rather than "a cave of Ali Baba" to be raided as a data bank for each historian's disparate needs. Chiffoleau views the will as "a veritable expression of civilization." From the rise of Europe's urban society in the twelfth century, the will has been "one of the essential instruments that allowed society to reproduce itself," organizing continuity and "redefining little by little the connections between individual and family, the relations between living and dead, the boundaries of religious influence, the frontiers of the sacred and the profane."[20]

Underlying all the messages that Jewish wills contain, Shlomo Goitein discerned in his Geniza exemplars several tendencies and two intrinsic themes. Among the tendencies or principles of testaments was making peace with one's fellow men in preparation for one's meeting with God. This resolution meant paying all debts, rectifying and clarifying any transactions that would trouble others, and releasing yet others from potential liabilities or claims. Goitein notes: "The list of precautions taken out of consideration for one's fellow man is endless." A corollary principle was that a man's primary creditor was his wife, to whom the "debt" of a dowry and the deferred marriage gift demanded payment and for whom the widow's oath might need to be waived and various provisions and protections supplied.

Goitein sees another organizing principle as the "general human propensity" (in Jewish society "particularly pronounced") to establish financial security and family continuity for one's children. A married daughter was considered to be in another family but received a token gift to show love. An unmarried daughter represented a familial obligation on the testator. An only child, if female, became sole heir "by biblical law," but prudence in a gentile country might counsel explicit provision to that effect. The biblical double share for the firstborn son could be strengthened by specific legacies, but Goitein noted "in many cases" the tendency to provide equal shares to males and females, or not to seem to prefer one over another. Yet another principle in the Geniza wills was the "exaggerated preoccupation with interment" as echoing religious belief, conveying social status, and expressing personality. Finally, the principle of charity was a priority, even though wills generally expressed only minor philanthropic gifts or none at all, since such large or complex transfer of property was better accomplished in timely fashion before the confection of a will.[21]

Goitein's two underlying or defining themes, seen as much in preparations and later announcements as in the will itself, involved a staunch "assertion of the belief in the continuity of the body-soul existence," which "colored all ideas and images of life after death." In most wills this foundation would be implicit, a continuity of action. The second theme was "the communal aspect of death." This understanding was manifest in the presence and activity of the community as responsible or caring in the whole death process, including the will. It was equally manifest in the vision of bereavement and death as both "punishment of the community for its long list of sins" and atonement for sins, with the death of a holy person as "a vicarious sacrifice for the community." Goitein finds that "this concept of death as punishment and expiation as related to human behavior" coexisted with a contradictory sense of a "predetermined life span" finally played out, an idea he believes "essentially foreign to Judaism." The wills themselves were not the vehicles for expressing such attitudes, but those orientations of spirit belong to the wider meaning of the wills. Immemorial traditions and social energies of the community at large thus framed the simple act of drafting a will.[22]

Such larger horizons aside, the Latinate survivals constitute an important point of entry for the social history of Jewish communities in the realms of Arago-Catalonia and Majorca. Each such document has its autonomous significance, but in series as at Puigcerdá they can slowly accumulate to re-create the people and institutions of a given *aljama,* especially organizing and associating the isolated data available in greater mass from the many codices recording loans from Jews to Christians. Family genealogies can be constructed and eventually related, surnames grouped, and a basic prosopography attempted. The Latinate Jewish genre itself deserves to be studied as a separate topos, an action immemorially Jewish but (as communicated here in the structures, categories, and expressions of Roman law) a kind of juridical acculturation. A larger familiarity with the responsa literature and other mirrors of medieval Jewish life and law can tease further meaning from testamentary texts both as particular and as group phenomena. Even the pattern of inserts, pronunciations, false starts, and corrections in these hurried records can tell us something of the vernacular expression being translated and transformed into the official Latin.

Such isolated testaments resist discovery. They are random flashes, misprized and passed by as researchers flip the codex pages seeking other data. To search directly is to court tedium and risk minimal results. The best strategy is to alert archival searchers in all fields to ticket such finds and present them to view. This effort will eventually assemble a *testamentarium,* a body of medieval Jewish lore not otherwise accessible. Goitein laments that "a Geniza has not yet been found in Europe." Yet the Latinate Jewish wills with their collateral testamentary documentation from crown and society constitute a unique treasure trove, similarly intimate and domestic, much smaller so far, more modest in scope of content but more systematic and abundant in its own speciality.[23]

Appendix: Unpublished Documents

In these transcriptions I follow the Madrid *Normas de transcripción y edición de textos y documentos* (Madrid, 1944), with minor adjustments:

°[ ] for holes, requiring conjectural additions

\ / to set off words inserted above the line

<> to enclose deteriorated or partially reconstructed text, and [ ] for editorial intrusion

The forms *i* and *j* are not distinguished; the rare *y* is usually retained. For the incarnational calendar, both dates are given where appropriate, the preferred date outside the parentheses. As in the notes, abbreviations for the archives are

Arch. Cath. Barc.: Arxiu Capitular de la Catedral, Barcelona

Arch. Crown: Arxiu de la Corona d'Aragó, Barcelona

Arch. Dioc. Gerona: Arxiu Diocesà de Girona, Gerona

Arch. Hist. Gerona: Arxiu Històric de Girona

Arch. Hist. Nac.: Archivo Histórico Nacional, Madrid

Arch. Hist. Puigcerdá: Arxiu Històric Comarcal de Puigcerdà

1

Lérida 10 August 1260
Arch. Crown, Cancelleria, reg. 11, fol. 224v

Pero the son of Poncio Guillermo has a charter appointing him notary for the Jews of Jaca in Aragon.

Petrus filius Poncii Guillelmi de Iaccha habuit cartam: quod sit notarius publicus Iudeorum Iacce.

Datum Ilerde, IIII idus Augusti, [anno domini MCCLX].

2

Lérida 6 June 1263
Arch. Crown, Cancelleria, reg. 12, fol. 88

The deceased Salamó de Tortosa, a Jew of Barcelona, made his will in two charters, one Latin and one Hebrew, with three executors. His daughter Bellor is universal heir, with a guardian for her minority. King Jaume I confirms the will, its stages, and Bellor but leaves open challenges by potential legatees.

Quod cum supplic°[a]ndo propositum sit et ostensum coram nobis Iacobo dei gracia rege Aragonum etc. quod Salomon de Dertusa Iudeus Barchinone olim defunctus fecerit seu condiderit testamentum et ultimam voluntatem suam prout patet in duobus instrumentis, quorum unum est scriptum littera latina et roboratum a Petro de Castro Aziolo tenenti locum Guillelmi de Turrillis vicarii nostri in Barchinona, et aliud est littera eybrayca scriptum:

In quo testamento dictus Salomon elegit manumissores suos Biona Satelli, Isaacum filium quondam Boneti de Apiara, et Zarchum Modeci[1] Iudeos nostros Barchinone:

Et in eodem testamento instituit sibi heredem universalem Belor fil-

1. Régné, *Catalogue:* Malet.

iam suam pupillam, cui dimisit omnia bona sua quecumque habebat vel habere debebat ubique aliqua racione:

Et eciam dictus testator dedit et assignavit tutores et curatores dicte Belor filie sue manumissores predictos, prout in serie seu forma dicti testamenti lacius continetur:

Nos videntes et intelligentes predicta recte et diligenter fore facta: laudamus, concedimus, et confirmamus totam dictam ordinacionem seu seriem testamenti predicti, tam in eleccione manumissorum predictorum quam in institucione predicta, quam in tutela et cura quam in contraendo matrimonio de dicta Belor (cum consilio dictorum tutorum et curatorum et eciam matris sue), quam in omnibus aliis et singulis in eodem testamento contentis pariter et expressis.

Predictam itaque confirmacionem nostram facimus in hunc modum, quod si aliquis poterit ostendere se habere maiu[s] ius in bonis dicti Salomonis de Dertusa quam Belor filia sua pupilla, quocumque modo vel qualibet alia racione: quod racione dicte nostre confirmacionis, illi vel illis nullum preiudicium valeat generari. Immo illud sibi in omnibus salvum facimus, quocienscumque inde coram nostro baiulo vel vicario de dictis bonis duxerit conquerendum.

Et accipimus eandem Belor et omnia bona sua sub nostra proteccione, empara [=amparancia], custodia, manutenencia, et firmo ducatu. \Quicumque autem contra ipsam ordinacionem in aliquo venerit, iram nostram et indignacionem se noverit incursurum./

Mandantes vicariis et baiulis nostris Barchinone presentibus et futuris quod ordinacionem predicti testamenti inviolabilem faciant perpetuo observari, et non contraveniant in aliquo vel [contraveniri] permittant.

Datum Ilerde, VIII idus Iunii, anno domini MCCLX tercio.

3

Egea 1 December 1263
Arch. Crown, Cancelleria, reg. 12, fol. 131v

Confers "notariate of the Jews of Egea" on Simón Gil, which includes documents between these Jews and Christians from any place. Simón has a monopoly for life, may appoint a substitute, is to charge the usual fee, and must pay 20 Jaca sous a year in two installments.

Per nos et nostros damus et concedimus tibi Simono [=Simoni] Egidii de Exeya scribaniam Iudeorum Exeye diebus omnibus vite tue; <*ita*> quod tu vel substitutus a te conficiatis et faciatis omnia instrumenta debitorum et aliorum contractuum que inter Christianos ubique tam Exeye quam aliorum locorum et Iudeos Exeye erunt facienda seu conficienda. Et nullus alius preter te vel substitutus a te audeat de cetero facere seu conficere dicta instrumenta—quod si fecerint nullam optinent firmitatem.

Et pro censu dicte scrib<*anie*> dabis nobis et nostris, et loco nostri merino Exeye, annuatim diebus omnibus vite tue viginti solidos iaccenses; de quibus in festo Sancti I<*ohannis*> Babtiste[1] medietatem solvas, et in festo nathalis domini aliam medietatem. Et percipias pro tuo [lab(ore) *deleted*] officio et labore quantumcumque alii scriptores inde percipere et habere consueverunt.

Et sic habeas et teneas scribaniam predictam dum tibi fuerit vita comes, et dum bene et legaliter in dicto officio te habebis.

Mandantes merino, militibus, infancionibus, iusticie, iuratis, et universis aliis hominibus Exeye tam Christianis quam Iudeis presentibus et futuris: quod hanc donacionem nostram et graciam quam tibi facimus firmam habeant et observent et faciant ab omnibus inviolabiliter observari, et non contraveniant nec aliquem contravenire permittant aliquo modo vel aliqua racione, si confidunt de nostri gracia vel amore.

Datum apud Exeyam, kalendas[2] Decembris, anno domini MCCLX tercio.

4

Zaragoza 9 February (1263) 1264
Arch. Crown, Cancelleria, reg. 12, fol. 142v

Grants to the Jew Astruc Azarel for life the office of commercial weights at Lérida, with a rent of 20 sous to the crown each Christmas.

Per nos et nostros damus et concedimus tibi Astrugo Ascarelli Iudeo Ilerde in tota vita tua scribaniam pensi nostri Ilerde; ita quod tu sis

1. June 24 was his main feast, the nativity. August 29 as the beheading and September 24 as his conception do not allow for the six months until the December 25 payment.

2. Chancery usage, rarely *kalendis.*

scriptor dicti pensi, et habeas et teneas predictam scribaniam in tota vita tua dum bene et fideliter te habueris in eadem.

Tu tamen tenearis nobis et nostris dare quolibet anno in festo natalis domini XX solidos pro predicta scribania.

Et sic habeas et teneas dictam scribaniam, et iura eiusdem percipias in tota vita tua, dum bene et fideliter geras officium eiusdem. Mandantes etc.

Datum Cesarauguste, V idus Februarii, anno domini MCCLX tercio.

5

Villafranca del Panadés 3 September 1268
Arch. Crown, Cancelleria, reg. 15, fol. 116v

The deceased Jew Benvenist de Porta appointed as executors his wife Jamila, Jahudà de la Cavalleria, Astruc Sa Porta, Azmel (=Ismāʿīl) Ibn Venist of Morella, Mossé Sullam and Perfet de Sa Real, all "according to the custom of the Jews," in a will done in Hebrew. King Jaume here recognizes the Jewish custom and releases the executors from having "to show any inventory" of the deceased's goods.

Concedimus vobis Iafudano de la Cavaleria, Astrucha za Porta, Azmel Abenvenist de Morela,[1] Mosse Sullam, Perfeito de za Real, et Iamila uxori quondam Benvenist de Porta, manumissoribus ipsius Benvenist: quod ex quo secundum consuetudinem Iudeorum fuistis manumissores constituti predicti Benvenist et per ipsum, ut in suo testamento facto in ebrayco manifeste apparet, non teneamini de cetero aliud ostendere inventarium, in causa vel extra causam, nec eciam aliquam aliam racionem.[2]

Mandantes vicariis, baiulis, et aliis officialibus nostris presentibus et futuris quod vos contra predicta in aliquo non compellant; immo vos habeant et teneant et haberi ac teneri faciant pro manumissoribus, ut superius est dictum et ut continetur in testamento superius memorato.

Datum Villefranche Penitensis, III nonas Septembris, anno domini MCCLX octavo.

1. Régné reads Torela. Toralla near Lérida, or Morella in Valencia?
2. Not ablative.

6

Barcelona, Dominican house 3 September 1268
Arch. Crown, Cancelleria, reg. 15, fol. 117rv

A lawsuit before King Jaume I has the great Salamó Ibn Adret defend claims of his ward Belshom, son of the deceased Bonanat de Besalú, against the executors of the deceased Benvenist de Porta of Villafranca, namely, Mossé Sullam, Samuel Sullam, Ismael of Tudela, and Perfet de Sa Real. Bonanat died intestate, Ibn Adret charges, half of his goods going to his daughter Sara and half to Benvenist de Porta (not to Belshom). With Benvenist also now dead, leaving a son Vidal, the legacy of Bonanat (worth 48,000 gold morabatins) should go to Belshom. The trial went through "many maneuvers and objections and responses," and "some letters sealed with Our seal." The crown had seized the property of Bonanat, releasing the legacy to Benvenist (then bailiff of Barcelona and Gerona). The king, having perused Bonanat's will and the crown documents and heard the extensive arguments, concluded that Bonanat was not intestate and dismissed Ibn Adret's suit. The host of dignitaries at the sentencing included the great lawyer Ramon de Penyafort.

In nomine dei, amen.

Lis seu contraversia vertebatur coram nobis Iacobo dei gracia <rege Aragonum, Maioricarum et Valencie>, comite Barchinone et Urgelli et domino Montispessulani, inter Salamonem den [=de En][1] Adret \Iudeum/ tutorem Bellihominis Iudei filii Bonanasch Iudei de Bisulduno <agentem tutorio> nomine ex una parte, et Mosse Sulam et Samuel Sulam, Hizmael de Tudela, Perfectum de Regali Iudeos manumissores Benvenist de Porta Iudei de Villafrancha quondam defendentes ex altera, in hunc modum.

Proponit Salamon den [=de En] Adret, tutor datus Belshom filio Bonanasch Iudei de Bisuldu[no], quod pater ipsius Belshom decessit ab intestato, relictis duobus filiis scilicet Sarra et Belshom; et pars bonorum dicti Bonanasch ad illam Sarram filiam pervenit, ex [=et] altera

1. *Sic*, Catalan En as honorific, not ben as in Ibn Vives. Cf. later in the document: *den Bonasch*. See the discussion of En above, my introduction, under "Names."

pars bonorum pervenit ad Benvenist za Porta Iudeum de Villa-francha.

Qui Benvenist decessit, dimisso filio herede nomine Vidal, et relictis manumissoribus scilicet Iahudano de Cavaleria, Mosse Sullam, et Perfeit de za Reyal, et Hizmael, et uxore superstite dicti Benvenist, et Samuele Sulam, et Astrugo de Porta fratre ipsius Benvenist.

Et predictus filius ipsius Benvenist et mater ipsius et manumissores ante dicti tenent bona ipsius Benvenist, ad quem bona den [=de En] Bon[an]asch[2] pervenerunt.

Unde petit sibi dari et deliberari a predictis bona que fuerunt den [=de En] Bon[an]asch que ad dictum Benvenist devenerant, et ipse habuit et recepit cum sit heres sui patris ab intestato in medietate bonorum suorum, cum sine causa habuit et percepit. Valent autem bona predicta quadraginta octo milia morabatinorum et amplius.

Super qua quidem peticione lis est contestata inter dictas partes. Et ad fundandam intencionem suam, utraque pars plures posiciones et excepciones et responsiones fecit. Et predicti manumissores testamentum conditum pro dicto Bo[na]nasch, et quasdam litteras sigillatas sigillo nostro, coram nobis in iudicio produxerunt.

In uno quorum fit mencio quod bona dicti Bo[na]nasch fuerunt adquisita et confiscata nobis pluribus de causis, de quibus bonis cessionem et donacionem dicto Benvenist feceramus prout in dicta littera continetur. Et in alia littera fit mencio quod nos volumus et mandamus dicto Benvenist, tunc baiulo Barchinone et Gerunde, quod nullo tempore teneatur prestare sive solvere aliquid aliquibus personis, racione pecunie que quondam fuit Bonanasch de Bisuldone, tam racione hereditatis legitime quam quibuslibet aliis modis.

Tandem nos Iacobus dei gracia rex Aragonum, Maioricarum et Valencie, comes Barchinone et Urgelli et dominus Montispessulani, visa et intellecta peticione pre°[sentat]a ut sup°[ra] in inicio huius cause, lite legitime contestata inter dictas partes, visis et intellectis posicionibus et excepcionibus et replicacionibus et responsionibus in hac causa factis a partibus supra dictis, viso et intellecto diligenter tenore testamenti dicti Bon[an]asch, et visis et intellectis tenoribus dictarum l°[iter]arum, visis et intellectis eciam racionibus utriusque partis, habentes deum pre oculis, sedentes predictis partibus in nostra presencia constitutis, attendentes quod dictus Bonanasch testatus decessit instituta sibi herede dicta Sarra filia sua ut apparet ex forma dicti testamenti et sic non est

2. Both forms appear in this document.

locus ab intestato, attendentes eciam quod si locus eciam ab intestato non improbatur, quod predicti manumissores teneant res petitas scilicet morabatinos petitos in libello, attendentes eciam quod dictus tutor non provavit [=probavit] dictum Belshom habere ius in dimidia bonorum dicti Bona\na/sch, attendentes eciam cessionem et donacionem per nos factam dicto Benvenist de[3] bonis que fuerunt dicti Bonanasch ut in carta sigillata sigillo nostro pendenti plenius continetur: hiis racionibus et multis °[a]liis que tangi possunt, dictos manumissores supra conventos pro se et aliis manumissoribus [*fol. 117v*] a peticione dicti tutoris de Bels[hom] impubere[4] ut supra duximus sentencialiter absolvendos.

Lata fuit hec sentencia in domo Fratrum Predicatorum Barchinone, anno incarnacionis domini MCCLX octavo, iii nonas Septembris, in presencia et testimonio domini Arnaldi episcopi Barchinone, Berengarii Arnaldi, Bernardi de Angularia, Guillelmi de Cervilione, Magistri Berengarii de Turri archidiaconis Barchinone, Guillelmi de Villafrancha, Iacobi Grunnii, Fratris Raimundi de Pena Forti; Fratris Arnaldi de Sagarra, et plurium aliorum testium.

7[1]

Villafranca del Panadés — 4 September 1268
Arch. Crown, Cancelleria, reg. 15, fol. 116v

Remits any future legal action by the crown against Vidal de Porta, son of the deceased Benvenist de Porta, and the executors, on account of Benvenist himself, his deceased son Perfet, or the deceased Bonanat of Besalú and his heirs. Confirms all charters given by the crown to Benvenist bearing on the goods of both Benvenist and Bonanat.

Per nos et nostros remittimus et diffinimus <tibi Vitali> de Porta filio Benvenist de Porta quondam, et manumissoribus dicti patris tui et vestris successoribus in perpetuum, omnem peticionem, questionem, et demandam quam facere possemus in bonis dicti patris tui, tam racione ipsius Benvenist quam racione Perfect[i]onis filii sui quondam, quam

3. Repeated: *de*.
4. Impubere: conjectural reading.
1. The first of three documents on fol. 116v, related to Régné's two documents of September 3.

eciam racione Bonanasqui de Bisulduno quondam seu heredum suorum.

Concedentes et confirmantes tibi Vitali predicto et successoribus tuis in perpetuum omnes donaciones, concessiones, stabilimenta et diffinimentes factas a nobis Benvenist predicto cum instrumentis nostris, tam de bonis ipsius Benvenist patris tui quam eciam de bonis Bonanasqui predicti, ut in eisdem instrumentis plenius et melius continetur; promittentes nos ratum et firmum habere quicquid in dictis instrumentis specialiter vel generaliter a nobis est concessum, et contra tenorem ipsorum instrumentorum in aliquo non venire.

Mandantes vicariis, baiulis, curiis, et aliis officialibus etc.

Datum Villefranche Penitensis, II nonas Septembris, anno domini MCCLX octavo.

8

Villafranca del Panadés 4 September 1268
Arch. Crown, Cancelleria, reg. 15, fol. 116v

Protects the executors of the deceased Benvenist de Porta, and his son Vidal, from any legal action by the son (Belshom) of the deceased Bonanat of Besalú or by any other persons, on any aspect of the testamentary trial just finished.

Concedimus vobis manumissoribus Benvenist de Porta quondam, et Vitali filio eiusdem Benvenist, quod non teneamini respondere nec facere ius filio quondam Bo[na]nasch de Bisulduno, nec tutori suo nec eciam aliquibus aliis personis, super aliquibus peticionibus vel demandis factis vel faciendis vobis, racione bonorum Benvenist predicti seu Bo[na]nasqui de Bisulduno superius memorati, extra villam Villefranche Penitensis. Nec aliquis vicarius vel baiulus seu alius officialis noster possit compellere vos[1] ad faciendum ius super predictis, nisi ut superius continetur.

Datum Villefranche Penitensis, II nonas Septembris, anno domini MCCLX octavo.

1. Deleted: *ad*. Repeated: *vos*.

9

Zaragoza 31 August 1271
Arch. Crown, Cancelleria, reg. 21, fols. 10v-11

King Jaume I confers on "Muḥammad son of the *faqīh* Ismāʿīl of Borgia" for his lifetime "the concession We made to your said father for his lifetime, of the offices of *faqīh, amīn,* and scribe of the Saracens of Borgia, with a charter as is contained therein." The king also "approves and confirms to you the concession that the *aljama* of Borgia made to your father of the office of *ṣāḥib al-ṣalāt* of the town of Borgia for your lifetime," as detailed in their document of appointment.

°[Per] nos et nostros laudamus, concedimus, et confirmamus tibi Mahometo, filio alfaquimi Ismaeli de Borgia, \diebus omnibus vite tue concessionem, quam/ concessionem[1] feceramus \°[dict]o patri tuo/ in °[vit]a sua, de alfaquimatu, alaminatu, et scribania Sarracenorum de Borgia, cum[2] carta nostra ut in ea continetur.

Laudamus eciam et confirmamus t°[ibi] concessionem quam aliama Sarracenorum de Borgia fecerunt[3] patri tuo quondam de çab°[a]çalanatu ville de Borgia in vita °[sua] ut in carta quam dicti Sarraceni aliame predicte inde sibi fecerunt plenius continetur.

Ita scilicet quod tu habeas et teneas officia ante dicta [*fol. 11*], et ipsis utaris toto tempore vite vestre ut in cartis predictis \patri tuo inde factis/ plenius continetur, dummodo te in dictis officiis bene et fideliter habueris.

Concedentes tibi quod habeas et percipias pro tuo officio et labore quicquid \predictus pater tuus consuevit inde percipere et habere pro suo officio et labore/.[4]

Datum Cesarauguste, II kalendas Septembris, anno domini quo supra [anno domini MCCLXX primo].

1. Probably meant to be deleted, as is *quam tibi* here.
2. Deleted: *alia.*
3. Deleted: *Ismaelo.*
4. Deleted: five words.

10

Gerona 4 September 1271
Arch. Crown, Cancelleria, reg. 37, fol. 26v

Prince Pere gives a privilege to the Jews of Gerona, Besalú, and their collectory area to draft marriage documents, including dowry documents and "all that pertains to nuptial contracts," according to Jewish custom, as either "Christianic or Hebraic" charters. The same applies to contracts of sale, purchase, or rental between Jews and Christians or Jews and Jews. Notifies the notaries and the Jewish scribes "who draft documents in Hebraic mode" to that effect.

Noverint universi quod nos infans Petrus etc. damus, concedimus et indulgemus vobis universis Iudeis Gerunde et Bisuldoni et aliorum locorum ad vestram colleccionem[1] pertinencium, quod in vestris contractibus nupciarum seu coniugii inter aliquem et aliquam faciendas, faciatis et facere possitis instrumenta christianica[2] vel ebrayca ad morabatinos, tam de dotis promissione, sponsalicio, augmento, donacione debita propter nupcias dotis quam de omni eo quod redire debet patri vel matri vel parentibus de muliere que mortua sine infantibus fuerit de dote donata, et generaliter de omnibus aliis que pertineant ad contractus nupciales ut moris est inter vos imposterum faciendos.

Item donamus, concedimus, et eciam indulgemus vobis eisdem Iudeis ex nostra gracia speciali quod de honoribus et possessionibus vestris presentibus et futuris et de honoribus seu possessionibus quas emetis ab aliquibus Christianis vel vos eisdem venderitis, faciatis et facere possitis instrumenta vendicionum, empcionum, et stabilimentorum, et censum eorum prestandum perpetuo ad aureos tam inter Iudeum et Christianum quam inter Iudeum et Iudeum.

Mandantes scriptoribus qui conficiunt ebrayce instrumenta et notariis Gerunde et Bisuldoni et aliorum locorum, ut huiusmodi instrumenta conficere vel scribere, quia eos ac eciam fideiussores et testes qui in eis nominati fuerint absolvimus et indulgemus.

1. Not here *collectam,* the usual term to indicate a district for gathering Jewish taxes.
2. Unusual form, influenced by *ebrayca.*

Datum Gerunde, pridie nonas Septembris, anno domini MCCLXX primo.

11

Perpignan 23 May 1272
Arch. Crown, Cancelleria, reg. 21, fol. 38

King Jaume awards Bartomeu Tomàs for life the notarial office of Barbastro "both for Christians and Jews." The city jurates and council are to recognize this monopoly. Bartomeu may appoint a substitute or colleague and must pay the crown 4 gold morabatins every Christmas.

Noverint universi quod nos Iacobus dei gracia rex Aragonum, Maioricarum et Valencie, comes Barchinone et Urgelli et dominus Montispessulani, per nos et nostros damus et concedimus tibi Bartholomeo Tomasii in tota vita tua scribaniam ville Barbastri tam Christianorum quam Iudeorum.

Ita videlicet quod tu, vel quem seu quos volueris loco tui, conficiatis et scribatis acta, testamenta, et quelibet <alia> publica instrumenta que in villa Barbastri Christiani vel Iudei facere habebunt, dum tamen tu seu ille vel illi quem vel quos deposueris loco tui habeatis vos in ipso officio fideliter atque bene.

Mandantes firmiter iuratis et consilio Barbastri quod te vel quem seu quos volueris loco tui habeant et teneant pro scriptore publico de Barbastro de cetero et non aliquem alium, dum vos in ipso officio fideliter et bene habueritis ut est dictum; et predicta firma habeant et non contraveniant aliqua racione.

Est tamen sciendum quod pro tributo predicte scribanie debes dare nobis et nostris singulis annis quattuor morabatinos alfonsinos boni auri et recti pensi in unoquoque festo natalis domini.

Datum Perpiniani, X kalendas Iunii, anno domini MCCLXX secundo.

12[1]

Montpellier 13[2] August 1272
Arch. Crown, Cancelleria, reg. 21, fol. 55v

Releases the persons and properties of the Jews Botina, Vives Vidal, and Astruc of Beaucaire, executor-guardians of Mossé, the child-heir of the deceased Salamó Samiel (also called Bonisac Samiel of Carcassonne) and of his wife the same Botina. Also releases the administrative reviewers added to their number by the crown—Samiel of Béziers, son of the deceased Cresques of Béziers, and Bonifós Mossé of Narbonne. The release excludes any audit or accounting to the crown concerning their ward Mossé as well as any civil or criminal action by the crown against them.

Per nos et nostros absolvimus et diffinimus ac remittimus vos Botinam Iudeam et Vives Vitalis et Astrugum de Belcaire Iudeos, tutores testamentarii \Mosse/ filii impuberis et heredis Salomonis Samielis quondam aliter vocati Bonisac Samielis de Carcassona et viri Botine predicte, et vos Samielem de Biterris filium Cresches de Biterris quondam et Bonafos Mosse de Narbona per nos additos et constitutos ad regimen et administracionem impuberis predicti et suorum bonorum, et vos et omnia bona vestra presencia et futura a reddicione computi amministracionis seu tutele dicti Mosse nobis seu alicui alii loco nostri inde faciendi; et ab omni eciam peticione et demanda ac pena cuiuslibet [= civilibus] et criminalibus, quas contra vos et unumquemque seu alterum vestrum vel bona vestra facere vel movere, imponere, seu infligere possumus vel possemus imposterum nos vel nostri racione predicta vel racione male administracionis seu fraudulente vel dolose, quod dicebatur nos esse contentos[?] de predictis quantum ad nos pertinet; facientes inde vobis et vestris imperpetuum per nos et nostros bonum finem [et] firmum pactum de non petendo.

Ita videlicet quod \de/ predicta tutela sive administracione eiusdem aut bonorum dicti Mosse non teneamini nobis vel nostris seu alicui seu

1. This run of six documents, on the same matter and in the same hand, gives the date on this last charter.

2. Régné: 16 August. Chancery usage: *idus,* rarely *idibus.*

aliquibus nomine vel loco nostri reddere de cetero vos vel alter vestrum seu vestri compotum aliquod vel racionem. Nec nos vel nostri pro predictis vel eorum aliquo peticionem aliquam vel demandam contra vos vel vestros aut res vestras possimus facere vel movere nec aliquam penam civilem vel criminalem in personas seu res vestras imponere seu infligere ullo modo pro predictis. Set sitis inde vos et vestri quantum ad nos et nostros liberi et inmunes ac penitus perpetuo absoluti sicut melius [dici] vel intelligi potest etc.

Dictam vero solucionem et remissionem vobis facimus de predictis iure, scripto, vel consuetudine aliqua non obstante, cum hoc de certa sciencia faciamus: vos vero teneamini de predictis omnibus et singulis reddere computum et racionem Mosse predicto filio et heredi Salomonis Samielis quondam superius memorati.

Mandamus itaque firmiter baiulis, curiis etc.

[Datum in Montepessulano, idus Augusti, anno domini millesimo CCLXX secundo.]

13

Montpellier 13[1] August 1272
Arch. Crown, Cancelleria, reg. 21, fol. 55v

Crown pardon or waiver to Mossé, the son and heir of the deceased Salamó Samiel ("long known as Bonisac Samiel, a Jew of Carcassonne") for all civil and criminal action, or confiscation, against him or his inheritance, by reason of public or private delict or crime against the crown or others.

Per nos et nostros absolvimus et diffinimus ac remittimus te Mosse filium et heredem Salomonis Samielis quondam vocati ab olim Bonisac Samielis Carcassone Iudei et tuos, ac omnia bona tua mobilia et inmobilia presencia et futura, ab omni nostri et nostrorum peticione et de-

1. Régné: 16 August. No date appears on the first of these documents in series, or the second, or on the present document (the third), or on the following two. I have borrowed the date on the next in line, which is on a different topic than the set of five. If the date on the charter previous to the whole undated set of five is used (though also on a different topic), read: [*Datum in Montepessulano, XVII kalendas Septembris, anno domini MCCLXX secundo*] or 16 August 1272.

manda ac pena civilibus et criminalibus, quas contra te vel bona tua seu que fuerunt dicti patris tui quondam habemus et habere vel movere, imponere seu infligere possumus seu possemus racione alicuius delicti publici vel privati seu criminis vel delictorum seu criminum a dicto patre tuo quondam commissi seu commissorum contra nos vel alios quoscumque quantum ad nos pertinet tam facto quam verbo quocumque modo, ex quo vel quibus bona dicti patris tui possent aut deberent nobis aut nostris confiscari in totum [=toto] vel in parte seu [i]n eis ius seu peticionem aliquam haberemus; facientes inde tibi et tuis bonum finem et firmum pactum de non petendo.

Ita videlicet quod, racione alicuius delicti vel criminis a dicto patre tuo olim commissi verbo vel facto quocumque modo, non possimus tibi vel tuis aut contra bona tua vel que dicti patris tui fuerunt, facere vel movere nos vel nostri peticionem aliquam sive demandam, nec ali°[quam] penam civilem vel criminalem imponere seu infligere ullo modo; set sitis inde, quantum ad nos pertinet, tu et tui °[c]um omnibus bonis tuis presentibus et futuris liberi et immunes ac penitus perpetuo absoluti, sicut melius dici vel intelligi potest etc.

[In Montepessulano, idus Augusti, anno domini mille CCLXX secundo.]

14

Montpellier 5 November 1272
Arch. Crown, Cancelleria, reg. 21, fol. 71v

King Jaume awards to "Mossé el Neyto, Jew of Jaca," for life the notariate of the public granary or exchange (*almudí*), and the office of measuring there, at a salary of 4 pence daily.

Noverint universi quod nos Iacobus dei gracia rex etc. per nos et nostros damus et concedimus tibi, Mosse el Neyto Iudeo Iacce, in tota vita tua scribaniam almudini et officium rasore ipsius almudini ville Iacce.

Ita scilicet quod tu toto tempore vite tue, dum bene et fideliter in ipso officio te habueris, scribas ea que scribenda fuerint in ipso almudino vel racione ipsius; et radas mensuras bladi et aliorum que in dicto almudino mensurabuntur et radi[1] debebunt; et exerceas predicta sicut alii ipsa tenentes temporibus preteritis ea melius exercere consueverint.

Concedentes eciam tibi pro officio et labore tuo predictorum [quod] habeas et recipias singulis diebus in tota vita tua dum predicta tenueris quattuor denarios Iacce de redditibus eiusdem almudini.

Hanc autem donacionem tibi facimus sine preiudicio alterius. Mandantes etc.

Datum in Montepessulano, nonas[2] Novembris, anno domini MCCLXX secundo.

15

Montpellier 15 November 1272
Arch. Crown, Cancelleria, reg. 21, fol. 74

Previously the crown had "associated" the Jews Samuel Cresques and Bonafós Mossé of Narbonne as supplementary executors for the deceased Salamó Samiel (called Bonasac Samuel of Carcassonne), a Jew of Perpignan, to the official executor-guardians of the child-heir Mossé—namely, the widow Botina, Astruc of Beaucaire, and Vives Vidal, all also Jews. Now King Jaume gives the original three executor-guardians, with the advice and concurrence of the extra two, authority to buy for young Mossé's benefit properties in Perpignan and the Roussillon region to the amount of 10,000 Valencian sous. Anyone else doing so incurs a fine of 1,000 sous.

Noverint universi quod cum nos Iacobus dei gracia etc. associaverimus ac dederimus vos, Samuelem Cresches de Biterris et Bonafos \Mosse/ de Narbona Iudeos, Butine uxori \Salomonis Samielis aliter (vocati/ Bonisachi Samuelis de Carcassona) Iudei Perpiniani quondam, et Astrugo de Belcayre ac Vives Vitalis tutoribus testamentariis Mosse filii impuberis Bonisach quondam et Botine predictorum, cum alia carta nostra prout in ea plenius continetur: nunc siquidem cum presenti carta damus et concedimus, vobis Botine et \Astrugo de Belcayre [et] Vives

1. MS: *radd-*; above, *rad-*.
2. Chancery usage, rarely *nonis*.

Vitalis predictis/,[1] licenciam et potestatem emendi in Perpiniano et terra Rossillionis, nomine et racione et ad utilitatem dicte Mosse impuberis, hereditates et posse[ssione]s pro X milibus solidorum regalium, simul vel separatim, consilio \et voluntate Samuelis Cresches et Bonafos Mosse de Narbona predictorum/,[2] sine impedimento et contradiccione alicuius persone.

Et \vos tutores iamdicti teneamini solvere et solvatis/,[3] de bonis eiusdem Mosse denarios ante dictos, quando empcio seu empciones hereditatum vel possessionum fient per vos ut superius continetur, usque ad summam scilicet decem milium solidorum.

Statuentes et mandantes quod aliqua persona non emat nec audeat emere extra villam Perpeniani[4] vel terram Rossilionis hereditates vel possessiones aliquas de bonis dicti pupilli, nisi hoc faceret de voluntate et assensu \vestrum omnium predictorum ut superius est expressum/.[5]

Et si quis contra hoc venire attemptav[er]it, penam mille solidorum incurret quocienscumque hic duxerit attemptandum, predictis in suo robore nichilominus duraturis. Mandantes etc.

Datum in Montepessulano, XVII kalendas[6] Decembris, anno domini MCCLXX secundo.

16

Montpellier 15 November 1272
Arch. Crown, Cancelleria, reg. 21, fol. 74v

The deceased Jew of Perpignan Salamó Samiel ("likewise called Salamó Samiel of Carcassonne") had appointed as guardians for his child-heir Mossé the boy's mother Botina and the Jews Vives Vidal and Astruc of Beaucaire. Further to protect young Mossé, King Jaume had added two executors-overseers, Samuel Cresques of Béziers and Bonafós Mossé of Narbonne. To keep Mossé's inheritance intact, the king now forbids

1. Above deleted *Samueli Cresques et Bonafos de Narbona predictis.*
2. Above deleted *Astrugui de Belcayre et Vives Vitalis contutorum predictorum.*
3. Above deleted *manumissores dicti Bonisachi \Salamonis Samielis . . . / et tutores quidem Mosse filii eius teneantur solvere et solvant.*
4. *Sic.*
5. Above deleted *vestrum.*
6. Deleted: *Septembris.*

any money or goods of Mossé to be moved outside Perpignan and the Roussillon district without the executors' permission, until Mossé is over eighteen years. Penalty for noncompliance will be 1,000 Melgueil sous each time, plus restitution.

Noverint universi quod cum \Salamon Samielis vocatus aliter/ Bonisacus Samielis de Carcassona Iudeus Perpiniani quondam assignavisset in sua ultima voluntate filio suo Mosse impuberi in tutores Botinam uxorem suam et matrem dicti Mosse et Vives Vitalis et Astrugum de Belcayre Iudeos, nosque Iacobus dei gracia rex Aragonum etc. ad utilitatem impuberis predicti associaverimus et addiderimus eisdem tutoribus Samuelem Cresques de Biterris et Bonafos \Mosse/ de Narbona <cum carta> nostra ut in ea continetur:

Nichilominus tamen nos Iacobus dei gracia rex predictus ad maiorem predicti Mosse impuberis utilitatem, et ne bona ipsius <possint> dissipari, cum presenti carta volumus et statuimus quod aliqua bona dicti impuberis (denarii scilicet vel alie res seu peccunia) °[non] <extrahantur> vel mutentur aut portentur extra Perpinianum vel terram Rossilionis ab aliqua persona vel personis absque voluntate dicte Botine et Samielis et Bonafos \et Vives Vitalis et Astrugii de Belcayre/, donec scilicet dictus Mosse impuber etatem excessit decem et octo annorum.

Quicumque autem contra hoc fecerit vel venire temptaverit, incurret penam mille solidorum melgoriensium nobis quocienscumque hoc fecerit vel noverit persolvendam, dicta peccunia prius seu rebus ipsis dicti impuberis (quos seu quas contra °[h]oc mandatum nostrum de terra Rossilionis extracxerit) persolutis. Mandantes etc.

Datum in Montepessulano, XVII kalendas Decembris, anno domini MCCLXX secundo.

17[1]

Montpellier 10 January (1272) 1273
Arch. Crown, Cancelleria, reg. 21, fol. 81v

The deceased Vidal Astruc, a Jew of Perpignan, had made a will under the authority [*posse*] of Prince Jaume. King Jaume now approves the will itself and the arbitration or compromise on it arranged between

1. Washed away and stained down right side, obscuring text.

Vidal's children and Bondia of Lunel (the legal guardian appointed in Vidal's will) as well as the audit of the inheritance presented before Prince Jaume or his substitute Pere Rubi.

Quod nos Iacobus etc. intelligentes quod Vitalis Astruc Iudeus Perpiniani quondam, in posse karissimi filii nostri imfantis[2] Iacobi <primogeniti>,[3] condidit testamentum: ideo ipsum testamentum cum presenti carta duximus confirmandum.

Et similiter intelligentes quod composiciones et ordi<naciones> seu peticiones facte, inter filios prefati Vitalis Astruc condam [=quondam] et Bondiam de Lunello tutorem et procuratorem constitutum in testamento prefato dicti Vitalis Astruc quondam (et eciam computum, quod super predictis denariis Bondia reddidit coram dicto filio nostro vel c<oram> Petro Rubei loco eius) laudate et confirmate fuerunt et sunt per predictum filium nostrum infantem Iacobum: ipsas similiter de certa sciencia concedimus et confirmamus, prout melius et plenius dicte composiciones, ordinaciones, particiones, et computum confirmate sunt per filium nostrum infantem Iacobum. Mandantes etc.

Datum in Montepessulano, IIII idus Ianuarii, anno domini MCCLXX secundo.

18

Perpignan 9 April 1274
Arch. Crown, Cancelleria, reg. 19, fol. 122v[1]

King Jaume grants a privilege to the Jews Astruc of Beaucaire and Vives Vidal, together with the widow Botina the guardians for the child-heir of the deceased Salamó Samiel, also called Bonisac Samiel of Carcassonne: if Botina dies, she cannot be replaced by another guardian as long as they live, unless they will be legally convicted of misusing their office.

Noverint universi quod nos Iacobus dei gracia etc. concedimus vobis Astrugo de Belcayre et Vives Vitalis Iudeis, tutoribus datis Mosse pu-

2. Sic.
3. Conjectural.
1. Régné: 122.

pillo filio et heredi universali \Salamonis/ Samielis[2] (alio nomine vocati Bonisachi Samielis de Carcassona) quondam Iudei, per dictum Salamonem in testamento suo, una cum Botina quondam uxore Salamonis et matre dicti pupilli: qualiter [=quia] dicta Botina (que erat una vobiscum data tutrix per dictum Salamonem in dicto testamento, ut dictum est) sit mortua, alius tutor vobis viventibus non possit dari, nec detur dicto pupillo nec adiungi in dicta tutela curator aliquis vel tutor, nisi probatum primo esset contra vos in posse nostro quod vos in eadem tutela minus bene haberetis; immo vos ambo geritis et aministratis tutelam dicti pupilli et bona eius universa, secundum quod simul cum dicta matre sua quondam fecistis, nisi tamen probari posset ut est dictum quod minus bene vos haberetis in eadem. Mandantes <etc.>

<Datum Perpiniani>, V idus Aprilis, anno domini MCCLXX quarto.

19

Perpignan June/July 1274[1]
Arch. Crown, Cancelleria, reg. 19, fol. 141rv

King Jaume confirms the agreement reached by the arbitrators Salamó Sullam de Porta, Vidal Provençal, Salamó Cohen, and Astruc Salamó, with the counsel of Pere Rubi "a judge of Perpignan and Roussillon," between Astruc Vidal, the son of the deceased Jew of Perpignan Vidal Astruc, and his brother Abraham as party of the first part, and Vidal Astruc's widow Colasana (Tolosana?), Perfet Garcia, Todros Garcia (Gracià?), and Vidal (brothers of Colasana), on behalf of Vidal Astruc's daughter-heirs Nina and Petita on the other part, concerning their goods and inheritance.

Iacobus dei gracia etc. per nos et nostros laudamus, concedimus, et confirmamus composicionem per Salamonem Sullam de Porta et per Vitalem Provencalem et per Salamonem Cohen[2] et Astrugum Salamonis Iudeos, arbitros factos, consilio Petri Rubi iudicis Perpiniani et

2. Deleted: *Samuelis.*

1. No day or month. The following document is 6 nones of July (July 2), the previous document is 4 kalends of July (June 28), both at Perpignan. About a third to a half of this charter is abominably scribbled and water-damaged. Régné: *fin juin.*

2. Régné: Cohta.

Rossillionis, inter Astrugum Vitalis filium Vitalis Astrugii Iudei Perpiniani quondam et Abraham fratrem eius ex una parte et eciam Colasanam uxorem dicti Vitalis Astrugii quondam, et Perfeytum Garcia et Toroz Garcia ac Vitalem fratres dicti Colasane nomine seu racione Nine et Petite filiarum Vitalis Astrugii quondam ex altera, super bonis scilicet et hereditate Nine et Petite predictarum prout in cartis inde factis melius <et plenius continetur>.

20

Lérida 14 November 1275
Arch. Crown, Cancelleria, reg. 20, fol. 298

King Jaume notifies all the notaries of Egea in Aragon that the Jews there, present and future, may draw up their documents with any public notary of Egea, including debts (purchases) or any other kind of charter, and they need not use one designated notary. For this privilege the notaries as a body must pay the crown 30 Jaca sous on the yearly feast of St. Michael.

Per nos et nostros damus et concedimus vobis universis et singulis scriptoribus ville Exee tam presentibus quam futuris: quod Iudei Exee presentes et futuri possint, cum quocumque scriptore publico Exee voluerint, conficere suas cartas debitorum suorum et alias quascumque cartas quas facere habuerint sive facient cum quibuscumque personis.

Et non teneantur nec possint compelli ad conficiendum suas cartas predictas cum uno solo scriptore seu [=sed] quocumque seu quibuscumque scriptoribus publicis dicte ville voluerint, non obstante donacione a nobis alicui facta in contrarium.

Hanc vero concessionem facimus vobis ita videlicet ut vos et vestri successores, qui pro tempore fuerint scriptores publici dicte ville, teneant [dare] nobis et nostris singulis annis de cetero in unoquoque festo Sancti Michaelis[1] triginta solidos iaccenses, pro censu sive tributo concessionis predicte. Mandantes etc.

Datum Ilerde, XVIII kalendas Decembris, anno domini MCCLXX quinto.

1. September 29 was his main feast.

21

Barcelona 27 September 1278
Arch. Crown, Cancelleria, reg. 40, fol. 262v

King Pere orders ʿAlī the *faqīh* of Calatayud, resident at Saviñan, to go to Calatayud on the schedule his predecessors had followed, "for the purpose of judging lawsuits and cases which have been or will be brought by Christians and Jews against Saracens of your *faqīh* jurisdiction," and to conclude such cases. The king also authorizes ʿAlī "that you make all the Arabic ["Saracenic"] documents, and no other *amīn* or *ṣāḥib al-ṣalāt* throughout the entire land of your *faqīh* jurisdiction." All of this is in accord with the privilege ʿAlī already holds.

Petrus dei gracia rex Aragonum fideli suo Aly alfaquimo Calataiubi, habitatori de Savinyan, salutem et graciam.

Mandamus vobis quatenus in diebus in quibus predecessores vestri consueverunt intrare Calataiubum, causa iudicandi contenciones et casus que mote sunt vel fuerint per Christianos et Iudeos contra Sarracenos vestri alfaquimatus, intretis et veniatis vos personaliter diebus quibus consuetum est ad predictam villam Calataiubi, ut de predictis Sarracenis possitis facere querelantibus iusticie complementum.

Mandamus eciam vobis quatenus \vos/ faciatis omnes cartas sarracenicas, et non alius alaminus nec çaveçalanus, per totam terram alaminatus vestri.

Et predictas exerceatis secundum tenorem privilegii vestri quod inde habetis.

Datum Barchinone, V kalendas Octobris, anno domini MCCLXX octavo.

22

Barcelona 20 November 1278
Arch. Crown, Cancelleria, reg. 41, fol. 16

The crown bailiff Bartolomé Tomás has confiscated the office of *ṣāḥib al-wathāʾiq* or scribe for the city and district of Huesca from Ibrāhīm

b. ʿAbd Allāh. King Pere here orders his restoration as scribe, "to use [the office] just as he has done heretofore," until the king can investigate further. Ibrāhīm holds the post "with a charter" from the previous king, Jaume I.

Fideli Bartholomeo Thomasii.

Mandamus vobis quatenus, super scribania Sarracenorum Osce quam vos de mandato nostro emparastis Abrahim filio Abdille Avincentrel,[1] qui eandem scribaniam tenet ad tributum cum carta illustrissimi patris nostri: nullum impedimentum seu contrarium faciatis.

Set ipsum Abrahim permittatis uti dicto officio prout consuevit hucusque, donec nos viderimus super eo.

Datum Barchinone, XII kalendas Decembris, anno predicto [anno domini MCCLXXVIII].

23

Barcelona 10 January (1278) 1279
Arch. Crown, Cancelleria, reg. 41, fol. 138

A form letter to Ferrer Maiol the crown vicar of Barcelona, with copies to nine other vicars throughout Catalonia, ordering them to have heralded or cried in their vicariates that only notaries authorized by the crown may draft public documents, except for wills and dowries, under penalty of 100 morabatins. After that announcement, such unauthorized documents are null and void.

Fideli suo Ferrario Mayol vicario Barchinone, salutem et graciam.

Mandamus vobis quatenus faciatis preconitzari publice per totam vicariam quam vos pro nobis tenetis, sub pena C morabatinorum, ne aliquis scriptor preter eos qui habent auctoritatem a domino rege patre nostro, vel a nobis, audeant uti officio tabellionis, exceptis testamentis et cartis dotaliciis.

Mandamus eciam vobis quatenus faciatis preconitzari sub dicta pena quod nullus audeat, apud ipsos tales scriptores, alias cartas conficere vel firmare preter predictas; quoniam nos omnes cartas quas post predictam

1. Avinçoncol?

preconizacionem fecerint, preter testamenta et cartas dotalicias, irritas decernimus et inanes.

Datum Barchinone, IIII idus Ianuarii, anno etc. [domini MCCLXXVIII].

Petrus Marchesii

Vicario Villefranche
Vicario Cervarie
Vicario Minorise et Vici
Vicario Barchinone
Vicario Terrachone et Campi
Vicario Bergatane[1]
Vicario Montisalbi
Vicario Ilerde
Vicario Rippecurcie et de Payllars

Has tulerunt Bonetus et Dominicus de Montanyana.

24

Valencia 17 April 1282
Arch. Crown, Cancelleria, reg. 44, fol. 226

Notifies Sebastian Manso, crown subvicar of Tortosa, that the trial delegated to the crown court there, between Astruc Jacob Xixó (= Shashon/Sasson) and his in-law Jucef Cohen, concerning an affair of espousal documents and testaments, is to be resolved "by the Hebrew Sunna." Having entered a crown court with Jewish law, it should finish by it.

Sebastiano de Manso subvicario Dertuse.

Quod causam que sub audiencia eius vertitur ex delegacione domini regis, inter Astruch Iacob Sicxoni ex una parte et Iuceff Cohen generum[1] suum ex altera, super facto sponsaliciorum et testamentorum, terminet per zunam ebraicam.

Si eam cognoverit per zunam, debet terminari prout ut fuerit faciendum.

Datum Valencie, XV kalendas Madii, anno [domini] MCCLXXX secundo.

1. Catalan Berguedà. Deleted here: *Vicario Terrachone.*
1. Classical son-in-law, later rather brother-in-law, father-in-law, or even other relative.

25

Zaragoza 13 February (1284) 1285
Arch. Crown, Cancelleria, reg. 56, fol. 5

King Pere orders the Lérida bailiff and his lieutenant, in the matter of a will by the deceased Jahudà of Limós (modern Limoux) and the inheritance from him to his widow Bonadona, that she must not be illegally harassed as long as she is willing to respond to charges made at law.

Baiulo Ilerde vel eius locum tenenti.

Mandamus vobis quatenus super testamento condito per Iahudanum de Limos quondam, et super bonis legatis per ipsum Bonedone uxori suo, non permittatis ipsam B°[on]amdonam ab aliquo vel aliquibus contra iusticiam aggraviari, ipsa tamen faciente querelantibus de se super predictis iusticie complementum.

Datum Cesarauguste, idus[1] Februarii, [anno domini MCCLXXXIV].

26

Zaragoza 24[1] February (1284) 1285
Arch. Crown, Cancelleria, reg. 56, fol. 9

King Pere notifies the bailiff of Lérida Esteve de Cardona about the charge that Bonadona had maneuvered her dying husband Jahudà of Limós (modern Limoux) a Jew of Lérida into making a last testament against his usual reason and wishes, to the prejudice of other relatives. The bailiff must investigate and if appropriate prosecute.

Petrus dei gracia etc. fideli suo Stephano de Cardona baiulo Ilerde, vel eius locum tenenti.

1. Chancery usage, rarely *idibus*.

1. Régné: 23. For 1285 the sixth kalends is February 24; if the stated year 1284 had prevailed, its leap year date would have been February 25.

Intelleximus quod cum Iahudanus de Limos Iudeus Ilerde laboraret in extremis et vellet condere testamentum, Bonadona uxor eiusdem Iahudani et aliqui Iudei de parentela sua fraudulenter et per vim fecerunt ei condere testamentum ultra quod °[sana] mente gereret et contra voluntatem suam, in preiudicium aliquorum aliorum affinium eiusdem Iahudani.

Quare mandamus vobis quatenus super hoc inquiratis diligenter veritatem; et quoscumque adveneritis culpabiles de predictis, procedatis contra eos iusticia mediante.

Datum Cesarauguste, ut supra [VI kalendas Marcii, anno domini MCCLXXXIV].

27

Barcelona 5 September 1285
Arch. Crown, Cancelleria, reg. 57, fol. 198

King Pere takes up with the bailiff of Lérida Esteve de Cardona the case of the widow Bonadona and her accomplices, accused of fraudulently maneuvering her dying husband Jahudà of Limós, a Jew of Lérida, into making an improper will. Cardona has sent the investigatory record to the king, but it is confused by dishonest and vacillating witnesses. Cardona must reopen the case, bring it to a clear conclusion, and send the results to the king.

Stephano de Cardona baiulo ilerdensi.

Super inquisicionis cuiusdam negocio, quam contra Bonamdonam uxorem quondam Iahudani de Limos Iudei ilerdensis et alios consortes suos vobis faciendam commisisse recolimus, super quadam fraude per eos in testamento dicti Iahudani commissa ut dicitur (tam dicta seu deposiciones eorum contra quos fiebat inquisicio quam quorundam testium super quibusdam articulis ipsum negocium contingentibus productorum), vos intelleximus recepisse.

Accepimus insuper quod, tam hii contra quos fit inquisicio quam testes predicti, iureiurandi religione contempta ac suis deposicionibus vacillantes, dicta sua fraudulenter variant, suborn°[a]ti adeo quod veritate sepulta non potestis commode ipsum inquisicionis negocium terminare.

Ideoque vobis dicimus et mandamus quatenus si ex presumpcionibus verisimilibus vel notabilibus argumentis vobis consuggerit prefatos, contra quos fit inquisicio et eciam contra ipsos productos seu eciam producandos, subornatos existere vel in suis deposicionibus variare vel alias de veritate dicenda suspectos: vos ipsos et eorum dicta iterum examinare curetis. Et si vobis visum fuerit ex racionibus supra dictis, eos ad questiones ponatis, curantes omnino ut veritatem facti plenariam habeatis.

Et sic in dicto inquisicionis negocio usque ad diffinitivam sentenciam, absque diffugiis, libere procedatis; et ex tunc, infecto negocio, ad nos ipsum ubi fuerimus remittatis.

Datum Barchinone, nonas[1] Septembris, anno domini MCCLXXXV.

28

Valencia 3 February (1285) 1286
Arch. Crown, Cancelleria, reg. 63, fol. 39v

The crown orders authorities to protect Astruga, daughter of the deceased Astruc of Gerona formerly of Murviedro, and Astruguet his nephew, both minors, in the inheritance he left them in his will. Should anyone seize any of this, the authorities must recover it for them, all according to the "law and custom or Sunna of the Jews."

Mandamus vobis quatenus manuteneatis et defendatis Astrugam filiam quondam Astrugui de Gerunda quondam Muriveteris, et Astruguetum nepotem prefati Astrugui pupillas, in possessione que sunt[1] de bonis que dictus Astrugus eisdem pupillis legasse dicitur in testamento suo; nec permittatis ipsos pupillos expelli sine cause cognicione de possessione ipsorum bonorum, ipsis facientibus querelantibus de se iusticie complementum.

Et si forte expulsi sunt sine cause cognicione de possessione predictorum bonorum vel partis ipsorum, faciatis eos in eandem possessionem reduci, prout hec de iure et foro seu açunna Iudeorum fuerint facienda.

1. Chancery usage, rarely *nonis.*
1. Sic. For *illorum que sunt de?*

Datum ut supra [Valencie, III nonas Februarii, anno domini MCCLXXX quinto].

29

Barcelona 21 February (1285) 1286
Arch. Crown, Cancelleria, reg. 63, fol. 67

King Alfons orders both the Barcelona bailiff and the Cervera bailiff independently to force the Jews Biona Saltell and Isaac Sa Porta, executors for the will of the deceased Astruc de Porta a Jew of Besalú but resident of Barcelona, to render an accounting to the children or heirs and to their legal guardians about the inheritance. If the executors delay, the officials must make them pledge security, lest the legacies be diminished, and must make them return to heirs or guardians whatever the audit indicates to be returned.

Baiulo Barchinone ac vicario et baiulo Cervarie.

Mandamus vobis quatenus quilibet vestrum sub districtu suo compellatis °[B]iona Saltellis[1] et Isach Sa Porta Iudeos, manumissores testamenti et rerum Astrugi de Porta Iudei Bisulduni quondam habitatori Barchinone, ad reddendum compotum seu racionem filiis seu heredibus dicti defuncti, vel eciam eius curatori seu curatoribus, de hiis que amministraverint de bonis dicti defuncti.

Et si forte dictum compotum haberent retard°[ar]i, faciatis ipsos cavere idonee in posse vestro, taliter quod ipsa bona nequeant dissipari.

Mandamus eciam vobis quatenus compellatis dictos ma°[nu]missores et bona eorum ad tornandum dictis heredibus seu eorum curatoribus quecumque facto computo tornare teneantur.

Datum Barchinone, IX kalendas Marcii, [anno domini MCCLXXXV].

1. Régné: Alcolf.

30

Barcelona 25 February (1285) 1286
Arch. Crown, Cancelleria, reg. 63, fol. 68v

King Pere had ordered the Lérida bailiff Esteve de Cardona to conduct an investigation against Bonadona the wife of the deceased Jew of Lérida Jahudà of Limós (modern Limoux) and her accomplices and against witnesses in the case who perjured themselves. Pere had insisted that Cardona must carry out the process to a final sentence and forward it to the king. Now King Alfons repeats Pere's orders and again demands a final sentence, to be forwarded immediately along with a set day for its reading before the king and the culprits, and for its execution.

Alfonsus fideli suo Stephano de Cardona ba°[iu]lo Ilerde.

Cum dominus rex inclite recordacionis Petrus, rex Aragonum pater meus, mandaverit vobis per litteras suas quod super negocio inquisicionis (quam de mandato dicti domini patris mei faciebatis) contra Bonamdonam uxorem quondam Iahudani de Limos Iudei Ilerde et alios consortes suos, racione fraudis per eos commisse ut dicitur in testamento dicti Iahudani, et contra quosdam eciam productos in ipso negocio qui in deposicionibus eorum variabant subornari, procederetis usque ad diffinitivam sentenciam, et postea processum ipsius inquisicionis ad eum remitteretis:

Mandantes vobis quatenus, iuxta mandatum dicti domini patris mei predicti, in ipso negocio usque ad diffinitivam sentenciam procedatis; et ipsum negocium seu processum nobis in continenti mittatis sub vestri sigilli munimine interclusi, assignando diem idoneam partibus qua coram nobis comparentur ad audiendam sentenciam super ipso negocio et ad procedendum prout fuerit faciendum.

Datum Barchinone, V kalendas Marcii, [anno domini MCCLXXXV].

31

Palma de Majorca — 6 July 1288
Arch. Hist. Nac., Clero, — [13 June 1292]
Dominicanos, Palma, carp. 89

The will of Salema, the son of Aaron b. Aarde, on his deathbed, analyzed at length above in chapter 4.

Hoc est translatum sumptum fideliter a quodam testamento cuius tenor talis est.

Quoniam nullus in carne positus mortem evadere potest, idcirco ego Zalema filius Aaron ben Aarde Iudeus, gravi detentus egritudine, pleno tamen sensu meo sanaque memoria, meum facio et ordino testamentum in quo eligo manumissorem meum Maymonam uxorem meam, cui rogando precipio et plenam confero ei potestatem quod (si me mori contigerit antequam aliud mihi condere liceat testamentum) ipsa petat, vendat, recipiat, distribuat, dividat, et ordinet omnia bona mobilia et immobilia prout in hoc meo testamento scriptum invenerit et ordinatum.

In primis eligo sepulturam meam in cimiterio Iudeorum. Item volo quod dentur quinque solidi amore dei.

Item dimitto Maazuga filie mee uxori den [=d'En] Horsa Iudeo pro complemento partis, hereditatis, et legitime sibi pertinentis in bonis meis: decem solidos regalium Valencie, in quibus et in eo quod sibi dedi tempore nupciarum suarum, ipsam michi heredem instituo.

Item dimitto Axera filie mee, uxori quondam Iacob ben Salmo Iudei, pro complemento partis, hereditatis, et legitime sibi pertinentis in bonis meis: decem solidos dicte monete, in quibus et in eo quod sibi dedi tempore nupciarum suarum, michi heredem instituo.

Item recognosco quod Maymonus filius meus habet medietatem in quadam Sarracena negra nomine Maymona, que fuit de Minoricha, quam ego emi a Raimundo Alber; et medietatem precii ipsius Sarracene solvit dictus Maymonus filius meus, quamvis instrumentum empcionis mee dicte Sarracene fiat meo nomine.

Item dimitto dicto Maymono filio meo pro complemento partis, hereditatis, et legitime sibi pertinentis in bonis meis: medietatem pro indiviso tocius medietatis <mee partis> domorum, quas ego et Marçoch ben Aaron Iudeus frater meus habemus medio per medium intus civitatem Maioricarum satis prope domos sinagoge. Et ipsas domos tenemus per Raimundum de Trilea; qui Raimundus de Trilea predictus predictas domos habeat pro alodio.

Item dimitto dicto Maymono filio meo medietatem tocius medietatis mee quarundam aliarum domorum, quas ego et dictus Marçoch ben Aaron frater meus habemus intus civitatem Maioricarum et tenent se cum predictis domibus maioribus superius nominatis; pro quibus duobus hospiciis tenemur ego et dictus Marçoch facere dicto Raimundo de Trilea (cuius sunt [=est] alodium) duos morabatinos censuales, de quibus duobus morabatinis censualibus [*illegible, 8 words*] medium morabatini.

Volentes quod dictus Maymonus filius meus teneatur dare Abrafim et Carime, filiis meis fratribus suis, in auxilium maritandi et nutriendi: triginta libras regalium Valencie, equis porcionibus. Quas triginta libras teneatur solvere dictus Maymonus predictis fratribus suis infra spacium trium annorum post obitum meum. Et si forte dictus Maymonus filius meus predictas triginta libras noluerit vel non poterit dare dictis filiis meis, fratribus suis s[c]ilicet Abrafim et Carime, non habeat nisi tantum terciam partem dicte medietatis mee dictorum duorum hospiciorum.

Laudo et concedo Maymone uxori mee suum sponsalicium, prout in instrumento suo dotalicio continetur.

Solutis legatis predictis et debitis meis persolutis, omnia alia bona mea mobilia et immobilia dimitto et concedo dictis Abrafim et Carime filiis meis—sub hac forma quod dicta Maymona, uxor mea mater eorum, teneat predictos [=pro dictis *etc.*?] infantes filios meos s[c]ilicet Abrafim et Carimam bona eorum; et vivat de dictis bonis simul cum dictis filiis meis quousque dicta Carima virum duxerit.

Et volo quod dicta uxor mea possit maritare de dictis bonis predictam Carimam, filiam mei et ipsius uxoris mee, cognicione ipsius uxoris mee et prout ipsa voluerit. Et in eo quod dicta uxor mea dabit de dictis bonis meis predicte Carime cum viro, ipsam Carimam michi heredem instituo pro parte, hereditate, et legitima sibi pertinente et pertinere debente in bonis meis.

Dono nutricem et curatricem dictis Abrafim et Carime filiis meis dictam Maymonam uxorem meam, que ipsos et eorum bona teneat, regat, procuret, et aministret, quousque dicta Carima pervenerit ad etatem quindecim annorum, et tunc dicta mater sua teneatur eam maritare. \Et maritata dicta Carima, totum residuum dictorum bonorum dimitto dicto Abraffim filio meo pro parte, hereditate, et legitima sibi pertinente et pertinere debente in bonis meis./ Et postquam dicta Carima maritata fuerit, sit ipsa uxor mea domina et potens omnium aliorum bonorum mobilium et immobilium dicto Abrafim filii mei, de tota vita ipsius uxoris mee.

Et si forte, cum dictus Abrafim filius meus pervenerit ad etatem viginti annorum, voluerit habere partem suam dictorum bonorum, recipiat dictus Abraffim filius meus medietatem omnium bonorum mobilium et immobilium que sibi dimitto, maritata prius dicta Carima.

Et solutis legatis meis predictis et debitis in qua medietate in dicto casu, ipsum michi heredem instituo pro parte, hereditate, et legitima sibi pertinente et pertinere debente in bonis meis.

Et alia medietas eorundem bonorum mobilium et immobilium sit dicte Maymone uxoris mee, ad omnes voluntates suas faciendas.

Recognosco quod dictus Maymonus filius meus tenet a me in commanda viginti et unam libras regalium Valencie cum carta, parum plus vel minus, quas solvere teneatur uxori mee, que ipsas viginti et unam libras ponat et teneat in bonis meis supra dictis.

Est enim certum quod, de predicta medietate dicte medietatis mee dictorum duorum hospiciorum quam superius dimitto dicto Maymono filio meo sub condicionibus ante dictis, feceram dividere [?] eidem Maymono donacionem cum carta que nondum perfecta et nec venit ad effectum.

Hoc est autem ultima voluntas mea, quam laudo et concedo et volo valere prout testamentum et iura ultime voluntatis mee; que si non valet iure testamenti, saltem valeat iure codiciliorum vel cuiuslibet alterius iuris ultime voluntatis.

Actum est hoc II nonas Iulii, anno domini MCCLXXX octavo.

Signum[1] Saleme filii quondam Aaron ben Aarde predicti, qui hoc meum testamentum laudo, concedo, et firmo.

Testes huius testamenti sunt Petrus de Algayre, Arnaldus Sureda, Petrus Martini, Berengarius Amenlerii, Felicius Maguenerii, Petrus Ollarii, Petrus de Vallibono,[2] Maymonus Abenono Iudeus, et Omar ben Annum Iudeus.

Sig+num Petri Rosseti notarii publici Maioricarum, qui hoc scribi fecit et clausit, cum litteris rasis et emendatis in linea XIIII ubi scribitur

1. The usual internal cross seems overwritten or corrected here.

2. A little apart, the last third of this line is in Hebrew. Transliterated, Norman Roth makes it out as: . . . *melamed ḥatamti s-r-a [s-q-a?] modeh ʿomar ʿed maimon ben noro [nuru?] ʿed*. Thus the names "Omar, witness," and "Maimon b. Noro, witness" seem clear.

"trium" et cum litteris apositis in linea XXIIII ubi scribitur "siti," et cum literis rasis et emendatis in linea XXVI ubi scribitur "supra dictis."

Sig + num Geraldi de Marina notarii publici Maioricarum, testis.

Signum Bernardi de Sancto Martino notarii publici Maioricarum, testis.

Sig + num Arnaldi de Sancto Martino notarii publici Maioricarum qui hec scribi et translatari fecit fideliter a suo originali testamento, et cum eodem diligenter comprobavit et clausit idus Iunii, anno domini millesimo CC nonagesimo secundo, cum scripto in XVII linea ubi dicitur "et ma," et in XVIII linea ubi scribitur "[ma]ritatata[3] dicta Carima, totum residuum dictorum bonorum dimitto dicto Abraffim filio meo pro parte, hereditate, et legitima sibi pertinente et pertinere debente in bonis meis."

32

Montpellier 8 November 1289
Arch. Crown, Cancelleria, reg. 80, fol. 95v

A lawsuit was in progress between Mossé b. Zabara ("Cabra") a Jew of Lérida and Chayim ("Kaim") or Hayyim Azarel and his son David, in connection with Mossé's previous marriage with the daughter of Chayim, "on which there are Hebrew documents." King Alfons orders the bailiff of Lérida to have the trial settled "according to Hebrew law and by Jews." If the situation has been properly understood by the king, the bailiff is to "assign as judge for this a Jew competent and not unacceptable to the parties" to hear and judge the matter.

Baiulo Ilerde.

Cum cause vertantur inter Mosse Avincabra[1] Iudeum Ilerde ex una parte et Kaim Azcarel et David eius filium ex altera, racione matrimonii olim contracti inter dictum Mosse et filiam dicti Kaim, super quibus sunt instrumenta ebraica, concedimus quod predicta habeant secun-

3. *Sic.*

1. Régné so reads; I have problems with the four letters and overstroke, without being able to offer an alternative reading. Arabic *ibn* indicates a Hebraic equivalent rather than Catalan or Occitan *cabra/cabrit* (see chap. 1, n. 26, and chap. 3, n. 31).

dum ius ebraicum terminari ut dicitur et per Iudeos, et quod sic est fieri etc.

Mandantes, si est ita, assignatis super premissis in iudicem unum Iudeum, sufficientem et partibus non suspectum, qui auditis partium rebus determinaret.

Datum ut supra [Datum in Montepessulano, VI idus Novembris, anno domini MCCLXXXIX].

33

Valencia 17 January (1291) 1292[1]
Arch. Crown, Cancelleria, reg. 192, fol. 74

King Jaume II grants to the Jewish community present and future of Valencia city that all Hebrew documents made about any agreements between Jews are to be mutually observed and have the force of law "just as those Hebrew charters or documents were accustomed to be observed and used in the times of the illustrious lords kings Jaume [I] and Pere [III]."

Iacobus etc. volumus et concedimus, vobis universitati aliame Iudeorum Valencie presentibus et futuris, quod omnes carte sive instrumenta ebrayca confecta sive conficienda super aliquibus contraccionibus initis seu ineundis inter aliquos Iudeos ad invicem observentur et roboris obtineant firmitatem: prout temporibus illustrium dominorum regis Iacobi etc. et domini regis Petri etc. ipse carte seu instrumenta hebrayca consueverant esse observata et usitata.

Mandantes per presentes universis officialibus nostris presentibus et futuris quod vobis unicuique vestrum observent et observari faciant omnia instrumenta et cartas ebraycas super contraccionibus °[initis seu ineundis], factis seu faciendis, prout temporibus dictorum dominorum regum consueverint observari.

Datum ut supra [XVI kalendas Februarii, anno domini mille CCXCI].

°[Signum Iacobi dei gracia regis] Aragonum etc.

1. From the preceding document's dateline.

34

Barcelona 21 April 1300
Arch. Crown, Cancelleria, reg. 197, fol. 106rv

Jaume II had learned that some Jews of the Zaragoza community, "fraudulently and with no small damage" to crown interests, had hidden possessions on which they ought to have paid taxes into "the chests or collecting point" for crown taxes. The king had then ordered Guillem Palasí "to compel the rabbis or scribes of the community who had exercised the office of scribe of the collections or tax-chests" both to show the financial documentation and to undergo an audit on tax receipts during his reign. Envoys now went to the king in person, showing a privilege given and sealed by Jaume I to the Zaragoza Jewry and "to all the communities of the Jews of Aragon" assuring them that "from now on forever he would never see or cause to be seen the writings, charters, and secret documents of the said Jews." The king consequently waives all charges up to the present against the "rabbis or scribes," the officials, and each and every Jew, including future claims ("except for grievances [legally brought] by one or more Jews of that community"). Witnesses include Guillem d'Anglesola, Pere Cornel, Berenguer d'Entença and Bernat Guillem d'Entença, and Ramon de Vilamalur.

Noverint universi quod, cum nobis Iacobo etc. per aliquos relatum fuisset quod aliqui Iudei aliame civitatis Cesarauguste fraudose et in nostri non modicum preiudicium absconderant aliqua bona sua, pro quibus solvere tenebantur in archis sive collectis que per ipsam aliamam fiebant pro solvendis tributo, peytis, et aliis exaccionibus regalibus (quas aliama dictorum Iudeorum nobis tenebatur solvere et debebat), et propterea nos per nostram litteram mandavissemus fideli scriptori nostro Guillelmo Palazini ut compelleret rabis sive scriptores aliame predicte, qui a tempore nostri regiminis citra exercuerunt officium scribanie collecte sive tallie archarum predictarum, ad hostendendum et tradendum sibi loco nostri albaranum sive scripta que prefati Iudei in archis seu collectis predictis solvere tenebantur; et quod eciam compelleret adenatatos seu collectores denariorum dictarum archarum et eorum bona ad accedendum eidem nomine nostro racionem et compotum de hiis que collegerunt et receperunt et amministrarunt infra tempus predictum, de collectis sive talliis vel archis predictis, et ad restituendum, si qua de predictis (recepto et facto compoto) constituere tenerentur: accesserunt ad nostram presenciam nuncii aliame Iudeorum Cesarauguste predictorum, et exhibentes ac ostendentes nobis quoddam [*fol. 106v*] privilegium tam ipsi aliame quam aliis aliamis Iudeorum Aragonie per recolende memorie dompnum Iacobum regem Aragonie avum nostrum concessum eis sigillo maiori cereo pendenti munitum, in quo prefatus dominus Iacobus avus noster statuit in perpetuum quod nunquam de cetero videret nec videri faceret scripta, cartas vel secreta dictorum Iudeorum, nobis humiliter supplicarunt ut a processu predicto desisti facere mandaremus.

Nos autem eorum supplicacionibus benignius inclinati, cum Iudeis aliame Cesarauguste predicte micius agere volentes, absolvimus, remittimus, et indulgemus per nos et nostros rabis seu scriptoribus aliame predicte, secretariis, collectoribus, necnon adelantatis, et universis et singulis Iudeis eiusdem aliame et bonis eorum perpetuo, omnem peticionem et demandam quam contra vos seu aliquos ex ipsis facere et movere possemus racione predicta, usque ad diem qua presens carta nostra conficitur; volentes eciam et concedentes eisdem quod de cetero nos et nostri contra ipsos vel eorum aliquem pro predictis in casu huiusmodi nullam peticionem seu demandam faciemus nec fieri mandabimus, nisi ad querimonia Iudeorum dicte aliame vel aliquorum seu alicuius eorum; et in eo capi procederemus, et procedi faceremus, in eis prout nobis videretur, non iniuriando Iudeis aliame predicte.

Mandamus itaque per presens privilegium nostrum universis officialibus et subditis nostris presentibus et futuris quod hanc remissionem, absolucionem, et indulgenciam nostram, et omnia alia et singula in presenti carta nostra contenta, firma habeant et observent et non contraveniant nec aliquem contravenire permittant aliqua racione.

Datum Barchinone, undecimo kalendas Madii, anno domini millesimo trescentesimo.

Sig + num Iacobi dei gracia regis Aragonum etc.

Testes sunt:	Bernardus Guillelmi de Entença	Raimundus de Vilamuro
Petrus Cornelis	Guillelmus de Angularia	Berengarius de Entença

35

Puigcerdá 23 October 1306
Arch. Hist. Puigcerdá
Protocols: M. d'Alb/B. Mauri,
Liber testamentorum, 1306–1307, fol. 12v

Last testament of Regina, wife of Bondia Coras (or Cresques?), analyzed at length above in chapter 5.

Regina uxor Bondia Coras Iudei condam, licet sim infirma etc., meum facio et condo testamentum de bonis meis, ordinando etc. [*deleted:* in quo constituo]. In primis iubeo corpus meum sepeliri.

Et iubeo dari Iuceff Choen C solidos, quos ei lego. Item dimitto Isaach de Soall XXX solidos. Item heredibus Iuceff de Soall, Iudei condam, XXX solidos. Item XX solidos Momete Iudeo. Item dimitto Mancose uxori Abrahe de la Rotxela Iudei condam, C solidos. [*Deleted:* Et volo iubeo quod secratarii].

Item dimitto Aster sorori dicte Mancose L solidos. Item iubeo fieri quandam caritatem pro anima mea, die obitus mei, cui faciendo assigno et dimitto C solidos.

Item dimitto Aster [*deleted:* uxori] filee mee, uxorique Fagim Bonet Iudei, pro parte et hereditate ei pertinentibus et pertinere debentibus in bonis meis C solidos barchinonenses; in quibus, et in illa dote quam habuit tempore nupciarum eius et dicti viri sui, ipsam heredem mihi instituo, et nisi aliud etc.

Item dimitto Gaux, filie mee et dicti viri mei condam, pro parte et iure ei pertinentibus in bonis meis, C [solidos]; in quibus, et in illa dote quam habuit tempore nupciarum eius et Astruch Iuceff viri eius, ipsam mihi heredem instituo, et nisi aliud etc.

Item dimitto elemosine Iudeorum Podiiceritani, amore dei pro anima mea, quendam lectum meum cum omnibus suis pannis et preparamentis, qui stet in scola Iudeorum predictorum. Et constituo manumissorem meum et exsecutorem huius mei testamenti Astruch Iuceff Iudeum pro[1] cui dono licenciam etc.

In residuis aliis bonis meis, ubicumque sint et quecumque, Bondia

1. *Sic.*

et Iuceff neptes meos filiosque Astruch Bondia Iudei condam mihi heredes universales instituo. Hanc autem etc.

Testes: Matheus de Oliana, Arnaldus Payleres, Raimundus Rahedor, Astruch de Besalu, Iacob Abrahe Choen, Bernardus Duran, Iuceff Abrahe, et Vitalis filius Astruch Crexent.

Debet V solidos Astruch Iuceff.

36

Puigcerdá 6 November 1306
Arch. Hist. Puigcerdá, ibid., fol. 15v

Last testament of Astruga, wife of Jucef Abraham "a Jew of Puigcerdá," analyzed in detail above in chapter 5.

Astruga uxor Iuceff Abrahe Iudei de Podioceritano, licet sim infirma etc., facio meum testamentum de voluntate dicti viri mei de bonis meis etc. In primis dimitto Fave matri mei DC solidos barchinonenses \ad suam voluntatem/ pro parte, hereditate, legitima, et iure sibi pertinentibus et pertineri debentibus in bonis meis.

Et volo et mando quod si dictus Iuceff Abrahe vir meus voluerit providere dicte matri mee in domo sua in cunctis suis corporalibus necessariis in tota vita sua, quod dicta mater mea non possit compellere dictum virum meum ad solvendum sibi denarios ante dictos, dum tamen dictus vir meus non ducat aliam uxorem et velit stare caste. Attamen si dictus vir meus duxerit aliam uxorem, volo quod dicta mater mea possit in continenti compellere dictum virum meum ad solvendum sibi denarios ante dictos.

Item dimitto corone \del/[1] rotle scole Iudeorum Podiiceritani L solidos barchinonenses.

Item dimitto Aster et Bonafylla, filiabus meis et dicti viri mei, omnia mea indumenta et preparamenta mea, quecumque habeo.

Et cum institucio heredis universalis capud sit et fundamentum cuiuslibet testamenti, in residuis omnibus aliis bonis meis mobilibus et immobilibus dictas Aster et Bonamfiliam filias meas mihi heredes universales instituo. Hanc autem etc.

Iuceff vir eius laudo.

1. *Sic.*

VIII idus Novembris.

Testes rogati: Petrus Salmes, Guillelmus Comdor, Bernardus Colomer, Iacobus Orig, Simon de Pinosa rector ecclesie de Castelar, Bondia Abrahe, Iuceff Coen.

Debet V solidos vir.

37

Puigcerdá 9 November 1306
Arch. Hist. Puigcerdá, ibid., fol.15

Last testament of Salamó Bedós, "a Jew who was from Mazères," analyzed in detail above in chapter 5.

V idus Novembris.

Salamo Bedoz Iudeus qui fuit de Matzeres, licet etc., meum facio et condo testamentum de bonis meis [*deleted:* ordinando et] de voluntate et laudamento Astruch Bedoz Iudei patris mei, ordinando etc.

In primis dimitto etc. Astruch Bedoz patri meo viginti turonenses argenti. Item iubeo eidem persolvi et reddi ex una parte septem turonenses argenti et ex alia parte unum florinum auri, quos et quem sibi debeo ex causa mutui.

Et volo [*deleted:* quod] et iubeo quod heredes mei universales subscripti teneantur eidem patri meo providere in comestione et potu bene et decenter, quousque eidem patri meo dictas pecunie quantitates persolverint plenarie. Et dicta provisio non computetur eidem in solutum dictarum pecunie quantitatum.

Item lego Baynole sorori mee decem solidos barchinonenses. Et confiteor insuper quod habui a Cobes uxore mea seu eius nomine, tempore nupciarum pro dote seu quinquaginta libras turonensium parvorum, quas eidem persolvi et reddi iubeo in continenti cum voluerit post meum obitum.

Et volo et mando quod dicta uxor mea sit domina et potens de heredibus meis universalibus subscriptis et bonis suis, dum vita fuerit sibi comes. Et \teneantur dicti heredes mei/ providere sibi in tota vita sua in suis omnibus corporalibus necessariis bene et decenter.

Item volo, iubeo atque mando quod heredes mei universales subscripti provideant et providere teneantur bene et decenter Bonatose filie mee et dicte uxoris mee in omnibus suis corporalibus necessariis, tantum et tamdiu quousque Vidas de Lunello Iudeus maritus dicte Bonatose cum ipsa habitabit et cum ea residenciam faciet continuam in una domo sub una commonia [=communia], expensa, et familiaritate. Et tunc temporis, cum dictus Vidas cum dicta Bonatosa habitabit, volo quod dentur sibi decem solidos barchinonenses quos eidem lego; in quibus, et in illa dote quam eidem Bonatose dedi cum dicto viro suo, ipsam mihi heredem instituo [*deleted:* et nichil aliud].

Attamen volo et mando quod si dictus Vidas de Lunello est mortuus vel eciam de cetero morienter [=morietur] infra spacium duorum annorum proximo subsequencium post meum obitum, quod heredes mei universales subscripti teneantur dictam filiam meam Bonatosam congrue maritare; et dent et teneantur ei dare pro dote sua tunc temporis viginti quinque libras turonensium parvorum, quoniam illas sibi lego sub dicta forma et modo pro parte, hereditate, et iure ei pertinentibus et pertinere debentibus in bonis meis, et nisi aliud etc.

Et cum institucio heredis universalis capud est etc., in residuis omnibus aliis bonis meis ubique sint et quecumque, Elias et Mosse Bedoz filios meos et dicte uxoris mee mihi heredes universales instituo.

Et substituo, volo, et mando quod si alter dictorum filiorum meorum decederet quandocumque sine prole legitima, quod pars bonorum parti utrique eorum legatorum remaneant et revertantur [=remaneat et revertatur] iure substitucionis alteri eorum vivo et superstiti et dicte Cubes uxori mee et dicte Bonatose filee mee, inter eos equis partibus dividenda. Hanc autem etc.

Astruch Bedoz pater dicti Salamonis laudat et confirmat.

Testes rogati: Salamo de Valencia, Deuslosal de Besaldu, Salamo Iuceff, Iacob Astruch, [*deleted:* Rotben] Ruben Iuceff—omnes Iudei. Arnau durg [=d'Urg] et Raimundus Serra, Christiani.

Debet XII denarios.

38

Puigcerdá 21 November 1306
Arch. Hist. Puigcerdá, ibid., fol. 17rv

Last testament of Gentil, wife of Jacob b. Abraham Cohen, analyzed in detail above in chapter 5.

XI kalendas Decembris

Gentill uxor Iacob Abrahe Choen Iudei, licet etc., meum facio et condo testamentum de bonis meis, ordinando etc.

In quo testamento constituo manumissorem meum et executorem huius mee ultime voluntatis dictum Iacobum virum meum qui [= cui] dono etc.

Item accipio mihi de bonis meis pro anima mea C solidos barchinonenses quos donari et distribui iubeo pro anima mea, ad noticiam dicti viri mei et heredum universalium subscriptorum \infra unum annum/.

Item dimitto Iudee filie mee uxori Fabib [*deleted:* Maymo] \Salamonis/ de Barchinona Iudei pro parte, hereditate, et iure ei pertinentibus et pertinere debentibus in bonis meis quinque solidos. In quibus, et in illa dote [*deleted:* qua] seu parte eiusdem dotis quam ego et dictus vir meus ei dedimus cum dicto viro suo \tempore nupciarum ut in instrumentis nupciarum vocatis [*or:* votatis?] plenius et melius continetur/, ipsam mihi heredem instituo, et nisi aliunde etc.

Item dimitto Regine filie Goyo filie mee condam [= quondam] pro parte, hereditate, et iure ei pertinentibus et pertinere debentibus successione et racione dicte matris sue in bonis meis V solidos barchinonenses. In quibus et in illa dote cuiuscumque quantitatis existat quam ipsa Goyo filia mea et Astruch Deuslosall Iudei viri eius viventis[1] habuerunt et receperunt tempore nupciarum de bonis meis et dicti viri mei ut [in] instrumentis nupciarum vocatis [*or* votatis] ad verba [?] inde confectis continetur melius, ipsam mihi heredem instituo, et nisi aliud etc.

Item dimitto Goyo [*deleted:* filie Adzero] et Atzero filiabus Adzero filie mee condam [= quondam], et Astruch Deuslosall viri eius adhuc viventis, pro parte, hereditate, et iure eis pertinentibus et pertinere debentibus in bonis meis, successione et racione dicte Adzero filie mee videlicet, utrique earum V solidos barchinonenses.

In quibus et in illa dote quam dicta mater earum habuit et recepit tempore nupciarum eius et dicti viri sui generis [mei] et dicti viri mei ut in instrumentis nupciarum vocatis [*or:* votatis?] nupciis inde confectis melius et lacius continetur, utramque earum mihi heredes instituo, et nisi aliunde petere possint etc.

Et quia institucio heredis universalis capud sit et fundamentum cuiuslibet testamenti, in residuis omnibus aliis bonis ubique sint et quecumque Abraham Iacob et Davit Iacob Choen, filios meos et dicti viri mei, mihi heredes universales instituo. Et volo et substituo atque

1. *Sic*, phrase in genitive.

mando quod, si alter eorum filiorum meorum heredum universalium decederet quandocumque sine prole legitima, quod pars bonorum pertinens utrique legatorum alteri eorum vivo et superstiti iure substitucionis remaneat et revertatur. Hoc autem etc.

Testes rogati: Bernardus Petri, Matheus den [=d'En] Bort, Iohannes Baiuli, Bernardus Collati, Guido de Piritis, Arnau Ponz, Durandus Salamonis, Salamon Iuceff.

39

Teruel 1 June 1310
Arch. Crown, Cancelleria, reg. 206, fol. 124rv

At the death of Samuel Ibn Vives, the official Arnau Cortit had sequestered his estate, on which the crown had claims because Samuel had stood surety on behalf of the Jew Ayhon (Aylon?) Ibn Menashe who had bought at auction the revenues and bailiate of Játiva. Salamó Ibn Vives (son of the Valencian Jew En Vives Salamó), with Jahudà Ibn Vives as accomplice, had removed a chest of the deceased, in the house of the Valencian Jewess Na Vives, and in defiance of the court seizure had carried away its contents. Worse, he had then forged "a Hebrew document" claiming that the deceased had appointed Samuel and Jahudà his executors. King Jaume II then appointed an investigative commission (the royal judge Jaume de Arters, the citizen Pere de Corell, and the Jew Jahudà Ibn Ḥasan), who cited all Jews with knowledge of the affair to give testimony under penalty of the ban (*alatma*), but the two culprits refused and incurred penalties of person and property. Now the king gives a pardon to Salamó and waiver of prosecution and penalties; but Salamó had to pay 4,000 Barcelona sous through the crown official Pere Martí, and must stand ready to respond at law to civil suits brought by others.

Nos Iacobus etc. attendentes quod tu Salamon Abenvives filius den [=de En] Vives Salamonis Iudei Valencie fuisti inculpatus quod, post emparam[1] pro parte nostra factam per fidelem portarium nostrum Arnaldum Cortit de bonis Samuelis Abenvives quondam Iudei Valencie (racione accionis quam curia nostra habebat contra bona ipsius de-

1. Cf. Catalan *empara,* sequestration.

functi, racione cuiusdam fideiussionis quam fecerat nostre curie pro Ayhono Abenmenax Iudeo, racione baiule Xative et reddituum eiusdem quam et quos olim dictus Ayhonus emerat in encanto) asservisti[2] contra dictam emparam una cum Iahudano Abenvives quandam caxiam dicti defuncti, que erat in domo de Na Vives Iude[e] Valencie, et inde extraxisti res que ibi erant; quodque tu et dictus Iahudanus, asserentes dictum Iudeum defunctum in suo obitu ordinasse te et dictum Iahudanum manumissores suos, fecistis post eius obitum instrumentum ebraycum confici in quo continebatur quod dictus defunctus te et ipsum Iahudanum manumissores suos constituerat:

Et cum de premissis inquireretur veritas per Iacobum de Arteriis iudicem curie nostre, Petrum de Coicilio[3] civem, et Iahudanum Abenhazen Iudeum Valencie a nobis assignatos super inquisicionem huiusmodi, [*fol. 124v*] et fecissent pro parte nostra alatmam poni Iudeis omnibus aliame dicte civitatis ut infra certam diem testimonium perhiberent de hiis que scirent super bonis dicti defuncti, tu contra dictam alatmam omisisti veritatem dicere super hiis que in predictis sciebas infra assignatum tempus in alatma predicta, ob quod penam corporis et bonorum incurrisse dicebaris:

Idcirco de speciali gracia absolvimus, diffinimus, et relaxamus tibi dicto Salamoni Abenvives et bonis tuis perpetuo omnem accionem, questionem, peticionem, et demandam et omnem penam civilem et criminalem et aliam quamlibet quam contra te vel bona tua possemus facere, proponere, vel movere aut eciam infligere nos vel officiales nostri racionibus supra dictis vel qualibet earundem.

Hanc autem absolucionem, diffinicionem, remissionem et relaxacionem facimus per nos et nostros tibi dicto Salamoni et bonis tuis perpetuo de predictis omnibus et singulis eorundem sicut melius dici et intelligi potest ad tuum tuorumque salvamentum et bonum intellectum; sic quod pro premissis vel premissorum aliquo non possis de cetero tu vel bona tua per nos vel officiales nostros requiri, demandari, puniri, seu in aliquo conveniri.

Immo sis inde penitus absolutus, te tamen faciente tuis querelantibus de predictis civilis iusticie complementum.

Pro hac autem absolucione et diffinicione solvisti et dedisti pro nobis fideli thesaurario nostro Petro Martini quattuor milia solidorum Barchinone.

Mandamus igitur per presentes, universis et singulis officialibus

2. For: *asservavisti?*
3. My reading unsure (e.g., Corilo?).

nostris presentibus et futuris, quod huiusmodi absolucionem, diffinicionem, et remissionem nostram teneant et observent et faciant inviolabiliter observari, et non contraveniant nec aliquem contravenire permittant aliqua racione.

In cuius rei testimonium presentem cartam nostram tibi fieri et nostro sigillo pendenti iussimus sigillari.

Datum Turolii, kalendas[4] Iunii, anno domini millesimo CCCX.

Bernardus de Fonte, mandato regio facto per Petrum Martini.

40

Lérida 24 October 1314
Arch. Crown, Cancelleria, reg. 211, fol. 220

Jaume II responds to the petition of the Jewish physician Rabbi Azaria, "the scribe or notary in the Jewry of the Jews of Zaragoza," who is unable to attend to his notarial duties because of his obligation to visit the ill. The king therefore allows him to exercise the notarial office "by a suitable substitute" the rabbi will appoint just as others were accustomed to do in that office. The king notifies the merino of Zaragoza and the Jewish officials (the *mukdamim,* here as *adelantati*).

Nos Iacobus, attendentes te Rabi Azariam fisicum, scriptorem seu notarium in iudaria Iudeorum Cesarauguste, quia habes intendere necessario circa visitacionem infirmorum, non potes [=posse] eo modo intendere circa exercicia officii notariatus predicti: idcirco ad humilem supplicacionem nobis pro parte tua, concedimus tibi quod dictum officium notariatus possis per ydoneum substitutum vel substituendum per te facere, deservire, ac eciam exercere, prout tempore aliorum qui dictum notariatus officium tenuerunt extitit fieri consuetum.

Mandamus itaque per presentem merino nostro Zaragoze et adelantatis Iudeorum predictorum, ac Iudeis ipsis presentibus et futuris, quod concessionem nostram huiusmodi firmam habeant et observent et contra eam non veniant aliqua racione.

In cuius rei testimonium presentem cartam tibi fieri iussimus atque tradi.

4. Chancery usage, rarely *kalendis.*

Datum Ilerde, IX kalendas Novembris, anno domini millesimo CCCXIIII.

Egidius Petri, mandato regio.

41

Valencia 27 February (1317) 1318
Arch. Crown, Cancelleria, reg. 232, fols. 352v–353

Jaume II leases in perpetuity at an annual rent, to Jahudà A(s)darra a Jew of Valencia, "the office of scribe of the community of Jews of Valencia," imposing him or his "suitable substitute" as the monopolistic notary there, for "all documents and other Hebrew writings of any kind of contract." Jahudà can sell, subrent, or alienate (though always preserving the crown ownership or overlordship, and allowing a thirty-day notice for the crown's reserved option to buy back). This notice to both Jahudà and the Jewish community was processed by Clement Salavert and the king's treasurer Pere Martí.

Nos Iacobus etc. cum presenti carta nostra per nos et nostros successores stabilimus et [in] emphiteosim[1] damus et concedimus tibi Iaffudano Acdarra[2] Iudeo Valencie et successoribus tuis in perpetuum officium scribanie aliame Iudeorum Valencie.

Ita quod tu solus et non alius sis scriptor dicte aliame, ac scribas ac scribi facias per substitutum idoneum omnia instrumenta ac alias scripturas ebraycas quorumcumque contractuum fuerint.

Hanc autem stabilicionem [=stabilimentum] et in emphiteosim, donacionem, et concessionem facimus per nos et successores nostros tibi et successoribus tuis perpetuo, sicut melius dici potest et intelligi ad tuum tuorumque salvamentum et bonum intellectum; sub tali tamen pacto, forma, et condicione quod pro censu dicte scribanie, quam tibi stabilimus et in emphiteosim damus et concedimus, detis et solvas nobis et nostris tu et tui, in primo venturo festo nathalis domini et deinde singulis annis in eodem festo, duos morabatinos auri alfonsinos.

In hiis autem non proclames necque facias tu vel tui alium dominium

1. Catalan *enfiteusi*, hereditary lease.
2. Cf. Adarra below in doc. 43.

nisi tantum nos et nostros; liceatque tibi et tuis post dies triginta ex quo in nobis vel baiulo generali regni Valencie fatigati fueritis, predictam scribaniam quam tibi stabilimus et in emphiteosim damus et concedimus vendere, stabilire, sive eciam alienare tuo consimili et tuorum, salvo tamen semper in predictis que tibi stabilimus et in emphiteosim damus et concedimus censum, iura, et dominio et faticha[3] nostri et nostrorum.

Mandantes per presentem cartam nostram baiulo generali regni Valencie universisque officialibus nostris presentibus et futuris quod concessionem et stabilimentum ac donacionem nostram predictam firmam habeant et observent, et ab aliis [*fol. 353*] faciant inviolabiliter observari ut est dictum; et non contraveniant nec aliquem contravenire permittant aliqua racione.

Mandantes nichilominus adelantatis ac universis aliis Iudeis aliame predicte quatenus observando stabilimentum et in emphiteosim, donacionem, et concessionem nostram huiusmodi, te ac substitutum tuum ydoneum habeant pro scriptore ipsius aliame et non alium ut superius continetur.

In cuius rei testimonium, presentem cartam tibi fieri iussimus, nostro pendenti sigillo munitam.

Datum Valencie, III kalendas Marcii, anno domini MCCCXVII.

Clemens de Salaviridi, mandato regio facto per Petrum Martini thesaurarium.

42

Puigcerdá — 20 November 1321
Arch. Hist. Puigcerdá
Protocols: M. d'Oliana/G. Hualart,
Liber testamentorum, 1321–1322, fol. 17

Last testament of Jacob b. Abraham Cohen, Jewish resident of Puigcerdá, on his deathbed, analyzed at length above in chapter 4.

Duodecim kalendas Decembris.

Iacobo Abrae \Coen/ Iudeus habitator Podiiceritani, detentus infirmitate, facio meum testamentum de bonis meis, in quo constituo

3. Wavers between accusative construction and ablative absolute for the four.

manumissores meos Abraam Iacob Choen et Daui Iacob Choen, filios meos et quondam Covallis uxoris mei, quibus dono licenciam divi et destri bona mea etc.

In primis dimitto Sancie neptis [=nepti] mee, filie Suore filie mee quondam, iure institucionis centum solidos.

Item dimitto \ad suum maritagium/ Regine neptis [=nepti] mee, filie dicte filie mee quondam, iure institucionis quinque solidos. Item Guoyo sorori eius neptis [=nepti] mee filie dicte filie mee quondam, iure institucionis V solidos; in quibus, ut [*deleted:* dono] dote quam [*deleted:* sibi] dedi dicte matri earum filee mee, ipsas neptas[1] meas mihi heredes instituo. Et nihil aliud in bonis meis petere valeant vel habere.

Item dimitto Iudee, filie mee et dicte uxoris mee quondam, iure institucionis quinque solidos; in quibus ut dote quam dedi, cum Philippo Maimo, ipsam mihi heredem instituo.

Item dimitto [*deleted:* Dauiu] Davidi nepti meo, filio dicte Iudee filie mee XX solidos.

Item confiteor quod habui in dotem a dicta uxore mea in dotem suam [*sic*] mille solidos, [*deleted:* in quibus et aliis bonis factis] \in quibus et in aliis/ dictos filios meos Abraee [*sic*] et Daviu filios meos heredes universales instituit testamentum. Quos mille solidos eis desolvi iubeo de bonis meis.

Item confido filio meo Abrae quod debeo sibi centum libras barchinonenses cum carta, quas sibi solvi iubeo de bonis meis.

Quibus omnibus solutis, in residuis aliis bonis meis, ipsos Abraam et Daviu filios meos [*canceled:* mihi] ipsos mihi heredes instituo. Hec autem etc.

Testes rogati: Petrus Percats sutor, Iacobus Brahl, Iacobus Borser, Philipus Celarer iunior, Guillem de Eyna, Vincencius de Eyna, et Petrus Ermengau et [*canceled:* Levi] Boniacip Levi Iudeus.

43

Barcelona — 1 April 1327
Arch. Crown, Cancelleria, reg. 229, fol. 274v

After receiving the monopoly on drafting Hebrew documents with notarial impact in Valencia city's Jewish community, both between local

1. First and third declension forms are medieval variants, here mixed.

Jews and with outsiders, Jahudà de Adarra substituted two Jewish scribes to do the actual work. These men grossly overcharged the customers and after payment did not always deliver but demanded a second fee. Responding to the community's plea for help, the king orders the bailiff together with the Jewish officials (*mukdamim,* here as *adelantati*) to ensure reasonable prices and faster service, under threat of removal and other penalties. Moreover, decrees or instructions made by the community as such, both on taxes and other affairs, must henceforth be done "by a Christian notary and not by a Jew, so . . . they can easily be found, and so nothing can be added or taken out or changed." Domènec de Biscarrués processed the charter.

Fideli suo baiulo regni Valencie generali, presenti et qui pro tempore fuerit, salutem etc.

Ex parte aliame Iudeorum civitatis Valencie fuit nobis expositum reverenter quod, cum Iahuda Adarra Iudeus aliame predicte ex concessione nostra (ad certum censum sibi factum) obtineat[1] scribaniam eorum [instrumentorum] que fiunt in ebrayco in iudaria civitatis predicte, inter Iudeos ipsius aliame ad invicem vel alios contrahentes, et dictus Iaffuda stabiliverit seu substituerit in dicta scribania duos Iudeos qui huius \Modi/ scripturas conficiunt: ipsi substituti immoderatum salarium recipiunt ab illis Iudeis quibus scripturas conficiunt supra dictas et eis eciam ipso persoluto salario nequeunt habere instrumenta ab eis confecta, immo habent iterum eis satisfacere pro eisdem.

Quocirca nobis fuit humiliter supplicatum ut super premissis dignaremur de congruo remedio providere.

Qua supplicacione benigne admissa, vobis comittimus et mandamus quatenus, una cum adenatatis aliame predicte qui sunt vel erunt pro tempore, taxeatis scripturas predictas; et aliter super premissis providere curetis quod salarium immoderatum non exigatur per dictos scriptores, et quod possint sine alia extorsione habere scripturas breviter et absque maliciosa dilacione illi qui eas confici fecerint per predictos—cum interdum dilacio circa talia questum sapere videatur.

Ad que omnia inconcusse servanda, per privacionem dicti officii seu eius exercicii, et aliam adieccionem penarum, illos fortiter compellatis.

Preterea volumus atque mandamus quod ordinaciones atque statuta de cetero facienda per dictam aliamam, tam super peytis et contribucionibus eorundem quam super aliis, conficiantur per notarium Chris-

1. *Sic,* though context suggests a past tense.

tianum et non per Iudeum, ut quicquid super premissis statutum et ordinatum fuerit possit faciliter inveniri, nec quicquam circa ea addi seu detrahi valeat aut mutari.

Presentes vero inde fieri iussimus, sigillo nostro pendenti munitas.

Datum Barchinone, quinto nonas[2] Aprilis, anno domini MCCCXX septimo.

Dominicus de Biscarra, ex peticione provisa in audiencia.

44

Gerona — 25 July 1343
Arch. Dioc., Registres episcopals, VIII, fol. 66

Isaac Astruc in a suit before Bishop Arnau de Montrodon of Gerona has placed in evidence a notarized charter, showing that Guillem Llorenç of Sant Miquel de Fluviá owed 72 Barcelona sous to Isaac and Abraham Astruc, Jews of Gerona, now overdue. Guillem had assigned as security "three copper pots," and Isaac asks the bishop to force Guillem to hand over the pots or else pay "the debt and its interest." Bishop Arnau therefore orders Guillem to surrender "the said pots" or pay the debt or else to appear on the fourth day after receipt of this notice before the episcopal court at Báscara to answer his creditors. If Guillem refuses, the bishop's court will prosecute him.

Noveritis quod, comparens coram presencia nostra Issachus Astruchi Iudeus Gerunde, nobis exhibuit et hostendit quoddam instrumentum publicum inter alia continens quod Guillelmus Laurencii de Sancto Michaeli de Fluviano in quodam debito septuaginta duorum solidorum barchinonensium est sibi et Abrae Astrugui Iudeo Gerunde principaliter obligatus.

Pro quibus eis exsolvendis certo termino, iam elapso, sibi obligavit; ac vobis eorum nomine readidit[1] tres ollas de cupro.

Verum cum de dicto debito, ut ipse Iudeus asserit, non sit eidem satisfactum, et a nobis petierit vos compelli per nos ad readendum a eis dictas ollas vel sibi satisfieri in debito supra dicto et lucro eiusdem, ide-

2. For: *kalendas Aprilis.*
1. *Sic*; not *reddo.*

irco vobis per presentes dicimus et mandamus quatenus ipsum debitum Iudeis ut convenit exsolvatis, vel tradatis sibi dictas ollas; aut quarta die a recepcione presencium in antea computanda, coram curia nostra de Baschera compareatis ipsis Iudeis in iusticia responsuri.

Alioquin contra vos procederemus, iusticia mediante.

Datum Gerunde, sub nostro sigillo minori, VII kalendas Iulii, anno predicto [MCCCXLIII].

45

Puigcerdá — 22 July 1348

Arch. Hist. Puigcerdá,
Protocols: B. Manresa/J. Montaner
Liber testamentorum, 1348–1349, fol. 10

Last testament of Mossé Ali Bedós, a Jew of Perpignan, analyzed at length above in chapter 4.

Mosse Ali Bedoz Iudeus Podiiceritanie, licet etc., facio meum testamentum de bonis meis etc. in quo constituo manumissores meos etc. Lomach Astruch et Mosse Ysach Choen Iudios Podiiceritanie, quibus dono etc.

Et eligo meo corpori sepulturam in fossario Iudeorum Podiiceritanie.

Et dito Astruch Bedoç et Salamo Bedoç fratribus meis, utrique pro parte etc., decem solidos. Item dito Salamoni, Mosse, et Mree filiis meis et [*deleted:* de] Regine uxoris mee iure institucionis etc. septem libras [et] decem solidos barchinonenses.

Et volo et substituo quod, si alter dictorum filiorum et filie meorum decederet quandocumque, quod pars [=partes] premortui alteris vivis et superstitibus revertantur iure substitucionis. Et si omnes decederent sine prole legitima, quod legata per me eis facta revertantur iure substitucionis dicte Regine matri eorum.

Item dito quinque solidos amore dei ad cognicionem dictorum meorum manumissorum.

Item dono pro azinis fossarii, III solidos.

Item dito omnes vestes meas amore dei ad cognicionem dictorum manumissorum.

Item dito pro luminaria scole II solidos.

In residuis aliis bonis etc. Reginam uxorem meam mihi heredem universalem instituo, que teneatur etc. Hanc autem etc.

Testes rogati: Franciscus Solerii, Bernardus Coloni, Iacobus Scribe, Bernardus Alo, Iacobus Vilauta, Petrus Vilauta, et Bernardus Maresa.

XXII die mensis Iulii.

Notes

Abbreviations

Arch. Cath. Barc.: Arxiu Capitular de la Catedral, Barcelona

Arch. Crown: Arxiu de la Corona d'Aragó, Barcelona

Arch. Dioc. Gerona: Arxiu Diocesà de Girona, Gerona

Arch. Hist. Gerona: Arxiu Històric de Girona

Arch. Hist. Nac.: Archivo Histórico Nacional, Madrid

Arch. Hist. Puigcerdá: Arxiu Històric Comarcal de Puigcerdà

Preface

1. On that collection see Sebastià Bosom i Isern, "Arxiu Històric Comarcal de Puigcerdà," *Guia dels arxius històrics de Catalunya,* 5 vols. to date (Barcelona, 1982–1992), 5:127–217, esp. 187–190; and Sebastià Bosom i Isern and Salvador Galceran i Vigué, *Catàleg de protocols de Puigcerdà,* Inventaris d'arxius notarials de Catalunya 4 (Barcelona, 1983).

Introduction

1. On the peculiarities, uses, and limitations of medieval wills as well as their bibliography, see Steven Epstein, *Wills and Wealth in Medieval Genoa 1150–1250* (Cambridge, Mass., 1984); Michael Sheehan, *The Will in Medieval England from the Conversion of the Anglo-Saxons to the End of the Thirteenth Century* (Toronto, 1963); Samuel K. Cohn, Jr., *Death and Property in Siena, 1205–1800: Strategies for the Afterlife* (Baltimore, 1988); Louis de Charrin, *Les*

testaments de la région de Montpellier au moyen âge (Ambilly, 1961); and Jacques Chiffoleau, "Les testaments provençaux et comtadins à la fin du moyen âge: Richesse documentaire et problèmes d'exploitation," in Paolo Brezzi and Egmont Lee, eds., *Sources of Social History: Private Acts of the Late Middle Ages* (Toronto, 1984), 132–152. For a wider context of perceptions and afterlife strategies, see Chiffoleau's earlier *La comptabilité de l'au-delà: Les hommes, la mort, et la religion dans la région d'Avignon à la fin du moyen âge (vers 1320–vers 1480)* (Rome, 1980), and Michel Vovelle, *La mort et l'occident de 1300 à nos jours* (Paris, 1983). See also the older Henri Auffroy, *Évolution du testament en France des origines au XIII*ᵉ siècle (Paris, 1899). On Catalan wills see the works below in chap. 2, n. 1; on Aragonese wills see chap. 1, nn. 22–25, and text.

The past decade has suddenly seen a spate of books on wills in early modern Spain, especially in the eighteenth century, notably Carlos M. N. Eire, *From Madrid to Purgatory: The Art and Craft of Dying in Sixteenth-Century Spain* (Cambridge, 1995). By the sixteenth century, however, the societal and testamentary context had become radically different, while the profession of notary had split into categories such as the esteemed class of governmental bureaucrats and the unesteemed class of drafters of private contracts and testaments.

2. For coping with Jewish name forms, Benzion Kaganoff's *A Dictionary of Jewish Names and Their History* (New York, 1977) is an essential starting point; Kaganoff's charming and erudite essays survey the whole field. Simon Seror's *Les noms des juifs de France au moyen âge* (Paris, 1989) is invaluable as a dictionary of each name and its variants, meticulously arranged by time and place, with source citation for each item. Seror is useful here especially for his Occitan resources, particularly for Catalan Roussillon and its neighboring regions. Very handy also is Alfred J. Kolatch, *The Complete Dictionary of English and Hebrew First Names* (Middle Village, N.Y., 1984); a more "popular" selection is in Kolatch's *The New Name Dictionary: Modern English and Hebrew Names* (Middle Village, N.Y., 1989). For Judeo-Arabic families and their variant-named branches, the nearly 1,200 pages of Abraham I. Laredo, *Les noms des juifs du Maroc: Essai d'onomastique judeo-marocaine* (Madrid, 1978), include much Spanish and Catalan material, down to specific individuals in each branch. Shlomo D. Goitein also takes up Judeo-Arabic names in his *A Mediterranean Society: The Jewish Communities of the Arab World as Portrayed in the Documents of the Cairo Geniza,* 6 vols. (Berkeley, Los Angeles, London, 1967–1993), 1:357–358; 2:237; 3:6–14, 63–64, 314–319; 5:396–397. Joaquim Miret i Sans and Moïse Schwab have several pages of comment on difficult names of Catalan Jews at the end of their "Documents sur les juifs catalans aux XIᵉ, XIIᵉ, et XIIIᵉ siècles," *Revue des études juives* 68 (1914): 190–196. The classic article by Irene Garbell, "The Pronunciation of Hebrew in Medieval Spain," *Homenaje a Millás-Vallicrosa,* 2 vols. (Barcelona, 1954–1956), 1:647–696, touches throughout on names, including Catalan names. For the problems in translating Latin names into Catalan and the many resources, see Robert I. Burns, S.J., *Society and Documentation in Crusader Valencia* (Princeton, 1985), chap. 15.

3. Kaganoff, *Jewish Names,* 49. The phenomenon of widespread use of

"gentile" names had its antecedents. Leonard Victor Rutgers presents a subtle revisionist examination of Jewish names in third- and fourth-century Rome, for example, where "the majority of names used were typically Late Ancient names rather than specifically Jewish ones" and that "typically Jewish names were not very popular." He concludes that this practice shows "a lively interaction between Jews and non-Jews" but not assimilation or fundamental acculturation since it occurred in a context of strong consciousness of Jewish identity on the part of Jews and recognition of that identity by gentile observers. See his "The Onomasticon of the Jewish Community of Rome: Jews vis-à-vis Non-Jewish Onomastic Practices in Late Antiquity" in his *The Jews in Late Ancient Rome: Evidence of Cultural Interaction in the Roman Diaspora* (Leiden, 1995), 139–175, quotations from pp. xix, 97.

4. Jean Régné, comp., *History of the Jews in Aragon: Regesta and Documents 1213–1327,* ed. Yom Tov Assis, indexed and improved facsimile reprint of French entries of Régné's "Catalogue des actes de Jaime I, Pedro III, et Alfonso III, rois d'Aragon, concernant les juifs (1213–1327)," *Revue des études juives* 60 (1910) to 70 (1920), with supplement for Jaime II, *Revue des études juives* 73 (1923) to 78 (1925) (Jerusalem, 1978). Assis's list of Jewish names is in Régné, *History of the Jews,* 668–703. Joaquim Miret i Sans, *Itinerari de Jaume I "el Conqueridor"* (Barcelona, 1918), list on pp. 588–629.

5. Seror, *Noms des juifs,* xv.

6. On money of the realms and its bibliography, see Burns, *Society and Documentation,* 108–110; Burns, *Medieval Colonialism: Postcrusade Exploitation of Islamic Valencia* (Princeton, 1975), chap. 2, sec. 3, pp. 28–34; Miguel Crusafont i Sabater, *Numismática de la corona catalano-aragonesa medieval (785–1516)* (Madrid, 1982). See also the standard classics, Aloïss Heiss, *Descripción general de las monedas hispano-cristianas desde la invasión de los árabes,* 3 vols. (Madrid, [1865–1869] 1975), 2:182–190, and Joaquim Botet i Sisó, *Les monedes catalanes: Estudi y descripció de les monedes carolingies, comtals, senyorials, reyals, y locals propries de Catalunya,* 3 vols. (Barcelona, [1908] 1976), 2:47–50. The booklet by Leandre Villaronga, *La moneda de Barcelona* (Barcelona, 1976), is a useful overview. And Thomas N. Bisson, *Conservation of Coinage: Monetary Exploitation and Its Restraint in France, Catalonia and Aragon (c. A.D. 1000–c.1225)* (Oxford, 1979), provides thorough background.

7. Burns, *Medieval Colonialism,* 30–31 and passim.

8. Richard Emery, *The Jews of Perpignan in the Thirteenth Century: An Economic Study Based on Notarial Records* (New York, 1959), 129 (quote), 130 (table).

Chapter 1: The World of the Wills

1. On the realms of Aragon see Thomas N. Bisson, *The Medieval Crown of Aragon: A Short History* (Oxford, 1986), with bibliographical essay, and for the thirteenth century Robert I. Burns, S.J., ed., *The Worlds of Alfonso the Learned and James the Conqueror: Intellect and Force in the Middle Ages* (Princeton, 1985), especially the opening chapter. See also Burns, *Muslims,*

Christians, and Jews in the Crusader Kingdom of Valencia: Societies in Symbiosis (Cambridge, 1984), his *Islam under the Crusaders: Colonial Survival in the Thirteenth-Century Kingdom of Valencia* (Princeton, 1973), and his *Society and Documentation in Crusader Valencia* (Princeton, 1985) with his other books in its bibliography.

2. Yom Tov Assis's *The Golden Age of Aragonese Jewry 1213–1327* is forthcoming from the Littman Library press in Oxford, and will become the standard general history. More briefly, see his "The Jews in the Crown of Aragon and Its Dominions" in *Moreshet Sepharad: The Sephardi Legacy,* ed. Haim Beinart, 2 vols. (Jerusalem, 1992), 1:44–102. The *Actes* of the *I Col·loqui d'història dels jueus a la corona d'Aragó* (Lérida, 1991), by over two dozen specialists, has extensive bibliographical and thematic background on the Jews of the realms. More focused is the collection *Mossé ben Nahman i el seu temps: Simposi commemoratiu del vuité centenari del seu naixement 1194–1994* (Gerona, 1994). Less impressive but useful are the studies in *Jornades d'història dels jueus a Catalunya* (Gerona, 1990), especially Asunción Blasco Martínez on Zaragoza and Christian Guilleré on Gerona. A comprehensive annotated bibliography for Catalonia is Jaume Riera i Sans, "Estudis sobre el judaisme català," *Calls* 1 (1986): 93–132 (years 1970–1984), 2 (1987): 181–207 (1929–1969), and 3 (1988–1989): 103–134. For wider bibliographical coverage, not by list but by judicious thematic essays, see Enrique Cantera Montenegro, *Los judíos en la edad media hispana* (Madrid, 1986). A useful survey is Lluís Marcó i Dachs, *Els jueus i nosaltres* (Barcelona, 1977), revised as *Los judíos en Cataluña* (Barcelona, 1985). The standard general survey by Yitzhak Baer, *A History of the Jews in Christian Spain,* 2 vols. (Philadelphia, 1971), continues to fill a void, as does the more interior and domestic survey by Abraham Neuman, *The Jews in Spain: Their Social, Political and Cultural Life during the Middle Ages,* 2 vols. (Philadelphia, 1948). An able survey from Roman times to the Ottoman diaspora and today is Jane S. Gerber, *The Jews of Spain: A History of the Sephardic Experience* (New York, 1992). Yitzhak Baer's *Studien zur Geschichte der Juden im Königreich Aragonien während des 13. und 14. Jahrhunderts* (Berlin, 1913) is newly accessible as *Historia de los judíos en la Corona de Aragón (siglos XIII y XIV)* (Zaragoza, 1985), while his three-volume *Die Juden im christlichen Spanien: Urkunden und Regesten* (1929–1936) is again available (Farnborough, 1970). The large and growing bibliography on the Jews of the realms of Aragon and particularly of the Catalan-speaking lands there will be drawn upon and cited below in connection with local and thematic materials. Especially noteworthy are Leila Berner's 1986 UCLA dissertation, "A Mediterranean Community: Barcelona's Jews under James the Conqueror," and the works by Yom Tov Assis, Robert Chazan, José Hinojosa Montalvo, J. R. Magdalena Nom de Déu, Jean Régné, Jaume Riera i Sans, David Romano, Bernard Septimus, and Joseph Shatzmiller (see bibliography below). Maurice Kriegel provides a wider interpretive framework in his *Les juifs à la fin du moyen âge dans l'Europe méditerranéenne* (Paris, 1979). Among doctoral dissertations in progress are Elka Klein on Barcelona's Jews from 1100 to 1276 (Harvard), those of Rebecca Winer and Philip Daileader (see below in chap. 4, n. 2), and that of Claude Denjean (see chap. 4 below, n. 18).

3. Yom Tov Assis, "Juifs de France réfugiés en Aragon (XIII–XIV siècles)," *Revue des études juives* 142 (1983): 285–322, and his "Les juifs de Montpellier sous la domination aragonaise," ibid., 148 (1989): 5–16 (second quote on pp. 15–16). King Alfonso is in Antoni Rubió y Lluch, ed., *Documents per l'historia de la cultura catalana mig-eval,* 2 vols. (Barcelona, 1908–1921), vol. 1, pp. 92–93, doc. 75 (11 June 1328): "gran dan"; "que·ls dits juheus son caxe e thesaur dels reys."

4. William Chester Jordan, *The French Monarchy and the Jews: From Philip Augustus to the Last of the Capetians* (Philadelphia, 1989), 234–238. Crescas Elias is translated by Yom Tov Assis in his "Jewish Attitudes to Christian Powers in Medieval Spain," *Sefarad* 52 (1992): 294, from the Hebrew text in Baer, *Juden im christlichen Spanien,* vol. 1, pp. 311–317, doc. 224a. On 13 August 1306 Jaume II arranged for the Barcelona Jews to receive "sexaginta judeos et uxores et infantes eorum cum omnibus bonis et rebus suis," whom "ipse rex expulit et expelli mandavit"; in 1307 the king sent similar letters to the Jewish communities of Gerona, Lérida, and Montclus: Arch. Crown, reg. 203, fol. 189v, in Eloy Benito Ruano, "La judería de Montalbán (Teruel)," *Medievalia,* 10 (1992): 56, listing also expulsions received from France in 1249, 1250, 1252, 1254, 1272, 1290, and 1291.

5. Bernard Septimus, *Hispano-Jewish Culture in Transition: The Career and Controversies of Ramah* (Cambridge, Mass., 1982), especially chaps. 1, 2, and 6, quotations from pp. vii and 1. See also his "Piety and Power in Thirteenth-Century Catalonia," *Studies in Medieval Jewish History and Literature,* ed. Isadore Twersky, 2 vols. (Cambridge, Mass., 1979), 1:197–230. On the Almohad persecution see Norman Roth, *Jews, Visigoths and Muslims in Medieval Spain: Cooperation and Conflict* (Leiden, 1994), chap. 4, esp. pp. 116–129; and Mark Cohen, *Under Crescent and Cross: The Jews in the Middle Ages* (Princeton, 1994), chap. 10, esp. pp. 166–167, 182–184.

6. The phenomenon of the Jewish crown bureaucrat and courtier, not only from the Arabic stratum, is elaborated for the brief reign of Pere el Gran in David Romano, *Judíos al servicio de Pedro el Grande de Aragón (1276–1285)* (Barcelona, 1983). On the *ḥakīm* as properly a savant, see Burns, *Muslims, Christians, and Jews,* 158–159. The Arabic translations are in Rubió y Lluch, *Documents,* vol. 2, p. 9, doc. 11 (2 March 1296): "scribi et translatari faciamus quosdam libros medicinales de arabico in romana lingua nobis valde necessarios . . . et solvatis dicto Vitali duos solidos barchinonenses qualibet die et dum ipse translataverit libros predictos," the crown providing all the paper; vol. 2, p. 22, doc. 29 (8 November 1313): "pro translatando et redigendo de arabico in romancio quodam libro scripto in arabico medicine vocato halçahahny"; vol. 2, pp. 13–14, doc. 16 (10 September 1302): "ad opus correccionis librorum medicinalium habeat necessarium quosdam libros arabicos medicinales quos aliqui judei terre nostre habent, ut posset inde facere corrigi pecias que sunt in dicto studio ilerdensi." See also vol. 1, pp. 142–143, docs. 137 and 138 (3 February 1349), Mestre Salamó translating (*aromançar*) a *libre sarrainesch.*

7. Robert Chazan, *Barcelona and Beyond: The Disputation of 1263 and Its Aftermath* (Berkeley, 1992), 211. Septimus, "Piety and Power," 1:197–230. See Moshe Idel, *Studies in Ecstatic Kabbalah* (New York, 1988), on Abulafia,

"a central figure" in Jewish mysticism with "a series of prophetic books" between 1279 and 1288. Idel argues for Abulafia's direct influence on Llull, ca. 1270; see his "Ramon Llull and Ecstatic Kabbalah, a Preliminary Observation," *Journal of the Warburg and Courtauld Institutes* 51 (1988): 170–174. See also Idel, "Abraham Abulafia and the Pope: An Account of an Abortive Mission" (in Hebrew), *Association of Hebrew Studies Review* 7–8 (1982–1983): 1–17.

8. Solomon Katz, *Exclusiveness and Tolerance: Jewish-Gentile Relations in Medieval and Modern Times* (New York, 1975), esp. 106, 108. Cooperman's essay is appended to Katz's *Tradition and Crisis: Jewish Society at the End of the Middle Ages,* rev. ed. (New York, 1993), 251 (quote). See too the remarkable reconstruction of interrelations between Jew, Muslim, and Christian in a specific *dhimma* society by Shlomo D. Goitein, "Interfaith Relations, Communal Autonomy, and Government Control," in his *A Mediterranean Society: The Jewish Communities of the Arab World as Portrayed in the Documents of the Cairo Geniza,* 6 vols. (Berkeley, Los Angeles, London, 1967–1993), 3:273–407. Even so simple a matter as food—its acquisition, processing, preparation, and consumption—became a principle of exclusion for both sides, a moral contaminant to avoid. Jaume Riera has explored this element in medieval Catalan Jewish life, with its constant vigilance by community leaders and the contention it occasioned between Christian and Jewish authorities, in his "La conflictivitat de l'alimentació dels jueus medievals," in *Alimentació i societat a la Catalunya medieval,* ed. M. T. Ferrer i Mallol (Barcelona, 1988), 295–311. Catalan Jews' meticulous fidelity to their observances and ceremonies found reflection in the fourteenth-century Catalan saying: "There are three remarkable things in the world—the Christians' faith, the Jews' observance, and the Moors' justice [*fe de cristians, colre festes a jueus, e justícia de moros*]" (p. 296). David Nirenberg's pioneering "Muslim-Jewish Relations in the Fourteenth-Century Crown of Aragon," *Viator* 24 (1993): 249–268, explores the equally complex social interaction between the two minorities, each defining itself also against the other and each reinforcing "the boundaries physically, legally, ritually, and violently" in "a constantly shifting triangle" of three communities. For cognate Occitania see Simon Schwarzfuchs, "L'image du chrétien dans les sources juives du Languedoc (XIIe–XIVe siècles)," in *Les juifs à Montpellier et dans le Languedoc à travers l'histoire du moyen âge à nous jours,* ed. Carol Iancu (Montpellier, 1988), 113–127.

9. On the very different experience with subject Muslims in the realms of Aragon, see Robert I. Burns, S.J., "Muslims in the Thirteenth-Century Realms of Aragon: Interaction and Reaction," in *Muslims under Latin Rule, 1100–1300,* ed. James M. Powell (Princeton, 1990), 57–102; the analogous situations in Castile and Portugal, Sicily, and Palestine are covered in the same volume, respectively, by J. F. O'Callaghan, David Abulafia, and Benjamin Kedar. The *dhimma* structure as applied by Jaume the Conqueror is thoroughly analyzed in Burns, *Islam under the Crusaders: Colonial Survival in the Thirteenth-Century Kingdom of Valencia* (Princeton, 1973), especially chaps. 6–11 and 17. The many combining influences that produced both Islam's expression of the *dhimma* and Europe's analogous structures, with their common roots and odd supportive causalities, are discussed in "The 'Protected Community':

Aliens within Islam and Christendom," in Burns, *Muslims, Christians, and Jews,* 54–60 and passim. For a revisionist view of the relative treatment of medieval Jews under Muslim and Christian governance, see Cohen, *Under Crescent and Cross,* though in chap. 6 he conceptualizes their position in terms of hierarchical marginality in the dominant society rather than, as here, exclusivist parallelism. For examples of the "Sunna of the Jews," see below, chap. 3, n. 2 and text. For Norman Roth see his "Dar 'una voz' " below, chap. 3, n. 7, with his "Civic State of the Jew" (ibid.), and Assis, "Jewish Attitudes," below in n. 32.

10. Asunción Blasco Martínez, "Los judíos del reino de Aragón: Balance de los estudios realizados y perspectivas," in *I Col·loqui d'història dels jueus a la Corona d'Aragó* (Lérida, 1991), 25. Míkel de Epalza has written penetratingly on the *dhimma* submission; see especially his "Islamic Fidelity (*amān*) to Pacts (*'ahd*) between Mudejar/Morisco Muslims and Spanish Christian Authorities," in Robert I. Burns, S.J., Paul E. Chevedden, and Míkel de Epalza, "Bilingual Surrender Treaties in Medieval Spain" (in preparation). Goitein notes that a certain measure of practical autonomy prevailed in the parallel societies in any Islamic state also by reason of the defective or extremely limited function of government then: "Their Muslim subjects, too, were left mostly to their own devices" (*Mediterranean Society,* 2:404), a situation even truer in Christendom.

11. This composite from current scholarship on the Jews of the realms of Aragon is from Blasco Martínez, "Judíos del reino de Aragón," esp. 65–75. The usual derivation of *call* from Hebrew *qahal* or community has now been challenged as coming from Latin *callis* for street or quarter by J. M. Magdalena Nom de Déu, "Etimologia no semítica de 'Call,' " *Calls* 2 (1987): 7–16. On rabbis see below, chap. 2, n. 44 and text.

12. On the conversionist movement see R. I. Burns, S.J., "Christian-Islamic Confrontation in the West: The Thirteenth-Century Dream of Conversion," *American Historical Review* 76 (1971): 1386–1434; revised, but with much of the notes dropped, in Burns, *Muslims, Christians, and Jews,* chap. 3. Robert Chazan, *Daggers of Faith: Thirteenth-Century Christian Missionizing and Jewish Response* (Berkeley, Los Angeles, London, 1989); and his *Disputation of 1263,* with review article by Burns in *Catholic Historical Review* 79 (1993): 488–495. Jeremy Cohen, *The Friars and the Jews: The Evolution of Medieval Anti-Judaism* (Ithaca, N.Y., 1982), with review article by Burns in *Catholic Historical Review* 69 (1984): 90–93. Jaume Riera i Sans, "Les llicències reials per predicar als jueus i als sarraïns (segles XIII–XIV)," *Calls* 2 (1987): 113–143. See also Mark D. Johnston, "Ramon Llull and the Compulsory Evangelization of Jews and Muslims," in *Iberia and the Mediterranean World of the Middle Ages: Studies in Honor of Robert I. Burns, S.J.,* ed. Larry Simon, Paul Chevedden, Donald Kagay, and Paul Padilla, 1 vol. to date (Leiden, 1995; vol. 2 forthcoming), 1: 3–37; and John A. Bollweg, "Sense of Mission: Arnau de Vilanova on the Conversion of Muslims and Jews," ibid., 50–71. For a wider framework, see especially James Muldoon, *Popes, Lawyers and Infidels: The Church and the Non-Christian World, 1250–1550* (Philadelphia, 1979); Benjamin Z. Kedar, *Crusade and Mission: European Approaches toward the Muslims* (Princeton, 1984); and A. H. Cutler and H. E. Cutler, *The Jew as Ally of the Muslim: Medieval Roots of Anti-Semitism* (Notre Dame, 1986), chaps. 4, 5.

13. Blasco Martínez, "Judíos del reino de Aragón," 26, currently endorses the golden age judgment for the two reigns: "es la Edad de Oro de la judería aragonesa desde todos los puntos de vista." For the discriminating and persecutory "shadows" specific to this time and place, Elena Lourie has gathered examples and placed them in a comparative perspective against the situation of the local Muslims, in her *Crusade and Colonisation: Muslims, Christians and Jews in Medieval Aragon* (Aldershot, 1990), part 7, pp. 51–69. For very different reasons intrinsic to the Jewish communities in Spain themselves, Yitzhak Baer repudiates the perception of a golden age, citing the taint of philosophical rationalism, the pampered Jewish courtier stratum too receptive to gentile currents, and a chasm between the affluent cosmopolitan upper class and the despised and ignorant lower classes more faithful to Judaism. See the lengthy discussion of Baer's historiography and underlying philosophy of Spanish Jewish history in David N. Myers, *Re-inventing the Jewish Past: European Jewish Intellectuals and the Zionist Return to History* (New York, 1995), chap. 5. For the lengthening shadows of the fourteenth century for the Jews of Arago-Catalonia and Occitania, especially for the period 1320–1350, see the revisionist approach on the paradoxical interdependence of violence and toleration there by David Nirenberg, *Communities of Violence: Minorities in Medieval Spain and France* (Princeton, 1996).

14. Goitein, *Mediterranean Society,* 5:131–132, and 542, n. 19; and on wills and their inventories 1:10, 180–181, 263–266; 2:36, 110–111; 3:42, 238, 251–255; 4:120–122, and especially 128–155. Reuven Yaron, *Gifts in Contemplation of Death in Jewish and Roman Law* (Oxford, 1960), quotations from pp. viii, 1, 2, 19, 32.

15. See the long essay by Shmuel Shilo, "Wills," *Encyclopaedia Judaica,* 17 vols. (Jerusalem, 1966–1981), 16:519–530. This study, along with over a hundred columns of related articles by specialists in the same encyclopedia, appears in "Family Law and Inheritance," in *The Principles of Jewish Law,* ed. Menachem Elon (Jerusalem, 1975), cols. 352–464, including "Firstborn" (434–435), "Ketubbah" (387–390), "Succession" (445–453), and "Widow" (399–403).

16. Goitein, *Mediterranean Society,* 5:131–132, 142–143, and on funerals 121–122.

17. A. M. Udina i Abelló, "Testament sacramental," *Documents jurídics de la història de Catalunya* (Barcelona, 1992), 43–50.

18. Goitein, *Mediterranean Society,* 1:265; 5:158–160, 165, 400–402. The burial societies are in Neuman, *Jews in Spain,* 2:172–176; Lérida is on p. 174. See now Yom Tov Assis, "Welfare and Mutual Aid in the Spanish Jewish Communities," in *Moreshet Sepharad,* vol. 1, esp. pp. 322, 333–340. Assis ascribes the rise of Jewish confraternities to the worsening economic situation in the fourteenth century, including "polarization and class struggle." Burial groups were the most important of these associations, dating from the end of the thirteenth century.

19. See the classic *Hebrew Ethical Wills,* ed. Israel Abrahams, 2 vols. in 1 (Philadelphia, [1926] 1976), esp. 2:163–210 for the Toledo wills of Judá b. Asher (1327). Goitein, *Mediterranean Society,* 5:143 and 1:10.

20. J. M. Millàs i Vallicrosa, ed., *Documents hebraics de jueus catalans* (Bar-

celona, 1927) [*Memòries* of the Institut d'Estudis Catalans, Secció Històrico-Arqueològica, I, fasc. 3, pp. 61–167], pp. 29–30 [*Memòries,* pp. 89–90], doc. 25 (14 May 1268), with fascsimile of the Hebrew text on plate 25, p. 149. See Leila Berner, "Barcelona's Jews," chap. 4. On the name Shealtiel see below, chap. 3, n. 26.

21. Even beyond Spain and its holocaust expulsion in 1492, a striking shift within the ideational foundations of European Jewry had begun before 1500. The discriminatory barriers to social mixing with Christians became so strong that the two peoples "were almost completely separated from each other," Jacob Katz explains; paradoxically, however, the consequent loss of Christian presence as threat or assimilative seduction allowed greater adaptability by Jews in intersocietal contacts, halakhic reinterpretations and dispensations, a shift from "hatred and contempt" for traditional Christian symbols to "rooted fear and abhorrence," and a conceptual reformulation of the very bases for social distancing, from merely credal to an underlying "deeper division in the biological-metaphysical or historical-metaphysical natures of the two camps" in Jewish thought (*Tradition and Crisis,* chap. 3, "Barriers against the Outside," esp. pp. 19–26).

22. José Cabezudo Astrain, "Testamentos de judíos aragoneses," *Sefarad* 16 (1956): 136–147; he cites two other wills of 1446 and 1484.

23. Marín Padilla, "Ultimas voluntades judías: Testamentos de Duenya Falaquera, Reyna Abenardit y Davit Rodrich (siglo XV)," from the notarial protocols of Zaragoza, Calatayud, and La Almunia, in *Anuario de estudios medievales* 15 (1985): 497–512.

24. Miguel Angel Motis Dolader, "Disposiciones *mortis causa* de los judíos de Epila (Zaragoza) en el ultimo tercio del siglo XV," *Homenaje al profesor emerito Antonio Ubieto Arteta* (Zaragoza, 1989), 475–498. Drawn from Zaragoza's Archivo Histórico de Protocolos, the wills are by Mossé Haddax the shoemaker and Nitzim Zanana. (The Hebrew name Hadas is from Aramaic for "myrtle," unless this is a form of Arabic Ḥaddād; Zanana is a variant of the Judeo-Arabic name Sammana; Nitzim is Hebrew Nissim, "miracles.") For wider context see his "La documentación notarial como fuente para la historia de los judíos aragoneses en el siglo XV," *El patrimonio documental y la historia* (Zaragoza, 1986), 249–260. Further widening the context, see María del Carmen García Herrero, "La muerte y el cuidado del alma en los testamentos zaragozanos de la primera mitad del siglo XV," *Aragón en la edad media* 6 (1984): 209–245; F. J. García Marco, "Tipología documental e investigación histórica: Las actas notariales como reflejo de la evolución de la sociedad aragonesa en la edad media," ibid., 9 (1991): 31–53; and Mariano Alonso y Lambán, "Las formas testamentarias en la alta edad media de Aragón," *Revista de derecho notarial* 5–6 (1954): 7–196 and 9–10 (1955): 241–399.

25. Asunción Blasco Martínez, "Mujeres judías zaragozanas ante la muerte," *Aragon en la edad media* 9 (1991): 77–120, a revision and amplification of her "Testamentos de mujeres judías aragonesas, 1401–1418," *Tenth World Congress of Jewish Studies: Proceedings* (Jerusalem, 1990), 7 vols., Div. B:2 (in press). See too her other articles on the Jews of Zaragoza and Aragon below in the bibliography as well as the long article there by M. A. Motis Dolader on Aragon's Jews from 1283 to 1479, "Los judíos aragoneses

en la baja edad media (1283–1479)," *Historia de Aragon* 6 (1987): 149–184.

26. Gabriel Secall i Güell has the 1410 testament of "Mossé Cabrit, draper filantrop de Valls i de Santa Coloma de Queralt (siglos XIV–XV)," *Aplec de treballs,* Centre d'Estudis de la Conca de Barberà, vol. 6 (1984), appendix, pp. 63–96 (Cabrit is Catalan for "kid"). The testaments of four members of the celebrated Vives family from 1436 to 1514 are all by *converso* Christians, in Angelina García, *Els Vives: Una família de jueus valencians* (Valencia, 1987), appendix 3–6, pp. 219–232. Gabriel Llompart has published the will of Regina, wife of the tailor Salamó (A)struc of Perelada, resident of Inca on Majorca, in 1388, in his "Documentos sueltos sobre judíos conversos de Mallorca (siglos XIV y XV)," *Fontes rerum balearium* 2 (1978): 188–189, doc. 3. Estanislao Aguiló transcribed "Documents curiosos del sigle XIV: Testament de Sayt Milí, juheu, fundador d'un hospital en el calle de Mallorca, 16 Agost 1377," in *Boletín de la Sociedad arqueológica luliana* 9 (1901–1902): 203–204. Also Majorcan is the 1467 will in Francisco Sevillano Colom, "Gabriel de Vallseca, cartógrafo mallorquín del siglo XV," in *Homenaje al Dr. D. Juan Reglá Campistol,* 2 vols. (Valencia, 1975), 1:159–162. Joaquim Sarret i Arbós provides only a translation from the Latin in "El testament d'un jueu, segle XIV," *Butlletí del Centre excursionista de la comarca de Bages* 25 (1929): 356–357, the will of Astruc Jucef at Manresa in 1391. Another translation, from the Latin of 1470, is Enrique Girbal, "Un testamento hebreo de la edad media," *Revista de Gerona* 5 (1881): 104–108. The Gerona documents of Luis Battle y Prats, "Judíos gerundenses en testamentarías medievales," of 1332–1458, are not wills but do include inventories; see *Anales del Instituto de estudios gerundenses* 4 (1949): 250–253. Also from Gerona, J. M. Madurell i Marimon has a will of 1462 by Benvenist Samuel Benvenist in "Jueus gironins i la seva aljama (1349–1498)," ibid., 22 (1974–1975): 42–44 (interior pagination 20–22), doc. 10, with his wife as "universal heir." While Ramon Corbella i Llobet, *L'aljama de jueus de Vic* (Vich, [1909] 1984), has no wills among his eighty documents, notice of an appeal about a will of 1284 (now lost) is transcribed as doc. 41, pp. 195–196. Castile must have its own scattering of Jewish wills; see, for example, Pilar León Tello, *Judíos de Toledo,* 2 vols. (Madrid, 1979), vol. 2, docs. 291 (s. XIV), 380 (1336), 576 (1374), 647 and 648 (1397), 662 (1398, published in 1624), 785 (1433), 804 (1442), 879 (1454), 1003 (1464), all still unpublished except for these notices and doc. 662 (1398); cf. also docs. 1003 (1464) and 1483 (ca. 1489). A fragment in Castilian but in Hebrew letters is in José Luis Lacave, "Un testamento hebraico fragmentario de Miranda del Ebro," *Sefarad* 46 (1986): 271–279. Manuel Serrano y Sanz improbably includes three late wills in his *Orígenes de la dominación española en América: Estudios históricos* (Madrid, 1918), 186–187, 477 (doc. 31 of 1446), 357 (doc. 18 of 1415), and 498 (doc. 3 of 1465, a *converso*).

27. Steven Epstein, *Wills and Wealth in Medieval Genoa, 1150–1250* (Cambridge, 1984), 15. The Sicilian will is in the *Registro* of Giovanni Maiorana; see note on p. 244 but also the new edition and facsimile edited by Aldo Sparti (Palermo, 1982), doc. 67 (14 April 1299). The only legible parts of the will inform us that he is a carpenter and has borrowed an ounce of gold and fifteen *tarin* coins to pay for his needs and present last illness and orders this money

repaid to his son "Helya" (Elijah/Eliyahu). Six Christians and two Jews serve as witnesses. For thorough community and notarial context see David Abulafia, "Una comunità ebraica della Sicilia occidentale: Erice 1298–1304," in his *Commerce and Conquest in the Mediterranean 1100–1500* (Aldershot, 1993), chap. 8.

28. Ariel Toaff, *The Jews in Umbria,* 2 vols. to date (1245–1435 and 1435–1484) (Leiden, 1993–1994), vol. 1, docs. 184 and 186; cf. doc. 165; vol. 2, doc. 953 (1439), doc. 1073 (1445), doc. 1244 (1457), doc. 1327 (1461), doc. 1685 (1475), doc. 1857 (1484) and the related doc. 891 (1435), doc. 1324 (1461), and doc. 1450 (1466). He notes, and has transcribed elsewhere, a very late will of 1423 where a banker is altering his previous provisions, making his wife his universal heir and giving each son 25 florins, an arrangement a Latinate will but not Jewish law could accommodate (vol. 1, doc. 771). Even for so late an era, there are only a dozen wills out of over a thousand notarial contracts. For similar late wills in Provence and Languedoc see the work of Danièle Iancu-Agou and Jacques Chiffoleau below in chap. 6, nn. 11 and 12.

29. See these and other testimony in the opening pages of Robert I. Burns, S.J., "Canon Law and the Reconquista: Convergence and Symbiosis in the Kingdom of Valencia under Jaume the Conqueror (1213–1276)," in *Fifth International Congress of Medieval Canon Law,* ed. Stephan Kuttner and Kenneth Pennington (Rome, 1980), 387–424.

30. Isidore Epstein, *The "Responsa" of Rabbi Solomon Ben Adreth of Barcelona (1235–1310) as a Source of the History of Spain* (New York, [1925] 1968), 47. On Jewish courts and on the relation of Jewish law and courts with Spanish, especially Arago-Catalan, royal courts see Neuman, *Jews in Spain,* vol. 1, chaps. 4, 5.

31. Neuman, *Jews in Spain,* 1:152.

32. Assis, in his "Jewish Attitudes to Christian Power in Medieval Spain," *Sefarad* 52 (1992): esp. pp. 298, 300–301.

33. Bernard Lewis, "Palimpsests of Jewish History: Christian, Muslim and Secular Diaspora," address to the Tenth World Congress of Jewish Studies, in its *Jewish Studies* 30 (1990): 9–10, with examples, and "strikingly even in theology."

Chapter 2: Mechanisms: Notary and *Sōfer*

1. Antoni M. Udina i Abelló, "El testament català en el segle XIII: Supervivencies i innovacions," *XIIe Congrés d'història de la Corona d'Aragó,* 3 vols. (Montpellier, 1987–1989), 2:157–165; see especially his more general *La successió testada a la Catalunya altomedieval* (Barcelona, 1984), a thorough study and edited collection of the surviving 137 wills up to 1025, with excellent bibliography; chap. 2 reviews the subject of wills in early Europe. See also Jean Bastier, "Le testament en Catalogne du IXe au XIIe siècle: Une survivance wisigothique," *Revue historique du droit français et étranger* 3 (1973): 374–417. Manuel M. Pérez de Benavides, *El testamento visigótico: Una contribución al estudio del derecho romano vulgar* (Granada, 1975). Of related interest is Joana Canals i Ramon, *L'hereu—una institució en crisi?* (Barcelona, 1985). For a sys-

tematic survey of wills in Spain, in 33 sections with bibliographical orientation, see Alfonso García-Gallo, "Del testamento romano al medieval: Las lineas de su evolución en España," *Anuario de historia de derecho español* 47 (1977): 425–497. Two recent contributions on Castilian wills are Jesús Coria Colino, from wills at Zamora in Castile in 1220–1533, "El testamento como fuente sobre mentalidades (s. XIII al XV)," *Miscelánea medieval murciana* 9 (1982): 193–219; and A. L. Molina Molina and Amparo Bejarano Rubio, "Actitud del hombre ante la muerte: Los testamentos murcianos de finales de s. XV," ibid., 12 (1985): 185–202, from 78 wills in the Murcian region. For Catalonia see Jordi Günzberg, "Testamentos del siglo XIV del Archivo histórico de protocolos de Barcelona (AHPB) y su applicación a la demografía histórica: Estudio archivistico-metadológico," *Acta historica et archaeologica mediaevalia* 10 (1989): 89–98; Imma Ollich, "La història medieval i les noves tècniques d'anàlisis per ordinador: Els testaments de Vic del segle XIII," ibid., 1 (1980): 11–27; and the thorough book-length analysis of testamentary formulas, item by item through 50 wills, by M. J. Arnall i Juan, "Testaments de fons monacals gironins existents a l'Arxiu de la Corona d'Aragó (segles XI–XV)," *De scriptis notariorum (s. XI–XV),* ed. Josefina Mateu Ibars (Barcelona, 1989), 39–159. An intensive analysis of some two thousand wills before 1200 is N. L. Taylor, "Medieval Catalonian Wills: Family Charter Evidence in the Archives," in *Discovery in the Archives of Spain and Portugal: Quincentenary Essays, 1492–1992,* ed. L. J. McCrank (Binghamton, N.Y., 1994), chap. 3. For a detailed analysis of an elaborate thirteenth-century will, see Robert I. Burns, S.J., "Daughter of Abū Zayd, Last Almohad Ruler of Valencia: The Family and Christian Seigniory of Alda Ferrándis, 1236–1300," *Viator* 24 (1993): 143–187.

2. Alfonso X el Sabio, *Las siete partidas,* 3 vols. (Madrid, [1807] 1972), *Partida* 6: e.g., drafting a will (law 303); anyone can make a will unless expressly forbidden (law 13); a Christian who *becomes* a Jew cannot make a will (law 9). Some aspects of succession and inheritance not touched on in this *partida* can turn up indirectly in others. For background see Robert I. Burns, S.J., ed., *Emperor of Culture: Alfonso the Learned of Castile and His Thirteenth-Century Renaissance* (Philadelphia, 1990), chaps. 1, 12, and index under "law."

3. *Fori antiqui Valentiae,* ed. Manuel Dualde Serrano (Madrid, 1967), rubrics 82 (38 laws), 85 (9 laws), 86 (39 laws), 87 (7 laws), 88 (7 laws), 89 (4 laws), 90 (6 laws), 92 (20 laws). The full Puigcerdá schedule is in Sebastià Bosom i Isern and Salvador Galceran i Vigué, *Catàleg de protocols de Puigcerdà* (Barcelona, 1983), 14–16.

4. On the Muslim scribe, see R. I. Burns, S.J., *Islam under the Crusaders: Colonial Survival in the Thirteenth-Century Kingdom of Valencia* (Princeton, 1973), 398–399, with appointments to the post and a surviving exemplar from Murviedro. See also R. I. Burns, S.J., *Society and Documentation in Crusader Valencia* (Princeton, 1985), 126, 132, and the edition by Burns and Paul Chevedden in "Al-Azraq's Surrender Treaty with Jaume I and Prince Alfonso in 1245: Arabic Text and Valencian Context," *Der Islam* 66 (1989): 1–37. Wilhelm Hoenerbach has an introductory essay on the "notarial" Islamic scribe and on the *kātib* in his *Spanisch-islamische Urkunden aus der Zeit der Naṣriden*

und Moriscos (Berkeley and Los Angeles, 1965), xxi–xxxv. M. C. Barceló Torres has collected 270 published and unpublished Mudejar/Morisco Arabic documents from 1366 to 1595, not all of course from public scribes, in *Minorías islámicas en el país valenciano: Historia y dialecto* (Valencia, 1984); on the post or function of translator of tax and public records from Arabic, see pp. 138–139; on Muslims' declarations before Christian notaries, see p. 414; and on those who wrote "de pròpria mà," see pp. 141–143. For background in Hispano-Arabic "notarial" practice (*shurūṭ*) see the edition by Pedro Chalmeta and Federico Corriente of Ibn al-ʿAṭṭār (d. 1009), *Kitāb al-Wathāʾiq wa-siǧillāt,* in Arabic with extensive Spanish introduction as *Formulario notarial hispano-árabe por el alfaquí y notario cordobés Ibn al-ʿAṭṭār (s. X)* (Madrid, 1983).

5. Ibn ʿAbdūn, *Séville musulmane au début du XII*[e] *siècle: Le traité d'Ibn ʿAbdūn,* ed. Évariste Lévi-Provençal (Paris, 1947), pp. 27–28, no. 17. Cf. Burns, *Islam under the Crusaders,* 398–399. For Canellas López, see his "El notariado en España hasta el siglo XIV: Estado de la cuestión," in *Notariado público i documento privado: De los orígines al siglo XIV* (VII Congreso Internacional de Diplomática), 2 vols. (Valencia, 1989), 1:104 ("curiosamente en Hispania adquiere singular difusión"). Francesc Carreras i Candi, "Desenrotllament de la institució notarial a Catalunya en lo segle XIII," *I Congrés d'història de la corona d'Aragó,* 1 vol. in 2 (Barcelona, 1909–1913), 765. For Jews commissioned for Arabic contracts, see below, pp. 35, 40–41.

6. Arch. Crown, reg. 21, fols. 10v-11 (31 August 1271), transcribed below in appendix, doc. 9, for Jaume's Muḥammad. Ibid., reg. 40, fol. 166 (1 October 1278): "tibi Foçan filio de Pharach Avinlatro Sarraceno Cesarauguste donacionem quam dominus Iacobus inclite recordacionis rex Aragonum pater noster tibi fecit de alcaydia et scribania Sarracenorum Cesarauguste et omnium terminorum Cesarauguste et de faciendis omnibus instrumentis sarracen[ic]is et açidaqes . . . Teneas eciam et habetis alhabeçes; et omnia iura alcaidie et scribanie integriter percipias." Angel Canellas López publishes this document, with slight differences from my transcription, in his *Colección diplomática del consejo de Zaragoza,* 2 vols. and album (Zaragoza, 1972–1975), vol. 2, p. 84, doc. 59; my supplied date differs from his "October 1–5." Sixteen years later in 1294 these same offices are linked in a tax report from Borgia's Muslims: "los officios de alfaquinado e de çabçala e de escrivania e de alaminatge de los moros" (Burns, *Islam under the Crusaders,* 379, 383, 386, and *Society and Documentation,* 127n.).

7. Arch. Crown, reg. 41, fol. 16 (20 November 1278), transcribed below in appendix, doc. 22. The appointment itself for life to the "scribaniam Osce et terminorum suorum" is on fol. 161.

8. See both crown charters cited in Burns, *Society and Documentation,* 126–127.

9. Arch. Crown, reg. 40, fol. 262v (27 September 1278), transcribed below in appendix, doc. 21. The same ʿAlī appears again on fol. 161v (21 October 1279).

10. Ibid., reg. 19, fol. 161v (17 August 1274): "vobis universis et singulis Sarracenis habitantibus seu habitandis in civitate Ilerde: quod si forte contigerit

aliquem Sarracenum masculum vel mulierem in Ilerda habitantem seu habitaturum mori sine herede, quod medietas tocius omnium bonorum ipsius Sarraceni sine herede morientis devolvatur ad nos et nostros, et alia medietas devolvatur ad [al]jamam predictorum Sarracenorum Ilerde." The full document, with some variant readings from my own, is now in Josefa Mutgé i Vives, *L'aljama sarraïna de Lleida a l'edat mitjana: Aproximació a la seva història* (Barcelona, 1992), p. 199, doc. 8.

11. Basañez Villaluenga, *La aljama sarracena de Huesca en el siglo XIV* (Barcelona, 1989), 16–20, 27–29, with archival references (docs. of 1301, 1340, 1361, 1370–1371). See especially in her documentary appendix doc. 86 (20 June 1391) where the Huesca *aljama* wins from the crown the permanent right to refuse to serve as substitute scribe, *amīn,* or *qāḍī* for the absentee holder of those titles; and doc. 90 (24 November 1391) dismissing ʿAlī Bellvis from all three offices for "excesses and crimes" including immoderate fees "pro scripturis eciam et contractibus, qui nostris provisionibus sunt taxati." Barceló, *Minorías,* 137–139. Mutgé, *L'aljama sarraïna de Lleida,* 40, 197–198, 348–349. Mercedes García Arenal and Béatrice Leroy, *Moros y judíos en Navarra en la baja edad media* (Madrid, 1984), 37–38. John Boswell, *The Royal Treasure: Muslim Communities under the Crown of Aragon in the Fourteenth Century* (New Haven, 1977), 92–95, 457–458, 491–492. M. T. Ferrer i Mallol, *Les aljames sarraïnes de la governació d'Oriola en el segle XIV* (Barcelona, 1988), 24, 292–295.

12. Asunción Blasco Martínez, "Notarios mudéjares de Aragón (siglos XIV–XV)," *Aragón en la edad media (Homenaje a la profesora emérita María Luisa Ledesma Rubio)* 10–11 (1993): 109–133, quotations from pp. 110, 113, 114, 123, 124. On the Mudejar *faqīh* see Burns, *Islam under the Crusaders,* 220–223, 378, 382–384.

13. David S. Powers, *Studies in Qur'an and Ḥadīth: The Formation of the Islamic Law of Inheritance* (Berkeley and Los Angeles, 1986), with background references to the books of Asaf Fysee (1974) and Noel Coulson (1971), quotations from pp. 9–10. The first quotation is from Shlomo Goitein (above, in introduction, n. 2) who applies his phrase both to Muslim and Jewish wills. Ibn Khaldūn's quote is from his *Muqaddimah,* trans. Franz Rosenthal (Princeton, 1967), 3:22–23, cf. pp. 127–129. See also now *Un tratado catalán medieval de derecho islámico: El Llibre de la Çuna e Xara dels moros,* ed. Carmen [M. C.] Barceló (Córdoba, 1989), on wills pp. 26–34 (chaps. 105–133), 58 (chap. 222), 63–65 (chaps. 238, 240–241), 83 (chap. 291), and 93 (chaps. 329–330).

14. On the disposition and respective characters of the several Mudejar populations in each kingdom and region of the realms at this time, see Burns, "Muslims in the Thirteenth-Century Realms of Aragon: Interaction and Reaction," in James M. Powell, ed., *Muslims under Latin Rule, 1100–1300* (Princeton, 1990), 57–102. The Eslida-Uxó case and appeals or Christian intervention are discussed at length in Burns, *Islam under the Crusaders,* chap. 11, "Christians and the Islamic Judiciary." Shlomo D. Goitein, *A Mediterranean Society: The Jewish Communities of the Arab World as Portrayed in the Documents of the Cairo Geniza,* 6 vols. (Berkeley, Los Angeles, London: 1967–1993), 5:131–132 (quote), and 542 n. 19.

15. See the review of this office and introduction to its extensive bibliography in Burns, *Society and Documentation,* chap. 5 ("The Notariate"), chap. 6 ("Chancery Procedures"), and chap. 22 on rhetoric and style. Other chapters treat script, mechanics such as chronology and onomastics, use of paper, witnesses, authentication, and the like. See too the magisterial study and bibliographies of José Bono, *Historia del derecho notarial español,* 2 vols. to date (Madrid, 1979–1982), with various sections on Arago-Catalan regions. The seventh Congreso Internacional de Diplomática, at Valencia in 1986, brought together experts on all aspects of the notariate up to the fourteenth century, its acts published as *Notariado público* (see above, this chap., n. 5), over half on Spain by some two dozen scholars, though virtually nothing was offered on Jewish or Muslim scribal analogues (see 1:104, 308). Especially relevant to the present paper are the introductory "Estado de la cuestión," by Canellas López (1:99–139); Rafael Conde with Francisco Gimeno, "Notarías y escribanías de concesión real en la corona de Aragón" (1:281–329), especially the typology of crown notaries on pp. 284–285; and the more local "El documento notarial en derecho valenciano hasta mediados del siglo XIV" by Arcadio García Sanz (1:177–199). The I Congrés d'Història del Notariat Català was held in November 1993 under the auspices of the Fundació Noguera. Publication of its acts and those of subsequent congresses will mark a turning point for Catalan notarial history. For the upland Kingdom of Aragon proper, see especially Angel Canellas López, "El documento notarial en la legislación foral del reino de Aragón," *Medievalia* 10 (1992): 65–81. (Estudios dedicados al profesor Federico Udina i Martorell, 4). In the *Siete partidas* (part 3, title 18, law 8) the king invests each new notary with a writing case and pen as symbols of office.

16. Daniel Waley, *The Italian City-Republics,* 3d ed. rev. (New York, 1988), 15. Steven Epstein, *Wealth and Wills in Medieval Genoa, 1150–1250* (Cambridge, 1984), 60–61, including a breakdown table of 431 wills by hour and site of drafting. Bensch, *Barcelona and Its Rulers, 1096–1291* (Cambridge, 1995), 39–41, 378. Josiah Cox Russell's *Medieval Regions and Their Cities* (Bloomington, 1972) assembles the evidence and methodologies by which the Barcelona population can be reckoned, estimating 48,000 souls "just before the plague" (p. 170). Though somewhat late for our present focus, see the model study by Benjamin Kedar, "The Genoese Notaries of 1382: The Anatomy of an Urban Occupational Group," *The Medieval City,* ed. H. A. Miskimin et al. (New Haven, 1977), 73–94.

17. Arch. Crown, reg. 41, fol. 138 (10 January [1278] 1279), transcribed below in appendix, doc. 23. The vicariates shifted in this formative period. Not given here are Gerona (with Besalú), Tárrega, Tortosa, and of course such Pyrenean areas as Seo de Urgel and Cerdanya, then under the kingdom of Majorca. Some of the missing may have been subvicariates or dependencies of others given here. Presumably a similar series went to the Aragon and Valencia kingdoms.

18. Ibid., reg. 48, fol. 15v (12 May 1280): "testamenta et instrumenta matrimonialia." On February 20 the king wrote to the people of Manresa that he had just learned that their church held the right to appoint their own notary; they could continue the practice until the king arrived to sort things out per-

sonally (fol. 43v). After a general letter on notaries, with consequent uproar among Barcelona's notaries, the king similarly advised them to continue as before "donec simus Barchinone personaliter constituti" to take up the matter with "universis tabellionibus Barchinone" (reg. 41, fol. 38v). On notarial powers and procedures for a cleric within his own parish, as well as notaries of the bishop's curia, the deans and the like, see the detailed treatment by Kristine Utterback, *Pastoral Care and Administration in Mid-Fourteenth Century Barcelona: Exercising the "Art of Arts"* (Queenston, Canada, 1993), 71–73 and, on testamentary practice, 164–178.

19. Ibid., reg. 12, fol. 142v (9 February [1263] 1264), transcribed below in appendix, doc. 4. On other special notariates, as for saltworks, a group of royal mills, or each war galley, see Burns, *Society and Documentation*, 37 and note. The name "Azcarel" has a soft *c*, biblical Azarel.

20. Arch. Crown, reg. 21, fol. 71v (5 November 1272), transcribed below in appendix, doc. 14. Joseph Jacobs's suggestion that Mossé's name is from Nieto in Murcia doesn't seem to fit its form or spelling.

21. Antoni Rubió y Lluch, *Documents per l'historia de la cultura catalana mig-eval*, 2 vols. (Barcelona, 1908–1921), 1:11–12, doc. 12 (13 December 1294): "conficiendum instrumenta debitoria, arabice facienda per Sarracenos, per illos scilicet qui profici[sc]untur ad partes Sarracenorum vel qui se obligant aliquibus personis pro certis quantitatibus in ipsis partibus exolvendis, et instrumenta ipsa melius exponi et intelligi apud dictos Sarracenos si scripta fuerint arabice pocius quam latine." On the name Bonsenyor see below, chap. 3, n. 21.

22. See, for example, the notarial appointments transcribed by Conde and Gimeno, "Notarías y escribanías," appendix, doc. 3 (28 March 1263), though the notary must sign all the documents; doc. 4 (27 April 1263): "tenere discipulos scriptores quoscumque . . . per te vel per ipsos," the notary again signing all; doc. 5 (28 June 1263): "possis habere sub manu tua quoslibet scriptores qui loco tui et nomine et auctoritate tuo instrumenta . . . redigant in publica forma et scribant"; doc. 6 (9 April 1274): "possis substituere scriptores qui loco et vice tua subscribant"; doc. 8 (8 January 1258): "quod tu et ille ac illi quos tu ibi posueris loco tui scribatis et conficiatis"; doc. 14 (8 June 1294): "vos vel quem volueritis loco vestri"; doc. 16 (8 March 1264): "in officio scribanie predicte curie . . . possis ponere et constituere scriptorem sive scriptores qui, tam in absencia quam in presencia tui, scribant et conficiant vice et nomine tuo scripturas ad dictas curias necessarias."

23. A number of these have been edited, excerpted, or studied. See, for example, Montserrat Casas i Nadal, "El 'Liber Iudeorum' de Cardona (1330–1334), ediciò i estudi," *Miscel·lània de textos medievales* 3 (1985): 121–350.

24. Ambrosio Huici Miranda, ed., *Colección diplomática de Jaime I, el Conquistador*, 3 vols. in 6 (Valencia, 1916–1920), vol. 2, p. 147, doc. 681; in new edition by M. D. Cabanes Pecourt, *Documentos de Jaime I de Aragón*, 5 vols. to date (Valencia, 1976–), vol. 3, p. 326, doc. 882 (19 December 1257): "omnia instrumenta debitorum vestrorum facta et facienda per manus presbiterorum vel quarumlibet aliarum personarum ecclesiasticarum ad scribanie officium constitutarum et firmamenta eciam . . . plenam roboris obtineant firmamentem [= firmamentum] in omnibus tam in iudicio quam extra iudicium ac si essent facta per manus publicorum tabellionum in curiis nostris iuratorum."

25. Huici Miranda, *Colección,* vol. 2, p. 221, doc. 778; Huici-Cabanes, *Documentos,* vol. 4, p. 132, doc. 1042 (9 August 1258); "universitati Barchinone, christianorum scilicet et iudeorum, salvare et conservare pristinas libertates"; "cum quibuscumque tabellionibus sive notariis volueritis Barchinone, non obstante aliqua concessione a nobis facta alicui de scribania speciali; nos enim revocamus de presenti collacionem sive concessionem quam feceramus de scribania speciali iudeo[rum] Petro de Columbario et quamcumque aliam donacionem alicui fecimus de speciali scribania in Barchinona . . . christianorum seu eciam iudeorum"; any future attempt by himself or his successors will be "irritam et inanem." This transcription from Arch. Crown, reg. 9, fol. 62v, is to be preferred over that of Francesc Carreras i Candi from the municipal archives, whose infelicities include a missing phrase of fourteen words ("Institució notarial," p. 774, doc. 2; reprinted in his *Miscelanea histórica catalana,* 2 vols. [Barcelona, 1905], 2:346).

26. Arch. Crown, reg. 11, fol. 224v (10 August 1260), transcribed below in appendix, doc. 1.

27. Ibid., reg. 12, fol. 131v (1 December 1263), transcribed below in appendix, doc. 3.

28. Ibid., reg. 20, fol. 298 (14 November 1275), transcribed below in appendix, doc. 20.

29. Ibid., reg. 21, fol. 38 (23 May 1272), transcribed below in appendix, doc. 11.

30. David Abulafia, "From Privilege to Persecution: Crown, Church, and Synagogue in the City of Majorca, 1229–1343," in *Church and City 1000–1500: Essays in Honor of Christopher Brooke,* ed. David Abulafia et al. (Cambridge, 1992), 115n. See Goitein, *Mediterranean Society,* 1:15 and 3:52, on the origins and early context of *aljamiado* texts, and the role of Aramaic, in ancient times the language of the Jewish courts, as a safeguard for formulas. See too the chapter "Language" in Paloma Díaz-Mas, *Sephardim: The Jews from Spain* (Chicago, 1992); *aljamiado* writings are not to be confused with the artificial Ladino, "really a calque-language of Hebrew" to translate liturgical texts (pp. 75–77). The surviving partial will in Hebrew in the early realms is above in chap. 1, n. 20.

31. Goitein, *Mediterranean Society,* 1:14–15, on the language of the Jewish courts in Arabic lands in the twelfth and thirteenth centuries; 2:179 for quotes on extent of writing; 2:228–230 on scribes; 3:348–349 on al-Wuḥsha; and 3:109, 354–357 on literacy. See Neuman, *The Jews in Spain: Their Social, Political and Cultural Life during the Middle Ages,* 2 vols. (Philadelphia, 1948), 2:94, the negative testimony of Mordecai Qimhi and Abraham Abulafia in the thirteenth century against the more sanguine eleventh-century Moses Ibn Gikatilla on Catalan Jews' proficiency in Hebrew. J. R. Magdalena Nom de Déu argues that outside the liturgical, scholarly, and literary use of Hebrew in the several realms of Arago-Catalonia the "ordinary" man in the street had "a limited, sometimes rudimentary, knowledge of Hebrew" for personal or professional notes: "The majority learned the Hebrew alphabet at an early age." It is difficult to guess how good was this popular Hebrew, and it is "impossible to estimate even in approximate fashion the percentage of Jews who wrote in Hebrew." See his introduction to *Judeolenguas marginales en Sefarad antes de*

1492: Aljamía romance en los documentos hebraiconavarros (siglo XIV), ed. Yom Tov Assis et al. (Barcelona, 1992), 7–8. See also Jordi Ventura i Subirats, "El coneixement de l'hebreu entre els conversos valencians de la fi del segle XV," *Revista de llengua i dret* 20 (1993): 7–48.

32. Bodies of formal replies by eminent rabbinic scholars to halakhic and other religious queries from near and far.

33. Isidore Epstein, *The "Responsa" of Rabbi Solomon Ben Adreth of Barcelona (1235–1310) as a Source of the History of Spain* (New York, [1925] 1968), 40–42. On the Jewish "notary," especially in the late fourteenth century, see the brief segment by Jaume Riera i Sans, "Notaris jueus i sarraïns," in M. T. Ferrer i Mallol and J. Riera i Sans, "Miscel·lània de documents per a la història del notariat als estats de la corona catalano-aragonesa," *Estudios históricos y documentos de los archivos de protocolos* (Miscelànea en Honor de Raimundo Noguera de Guzmán) 4 (1974): 434–438; and Asunción Blasco Martínez, this chap., below, n. 50. In her exhaustive bibliographical-thematic "Los judíos del reino de Aragón" in the *I Col·loqui d'història dels jueus a la Corona d'Aragó* (Lérida, 1991), Blasco Martínez remarks that "de los notarios [judíos] escribanos apenas se sabe nada" (p. 70). The judgment is echoed by David Romano in his "Els juheus de Lleida" in the same colloquium: "del segle XIII, no tenim dades de notaris jueus, tampoc en queda cap del segle XIV" (p. 119). See also the very late notice in Miguel Motis Dolader, "Los notarios i la documentación judía a través de las Taqqanot otorgadas por el infante Alfonso V y la aljama zaragozana en 1415," *El patrimonio documental aragonés y la historia*, ed. Guillermo Pérez Sarrión (Zaragoza, 1986), 261–271.

34. As in the Hebrew will above, p. 26. The celebrated cartulary *Liber feudorum maior* at the Arch. Crown has a set of instructions about calendars for Christian royal scribes, describing also the Jewish calendar: "Del compte del canelar [=calendar] dels juheus: le compte del kalendari dels jueus es del començament del mon, e es tro al primer dia de Septembre del any MCCCLXII compt<e hom> que ha cinch milia cent vint tres anys." I have not been able to find this late note in the published version of the manuscript.

35. María Cinta Mañé, comp., *The Jews in Barcelona 1213–1291: Regesta of Documents from the Archivo Capitular*, ed. Yom Tov Assis (Jerusalem, 1988), p. 21 and docs. 149, 379, and 398.

36. Fidel Fita and Gabriel Llabrés, eds., "Privilegios de los hebreos mallorquines en el códice Pueyo," *Boletín de la Real academia de la historia* 36 (1900): 387–388, doc. 88 (23 June 1372): "recepistis ab eis [secretariis] certos libros administrationum secretariorum preteritorum aljame ipsius," to make copies; "portari faciatis ad communem sinagogam ipsius aljame et immitti intus aliquam caxiam inibi existentem, quam claudi volumus, et super ipsius clausura vestrum sigillum apponi."

37. Josep Pons i Guri et al., eds., "Manual d'Alcover (anys 1228–1229)," in *De scriptis notariorum (s. XI–XV)*, ed. Josefina Mateu Ibars (Barcelona, 1989), Rubrica 3, p. 182.

38. Bono, *Historia del derecho notarial español*, 1:334.

39. *Fori antiqui Valentiae*, see especially rubrics 43 (*De peticione hereditatis*), 49 (*De divisione coheredum*), 62 (*De testibus*), 82 (*De tutela testa-*

mentaria), 85 (*Qui facere testamenta possunt*), 86 (*De testamentis*), 87 (*De intestatis*), 88 (*De heredibus instituendis*), 90 (*De repudianda hereditare*), 92 (*De legatis et fideicommissis*). The seven witnesses expected by the code of the emperor Justinian and reflected in the *Siete partidas* code of King Alfonso X of Castile in our period or the five witnesses stipulated by the code of the emperor Theodosius tended to beome fewer under the influence of medieval canon law, which allowed three. Louis de Charrin in his study of medieval wills at Catalan (and later, French) Montpellier found that the number of witnesses fell from seven to three, with most wills before 1340 having three to five witnesses, rising only thereafter to six to seven. Roman law required only males and excluded the immediate family and legatees. See Charrin, *Les testaments de la région de Montpellier au moyen âge* (Ambilly, 1961), 44, 50.

40. Arcadio García Sanz, "El documento notarial en derecho valenciano hasta mediados del siglo XIV," in *Notariado público y documento privado: De los orígenes al siglo XIV*, VII Congress Internacional de Diplomática, 2 vols. (Valencia, 1989), 1:188. This is true of the Valencian *Repartiment* codex, for example, but the ubiquitous notarial codices surviving from the late thirteenth century onward seem to hold the main juridical entry, abbreviating only some negligible formulas.

41. Neuman, *Jews in Spain*, 1:117.

42. Epstein, *Responsa of Ben Adreth*, 47–48, 55.

43. Arch. Crown, reg. 37, fol. 26v (4 September 1271), transcribed below in appendix, doc. 10. The odd and perhaps unique Latin adjective *christianicus* has no corresponding English "Christianic" but obviously does not translate as simply "Christian." Like its correlative here, *ebraycus*, the term designates a category at once linguistic and legal. In that context *christianicus* seems a Latinization of Old Catalan *crestianesch*, meaning proper to Christian language and culture.

44. Blasco Martínez, "Judíos del reino de Aragón," 71, on crown references; and Nirenberg, "A Female Rabbi in Fourteenth-Century Zaragoza?" *Sefarad* 51 (1991): 180 and n. Asher b. Yehiel around 1300 defined the Sephardic rabbi as a sage "whose occupation is the learning of the law, and who makes it permanent and [makes] his trade part-time, and who studies the Torah continuously and does not interrupt it in order to deal with futile objects but only to pursue his livelihood . . . [that man] belongs to the class of the rabbis"; see Simon Schwarzfuchs, *A Concise History of the Rabbinate* (Oxford, 1993), 66. Ibn Adret distinguished such men from "rabbis who have been appointed by the king and cannot study or teach [the law] properly" (Schwarzfuchs, *Rabbinate*, 48); see chap. 6 on the very different evolution and meanings of the Sephardic rabbi as against the Ashkenazic, with no specialization (p. 74) and with a common distinction between the rabbinic judge or *dayyan* (Catalan *jutge o rap*) and the synagogue rabbi. Cf. Goitein, *Mediterranean Society*, 2:211–212, "rabbi" in the East not as spiritual leader but "a prominent scholar whose legal opinions were regarded as authoritative." Cf. also the spiritual leader of the Jews at Vich in Catalonia in a document of 1336: "per eorum rabinum sive capellanum" (in Ramon Corbella i Llobet, *L'aljama de jueus de Vic* (Vich, [1909] 1984), p. 202, doc. 50.

45. Arch. Crown., reg. 197, fol. 106rv (21 April 1300), transcribed below in appendix, doc. 34.

46. Ibid., reg. 232, fols. 352v-353 (23 February [1317] 1318), transcribed below in appendix, doc. 41. The Hebrew name Adar (feminine Adara) means "noble"; the *a* ending here may be a scribal or Latinate addition. The ms. has Acdarra here but Adarra in doc. 43. The surname may be the distinguished Judeo-Arabic Adar'i family of Moroccan origin which had representatives in Barcelona.

47. Ibid., reg. 229, fol. 274v (1 April 1327), transcribed below in appendix, doc. 43.

48. Yitzhak Baer transcribes fourteenth- and fifteenth-century documents on the Arago-Catalan Jewish notariates: *Die Juden im christlichen Spanien: Urkunden and Regesten,* 3 vols. (Farnborough, [1929–1936] 1970), vol. 1, p. 202, doc. 164 (Játiva, 15 January 1311), on "Rabi Joce Avenjacob, scrivano dela dita aljama" (Joce being an Aramaic variant of Hebrew Yosef, popular in Spain); p. 290, doc. 210 (Zaragoza, 31 January 1340); p. 388, doc. 272 (Zaragoza, 16 October 1364): "judei parrochiani synagoge maioris judeorum Cesarauguste" on the "officia judarie civitatis Cesarauguste, sicut notarii, albedin, et el rabi qui decollat in macello, et los rabis qui faciunt orationem in synagogis"; p. 515, doc. 342 (Valencia, 10 March 1382): "salaris de avocats, escrivans"; p. 765, doc. 472 (Barcelona, 25 June 1400): "hauran a fer necessariament cartes e scriptures judaycas"; p. 854, doc. 531 (1423); p. 858, doc. 534 (1431). Documents for Navarre follow: see, e.g., p. 941, doc. 584 (1265); p. 946, doc. 585 (1270); pp. 1026 and 1028 (*fueros*). The Uncastillo case is in Ferrer Mallol and Riera i Sans, "Miscel·lània de documents," pp. 444–445, doc. C-2 (16 February 1391), to Zecharya Sarug ("Zaquariam Ceruc"): "sis rabinus aljame . . . et scriptor etiam instrumentorum . . . inter judeum et judeum," a monopoly enforced by a penalty of a hundred gold florins per violation. On Ceruc see also Irene Garbell, "The Pronunciation of Hebrew in Medieval Spain," in *Homenaje a Millás-Vallicrosa,* 2 vols. (Barcelona, 1954–1956), 688.

49. Arch. Crown, reg. 211, fol. 220 (24 October 1314), transcribed below in appendix, doc. 40. Azariya/Azaria is a biblical Hebrew name.

50. Asunción Blasco Martínez, "Notarios-escribanos judíos de Aragón (siglos XIV–XV)," *Rashi 1040–1990, hommage à Ephraïm E. Urbach: Congrès européen des études juives,* ed. Gabrielle Sed-Rajna (Paris, 1993), 645–656; "una tema sistemáticamente marginado" (p. 645), and see the four-page commentary of Riera above in this chap., n. 33. The appointment of March 1424 is transcribed in an appendix: "te dictum Açach in çoferium seu notarium aljame judeorum"; cf. also n. 19 of the article (1400). Of the doubly recognized *sōfer*-notary given authoritative standing by the king, Blasco Martínez concludes that at first in the fourteenth century some communities had one and some not; some chose their own, others received the person or office from the king; some acted for council or courts, others for private business; some were entrepreneur appointees who hired qualified experts for the actual work, while others were true *sōferīm* who might also appoint assistants. In 1380 at Zaragoza the clerk-recorder in court received no salary but took fees from both litigants (p. 648n.). In 1410 there a debt-receipt was cited as "scripto en ebrayco et romanceado en christianego" (p. 652n.). And in 1405 the testament of the Jew

Sento "fue reduzido de ebrayco en romanç" at the order of Huesca's justiciar (p. 653n.).

51. Neuman, *Jews in Spain,* 1:152.

52. Arch. Cath. Barc., perg., 1-6-384 (18 August 1273): "ego Bonyuas nutrita quondam Bondie Farnerii confiteor," with her *signum* below. Maria Cinta Mañé, comp., *The Jews in Barcelona 1213–1291: Regesta of Documents from the Archivo Capitular,* ed. Yom Tov Assis (Jerusalem, 1988), no. 304, reads Bonaivas, but the accented *y* is clear. Bonjudà(s) or Bonyueu was a not uncommon Catalan Jewish name.

53. Arch. Cath. Barc., perg. 1-6-181 (28 June 1290): "cursores publici et iurati civitatis Barchinone"; "de precio domorum et orti . . . in burgo eiusdem civitatis Barchinone prope ecclesiam Sancte Marie de Mari"; "et Issachus Levi Iudeus." Leila Berner's "A Mediterranean Community: Barcelona's Jews under James the Conqueror" (Ph.D. diss., UCLA, 1986, soon to be published, will transcribe the document in full and contextualize it). The document's *cursores publici et iurati civitatis* were the *corredors de Consell*; there were several subdivisions of brokers, such as *corredors de comerç* and *corredors de canvi.* The Mañé *Regesta,* no. 483, makes both principals Jews, but "Iudeus" is singular while Romeu de Sabadell is anyway a Christian name. The Jew "Rouen" is Catalan Rubén and Rovén, biblical Reuven.

54. Arch. Cath. Barc., perg. 1-6-374 (19 June 1286 within doc. of 30 June 1290). Berner transcribes and contextualizes this charter too in "Barcelona's Jews."

55. Arch. Cath. Barc., perg. 1-6-569 (4 August 1278): "confitemur et recognoscimus tibi Salamoni filio quondam Abrahe de Adreto . . . de pecunia heredum Isachi Adreti quondam." Hebrew letters are on the dorse (reverse of the parchment) but difficult to see. Berner treats the episode fully in "Barcelona's Jews."

56. On the courtesy title En, see my introduction above, "Names." The Arxiu Diocesà of Gerona contains similar documentation connected with Christian, and sometimes Jewish, wills. See the catalog entries in *Documents dels jueus de Girona (1124–1595): Arxiu històric de la ciutat, Arxiu diocesà de Girona,* ed. Gemma Escribà i Bonastre and Maria Pilar Frago i Pérez (Gerona, 1992), especially docs. 1 (1124), 52 (1295), and 65 (ca. 1320). Careful search in it to the mid-fourteenth century reveals no Jewish wills, but doc. 149 (1 September 1339) shows the bishop, on appeal from two Jewish minors, removing for fraud one of three administrators designated by a previous Hebrew will. The notarial codex for 1351 recently published, *El protocol del notari Bonanat Rimentol (1351),* ed. Laureà Pagarolas i Sabaté (Barcelona, 1991), has many documents on or for Jews but no Latinate testaments that year; it does offer Jewish post-testamentary materials, sometimes in business involving Christians (see docs. 31, 47, 49, 143, 165, 166, 192).

Chapter 3: The Role of Kings and Courts

1. Ambrosio Huici Miranda, ed., *Colección diplomática de Jaime I, el Conquistador,* 3 vols. in 6 (Valencia, 1916–1922), vol. 1, pp. 196–197, doc. 424.

M. D. Cabanes Pecourt, ed., *Documentos de Jaime I de Aragón,* revised version of Huici Miranda, 5 vols. to date (Valencia, 1976), vol. 3, pp. 75–76, doc. 601 (8 May 1252): "universis iudeis civitatis et insule Maioricarum . . . quod quilibet vestrum possit facere sponsalicium uxori sue cum carta hebraica ad aurum vel argentum sicut hoc possunt facere christiani Maioricarum uxoribus suis cum cartis christianis et . . . instrumenta vestra iudaica ad modum predictum facta eamdem obtineat firmitatem ac si essent facta per publicos notarios christianos." On "Hebrew" as including *aljamiat* texts of other languages in Hebrew script, see above, p. 43.

2. Angel Canellas López, ed., *Colección diplomática del consejo de Zaragoza,* 3 vols. (Zaragoza, 1972–1975), vol. 1, p. 211, doc. 108 (27 April 1264): "instrumenta dotium et sponsaliciorum inter alios aljame judeorum Cesarauguste confecta vel de cetero facienda per manum cuiuslibet scriptoris judei qui non sit publicus, observent, ita bene sicut essent facta per manum publici scriptoris, dum tamen sint ibi duo testes judei ex quo fieri *petit* secundum consuetudinem judeorum. . . . per azunam judeorum recipiat ius ab eis." For the word I've italicized, *petit,* my reading is *potest* (Arch. Crown, reg. 13, fol. 163). On "Sunna" in Jaume's realms and its use for Jews, see R. I. Burns, S.J., *Islam under the Crusaders: Colonial Survival in the Thirteenth-Century Kingdom of Valencia* (Princeton, 1973), pp. 221, 227–228.

3. Antonio Pons, *Los judíos del reino de Mallorca durante los siglos XIII y XIV,* 2 vols. (Palma de Mallorca, [1958–1960] 1984), with appendices of 212 documents, vol. 2, pp. 207–208, doc. 8 (25 May 1278): "quod testamenta omnia et instrumenta nuptialia, que dicti judei et judee de cetero fecerint et facere voluerint inter eos, possint fieri et scribi per scriptorem seu scriptores judeos in littera hebraica et cum testibus judeis tantum, si voluerint . . . [et] rata et firma et pro publicis habeantur ac si per notarium seu notarios publicos cristianos essent facta, et . . . prout de testamentis et instrumentis factis per notarios publicos cristianos uti potest." This is also in Fidel Fita and Gabriel Llabrés, "Privilegios de los hebreos mallorquines en el códice Pueyo," *Boletín de la Real academia de la historia* 36 (1900): 27–28, doc. 11.

4. Arch. Crown, reg. 192, fol. 74 (17 January [1291] 1292), transcribed below in appendix, doc. 33.

5. R. I. Burns, S.J., *Society and Documentation in Crusader Valencia* (Princeton, 1985), 22.

6. Francesc de Bofarull i Sans, "Jaime I y los judíos," *I Congrés d'història de la corona d'Aragó,* 2 vols. paginated as 1 (Barcelona, 1909–1913), appendix, p. 940, doc. 161 (24 June 1275): "attendentes quod dampnum et periculum imminent vobis fidelibus nostris Perpiniani, Ceritanie, Confluentis et aliorum locorum ad collectam vestram spectancium in instrumentis graciarum et privilegiorum que a nobis habitis [= habetis] . . . cum propter fraccionem sigillorum cum propter aque madefaccionem cum eciam propter amissionem et alia diversa pericula que noscuntur cotidie evenire"; he allows "quod omnia translata que fient et sumentur ex dictis instrumentis in posse scriptoris proprii vel scriptoris Curie eiusdem loci et sigillata cum sigillo Curie obtineant in omnibus roboris firmitatem in judicio et extra judicium sicut originalia eorundem." It is confusing that this study and collection of 168 documents has also entered the bibli-

ography as an offprint in the guise of a virtually unobtainable book retitled *Los judíos en el territorio de Barcelona (s. X–XIII)* (Barcelona, 1911).

7. Abraham A. Neuman, *The Jews in Spain: Their Social, Political and Cultural Life during the Middle Ages,* 2 vols. (Philadelphia, 1948), vol. 1, pp. 154 (quote), 155. Norman Roth, "Dar 'una voz' a los judíos: Representación en la España medieval," *Anuario de historia del derecho español* 56 (1986): 943–952. See also his revisionist "The Civic State of the Jew in Medieval Spain," in *Iberia and the Mediterranean World of the Middle Ages: Studies in Honor of Robert I. Burns, S. J.,* ed. Larry Simon et al., 1 vol. to date (Leiden, 1995), vol. 2, forthcoming.

8. Arch. Crown, reg. 66, fol. 203v (18 September 1286). "Ex parte Astrug Samuelis Abenafia et Jamile uxoris Iuceffi Abenafia filiorum Abraphim Abenafia Iudei Valencie coram nobis propositum, conquerentes quod cum dictus Abrahim pater eorum dedisse eisdem cum cartis ebrayce tunc confectis ius quod habet in alchariis de Rascayna et de Alcudia et de Benimaclet"; "quod in dictis cartis ebraicis continetur . . . et eciam alia instrumenta ebraica confecta inter Iudeos super . . . aliis contractibus observetis Iudeis."

9. Ibid., reg. 80, fol. 5 (8 July 1289, referring back to the time of Pere the Great): "Solomon Bahie Iudeus vicinus Muriveteris . . . emisse erbaticum rengni [*sic*] Valencie uti in carta iudayca inde confecta plenius continetur, et in dicta carta iudayca dicti Salamonis . . ." The Judeo-Arabic name here seems to belong to the son of the famous "Bahiel," Arabic secretary to Jaume the Conqueror and patriarch of Zaragoza's Alconstantini clan; see R. I. Burns, S.J., *Muslims, Christians, and Jews in the Crusader Kingdom of Valencia: Societies in Symbiosis* (Cambridge, 1984), 160–161.

10. Arch. Crown, reg. 80, fol. 75 (23 October 1289): "per instrumentum publicum iudaycum inde confectum."

11. Ibid., reg. 80, fol. 91 (31 October 1289): "Çalema Malagi" and "Astrugus Maleci," "racione quarundam domorum et logerii earundem sitarum in iudaria barchinonensi"; "secundum ius ebraycum et çunam Iudeorum." The "adenantati aliame Iudeorum" were to select as arbitrator "unum Iudeum ydoneum et partibus non suspectum invidie." On Islamic "Sunna" for Jewish law see above, this chap., n. 2 and text, p. 52. Salema is a form of Arabic Salimah and Salāmah; Malagi is Arabic Malīkī, not Hebrew Malachi.

12. Ibid., reg. 80, fol. 95v (8 November 1289), transcribed below in appendix, doc. 32. Though Catalan *cabra* means "she-goat" and provides a Christian surname as Cabrer or goatherd, the *c* in both Jewish surnames here is soft, yielding Arabic ibn Zabr and biblical Azarel. The son may be Catalan David or Daviu.

13. Bofarull, *Los judíos,* pp. 854–856, doc. 2 (21 May 1227): "quod nos Bonastrug, Saloman, Bonjuda, Bonafos filii Saltelli et nos Cresches, Mosse et Perfectus filii Vitalis Graciani, nos omnes septem heredes Perfecti et quondam nepotes eius, quia vos dominus Iacobus rex Aragonum . . . reddidistis nobis bona Perfecti memorati avunculi nostri que ipse nobis dimiserat in suo testamento, que ex parte vestra nobis emparaverat fidelis vester Berengarius Durfortis"; "et omnia alia debita tam nova quam vetera que vos vel dominus pater vester bone memorie vel comes Sançius patruus vester . . . ipsi Perfecto debu-

istis tam in cartis quam sine cartis"; "ac suscipimus in nobis omnia debita quecumque ipse Perfectus debebat pro vobis macellariis, panificis, vinaceriis, draperiis et aliis omnibus hominibus"; "hec difinicio semper obtineat firmitatem omni cuilibet iuri tam latino quam ebrayco." A line of Hebrew signatures in different hands is fitted into a large space between the text and the Christian witnesses. (I have made minor corrections from the Arch. Crown original, perg. 326.) Leila Berner explicates the background and implications of this remarkable charter in her "A Mediterranean Community: Barcelona's Jews under James the Conqueror," Ph.D. diss., UCLA, 1986; the Gracià (Hebrew *Ḥen*) as a notable family is prominent there. Latin *nepos* is not classical "grandson" here but medieval "nephew," clarified by *avunculus;* see the discussion on p. 86.

14. Arch. Crown, reg. 15, fol. 116v (3 September 1268), transcribed below in appendix, doc. 5. On the reading "Morella," see note in appendix, doc. 5. The name Sullam, though seeming to echo Arabic Sulami, is a diminutive of biblical Hebrew Meshullam; see Simon Seror, *Les Noms des juifs de France au moyen âge* (Paris, 1989), 259–260. Arabic Jamīla was a not uncommon name among Spanish Jewish women. Sa or de Real was a Catalan Christian as well as Jewish surname, either for Romance "royal" or from Arabic toponymic *raḥl.* The great Levi clan of Zaragoza took their surname Cavalleria/Caballería from their role as tenant-vassals of the Knights Templar at Zaragoza, often renewing from the crown the privileges they shared with Muslim and Christian tenants of the Order.

15. Arch. Crown, reg. 15, fol. 117rv (3 September 1268), transcribed below in appendix, doc. 6. The name Bonanasc involves the present indicative of Catalan *nàixer* ("he is born") with *bo* conveying "well" or "in a good hour," as the name Bonanat is the verb's passive participle, in the medieval inflection. Bel(s)hom is Catalan for a man of physical or moral perfection; exclusively a Jewish name during the reign of Jaume I, it doubtless is a cognate or crossover for a Hebrew equivalent. On Vidal as Romance for Hebrew Hayyim ("life"), see my introduction above.

16. Arch. Crown, reg. 15, fol. 116v (4 September 1268), transcribed below in appendix, doc. 7.

17. Ibid., separate document (4 September 1268), transcribed below in appendix, doc. 8.

18. Antoni Rubió y Lluch, ed., *Documents per l'historia de la cultura catalana mig-eval,* 2 vols. (Barcelona, 1908–1921), vol. 2, pp. 82–83, doc. 83 (5 April 1347): "inter filios Astruchi de Beers quondam et prime uxoris eius, ex una parte, et filios eiusdem Astruchi et secunde uxoris eius ex alia"; "quendam hospicium et unum locum sinagoge, quos pater eius habebat et habuerat Barchinone, et quandam bibliam et unum librum seu volumen Moysi de Egipto in se quatuordecim libros continentem"; "eligatis tercium extimatorem seu arbitratorem." This is the only document in which I have encountered the surname de (and plural des) Beers. It does not seem Hebrew Be'er or Arabic Bir; nor do Catalan names like Ber fit. It may be a toponym, as for example a variant of Besers/Besés (Catalan for Bézier), or a mistranscription. On plural wives or polygamy in Barcelona then, see Burns, *Islam,* 214–215; Yitzhak Baer, *A His-*

tory of the Jews in Christian Spain, 2 vols. (Philadelphia, 1971), 1:254; and Isidore Epstein, *The "Responsa" of Rabbi Solomon Ben Adreth of Barcelona (1235–1310) as a Source of the History of Spain* (New York, [1925] 1968), 87. In a noted case King Jaume I in 1267 recognized that "secundum legem judeorum licitum est uniquique [=unicuique] judeo habere eodem tempore plures uxores" in his realms, and that children from such unions were legitimate, "licet secundum jura contrarium existat"; he added his own legitimation in that inheritance case "non obstante aliquo jure ebraico" to end the dispute and facilitate the inheritance. See the charter in Bofarull, "Jaime I y los judíos," p. 887, doc. 62 (1 April 1267).

19. Yitzhak Baer, ed., *Die Juden im christlichen Spanien: Urkunden und Regesten,* 3 vols. (Farnborough, [1929–1936], 1970), vol. 1, part 1, pp. 256–259, doc. 190 (3 October 1327): "tota eius hereditas ad nos devolveretur"; "quasdam alias condiciones prohibitorias tibi dicto filio suo adiecit . . . multum tibi onerosum et periculosum." Barri as a Catalan surname (toponym) means a neighborhood or a section of houses. Catalan Colliure or Cottlliure is today a French port, Collioure on the Mediterranean. Daví in the document and its plural Davins, for David, also serves as a Catalan Christian surname. Bonjorn is a Catalan synonym for Bondia, a crossover name for Hebrew Yom Tov ("holy day"); he seems to be related to the celebrated maker of astronomical instruments for Pere IV at Perpignan, Bonet Daví Bonjorn de Barri.

20. Ibid., pp. 334–335, doc. 241 (5 March 1349): "non nulli judei de ditioribus et majoribus peytariis ipsius aljame"; "occasione generalis mortalitatis, que viguit hactenus in dicta villa"; "de foro seu ritu judeorum."

21. Ibid., pp. 336–337, doc. 242 (19 March 1349): "Mira, uxor quondam Salamonis Mordofay, judei quondam Barchinone, amita [=amica] exponentis predicti, gravi nuper egritudine constituta"; "dicitur esse nullum, et juxta legem ebraycam carrere debeat viribus et effectu et . . . dos dicte judee proximioribus sibi in linea parentele dividi debeat equis porcionibus"; "juxta ritum judeorum et legem et justitiam"; "vobis super hiis plenarie vices nostras committimus per presentes." The surname Cortal (Cortalls and variants) means "corral" and as a toponym is found in Cerdanya, near Castelló de Ampurias, and elsewhere, often as plural. For the names Astruc, Cresques, Jahudà, and Salamó, see my introduction above. Though Bonsenyor ("good lord") might have originated as an honorific (cf. Senyor), its exclusive use as a name by Jews suggests a crossover for a Hebrew equivalent.

22. Arch. Crown, reg. 56, fol. 5 (13 February [1284] 1285), transcribed below in appendix, doc. 25. The name Bonadona, though it appears only three times in Régné's indexes (see n. 30 below, this chap.), was a usual feminine Jewish name, a female equivalent of Bonsenyor (see n. 21, this chap.).

23. Ibid., reg. 56, fol. 9 (24 February [1284] 1285), transcribed below in appendix, doc. 26; on the corrected date, see note there.

24. Ibid., reg. 57, fol 198 (5 September 1285), transcribed below in appendix, doc. 27.

25. Ibid., reg. 63, fol. 68v (25 February [1285] 1286), transcribed below in appendix, doc. 30.

26. Ibid., reg. 63, fol. 67 (21 February [1285] 1286), transcribed below in

appendix, doc. 29. Régné reads "Alcolf" for Saltel. On the Astruc/Bonastruc identifications, see Robert Chazan, *Barcelona and Beyond: The Disputation of 1263 and Its Aftermath* (Berkeley, Los Angeles, London, 1992), 199–203. On the names Astruc and Isaac, see my introduction above. Though Seror explains Saltiel as coming from French *saut(el)* (*Noms des juifs,* 238), it is rather the biblical Shealtiel (variants Shaltiel, etc.). Biona is a form of biblical Jona.

27. Arch. Crown, reg. 46, fol. 217v (30 June 1284): "quod Boneta Iudea . . . intendens filiam suam uxorem dicti Bondavid bonorum subsidio defraudare ac legitima porcio quam de bonis matris eiusdem habere debet tempore mortis sue, ipsa Boneta oblita sua sanguine, contra pietatis officium et in fraudem atque iniuriam filie sue memorate vobis tradidit bona mobilia omnia que habebat, que quidem bona vos in vestrum dominium adeo convertistis, negociando et contrahendo ac mutuando . . ." Bonet is diminutive or feminizing of Bon ("good"); Benzion Kaganoff sees it rather as a variant of Bonat/Bonanat and therefore the *kinnui,* or Romance name for daily life, for Yom Tov as "holy day," *A Dictionary of Jewish Names and Their History* (New York, 1977), 131. Catalan could have either Bondavid or Bondaviu for the Latin here.

28. Arch. Crown, reg. 64, fol. 106v (27 August 1286): "absolvimus \ dimittimus et / diffinimus tibi Soli, uxori Avayu Avenrodrich, Iudee Turolii et tuis perpetuo . . . pro eo quia occultastis testamentum dicti mariti tui, in quo (ut dicitur) legaverat patri nostro quattuor mille morabatinos auri." Repeated in the review to his official, with: "mandamus quatenus dictam Iudeam absolvatis, et bona sua mobilia et inmobilia que ab ea cepistis et emparastis eidem restituatis et desemparetis." David Romano transcribes all four documents in his "Legado de un judío al rey Pedro el Grande," *Sefarad* 17 (1957): 144–149, also in his collected articles, *De historia judía hispánica* (Barcelona, 1991), 93–99.

29. Arch. Crown, reg. 206, fol. 124rv (1 June 1310), transcribed below in appendix, doc. 39. For the given name, could the Hebrew biblical Aylon be meant? Seror found a Jewish Ayon at Avignon in 1375 (*Noms des juifs,* 274). Vives (also a Christian Catalan name) is the subjunctive-imperative "live!" (probably for Hebrew Hayyim). Arabic Ḥasan is Hebrew biblical Yefet (English Japhet). For the courtesy title Na, see the introduction above, under "Names."

30. Rubió y Lluch, *Documents,* vol. 1, pp. 88–89, doc. 71 (23 February 1328): "in suo testamento ultimo ordinavit fieri quoddam studium ad opus scolarium judeorum pauperum, cui studio quoddam hospicium suum situm in judaria Dertuse legavit nec non plures libros et mille solidos barchinonenses pro provisione dicti studii"; "quod testamentum Bonadona uxor dicti Juceffi laudavit et eciam approbavit"; "per sexdecim annos et ultra, qui Açim ut dicitur male administravit studium predictum"; "quod ipse ut conjuncta persona dicti testatoris debet visere et administrare dictum studium et bona eius et complere ultimam voluntatem dicti testatoris cum ad eum pertinere dicatur ut proximiorem dicti testatoris." Though Cohen and Choen seem preferred spellings in Catalonia, there were several variants within that pattern; Seror's *Noms des juifs* lists a half-dozen Occitan variants from Cohel to Cahe (pp. 68–69). Aaron is Catalan for Hebrew Aharon, with variants such as Haron. On Bonadona as a name see above, this chap., n. 22. The Egea episode is in Rubió y Lluch, *Docu-*

ments, vol. 2, p. 123, doc. 123 (3 February 1357): "pietatis intuitu et pro redempcione anime sue et parentum suorum . . . quasdam domos suas situatas ante sinagogam judeorum dicte ville"; "et certos libros ebraycos"; "quod quidem magister vel rabi dicte aljame"; "non nulli judei dicte aljame, habentes odio dictum Abrahim." For Mayl as a variant of Meir, see Mayl/Mayr in Jean Régné's catalog, *History of the Jews in Aragon: Regesta and Documents, 1213–1327,* ed. Yom Tov Assis (Jerusalem, 1978), nos. 244 and 255.

31. Rubió y Lluch, *Documents,* vol. 2, pp. 111–112, doc. 117 (2 December 1355): "sibi fuerint dimissi per dictum patrem suum certi libri inter quos erat unus liber vocatus Evicenna, scriptus in pergameneis vitulinis delicatis littera rotunda, alias vocata inter judeos cadrada, et dictus liber tempore mortalitatis fuerit sibi surreptus seu abstractus a domo sua, et nunc repererit eum in posse cuiusdam judei cirurgici Barchinone vocati magister Boniuha Cabrit"; "procedendo sine omni litte et scripturis solemnibus solaque facti veritate attenta et maliciis omnibus proculpulsis." The editor's "Cerques" is Catalan plural of *cerque,* a circle, especially of persons; Cercs is also a Catalan family name and town, ultimately from Latin *quercus;* but here it is a misreading of Cresques. Cabrit is Catalan for kid or young goat. Hebrew Meir is found in Catalan documents then under such forms as Mahir and Mayr. Bonjua (Latin *bonus iudeus*) appears in Catalan/Occitan versions also as Bonjuas, Bonjuda(s), Bonjues, and Bonjuses. The somewhat misnamed "Square Script" in Hebrew, as against the generally rounded cursive, had a Sephardic subform. Latin *magister* here, Catalan *mestre,* though it could denote an artisan or a university graduate, also had the meaning of teacher and was frequently used as here for physician and as an honorific.

32. Baer, *Juden: Urkunden,* vol. 1, part 1, pp. 332–333, doc. 239 (1348): "laborans tamen egritudine, fecit legata distribuenda tam elemosinarie quam aliis, de certa quantitate olei, in quo dictus Hizquia nullum ius habebat, . . . et in butica et pro ipso extabat et tenebatur"; "dictam buticam invadendo et aperiendo extraxistis inde." Bofill (Latin *bonus filius*) can also be Bonfil(l).

33. Bofarull, *Los Judíos,* p. 918, doc. 117 (8 August 1272), but reading "Bonifac." Also in Huici Miranda, *Colección diplomática,* vol. 3, p. 374, doc. 1383. My introduction above touches on the name-forms Astruc, Bonisac ("Bon Isaac"), Cresques, Mossé, Salamó, Samiel, and Vidal given in this paragraph; for Vives see n. 29 above, this chap. Catalan *botina* is a half-boot, and Christians too bore Botinas as a surname. Régné's index indicates that this is its only appearance in all the 3,450 crown register documents on Jews from 1213 to 1327. Seror cites a very few male (Botin) and female uses in Occitania. Bonafós has occasioned several conjectures as to origin, including Bon Anfós in Catalan, but seems simply the formula of blessing: "bona fos!"

34. Bofarull, *Los judíos,* p. 918, doc. 118 (13 August 1272), but reading "Bonne" for "Botine." Also in Huici Miranda, *Colección diplomática,* vol. 3, p. 375, doc. 1384.

35. Régné, *Jews in Aragon,* appendix, transcribed documents, pp. 420–421, doc. 6 (16 August 1272).

36. Arch. Crown, reg. 21, fol. 55v (13 August 1272), transcribed below in appendix, doc. 12.

37. Ibid., separate document (13 August 1272), transcribed below in appendix, doc. 13.

38. Bofarull, "Jaime I y los Judíos," 919 (16 August 1272).

39. Arch. Crown, reg 21, fol. 74 (15 November 1272), transcribed below in appendix, doc. 15.

40. Ibid., reg. 21, fol. 74v (15 November 1272), transcribed below in appendix, doc. 16. See also Richard Emery's *The Jews of Perpignan in the Thirteenth Century: An Economic Study Based on Notarial Records* (New York, 1959), 30, 43–45, 54, 57, 69, 104–105, 124, 135, 156, 166.

41. Arch. Crown, reg. 21, fol. 74v (15 November 1272): "ab aliqua persona vel personis extra Perpinianum vel terram Rossilionis ad aliquas partes sine voluntate matris sue"; "donec scilicet idem Mosse etatem accesserit X et octo annorum."

42. Ibid., third separate document (15 November 1272): "non audeat nec possit uxorem aliquam desponsare iamdicto Mosse nec inter ipsum et aliquam iudeam matrimonium facere vel firmare, donec dictus Mosse etatem excesserit decem et octo annorum."

43. Ibid., fourth separate document (15 November 1272): "attendentes racioni esse consonum atque iuri, ut mater filios suos impuberes, mortuo patre, nutrire debeat . . . cum presenti carta volumus et statuimus quod dicta Botina [sit] mater et nutratrix dicti Mosse impuberis, donec etatis [= etatem] pervenerit decem et octo annorum, nisi tamen ipsa interim ducat maritum."

44. Ibid., reg. 19, fol. 122v (9 April 1274) transcribed below in appendix, doc. 18. The scribe writes the name first as Samuel, then corrects it to the form Samiel.

45. Ibid., reg. 19, fol. 141rv (June/July 1274) transcribed below in appendix, doc. 19. See note there correcting Régné's catalog on the date; Régné also mistranscribes Cohen as "Cohta" and Colasana/Tolasana as Calasana. The charter itself is clumsily worded. By one choice of punctuation (Régné's) the judge chose the arbitrators, who then reached an agreement on their own; by another choice (mine), the arbitrators reached their agreement with the advice of the judge, who presumably did not himself appoint them. A like problem makes it difficult to say whether Colasana was with the first party ("et eciam Colasana") or with the second. On the name-forms Abraham, Astruc, Salamó, and Vidal see my introduction above; on Cohen see above, this chap., n. 30. Though Catalan Tolosana and Tolsà mean a woman from Toulouse, a not uncommon name, the scribe seems to have confused *c* and *t* as is easily done in this script, yielding the form Colasana. Seror has no other citation than our present document as noted in Régné's catalog; seeing the Régné reading "Calasana," Seror argues for a larger cacography. Catalan Garcia, though common in the realms and not intrinsically alien to adaptation by Jews, is in fact almost unheard of among Jews this early in Catalonia or Occitania (again Seror's citation is from our document, through the Régné catalog); as a surname it prompts the suspicion that the scribe should have put Gracià (Hebrew Ḥen), a distinguished Catalan Jewish family (see above, this chap., n. 13). Toros is a variant of Todros, an ancient Jewish name adapted from the Greek ("gift"). Nina or Nena is Catalan for little girl and bears echoes here of Hebrew Nina

for granddaughter. Petita is Catalan for small woman or petite. Perfet is the past participle of Catalan *perfer*, meaning whole or complete and "translating" (as does Benvenist) Hebrew Shalom as a crossover name; other forms include Barfat. Seror argues that it is a variant of Profiat, for "profit" (*Noms des juifs*, 221; but see Kaganoff, *Jewish Names*, 13). Provençal/Proençal is Catalan for Provençal. Sullam is a diminutive for Hebrew Meshullam (see above, this chap., n. 14). Emery provides further information on this cast of characters in his *Jews of Perpignan*, though only one of the claimants is there: see Astruc Vidal on pp. 30, 41, 44, 69, 77, and 136, and his father Vidal Astruc on pp. 30, 69, 73, 77. Vidal Provençal is on pp. 36 and 154, Astruc Salamó on p. 76n., and Salamó Sullam de Porta extensively on pp. 17–18, 21, 47, 56, 72, 116, 137, 144, 154, and 160.

46. Arch. Crown, reg. 21, fol. 81v (10 January [1272] 1273), transcribed below in appendix, doc. 17. Bondia Cohen de Lunel appears in Emery's *Jews of Perpignan*, 30, 41, 47, 78, 124, 137, 139–140, 144–145, 159, 172, and 183–184.

47. Arch. Crown, reg. 44, fol. 226 (17 April 1282), transcribed below in appendix, doc. 24. On the kind of in-law see the note to the document. On Islamic Sunna for Jewish law, see above, this chap., n. 2 with text. Lunel is southwest of Nîmes. Abraham Laredo traces two Judeo-Arabic distinguished families of Spain and places our notable in the first: Shashon (from Hebrew Shoshan for "lily" or "lotus") with variants such as Susan and Sasson, with 77 famous members listed, and Sassoon/Sas(s)on (from Hebrew Sason for "joy"). The second lineage, however, appears only in 1392, and both lists appear to be the same family (see his *Les noms des juifs du Maroc: Essai d'onomastique judeo-marocaine* [Madrid, 1978], 885–886, 1111–1117, and 1146–1151). Catalan pronunciation of Xixó transliterates closely as Shashon, allowing the usual interchange of *i* and *a* (ibn/aben). See also Burns, *Muslims, Christians, and Jews*, 154–155. The Catalan name Bondia for good or lucky day among Christians was common among Jews here as a *kinnui* for Yom Tov; cf. Bonjorn above, this chap., n. 19.

48. Arch. Crown, reg. 63, fol. 39v (3 February [1285] 1286), transcribed below in appendix, doc. 28. On *nepos* as "nephew" here, not "grandson," see above, p. 86 and this chap., n. 13.

49. Ibid., reg. 12, fol. 88 (6 June 1263), transcribed below in appendix, doc. 2. On the name Biona as Jona, see n. 26, and on Bonet see n. 27, both in the chapter. Zarc, found at Barcelona and Perpignan, is a form of the Hebrew name Zerach, or "light" (variants Zarchi, Zarac). Bellor is Catalan for beautiful. Modec is a diminutive of Hebrew Mordechai (as with Mode and Moteff today). Saltiel must be a variant of Hebrew Shealtiel, on which see n. 26, this chap. On the *guiatge* see Robert I. Burns, S.J., "The *Guidaticum* Safe-Conduct in Medieval Arago-Catalonia: A Mini-Institution for Muslims, Christians and Jews," *Medieval Encounters: Jewish, Christian, and Muslim Cultures in Confluence and Dialogue* (Leiden) 1 (1995), 51–113. On oral dictation see below pp. 102–103.

50. Joaquim Miret i Sans and Moïse Schwab, eds. "Documents sur les juifs catalans aux XIe, XIIe, et XIIIe siècles," *Revue des études juives* 68 (1914): 184–

185, doc. 22 (7 November 1263 in copy of 17 July 1293): "domos meos cum solis et superpositis . . . viginti et quatuor libros hebraycos et locum quem habeo in sinagoga"; "convertantur in helemosinam pro remedio anime mee"; "orta que dicitur de Queralto Elemosine." The Scandarini family will be discussed in Leila Berner, "Barcelona's Jews." The root Alexander (and Sander, Sender) was among the "sacred names" taken directly, not a *kinnui*; see Kaganoff, *Jewish Names,* 49.

51. Joseph Jacobs, *An Inquiry into the Sources of the History of the Jews in Spain* (London, 1894), summary on p. xxv. Classical Latin *hereditas* kept the note of heir and succession; Spanish split the concept into *herencia* (inheritance) and *heredad* (a property, even one not received by inheritance), Catalan *heretat* can have either meaning. On the name Bonadona, see n. 22, this chap.

52. For the case of the copper pots, see doc. 44 (25 July 1343) transcribed below in appendix. A number of debt transactions and one brawl between Jews and Christians are among the ten or so pertinent episcopal cases in *The Register Notule communium 14 of the Diocese of Barcelona (1345–1348): A Calendar with Selected Documents,* ed. Jocelyn Hillgarth and Giulio Silano (Toronto, 1983); see nos. 34, 38, 213, 336, 415, 422, 425, 432, 484, 544, and 642.

Chapter 4: Wills: Palma, Perpignan, and Puigcerdá

1. See the comprehensive *A Mediterranean Emporium: The Catalan Kingdom of Majorca* (Cambridge, 1994) by David Abulafia as well as his "The Problem of the Kingdom of Majorca," *Mediterranean Historical Review* 5 (1990): 150–168 and 6 (1991): 35–61, and his "A Settled Frontier: The Catalan Kingdom of Majorca," *Journal of Medieval History* 18 (1992): 319–333. See too J. N. Hillgarth, "Majorca 1229–1550: The Economic and Social Background," in his *Readers and Books in Majorca 1229–1550* (Paris, 1991), vol. 1, chap. 1. See also Larry Simon, "Society and Religion in the Kingdom of Majorca, 1229–c. 1300," based on his doctoral dissertation (UCLA, 1989), currently being prepared for publication, esp. chap. 2, "Wills as Documents, and the Testator Population," with an appendix of transcribed wills. The standard multiauthor history is *Historia de Mallorca,* ed. Josep Mascaró Pasarius, 10 vols. (Palma de Mallorca, 1978), esp. articles there by Alvaro Santamaría Arández in vol. 3. Santamaría Arández also has an extensive bibliographical-thematic monograph, "Mallorca en el siglo XIV," *Anuario de estudios medievales* 7 (1970–1971): 164–238, as well as a volume of some 650 pages exploring all the problematics, themes, and bibliography of this odd kingdom: *Ejecutoria del reino de Mallorca, 1230–1343* (Palma de Mallorca, 1990). See also Pablo Cateura Bennasser, *Sociedad, jerarquía, y poder en la Mallorca medieval* (Palma de Mallorca, 1984), and the wide-ranging fiscal-commercial study by Antoni Riera Melis, *La Corona de Aragón y el reino de Mallorca en el primer cuarto del siglo XIV,* 1 vol. to date (Madrid, 1986), including background chapters.

2. On the kingdom's Jews, see David Abulafia, *A Mediterranean Emporium, chap. 5;* his "A Settled Frontier: The Catalan Kingdom of Majorca"; and his "From Privilege to Persecution: Crown, Church, and Synagogue in the City

of Majorca, 1229–1343," in *Church and City 1000–1500: Essays in Honor of Christopher Brooke,* ed. David Abulafia et al. (Cambridge, 1992), 111–126. Simon, "Society and Religion," chap. 6, has a comparative study of Majorca's Muslims and Jews. Richard W. Emery, *The Jews of Perpignan in the Thirteenth Century: An Economic Study Based on Notarial Records* (New York, 1959), includes some 150 documents transcribed. Josep Mascaró Pasarius has a book-length general study "Judíos i descendientes de judíos conversos de Mallorca" in his *Historia de Mallorca,* 10:44–180. The celebrated codex of Jewish privileges for Majorca is transcribed by Fidel Fita and Gabriel Llabrés, "Privilegios de los hebreos mallorquines en el códice Pueyo," *Boletín de la Real academia de la historia* 36 (1900): 13–35, 121–148, 185–209, 273–306, 369–402, 458–494. Valuable for its documents also is Antonio Pons, *Los judíos del reino de Mallorca durante los siglos XIII y XIV,* 2 vols. (Palma de Mallorca, [1958–1960] 1984). For the Jews of Cerdanya and Puigcerdá, see below, this chap., n. 18. My doctoral student Rebecca Lynn Winer is finishing her dissertation at UCLA "Women, Commerce, and Family in Perpignan 1250–1325" from extensive archival researches, including a chapter on the experience of Jewish women and their roles and autonomy in Perpignan society; new Jewish Latinate testaments will be recovered and analyzed there. Philip Daileader, Jr., has in hand an archival dissertation under Thomas Bisson at Harvard University, "Community, Government, and Power in Medieval Perpignan 1162–1397," with a chapter "The Jews of Perpignan."

3. Abulafia, "From Privilege to Persecution," 118.

4. Fita and Llabrés, "Privilegios," pp. 133–134, doc. 25 (21 July 1319): "ad civitatem et regnum Majoricarum concurrunt passim judei et judee alienigeni vagabundi . . . [et] ponunt discordias et inimicitias inter judeos nostros dicte aljame."

5. Ibid., pp. 199–200, doc. 46 (11 February 1328): "et cum judei dicte aljame mercantiliter vivant pro parte majore," the king allows that any Christian or Jew in debt "to any Jew or Jewess" there "by any mercantile contract or by partnership [*comanda*] or otherwise than by an interest loan [*contractus usurarius*]" may be arrested at the request of the Jewish creditor.

6. Arch. Hist. Nac., Clero Secular y Regular, Dominicanos: Palma, carp. 89 (6 July 1288, in 13 June 1292), transcribed below in appendix, doc. 31. This parchment version was doubtless generated from a notarial original, its paper codex now lost.

7. Shlomo D. Goitein, *A Mediterranean Society: The Jewish Communities of the Arab World as Portrayed in the Documents of the Cairo Geniza,* 6 vols. (Berkeley, Los Angeles, London, 1967–1993), 3:317. Omar for ʿUmar is not Omer, a new Hebrew name today in Israel.

8. Emery, *Jews of Perpignan,* 11, 102 (quotes). There were Jews here from at least 1160. Emery's notarial documents are from Perpignan's Archives Départementales des Pyrénées-Orientales, séries E, fonds des notaires, regs. 1–17.

9. Emery, *Jews of Perpignan,* 99, 106–107 (quotes); see also p. 14.

10. Ibid., 106–107.

11. Ibid., pp. 134–135, doc. 4 (27 February 1273): "Bonisachus Fagim judeus etc . . . dimitto jure institutionis et nomine hereditatis sue de dictis bonis

meis Bonedomine filie mee M.DCCC.LXX. V. sol. Bar. de qua etc. et dono dicte filee mee in curatorem et gubernatorem Juceffum de Crassa . . . item dimitto Regine filie mee jure institutionis . . . et totum quod sibi dedi tempore nuptiarum suarum cum viro suo . . . item volo et mando quod Bonafilia uxor mea habeat et reciperet suam dotem sicut continetur in instrumentis nuptialibus judaycis . . . instituo mihi heredes universales Vitalem Bonissac et Fagim Bonissac filios meos." On (Sa) Grassa see also pp. 18, 27n., 30, 147, 155, and 163–164. The name Bonisac as Bon Isaac, as well as Vidal and Mossé, have been noted in my introduction. On Bonadona see chap. 3, n. 22. Irene Garbell, "The Pronunciation of Hebrew in Medieval Spain," *Homenaje a Millás-Vallicrosa,* 2 vols. (Barcelona, 1954–1956), 1:662, 682. Simon Seror, *Les noms des juifs de France au moyen âge* (Paris, 1989), 235, 274.

12. Emery, *Jews of Perpignan,* p. 167, doc. 98 (10 October 1283). Gaugs is a Provençalism in Catalan.

13. Ibid., pp. 138–139, doc. 19 (9 August 1273): "quendam librum meum in quo sunt scripti [V libri] legis Moysi quem penes se habet"; "omnes libros meos quod penes me habeo"; "teneatur providere dicte Massipe filee mee in comestione et potu et indumentis et calciamentis usque quod dicta filia mea virum accipiat"; "solvatur Argote uxori mee tota dos sua prout in instrumento ebraico nuptiali facto inter me et ipsam"; "uxori mee Argote omnia indumenta sua et pannos meos omnes et totam bascolam meam que est in domo mea exceptis vasis vinariis et tina mea"; "dimitto helemosine obalorum judeorum infirma[n]cium VI sol. III den. Bar." I have made "generos meos" simply "in-laws"; the classical usage as son-in-law had by now become brother-in-law, father-in-law, or sometimes relative. Argota's name may relate to Catalan *agut,* feminine *aguda,* "animated" or "lively." The name Profait is a puzzle. Seror lumps it with Perfet (see above, chap. 3, n. 45) as meaning "(moral) profit," not a plausible joining. If Perfet is Catalan for "complete" and translates Hebrew *shalom,* and *profiat/porfiat* means "tenacious," there is still also room for conjecturing Catalan *profit* (for "profit") for Profait as in note 45, chap. 3, above. On the "coronat" *diner de tern* in this document, see my introduction, above, under "Moneys."

14. Ibid., pp. 149–151, doc. 49 (10 February 1277): "[si] voluerit venire apud Perpinianum morari una cum dictis heredibus meis et cum eis habitare"; "in tota vita sua tantum totum mansum meum in quo inhabito qui est in podio ville Perpiniani in callo judeorum"; "uxori mee omnes pannos meos et archas et vasa vinaria et alia utencilia domus mee . . . [et] instrumenta et alia que sint in dictis archis"; "dimitto amore Dei in remissione pecc[at]orum meorum DCXXV sol. Bar. coronatos . . . quolibet anno in festo quod judayce vocatur cabanes"; "amore Dei operi pontis Thetis Perpiniani"; "et ordino quod nec aliqua dictarum filiarum mearum nec etiam alia persona nisi tamen dicta uxor mea transcriptum sive translatum huius presentis testamenti mei possit habere nec sibi detur nec dicti heredes mei teneantur sibi dare." A number of persons involved here can also be traced in nontestamentary business in Emery's text and documents; his quote on Samiel is on pp.103–104. Perpignan got its first stone bridge, the Pont de Nostra Dona, in 1195; the legacy here may be for its maintenance (*operi*) or for a new construction. The Scal toponym for one wit-

ness may be any of four Occitan places or L'Escala on the Ampurian coast (cf. Seror, *Noms des juifs*, 249–250). The transcription Scal, as Seror found for another of this name in Emery, may be Soal, for which I suggest the biblical names Shual ("fox") and Shoval ("way") or a Catalan toponym like Escala. Kolatch's tracing of Meirona to Aramaic ("sheep") or Hebrew ("troops") is unnecessary in the Catalan context as above. On the equivalence of Asher and Asser in medieval Spain, see Garbell," Pronunciation of Hebrew," 666. The will of Benvenist is above in chap. 1, n. 26.

15. Emery, *Jews of Perpignan*, pp. 187–188, doc. 137 (24 September 1286): "manumissores meos scilicet Profaytum Davini de Capitestagno et Durandum de Malgorio habitatorem de Biterris"; "quasdam domos meos contiguas que sunt in civitate Narbone in fusteyria . . . et de eis semper quolibet anno in perpetuum doceri faciant infantes judeos pauperes de schientia ebraica quoscumque voluerint tam de Biterris quam de villa Perpiniani quam aliunde et specialiter de genero meo et dicti mariti mei . . . [et] emantur libri judaici"; "duos libros meos judaicos in quibus continentur V libri legis Moysi" (Genesis, Exodus, Leviticus, Numbers, Deuteronomy); "Blanche filie Abrae de Magalas ad opus sui maritamenti XX sol. Melg."; "in omnibus vero aliis bonis meis quecumque sint et unacumque [= ubicumque] instituo mihi heredem universalem dominum Deum amore cuius solvetis . . . amore Dei ad pauperes judeas maritandas." The manuscript's spelling of the names involved is Sara, Davinus de Capitestagno, Profaytus Davini, Durandus de Malgorio de Biterris, Mayrius, Juceffus, Cresques, Salamonus, Sima, Saverdia, Magalas, Mosse, Opidus (Latin for Opol in Roussillon). Sancho's toponym must be Vilallonga de la Salanca on the Tet river near Castellrosselló. The witnesses' occupations include *ganterius* (Catalan *guanter*) and *bracerius* (Catalan *bracer*). The toponym Cabestany is Capestang, west of Béziers in Occitania. For the names Cresques, Jucef, Mossé, and Salamó see above, my introduction; Profet is discussed above in this chap., n. 13, Bonsenyor in chap. 3, n. 21, and Daví in chap. 3, n. 19.

16. Emery, *Jews of Perpignan*, pp. 189–191, doc. 139 (8 November 1322): "duo milia sol. Bar. ad opus eius maritamenti . . . et quod interim heres meus subscriptus provideat et sibi providere teneatur intus domum suam de bonis suis in victu vestitu et aliis suis necessariis bene et decenter"; "filie mee omnes vestes sui corporis et omnes vestes que fuerunt dicte uxoris mee cum earum ornamentis, preparamentis, et jocalia sua et ligamenta ubicumque sint"; "falcidia ac trabelliamea locum non habeat in premissis"; "volo et mando totam predictam hereditatem et bona eiusdem integraliter et sine diminutione aliqua devenire ac reverti illustrissimo domino regi Majorice et suis"; "ymo ipsum legatum in eo casu volo fore cassum et nullum ac irritum . . . volo rationem et veritatem eis reddi et dici et in hoc testamento inseri ad eternam rey memoriam, videlicet quod omnia legata, lucra, et emolumenta per dictum patrem meum eis facta habuerint et receperint tam illustrissimus dominus rex Majorice quam illustris dominus rex Franchie in indempnationibus quas habere voluerunt a judeis in eorum dominationibus comorantibus"; "hospitium meum quo inhabito situm in callo." The manuscript name-forms in sequence are Asser Mosse Davi, Cohen, Bononis (both nominative and genitive, feminine), Astruchus, Bonusdominus, Samielis, Mayrona, Duran, Bonjuses Profayt, Vitalis Mayr,

Mosse Bonafos, and the Christian witnesses. On willing money to the king in Jewish wills, see pp. 57, 61, and 92; Norman Roth cites a legacy at Arévalo near Avila of 2,000 dinars "for the needs of the kingdom or the bishop," together with the gift of her houses to become a synogogue ("Bishops and Jews in the Middle Ages," *Catholic Historical Review* 70 [1994]: 14). Emery's text and documents add nontestamentary information on a few of the Perpignan principals (see the index); on *burgensis* see his p. 53. On the tension and background involving the kings of Majorca and France at this time, see Alvaro Santamaría Arández, "Tensión corona de Aragón-corona de Mallorca (1318–1326)," *En la España medieval* 3 (1982): 423–495. The names Astruc, Jacob, Mossé, Samiel, and Vidal are touched on above in the introduction; Maymona, Meirona, Belan, and Asher were treated earlier in this chapter. For Bonafós see chap. 3, n. 33; for Bonjueu and variants see n. 31 there; for Daví n. 19; and for Profet as perhaps "profit" n. 45 (cf. above, this chap., n. 13).

17. Emery, *Jews of Perpignan*, p. 149, doc. 48 (10 January 1277). See also p. 156, doc. 66 (8 January 1279): testamentary guardians had invested in loans; pp. 162–163, doc. 88 (1 September 1283): one testamentary guardian "non laudat" an arrangement; pp. 163–164, doc. 90 (5 September 1283): guardian approves a sale; pp. 169–170, doc. 107 (19 November 1283); p. 175, doc. 118 (17–26 March 1284); and pp. 175–176, doc. 119 (28 March 1284); among others here on executors or guardians.

18. On Puigcerdá and Cerdanya see Pau Vila, *La Cerdanya* (Barcelona, [1926] 1984), centered on its human geography; and Maties Delcor, *Estudis històrics sobre la Cerdanya* (Barcelona, 1977). Delcor gathered the "exiguous historical references to the Jewish community of Puigcerdá" in chap. 4, "Els jueus de Puigcerdá al segle XIII," previously published in *Sefarad* 26 (1966): 19–46. Emery's *Jews of Perpignan* provides valuable background, though he does not treat the neighboring region, Puigcerdá's Cerdanya. Emery transcribes five early wills, three of them quite long, in his "selected documents" appended: docs. 4 (1273), 19 (1273), 49 (1277), 137 (1286), and 139 (1322), and he includes a number of will-related documents. See also Emery's "Les juifs en Conflent et en Vallespir, 1250–1450" (regions adjoining Cerdanya), in *Conflent, Vallespir et montagnes catalanes*, LIe Congrès de la Féderation Historique du Languedoc Méditerranéen et du Roussillon (Montpellier, 1980), 85–91. The article of Pere Vidal "Les juifs des anciens comtés de Roussillon et de Cerdagne," *Revue des études juives* 15 (1887): 19–55, 16 (1888): 1–23, 170–203, gathered also as a book offprint (Paris, 1888), is available now as "Els jueus dels antics comtats de Rosselló i Cerdanya," *Calls* 2 (1987): 26–112, with translator's notes (see the discussion of fourteenth-century wills on pp. 35, 68–69). Despite his title, Vidal hardly refers to Puigcerdá and Cerdanya. Worse, Emery has exposed his "grave errors of transcription" (including *heredi* as Herod), his superficial acquaintance with the documentation, and his "entirely unbalanced" interpretations featuring "the bizarre rather than the typical" (*Jews of Perpignan*, 2–3). See too the guide by Sabastià Bosom i Isern, "Arxiu històric comarcal de Puigcerdà," in *Guia dels arxius històrics de Catalunya*, 5 vols. to date (Barcelona, 1982–1992), 127–217, and his *Catàleg de protocols de Puigcerdà* (Barcelona, 1983) mentioned in my introduction, n. 1.

Archaeological excavation of the early Jewish quarter (until moved around 1320) is currently going forward; see the progress report in *Acta historica et archaeologica mediaevalia* 14–15 (1993–1994): 386–387, and Claude Denjean et al., *Els jueus i els franciscans a Puigcerdà (segles XIII–XVI)* (Puigcerdá, 1994). Denjean is preparing a doctoral dissertation on the Jewish community of Puigcerdá; meanwhile, see her "Vivre sa judéité a Puigcerdà du milieu du XIIIéme siècle a la grande peste" in *Mossé ben Nahman i el seu temps: Simposi commemoratiu del vuitè centenari del seu naixement 1194–1994* (Gerona, 1994), 241–256. Demographics and locations for the Jewish community are in the erudite summation of history and archaeology by Sebastià Bosom i Isern and Oriol Mercadal i Fernańdez in the monumental series *Catalunya romànica* (Barcelona, 1944–), 23 vols. to date, vol. 7, *Cerdanya, Conflent,* 218–219, with an overlay map showing walls, antiquities, and Jewish districts.

19. Delcor, *Estudis sobre la Cerdanya,* 77–96, with thirty-five brief documents from it transcribed on pp. 102–110. This is the only specialized *Liber Iudeorum* at Puigcerdá for the thirteenth century; even for the fourteenth the Jews made extensive use of the general Christian notaries, though a mixed *Liber Iudeorum* can be found for 1326, 1330, and 1333. See Emery's opening chapter for the suggestions on Perpignan's size and on its Jewish names. On pressures from the north, see William Chester Jordan, *The French Monarchy and the Jews: From Philip Augustus to the Last of the Capetians* (Philadelphia, 1989), especially chap. 3. Emery stresses the opportunities opening, rather than French oppression, in the migration of southern French Jews (*Jews of Perpignan,* chap. 1).

20. Arch. Hist. Puigcerdá, protocols, Mateu d'Oliana and Guillem Hualart, *Liber testamentorum*, 1321–1322, fol. 17 (20 November 1321), transcribed below in appendix, doc. 42. Canceled with three vertical lines, for copy given. The wife's name may begin with *G* and have abbreviatory overstroke.

21. Biblical Levi is Catalan Leví. Boniacip is clear enough in the manuscript but may be a distortion of Romance Bo(n)macip (see p. 82 above); Hebrew Asif/Asiph does not seem comfortable here. Biblical and Catalan Jacob had French Jewish forms approximating or identical to the Christian: Jaque, Jacques, Jaccas (Simon Seror, *Les noms des juifs de France au moyen âge* [Paris, 1989], 140–141). David's name here is not the common Occitan variant Davin. The Covallis surname may relate to Cavaller? Catalan Felip, English Phillip, is uncommon and perhaps unprecedented as a Jewish name in these parts at this time.

22. Arch. Hist. Puigcerdá, protocols, Bernat Manresa and Joan Montaner, *Liber testamentorum,* 2 April 1348–31 August 1349, fol. 10 (22 July 1348), transcribed below in appendix, doc. 45. Three vertical lines cancel, suggesting that a copy was issued.

23. Carme Batlle, "Noticies sobre els jueus de la Seu d'Urgell: Els Bedoz (1336–1348)," *Urgellia* 10 (1990–1991): 375–406. Astruc with his wife Sarita and minor daughter Bonadoneta, included in the genealogical table in my text, appear in Batlle's study, e.g., on pp. 376 and 400. Seror, *Noms des juifs,* 96–97. Goitein, *Mediterranean Society,* 1:357.

Chapter 5: Women in Wills: Widows and Wives

1. Cheryl Tallen, "Opportunities for Medieval Northern European Jewish Widows in the Public and Domestic Spheres," in *Upon My Husband's Death: Widows in the Literature and Histories of Medieval Europe,* ed. Louise Mirrer (Ann Arbor, 1992), 116. Renée Levine Melammed, "Sephardi Women in the Medieval and Early Modern Periods," in *Jewish Women in Historical Perspective,* ed. Judith R. Baskin (Detroit, 1991), 122–123. She also notes that to avoid the prohibition against wives inheriting "it was not uncommon for husbands in many periods of Jewish history to have recourse to non-Jewish systems in order to leave a greater part of their estates to their wives" (p. 132n.). In the same volume see Judith Baskin, "Jewish Women in the Middle Ages," 94–114. On the rights and limitations of Jewish women "donors" or testators see Reuven Yaron, *Gifts in Contemplation of Death in Jewish and Roman Law* (Oxford, 1960), 138–140, and for the role of women as heirs/donees pp. 153–161; see also pp. 174–176 (widows) and 217–220 (dwelling rights). See too Enrique Cantera Montenegro, "Actividades socio-profesionales de la mujer judía en los reinos hispanocristianos de la baja edad media," in *El trabajo de las mujeres en la edad media hispana,* ed. Angela Muñoz Fernández and Cristina Segura Graiño (Madrid, 1988), 321–345; and ibid. for background Carme Batlle, "Noticias sobre la mujer catalana en el mundo de los negocios (siglo XIII)," 201–221. For wills of Jewish women in Aragon, see above, chap. 1, nn. 23–25. See also B. Z. Scherschewsky et al., "Widow," *Encyclopedia Judaica,* vol. 16, pp. 487–495, also published in *The Principles of Jewish Law,* ed. Menachem Elon (Jerusalem, 1975), cols. 399–403. The only study of widows in the area of the present book is Richard W. Emery, "Les veuves juifs de Perpignan," *Provence historique* 37 (1987): 559–569, a sociological analysis from some 850 notarial codices of Perpignan and other towns of Roussillon over a broad time range. He can document 285 widows, 555 married women, and 1,400 male Jews, but only 24 widowers. He estimates the Jewish population as fluctuating between 150 to 200 families, with widows numbering between 30 and 50, and he addresses such questions as marriage age and remarriage.

2. Arch. Hist. Puigcerdá, protocols, Mateu d'Alb and Bernat Mauri, *Liber testamentorum* 1306–1307, fol. 12v (23 October 1306), transcribed below in appendix, doc. 35. Canceled by three vertical lines, indicating a copy made. Initial X signals the start of a new document. In the left margin center: "debet V solidos." Cf. Richard W. Emery, *The Jews of Perpignan in the Thirteenth Century: An Economic Study Based on Notarial Records* (New York, 1959), name list on pp. 200–202 for comparisons.

3. Antonio Pons, *Los judíos del reino de Mallorca durante los siglos XIII y XIV,* 2 vols. (Palma de Mallorca, [1958–1960] 1984), vol. 2, p. 271, doc. 88 (8 August 1331), also in Fidel Fita and Gabriel Llabrés, "Privilegios de los hebreos mallorquines en el codice Pueyo," *Boletín de la Real academia de la historia* 36 (1900): 200–203, doc. 47: "iudei scolam habere valeant vel domum aliquam sive propriam sive conductitiam ad orandum iuxta legem Mosaycam ritus et consuetudines iudeorum in civitate predicta, ubi sinagogam curi-

osam et valde formosam et domum ad orandum alias habuerunt." The present *scola* is "potius antique reparatio et refectio, quam non sinagogam sed scolam aut domum ad orandum permittimus noncupari." Josep Millás Vallicrosa, "Esbozo histórico sobre los judíos en Barcelona," *Miscellanea barcinonensia* 12 (1966): 13–20.

4. Arch. Crown, reg. 202, fol. 202 (27 December 1304): "eo quia graviter excessistis, quia sinagogam vestram et almidraz construxistis et operati fuistis alcius et amplius quam fuisset licitus et debebat[ur]; quam quidem sinagogam et almidraz nos per vos ad statum debitum et pristinum reduci fecimus et mandavimus." On the circumstances of this synagogue see David Abulafia, "From Privilege to Persecution: Crown, Church, and Synagogue in the City of Majorca, 1229–1343," in *Church and City 1000–1500: Essays in Honor of Christopher Brooke,* ed. David Abulafia et al. (Cambridge, 1992), 124–125, and his *Mediterranean Emporium*, 90.

5. The manuscript gives the name forms as Abraham (in second declension), Aster, Astruch, Bondia, Bonet, Choen, Coras (?), Crexent, Fagim, Gaux, Jacob, Juceff, Mancosa, Mometa, Regina, Soall, Vitalis. On Aster as Est(h)er see above, chap. 4, p. 86. On Bondia see chap. 3, n. 47, on Bonet n. 27, on Cohen n. 30; on Creixent chap. 4, p. 82, on Fagim/Faqim p. 80, and on Gaugs/Gaux p. 98. Though Mancosa baffles Simon Seror (*Les Noms des juifs de France au moyen âge* [Paris, 1989], 171) it may well come from Catalan *mancús,* a facsimile or counterfeit Arabic gold coin minted at Barcelona by the counts; the first emission carried the minter's name "Bonnom hebreu," while the second was minted by the Jew Enees. The value, beauty, Jewish connection, and by the thirteenth century rarity of the exotic Arabic-Catalan coin must have led to this rare use of it as a name. Mometa is feminine for the masculine Momet/Mamet used among Jews at this time. Plausible origins are hard to discover, and Seror's *Noms des juifs* is not useful here. The Catalan and ancient Roman name Mamet/Mamert (including an Occitan St. Mamet) may afford a clue. The rest of the names here were touched on in my introduction, except for the puzzle of Coras/Comte/Cresques.

6. Arch. Hist. Puigcerdá, protocols, Alb/Mauri, fol. 15 (9 November 1306), transcribed below in appendix, doc. 37. Uncanceled. Mazères is seventy kilometers west of Toulouse, though less likely candidates can also be suggested.

7. *Fori antiqui Valentiae,* ed. Manuel Dualde Serrano (Madrid, 1967), rub. 82.

8. Cf. the Bedós will in chap. 4, n. 22, and related text. The manuscript gives the name forms throughout the document as Astruch, Baynola, Bedoz, Bonatosa, Cobes and Cubes, Deuslosal, Elias, Jacob, Juceff, Mosse, Ruben, Salamo, and Vidas, with toponym forms Besaldu, Lunellus, and Matzeres. Deulosal might also be seen as salutation, as Shalom. The phrase "domina et potens" in this will to mean full executor and administrator first appears in Catalan texts in 1192, though the reality of widows as executors was "much older"; see Stephen Bensch, *Barcelona and Its Rulers 1096–1291* (Cambridge, 1995), 273, with citations of testaments also from 1250.

9. Arch. Hist. Puigcerdá, protocols, Alb/Mauri, fol. 15v (6 November

1306), transcribed below in appendix, doc. 36. Canceled by three vertical lines, indicating copy made. At left margin middle, again: "debet V solidos." In paragraph three, adverbial *caste* used. Before Jucef (always Juceff in the manuscript) in the witness area: X.

10. Is Fava a form of Catalan Febe (English Phoebe; of Greek root)? Seror finds the name among Jews at Narbonne, Marseilles, and Perpignan, and also as a Christian name; he suggests an origin in French *fève,* as in *trouver la fève au gâteau* (to hit the mark, have a lucky find); see his *Noms des juifs,* 105. More simply, the Catalan surname Fava ("bean") may be its affectionate and whimsical source.

11. Shlomo D. Goitein, *A Mediterranean Society: The Jewish Communities of the Arab World as Portrayed in the Documents of the Cairo Geniza,* 6 vols. (Berkeley, Los Angeles, London, 1967–1993), 2:151. Alvin Kass, "Torah, Ornaments," *Encyclopedia Judaica,* vol. 15, cols. 1255–1258, and plates. The Sephardim used a wooden scroll-case, opening like a book, the rods coming up through its top.

12. The manuscript gives the various name forms as Abraham (in first declension), Aster, Astruga, Bonafylla and Bonafilia, Bondia, Coen, Fava, and Juceff. On Aster/Est(h)er see p. 86. For Bondia see chap. 3, n. 47, for Cohen n. 30.

13. Arch. Hist. Puigcerdá, protocols, Alb/Mauri, fol. 17rv (21 November 1306), transcribed below in appendix, doc. 38.

14. The manuscript gives the various name forms as Abraham (first declension), Adzero/Atzero, Astruch, Choen, Davit, Deulosal, Durandus, Fabib, Gentill, Goyo, Jacob, Juceff, Judea, Regina, and Salamon. On the name Asher see chap. 4, pp. 78, 83.

15. Gabriel Secall i Güell, *Els jueus de Valls i la seva época* (Valls, 1980), from the Arxiu Històric Arxidiocesà de Tarragona, with the four *libri Judeorum* described at length on p. 200. On the number of families and complete lists, see pp. 193, 204–206. The author reprinted this will in his *Les jueries medievals tarragonines* (Valls, 1983), appendix, pp. 554–555, doc. 19.

16. Ibid., pp. 188–191, with transcription on pp. 202–203 (1337–1338). Leila Berner, "A Mediterranean Community: Barcelona's Jews under James the Conqueror," Ph. D. diss., UCLA, 1986, pp. 144–162, 452–455.

17. Some of the phrases are "revocans omnia alia mea testamenta et ultimas voluntates per me olim conditas sive factas quondam"; "quod quingenti solidi distribuantur per eos ad puellas judeas maritandas"; "çafertora, quod quidem rotle sive çafertora volo dari et assignari scole sive sinagogue judeorum"; "item dimitto dicte Cerone terciam partem omnium pannorum meorum, tam lane quam lini quam stupe quam fustani quam eciam aliorum . . . et eciam ollarum mearum et mortariorum de cupro"; "absolvo et libero omnes judeos pauperes, qui mihi . . . debeant debita ascendencia usque ad quantitatem quindecim solidos terni"; "in hospicio quod ego et ipsa et eius filii insimul habitamus". (I have corrected some grammatical or typographical errors.) Seror, *Noms des juifs,* 100, on Serrona. On the *de tern* money here, see my introduction, above, under "Moneys."

18. The manuscript as transcribed presents the names in the will as Abraam, Asterona, Astrugua, Barzelay, Biona, Bonafilia, Bonetus, Boniua, Cap, Cerona,

Dulcich, Isach and Isçach, Leo, Maymo and Maymonus, Regina. On the name Biona see above, chap. 3, n. 26. On Maymó as Arabic Maimūn see above chap. 4, p. 77. Besides names discussed in the text, a number are in my introduction. The transcription errs as *filius* for *filios* in setting executors; name form and later reference to Astruga's sons clarify this. *Regino* and *Astero* are maltranscriptions, perhaps for the diminutives Reginona and Asterona. Note that there are two Maymos, one being the dead husband, the other being the legatee Maymó de Narbonne.

19. Baskin, "Jewish Women in the Middle Ages," 102.

20. Goitein, *Mediterranean Society,* 3:250–260, 278, 285–286.

21. Bensch, *Barcelona and Its Rulers,* chap. 6, especially the section "Marital Assigns and Widows' Rights," quotations from pp. 264 and 266.

22. Renée Melammed, "Sephardi Women," 23. Yitzhak Baer discusses the case in his *A History of the Jews in Christian Spain,* 2 vols. (Philadelphia, 1971), 1:318–319.

Chapter 6: The Search

1. Arch. Hist. Gerona, Pere Perrini of Castelló (Ampurias), manual no. 73, *Testamentos, 1326–1327,* ca. (unnumbered) fol. 19.

2. Arch. Crown, Pere IV, reg. canc. 1303, fol. 135rv (26 March 1341), also reg. 1304, fol. 96rv (18 October 1341), this time at Valencia, for Ismael (Hebrew Yishmael, Arabic Ismāʿīl). Bonastruges is a variant of Bonastruc. Oblitas was a Navarrese, later also an Aragonese, noble family.

3. Manuel Grau Montserrat, "Instrumenta judeorum (1327–1328)," *Amics de Besalú: V Assemblea d'estudis del seu comtat* (Olot, 1983), 155–156. Gabriel Secall i Güell, *La comunitat hebrea de Santa Coloma de Queralt* (Tarragona, 1986), appendix, docs. 17, 24, 46, 47.

4. Arch. Hist. Puigcerdá, protocols, Guillem Pere, *Compilacio omnium contractuum* (2 January–28 December 1370), fol. 105 (18 January 1370). "Sit omnibus notum quod ego Bonafilia, uxor magistri Jacob Bonet Iudei Podiiceritani . . . meum facio testamentum de bonis meis, ordinando super eisdem meam ultimam voluntatem"; "et in primis eligo meo corpori sepulturam in fossario Iudeorum Podiiceritani"; "item dono magistri [=magistro] Bernardo de Foix filio meo . . . quinque solidos barchinonenses"; "item lego Joye, filie Samuel Abrahe Cohen Iudee viginti solidos barchinonenses"; "decem solidos pro oleo deserviendo lampades escole Iudeorum"; "decem solidos barchinonenses alemosine del cal Iudeorum Podiiceritani."

5. Boniac is a variant of Romance Isaac in compound with Romance *bon* (Bonisac). Hebrew Yitzhar, not a variant of Yitzhak/Isaac, is a biblical name in its own right but less likely here. It does not appear in Simon Seror's *Les Noms des juifs de France au moyen âge* (Paris, 1989) for Occitania, but Bernat/Bernardus is on p. 36. On the name Bernard, cf. Catalan Felip used by a Jew (see chap. 4, n. 21, above). On the honorific "master," see above chap. 3, n. 31. On the name Aster/Est(h)er later in the will, see above chap. 4, p. 86; cf. below, this chap., n. 10.

6. Gabriel Llompart, "Documentos sueltos sobre judíos y conversos de

Mallorca (siglos XIV y XV)," *Fontes rerum balearium* 2 (1978): 188–189, doc. 3 (24 March 1388) from the Arxiu Històric de Mallorca. The transcription has Regino. Phrases include "sine strepitu iudicii et figura"; "coram tumulo dicti domini patris mei . . . bene et honorifice, more yudaico."

7. Arch. Hist. Puigcerdá, Joan de Conomines, *Liber testamentorum,* 18 April 1398–3 August 1408, fol. 1 (18 April 1398), including "quod omnes vestes mee dentur pauperibus parentibus meis ad cognitionem dictorum manumissorum meorum," and "pro oleo emendo quod deserviat ad honorem dei scole Iudeorum dicte ville." His codicil has as executor "magistrum Mahir [Hebrew Meir] Bonet, fisicum Iudeum" of Perpignan. On the name Boniac (Bon Isaac) see this chap., n. 5; on Bonet see above, chap. 3, n. 27; on Deulosal see above, chap. 5, n. 8 and text; on Cohen see above, chap. 3, n. 30; on Goyo see page 109; and on the honorific "master" see above, chap. 3, n. 31.

8. Arch. Hist. Puigcerdá, Bernat Manresa, 1398–1411, fol. 40 (27 February 1401): "quia nullus in carne positus mortem evadere potest . . . ego Vidal Bonafos pater, Iudeus ville Perpiniani, licet sim eger corpore tamen sanus mente facio, condo, et ordino meum testamentum de bonis meis"; "lego lampadem que ardet in sinagoga sive scola." See also above, chap. 1, n. 26 (cf. n. 22–24), for late fourteenth- and fifteenth-century wills from Majorca, Gerona, and elsewhere. On the name Bonafós, see above, chap. 3, n. 33.

9. Roger Aubenas, "À propos du testament d'un juif carcassonnais de 1305," in *Carcassonne et sa région,* XLIe Congrès d'Études Régionales Tenus par la Fédération Historique du Languedoc Méditerranéen et du Roussillon (Carcassonne, 1970), 165–171. This will of "Isaac medicus" (Catalan/Occitan Metge) is in the Bibliothèque Nationale in Paris, Collection Languedoc, Bénédictins, reg. 82, fols. 107 and 108 (August 1305), not an original but among the copies by Claude Devic and Joseph Vaissète, communicated to the editor by Philippe Wolff. The text has distributions "in festo cabanarum" and "in festo Paschae Domini" and "in festo Circumcisionis Domini dicto in hebraico Rossane"; it mandates "unam coronam qua [= que] alias utatur [= vocatur] in ebraico atara ad opus Rotuli" (besides the textual problems, the editor misunderstands this phrase); it leaves the grandsons "unam cameram et unam coquinam que sunt in passadorio juxta januam desupra stalario domus mee." The editor remarks that in his extensive research in southern French wills he has never encountered among the formularies a model for a Jewish will; the reason, as seen above, is that the Jews accommodated to the gentile world in these relatively few cases for special reasons, with consequent scribal clumsiness in their own adaptation.

10. Joseph Shatzmiller, *Shylock Reconsidered: Jews, Moneylending, and Medieval Society* (Berkeley, Los Angeles, London, 1990), 28–35, on Abraham and Bondaví, esp. 29–31 and 224 on the will. The will is transcribed in full in appendix 2, pp. 163–165, from the Archives de la Ville de Marseille, notaires II 19 between fols. 61 and 62. Both father and son are "cives Massilie," the son to act "tacitum et contentum, ita quod nichil amplius petere valeat in ceteris bonis meis"; "prohibeo quod dictus Bonus Davinus filius meus, pater dicti Abrameti, non habeat nec habere possit nec accipere fructus dicte vinee . . . non obstante quod dictus Abrametus esset post mortem meam in potestate

dicti Boni Davini." The "cloquaria argenti" can hardly be a belltower but perhaps a bell ornament like the other jewelry here. For local background see Adolphe Crémieux, "Les juifs de Marseille au moyen âge," *Revue des études juives* 46 (1903): 1–47, 246–268, and 47 (1903): 62–86, 243–261. Seror links the name Astes tentatively to Aster/Est(h)er (*Noms des juifs*, appendix 2). Besides the diminutives for Abraham, Bella, Blanca, and Salamó noted, see the name Bonadona above in chap. 3, n. 22, Bondaví there in n. 19, and Dolça on p. 112. Cresques is treated in my introduction. Deulocresca, "may God give him growth," involves the medieval subjunctive of the Catalan verb *créixer*, "to grow," as Cresques (*cresqués*) involves the optative. The name Profach, which Seror relates to Perfet and Profait, may rather be a variant of the Catalan given-name Profici, from Latin *proficere*, "to undertake, initiate." Cf. above, chap. 3, n. 45 and chap. 4, n. 13. Besides the identification Bellcaire = Beaucaire, there are Occitan and Catalan alternatives; see above, chap. 4, p. 85.

11. Daniele Iancu-Agou, "Autour du testament d'une juive marseillaise (1480)," *Marseille: Revue municipale trimesterielle* 133–134 (1983): 30–35, of Boniaqua Salamias, with facsimile; "L'inventaire de la bibliothèque et du mobilier d'un médecin juif d'Aix-en-Provence au milieu du XVe siècle," *Revue des études juives* 134 (1975): 47–80, a notary's testamentary inventory for Astruc de Sestiers at Aix in 1439, with explanation of the will itself of 21 July 1433 before a Marseilles notary; and "Une vente de livres hébreux à Arles en 1434: Tableau de l'élite juive arlésienne au milieu du XVe siècle," *Revue des études juives* 146 (1987): 5–62, with testamentary connections. Professor Shatzmiller introduced me to her work and tells me that she also has four wills from Orange in hand; he also informs me that Jacques Chiffoleau has a considerable number of later Jewish wills from Avignon.

12. Daniele Iancu-Agou, "Juives et néophytes aixoises: Leurs testaments, 1467–1525," *Eleventh World Congress of Jewish Studies*, 9 vols. (Jerusalem, 1994), division B, 1:165–172.

13. Monique Wernham, *La communauté juive de Salon-de-Provence d'après les actes notariés, 1391–1435* (Toronto, 1987), 26–38, 55–56, 77–81, 180, from the Archives Départementales des Bouches-du-Rhône. R. W. Emery notes but does not describe a will by the Jew Ali Abram at Arles-sur-Tech in 1347, from the Archives Départementales at Perpignan, register 284 of the notarial fonds, fols. 16–24, in his "Les juifs en Conflent et en Vallespir, 1250–1450," in *Conflent, Vallespir et montagnes catalanes*, LIe Congrès de la Federation Historique du Languedoc Méditerranèen et du Roussillon (Montpellier, 1980), 89. On the name Ali/Elias, see above, chap. 4, p. 99.

14. Shlomo D. Goitein, *A Mediterranean Society: The Jewish Communities of the Arab World as Portrayed in the Documents of the Cairo Geniza*, 6 vols. (Berkeley, Los Angeles, London, 1967–1993), 1:1–28 (introduction); quotes on pp. 10, 14–15.

15. Ibid., 3:188–191, 346–352; on coffins see 5:162. On the Eli/ᶜAlī name see above, chap. 4, p. 99. On Arabic Karīma, also in a Majorcan will above, see chap. 4, p. 78. I owe the *mamzer* suggestion to David Abulafia.

16. Ibid., 5:145–147 (year 1066), 144–145 (1090), 152–155 (1143), 147–149 (1150), 150–152 (1188).

17. Ibid., 5:139 (year 1040), 137 (1100), 138 (1201), 139 (1241).

18. Ibid., 5:152. A testamentary record on p. 140 has Abu'l-Ḥusayn Mūsā give his wife 50 dinars as the marriage gift plus 10 more as well as clothing and objects bought for her in the marriage but legally his as the husband. He waived the widow's oath of having nothing from his assets but only in return for her waiving replacement of the clothing listed in the marriage contract.

19. For these divisions and the rhetorical and legal training of the notary, see "Rhetoric and Style," in R. I. Burns, *Society and Documentation in Crusader Valencia* (Princeton, 1985), chap. 22, esp. n. 1.

20. Jacques Chiffoleau, "Les testaments provençaux et comtadins à la fin du moyen âge: Richesse documentaire et problèmes d'exploitation," in Paolo Brezzi and Egmont Lee, eds., *Sources of Social History: Private Acts of the Late Middle Ages* (Toronto, 1984), 151–152.

21. Goitein, *Mediterranean Society,* 5:141–142. On the historiography, methodology, and archaeology of Catalan Jewish cemeteries and their burials, see the thorough survey by David Romano, "Fossars jueus catalans," *Acta historica et archaeologica mediaevalia* 14–15 (1993–1994): 290–315.

22. Goitein, *Mediterranean Society,* 5:129–130.

23. Ibid., 2:403.

Glossary of Less Familiar Terms

*An asterisk indicates that the word is elsewhere in this list. Elements of surnames or given names are not included here. As is commonly done in English narrative, our text has omitted most Hebrew diacriticals, restored in this glossary. Entries in both Hebrew and Arabic appear in full capitals, on the model of the classic *Encyclopaedia Judaica* and *Encyclopaedia of Islam.*

ALAMINATUS. Latin. Office of the *AMĪN.**

ALATMA, or vet. Hebrew. A minor excommunication, or *niddui,* more lenient than the *ḥerem* in its promulgation, restrictions, and length.

ALFAQUINUS. Latin; Catalan *alfaquí.* See *FAQĪH.**

ALJAMA. Castilian, Catalan, Latin; from Arabic. Each local community of Muslims or Jews subject to the Christians in Spain, in its juridical personality as a semiautonomous corporation (*universitas*). Derived from the Arabic term for such a community's administrative council. Not the physical location (*CALL,** or *judería; morería* for MUDEJARS*). Several *morerías* or *juderías* could constitute a single *aljama.*

ALJAMIADO/ALJAMÍA. Castilian; Catalan *aljamiat;* from Arabic. Writing another language in the characters or letters of Arabic or Hebrew. Thus Hebrew could be written in Arabic script, while Aramaic, Arabic, Armenian, Catalan, or any other tongue might be expressed by transliterating into the Hebrew alphabet. Presumably the writer could speak other language(s) but he or his readers knew only one alphabet.

AMĪN. Arabic, "trustworthy." A minor official of a MUDEJAR* community, who grew in influence because of his role in tax collecting and especially as liaison with the Christian overlords.

ANTE MORTEM, DONATIO. Latin. See *MORTIS CAUSA.**

ʿAṬARA. Hebrew, "crown." Decoration covering the ends of the rods or staves on which the Torah scroll turned (see *SĒFER TŌRĀH**).

BĒT DĪN. Hebrew, "house of judgment." Medieval Jewish judiciary or courts of talmudic law in each local *ALJAMA,** a major source of community control and guarantor of Jewish traditions, touching on all civil, criminal, religious, and social aspects of individual and corporate life.

BĒT HA-MIDRĀSH. Hebrew, "house of study." Jewish community center for sacred study, open to all ages and classes, with prayer a subordinate activity. It could flank, merge with, or share quarters with the synagogue.

BURGENSIS. Latin. In the Perpignan early registers a man who lived on commercial or agricultural investments without entrepreneurial involvement (Richard Emery).

CALL. Catalan, either from Hebrew *qāhāl* for local communal organization or more broadly a "community," or else, as many now argue, from Latin *callis* for a narrow street. Section of a town reserved for Jews, around the institutions, facilities, and administrative offices encouraging their way of life. Also called a *judería.* Usually a privilege at this time, not a restrictive ghetto, with some Jews living elsewhere and some Christians in the *call.*

CHIROGRAPHUM. Latin. An indenture or bipartite document divided in half along an irregular line, often with a set of letters severed, to be validated later by rejoining the halves and the letters.

CONVERSO. Castilian; Catalan *convers.* An Iberian apostate or convert from Judaism to Christianity. The term is usually restricted to the conversion movement in the wake of the 1391 anti-Jewish riots and their fifteenth-century aftermath.

CORONAT. Catalan. Several varieties of coin showing a crowned king, but here especially the Valencian and Barcelonan pennies of that name under Jaume I (*diners de tern*) modeled on a Provençal coin.

CORREDOR. Catalan. A broker in agricultural, industrial, commercial, or other business.

CROAT. Catalan, "marked by a cross." The first *SOU** of the Arago-Catalan realms actually minted, in 1285, instead of being a ghost money of account.

DAYYĀN. Hebrew. Ordinary judge of the *BĒT DĪN** system of Jewish courts.

DHIMMA. Arabic. The status of the *dhimmī,* the Christians or Jews living as communities in Islamic lands. The *ahl al-dhimma,* or "people of the covenant," lived in subordinate but semiautonomous religious societies. Though noncitizens, *dhimmī* had rights and duties, enjoyed juridical and personal liberty, and related to the Islamic state through their own religious officials.

DĪNĀR. Arabic. Islamic coin modeled on the Roman *denarius,* consisting of 24 carats. Shlomo Goitein estimates that 2 Fatimid dinars could support a lower-middle-class family for a month.

DINER. Catalan, from Latin *denarius,* "penny." See *SOU.**

DONATIO. Latin. Free transfer of ownership with no requirement or reciprocal action. See *INTER VIVOS** and *MORTIS CAUSA.** Jewish pretestamentary gifts or transfers were bilateral, requiring the beneficiary's active response.

DOWER. See *SPONSALICIUM.**

DOWRY. See *KETŪBĀH.**

ENFITEUSI/EMFITEUSI. Catalan, from Greek. Temporary or perpetual alienation of property or an office (such as a notariate) at an annual fee, the original owner retaining direct dominion but ceding use of the property including the right to testamentary bequeathal of it.

EN. Catalan. Honorific from Latin vocative *domine.* Attached to Jewish or Christian names, akin to English "sir" or "Mr." *Na* is the feminine. Cf. Castilian *Don, Doña.*

ESPITAL/HOSPITAL. Catalan. An almshouse (also *almoina*) or hospice-hospital, whether Jewish or Christian.

ETHICAL WILLS. A genre of Jewish ethical literature, basically exhortatory injunctions. They were rarely real wills though sometimes misread as such.

FADIGA/FATIGA. Catalan and Latin. Option to repurchase a property when it again goes on the market, reserved to the former owner, especially in the case of *ENFITEUSI.**

FALCIDIAN FOURTH, from the Roman law *lex falcidia(na).* Decreed that legacies could constitute only three-fourths of an estate, leaving a fourth for the main heir. Thus the UNIVERSAL HEIR* could diminish other legacies so as to preserve his fourth. Not in Justinian's code, it entered the medieval Roman law revival late, coming into Barcelona only in the fourteenth century and in Catalan Perpignan by the early 1260s. Cf. TREBELLIANIC FOURTH.*

FAQĪH, AL-. Arabic. Theological jurist or scholar contributing to the religio-cultural jurisprudence and practical law. By MUDEJAR* times it could apply to anyone somewhat learned in koranic wisdom, of whom several might hold elected or appointed roles in local administration. See *ALFAQUINUS.**

FATWĀ. Arabic. Formal response by a theological lawyer in Islam, based on tradition rather than creative opinion, to a query from a judge or individual to help resolve a case or a conscience, including problems of inheritance. When a judge elicited a *fatwā,* the state enforced it. Scholars valued collections of responses.

FORUM. Latin. Law or law code, also used for Jewish biblical-talmudic law, as in *ius et forum et açunna Iudeorum.*

FUEROS. Aragonese and Castilian. Any municipal, regional, or royal code of customs, laws, and privileges. The *Fueros of Aragon* were especially the massive codification of laws of the upland Kingdom of Aragon by Vidal Canyelles in Latin (now lost) and Romance versions, promulgated by Jaume I in 1247. Cf. *FURS.**

FURS. Catalan. Romanized law code devised for Christian settlers arriving in the Valencian kingdom after its conquest from Islam. The local *Costum* version (by 1240) evolved into the *Furs* of 1261, applied to the whole kingdom by 1271. The Latin version is the *Fori.* Cf. *FUEROS.**

GENIZA. From Hebrew. A jumble of writings of any sort in Hebrew, discarded as useless but preserved for future burial either because the writings bear the name of God or because they are written in the godly language itself. The most celebrated is the Cairo Geniza at Fustat (Old Cairo) with over a quarter of a million pieces, now dispersed to libraries in Europe and America, of which some seven thousand are historical documents rather than literary pieces.

GUIATGE. Catalan; Latin *guidaticum.* A safeguard or passport to protect merchants, travelers, diplomats, or even ordinary MUDEJAR,* Jewish, or Christian individuals who could afford the fee. Popular for a variety of commercial, political, and social needs, its formulas could also be incorporated into any general charter.

ḤAKĪM. Arabic. Savant/physician, master of knowledge. As Catalan *alfaquim* and Castilian *alhaquín,* a Jewish courtier-diplomat for a Christian king, especially in Arabic matters. Cf. the very different *ALFAQUINUS,* *FAQĪH,** and *ḥākim* or judge.

HALĀKHĀH. Hebrew. The practices, observances, laws, and "whole legal system of Judaism" in the Talmud as against the homiletic, ethical, and aesthetic elements called the *aggada.*

HOSPICIUM. Latin. In these wills a residence or family house.

IN SOLIDUM. Latin, "for the whole." In Roman law the responsibility of each codebtor for the entire debt. Also as *plures rei promittendi.*

INTER VIVOS, DONATIO. Latin. In Roman law a gift not connected with a testament, while both donor and donee are alive. Cf. *MORTIS CAUSA, DONATIO.**

KABBALAH. Hebrew. The successive esoteric movements or teachings commonly called speculative Jewish mysticism, emphasizing an understanding or spirituality of contemplation, illumination, and inner truth as against a more traditional rational orientation. The term particularly refers to the expressions this approach assumed from the twelfth century, notably in thirteenth-century Provence and Gerona in Catalonia. *Kabbalah* differed in basics from Christian mysticism despite influences, borrowings, and some common elements.

KETŪBĀH. Hebrew. Marriage deed expressing the groom's traditional legal and financial obligations, particularly the money gift plus increment to be paid from his estate at his death, and describing as well the bride's dowry and its increment, also to be returned at his death. Cf. *TŌSEFET.**

KINNUI. Hebrew. A Romance secular first name used as an epithet or substitute name in business and daily life by Jewish males, in place of the sacred Hebrew given name (*shem ha-qodesh*) used for liturgical or religious purposes. The *kinnui* could translate or relate to the religious name; thus Bonat was a *kinnui* for Yom Tov.

LIBER IUDEORUM. Latin. Where the custom prevailed, a special notarial codex, the Book of the Jews, was reserved for Jewish clients or essentially Jewish business. Other notaries sometimes resisted this monopoly by one of their colleagues.

LEGITIMA. Latin. Portion of an estate removed by law from the free disposition of the testator, to go to children or other close relatives. In old Roman law the *legitima* could compensate for an unjust omission or defect in a will. A daughter's dowry could be reckoned as all or part of her *legitima.* By the emperor Justinian's code a third of the estate came under the *legitima* when there were several children, half the estate when more than four. The Visigothic version in Chindasvind's code set aside four-fifths, severely restricting the testator's freedom.

LIBER TESTAMENTORUM. Latin. Any notarial codex or manual reserved for wills alone.

LLIURA. Catalan. See POUND,* *SOU.**

*MAMZER.** Hebrew. An illegitimate child who also comes from a union severely prohibited by law (for example, from incest or double adultery), thereby incurring the liabilities of *mamzerūt* status, though the child keeps inheritance rights.

MANCÚS. Catalan. Eleventh-century Barcelonan counterfeit or facsimile of the Muslim gold *dīnār,* the first two emissions being by Jewish minters. Several other coins bore the same name.

MELGUEIL or Maguelone near Montpellier in Languedoc/OCCITANIA,* money of. See *SOU.**

MONEDA DE TERN. Catalan. The Barcelonan pennies of a ghost money *SOU.** Coined by Jaume I in 1258 with three parts of silver to nine of alloy.

MONEYS. See *CORONAT,* CROAT,* DĪNĀR,* DINER,* MANCÚS,** MELGUEIL,* *MONEDA DE TERN,** MORABATIN,* *RE(I)ALS,* SOU,* SUELDO,** TARIN,* TOURS.*

MORABATIN. Catalan *morabatí,* Castilian *maravedí* from Arabic *Murābiṭūn* (Almoravid dynasty). A counterfeit or facsimile gold *DĪNĀR** of Castilian origin worth six Valencian *SOUS** by the 1247 equivalency table of Jaume I. The Almoravid coin was worth 8½ sous. Other coins of this name in gold or silver are not relevant here. Cf. *MANCÚS.**

MORTIS CAUSA, DONATIO. Latin. In Roman law a gift by a donor expecting death but not expressed in a will and thus not a legacy. Void if the donee dies first and actually conferred in full at the donor's death. Cf. *INTER VIVOS, DONATIO.**

MUDEJAR. Castilian and English, from Arabic, "allowed to remain." A Muslim belonging to a community that surrendered under terms to Spanish Christians. His legal status resembled that in Islam's *DHIMMA.** "Mudejar" was not used in Catalan lands in our period, nor did any corresponding term designate subject Jews or Jewish communities.

NE'EMĀNĪM. Hebrew. The trustees or officials constituting the administrative board governing a local Jewish community in Catalan or OCCITAN* lands; in Christian Latin *secretarii.* In Aragon these officials were *mukdamīm,* with *ne'emānīm* as commissioners for specific duties.

NEPOS. Latin. In classical Latin a grandchild but possibly a nephew. In medieval Latin in the realms of Aragon usually nephew, but possibly grandchild. Catalan distinguishes *nebot* as nephew from *nét* as grandchild, vernacular terms a testator could introduce to clarify his Latin.

NISBA. Arabic. A Muslim's generic epithet indicating tribe or region, as distinguished from his *ism* or personal given name, his genealogical patronymic (with *ibn*), and his family referential *kunya* (with *abū*).

OBSERVANCIAS. Aragonese, Castilian. Interpretations and applications of the *FUEROS DE ARAGÓN,** gathered into collections from the first years of the fourteenth century.

OCCITANIA. Region of Oc-speaking Languedocians in southern France from the Atlantic to the border of Italy, with a troubadour culture cognate with that of Catalonia. Francia or Frankish northern France conquered or absorbed much of Occitania during the thirteenth and fourteenth centuries.

PORTER. Catalan; Castilian *portero*. Messenger and minor executive officer of the crown, especially in the royal household.

POST MORTEM SCRIBENDUM (TESTAMENTUM). Latin. A will indicated before witnesses orally, with the written version to be validated after death, a procedure from Visigothic law surviving into the thirteenth century. Cf. the *TESTAMENT SACRAMENTAL*.*

POUND. Latin *libra*, Catalan *lliura*. Twenty *SOUS** or 240 pennies in the Arago-Catalan money systems.

PRO ANIMA legacy. Latin. Testamentary gift to a charitable or religious institution or cause.

PUPILLUS or *impubes*. Latin. A minor below the age of puberty, requiring after the father's death a guardian (Latin *tutor*) over person and property. The guardianship could come by appointment in the will (Roman law *tutela testamentaria*) or according to the laws of family relationships (*tutela legitima*).

QĀḌĪ. Arabic. The main judge in an Islamic or MUDEJAR* community, especially of questions allied with religion, including testaments. The Mudejar *qāḍī* in each locality was appointed by the king or elected and was salaried by the crown.

QĀ'ID. Arabic, "leader." A military administrator or commander in charge of a fortress. In the MUDEJAR* community a local civil governor.

RE(I)ALS. Catalan, "royals." Here the generic term for the silver money of Valencia created by Jaume I in 1247. See *SOU*.*

RESPONSUM. Latin. A genre of rabbinic consultative opinion by correspondence, responding to queries or puzzles about *HALĀKHĀH** matters.

ṢĀḤIB AL-WATHĀ'IQ. Arabic. A general public scribe in Muslim and MUDEJAR* communities, especially widespread in Spain, whose activities were analogous but only analogous to those of the Christian notary and the Jewish *SŌFER*.* See also *SCRIBA*.*

SCOLA. Latin, "place of learning." Used commonly in the Middle Ages as a synonym for synagogue.

SCRIBA. Latin; Catalan *escrivà*. Generic term for a scribe or copyist but in its technical sense a publicly recognized and regulated drafter of contracts and documents, merging in thirteenth-century Arago-Catalonia into the more Romanized profession of notary. Used in Latin documents also for the analogous Jewish *SŌFER** and the Muslim *ṢĀḤIB AL-WATHĀ'IQ*.*

SĒFER TŌRĀH. Hebrew, "scroll of the Law"; Latin *çafertora*. The five books of Moses on a parchment scroll, used for reading in public worship.

SEPHARDIM. Hebrew and English. The Iberian Jews up to the Expulsion of 1492; thereafter their dispersed descendants.

SHEM HA-QODESH. See *KINNUI*.*

SHŌḤĒṬ. Hebrew. Ritual slaughterer licensed and appointed by a Jewish community.

SŌFER. Hebrew; Latin *çoferius* but more usually *SCRIBA*.* Salaried official authorized to draft documents in Hebrew and Aramaic for marriage, dowry, divorce, commerce, testaments, and community administration for his local Jewish community in the appropriate legalese and calligraphy. Though Christian authorities recognized his documents for the subject community as authentic, he was not a notary except by analogy.

SOU. Catalan. This shilling (Latin *solidus*) varied in value according to its Aragonese, Barcelonan, Melgorian (MELGUEIL*), Valencian, or other local origins. Twelve pennies (*diners*) made a *sou*, twenty *sous* a pound (*lliura*). The Aragonese *sou* was a *SUELDO*.* Until late in the thirteenth century only the penny was actually coined, the other denominations remaining a money of account. See *CORONAT*,* *CROAT*,* *DINER*,* *MONEDA DE TERN*,* *RE(I)ALS*.*

SPONSALICIUM. Latin. In medieval Roman law the dower or marriage gift from groom to bride, usually as a promise of later payment, evolving into the Catalan *excreix*, or addition to the bride's dowry (*exovar*), and becoming a claim or right as encumbrance over all the husband's property. For the analogous Jewish practice see *KETŪBĀH*,* *TŌSEFET*.*

SUELDO. Aragonese. Version of the *SOU** in the upland Kingdom of Aragon.

SUNNA "OF THE JEWS." Arabic. Gross misapplication of an Islamic term by the crown scribes in Arago-Catalonia to mean the religious system and law of subject Jews. In Islam the Koran, *Ḥadīth*, and *Sunna* formed a triple but unified source of revelation, with *Sunna* as the prophet Muḥammad's life and practice illuminating the Koran and with any *Ḥadīth* embodying such *sunna(s)* in a statement. Christian scribes expressed the Islamic religious system and law as *Sunna*, sometimes transferring the term also to the Jews.

TABELLIO. Latin. In Roman law a private but regulated scribe for drafting charters. In Arago-Catalonia a synonym for the official notary.

TARIN. Catalan *tarí*, Italian *tarino*. Etymology unknown. A silver money of Sicily circulating from the thirteenth to the fifteenth century.

TESTAMENT SACRAMENTAL. Catalan, "will by oath." Oral or written disposition of an estate without notary or formalities but before witnesses. In Valencia's *Furs* the disposition was oral before three male witnesses, to be validated by their oath before a judge within three months of the testator's death. The most celebrated form applied to the residents of Barcelona and Gerona.

TESTES ROGATI. Latin, "invited witnesses" as voluntary. Roman law required seven for a solemn testament, but the rule of three witnesses in ecclesiastical law influenced a trend to three or fewer than seven.

TŌSEFET. Hebrew. Increment added according to custom by the groom to his promise of a traditional sum to his bride (see *KETŪBĀH*). Also the increment the groom assumed responsibility to add when returning a bride's dowry (*tōsefet nedunya*).

TOURS, in France, money of. Popular in Catalan Montpellier and in OCCITANIA.* Fifteen pennies *tournois* equaled one Valencian *SOU*,* eighteen Barcelonan, fifteen Jacan, and sixteen of MELGUEIL* by the official rate of Jaume I in 1247.

TREBELLIANIC FOURTH. Latin *quarta trebelliana*, Catalan *quarta trebel·liànica*. Protects a fourth of the estate for the principal heir when a trust encumbers it. The heir in such a situation is a "fiduciary heir" for part or all of an estate, obligated to turn over that kind of trust-legacy to the "fideicommissary" trustee named as such in the will. Related to the *quarta pegasiana* in Rome after Justinian's reform. Cf. FALCIDIAN FOURTH.*

TUTOR. Latin. See *PUPILLUS*.*

UNIVERSAL HEIR. Latin *heres universalis.* The successor to the testator, "instituted" (designated) as the main heir, whether one person or several. Fundamental to Roman law wills: no will is valid without this heir, nor can such an heir exist outside a will. Appears in Catalonia around 1227 and spreads despite the rival system of VISIGOTHIC* equal shares.

VISGOTHIC testamentary law. Basically tribal custom codified with corrupt or Vulgar Roman law elements, Visigothic practice restricted the testator's freedom (as Roman law enlarged it) to distribute his estate, enjoined equal shares for all children male and female, rejected the UNIVERSAL HEIR,* and transferred most of the assets to the family. Despite the revival of Roman law and the crown's prohibition of Visigothic civil law in 1251, this older system survived as a lesser rival in Arago-Catalonia.

Bibliography

Archives

BARCELONA

1. Arxiu Capitular de la Catedral, pergamins
2. Arxiu de la Corona d'Aragó
   Cancelleria, Registres de Jaume I, Pere III, Alfons III, Jaume II, Alfons IV

GERONA

1. Arxiu Diocesà, registres episcopals
2. Arxiu Històric de Girona, protocols

MADRID

Archivo Histórico Nacional, clero: Dominicanos

PUIGCERDÁ

Arxiu Històric Comarcal, protocols

For other archives, see preface above.

Published Works

Abrahams, Israel, ed. *Hebrew Ethical Wills.* 2 vols. in 1. Philadelphia: Jewish Publication Society of America, [1926] 1976.

Abulafia, David. *Commerce and Conquest in the Mediterranean 1100–1500.* Aldershot: Variorum, 1993.

———. "From Privilege to Persecution: Crown, Church, and Synagogue in the City of Majorca, 1229–1343." In *Church and City 1000–1500: Essays in Honor of Christopher Brooke,* ed. David Abulafia et al., pp. 111–126. Cambridge: Cambridge University, 1992.

———. *A Mediterranean Emporium: The Catalan Kingdom of Majorca.* Cambridge: Cambridge University, 1994.

———. "The Problem of the Kingdom of Majorca." *Mediterranean Historical Review* 5 (1990): 150–168, 6 (1991): 35–61.

———. "A Settled Frontier: The Catalan Kingdom of Majorca." *Journal of Medieval History* 18 (1992): 319–333.

Aguiló, Estanislao. "Documents curiosos del sigle XIV: Testament de Sayt Milí, juheu, fundador d'un hospital en el call de Mallorca, 16 Agost 1337." *Boletín de la Sociedad arqueológica luliana* 9 (1901–1902): 203–204.

Albeck, Shalom. " 'The Law of the Kingdom Is Law' in the Jewish Communities of Medieval Spain." In *Sefer ha-yovel li-khevod ha-Rav Dr. Avraham Vais,* The Abraham Weiss Jubilee Volume, pp. 109–125. New York: Shulsinger Bros., 1964.

Alfonso X el Sabio, King of Castile. *Las siete partidas.* Ed. Gregorio López. In *Colección de códigos y leyes de España,* ed. Alberto Aguilera y Velasco, vols. 2, 3. Madrid: Imprenta de R. Labajos, 1865–1866. See also edition by Real Academia de la Historia. 3 vols. Madrid: [Imprenta Real, 1807] Atlas, 1972.

Alfonso, José María de. "Apreciación de la capacidad mental del testador: La intervención notarial y facultativa en el testamento abierto." *Revista jurídica de Cataluña* 72 (1973): 617–654.

Alonso y Lambán, Mariano. "Las formas testamentarias en la alta edad media de Aragón." *Revista de derecho notarial* 5–6 (1954): 7–196 and 9–10 (1955): 241–399.

Arnall i Juan, María J. "Testaments de fons monacals gironins existents a l'Arxiu de la Corona d'Aragó (segles XI–XV): Llurs clàusules diplomàtiques." In *De scriptis notariorum s. XI–XV,* ed. Josefina Mateu Ibars, Rubica 3, pp. 39–159. Barcelona: Universitat de Barcelona, 1989.

Assis, Yom Tov. *The Golden Age of Aragonese Jewry 1213–1327.* Oxford: Littman Library of Jewish Civilization. Forthcoming.

———. "Jewish Attitudes to Christian Power in Medieval Spain." *Sefarad* 52 (1992): 291–304.

———. "The Jews of the Crown of Aragon and Its Dominions." In *Moreshet Sepharad: The Sephardi Legacy,* ed. Haim Beinart, 1:44–102. 2 vols. Jerusalem: Magnes Press, 1992.

———. *The Jews of Santa Coloma de Queralt: An Economic and Demographic Case Study of a Community at the End of the Thirteenth Century.* Hispania Judaica 6. Jerusalem: Magnes Press/Hebrew University, 1988.

———, J. R. Magdalena Nom de Déu, and Coloma Lleal. *Judeolenguas marginales en Sefarad antes de 1492: Aljamía romance en los documentos hebraico-navarros (siglo XIV).* Barcelona: Universidad de Barcelona, 1992.

———. "Los judíos de Cataluña: Fuentes y posibilidades de estudio." In *I Col·loqui d'història dels jueus a la Corona d'Aragó: Actes*, pp. 139–155. Lerida: Institut d'Estudis Ilerdencs, 1991.

———. "Juifs de France réfugiés en Aragon (XIIIe–XIVe siècles)." *Revue des études juives* 142 (1983): 285–322.

———. "Les juifs de Montpellier sous la domination aragonaise." *Revue des études juives* 148 (1989): 5–16.

———. "The Papal Inquisition and Aragonese Jewry in the Early Fourteenth Century." *Medieval Studies* 49 (1987): 391–410.

———. "Synagogues in Mediaeval Spain." *Jewish Art* 18 (1992): 7–29.

———. "Welfare and Mutual Aid in the Spanish Jewish Communities." In *Moreshet Sepharad: The Sephardi Legacy*, ed. Haim Beinart, 1:318–345. 2 vols. Jerusalem: Magnes Press, 1992.

———. See also Mañé; Régné.

Aubenas, Roger. "À propos du testament d'un juif carcassonnais de 1305: Réflexions et programme de recherches." In *Carcassonne et sa région*, pp. 165–171. XLIe Congrès d'Études Régionales tenu par la Fédération Historique du Languedoc Méditerranéen et du Roussillon et la Fédération des Sociétés Académiques et Savantes de Languedoc-Pyrénées-Gascogne. Carcassonne: Congrès d'Etudes Régionales, 1970.

———. *Le testament en Provence, dans l'ancien droit.* Aix-en-Provence: Éd. P. Roubaud, 1927.

Auffroy, Henri. *Évolution du testament en France des origines au XIIIe siècle.* Paris: Éd. A. Rousseau, 1899.

Baer, Yitzhak [Fritz]. *Historia de los judíos en la Corona de Aragón (siglos XIII y XIV).* Zaragoza: Diputación General de Aragón, 1985. Translation of *Studien zur Geschichte der Juden im Königreich Aragonien während des 13. und 14. Jahrhunderts.* Berlin: Ebering, 1913.

———. *A History of the Jews in Christian Spain.* 2 vols. Philadelphia: Jewish Publication Society of America, 1971.

———, ed. *Die Juden im christlichen Spanien: Urkunden und Regesten.* 3 vols. Farnborough: Gregg, [1929–1936], 1970.

Barceló Torres, M. C. *Minorías islámicas en el país valenciano: Historia y dialecto.* Valencia: Universidad de Valencia, 1984.

———, ed. *Un tratado catalán medieval de derecho islámico: El Llibre de Çuna e Xara dels moros.* Córdoba: Universidad de Córdoba, 1989.

Basañez Villaluenga, Maria Blanca. *La aljama sarracena de Huesca en el siglo XIV.* Barcelona: Consejo Superior de Investigaciones Científicas, 1989.

Baskin, Judith R. "Jewish Women in the Middle Ages." In *Jewish Women in Historical Perspective*, ed. Judith R. Baskin, pp. 94–114. Detroit: Wayne State University, 1991.

Bastier, Jean. "Le testament en Catalogne du IXe au XIIe siècle: Une survivance wisigothique." *Revue historique du droit français et étranger* 3 (1973): 374–417.

Batlle, Carme. "Noticias sobre la mujer catalana en el mundo de los negocios (siglo XIII)." In Muñoz Fernández, Angela, and Cristina Segura Graiño, eds., *El trabajo de las mujeres en la edad media hispana,* pp. 201–221. Madrid: Asociación Cultural al-Mudayna, 1988.

———. "Noticies sobre els jueus de la Seu d'Urgell: Els Bedoz (1336-1348)." *Urgellia* 10 (1990–1991): 375–406.

Batlle y Prats, Luis. "Judíos gerundenses en testamentarías medievales" [1470]. *Anales del Instituto de estudios gerundenses* 4 (1949): 250–253. Also in David Romano Ventura, ed., *Per a una història de la Girona jueva,* 1:388–391. 2 vols. Gerona: Ajuntament, 1988.

Benito Ruano, Eloy. "La judería de Montalbán (Teruel)." *Medievalia* 10 (1992): 55–63. *Estudios dedicados al profesor Udina i Martorell,* vol. 4.

Bensch, Stephen. *Barcelona and Its Rulers, 1096–1291.* Cambridge: Cambridge University Press, 1995.

Berner, Leila. "A Mediterranean Community: Barcelona's Jews under James the Conqueror." Ph. D. dissertation, UCLA, 1986. Being revised for publication.

Bisson, T. N. *The Medieval Crown of Aragon.* Oxford: Oxford University Press, 1986.

Blasco Martínez, Asunción. *La judería de Zaragoza en el siglo XIV.* Zaragoza: Institución Fernando el Católico, 1988.

———. "Los judíos del reino de Aragón: Balance de los estudios realizados y perspectivas." In *I Col·loqui d'història dels jueus a la Corona d'Aragó: Actes,* pp. 13–97. Lérida: Institut d'Estudis Ilerdencs, 1991.

———. "Los judíos de Zaragoza: Un modelo para investigación." In *Jornades d'història dels jueus a Catalunya: Actes,* pp. 177–221. Gerona: Ajuntament, 1990.

———. "Mujeres judías zaragozanas ante la muerte." *Aragón en la edad media* 9 (1991): 77–120. Enlargement of her "Testamentos" (*q.v.*).

———. "Notarios-escribanos judíos de Aragón (siglos XIV–XV)." In *Rashi 1040–1990, hommage à Ephraïm E. Urbach: Congrès européen des études juives,* ed. Gabrielle Sed-Rajna, pp. 645–656. Paris: Éditions du Cerf, 1993.

———. "Notarios mudéjares de Aragón (siglos XIV–XV)." *Aragón en la edad media* [or *Homenaje a la profesora emérita Maria Luisa Ledesma Rubio*] 10–11 (1993): 109–133.

———. "Testamentos de mujeres judías aragonesas, 1401–1418." In *Tenth World Congress of Jewish Studies,* division B, vol. 2, 7 vols. Jerusalem: Magnes Press/Hebrew University, 1990. Vol. 2, in press. See her "Mujeres" above.

Bofarull i Sans, Francesc de. "Jaime I y los judíos." In *I Congrés d'història de la Corona d'Aragó,* pp. 819–943. 2 vols. paginated as 1. Barcelona: F. Altés, 1909–1913. Offprint book as "Los judíos en el territorio de Barcelona (siglos X al XIII), reinado de Jaime Ier" (1911).

Bollweg, John A. "Sense of Mission: Arnau de Vilanova on the Conversion of

Muslims and Jews." In *Iberia and the Mediterranean World of the Middle Ages: Studies in Honor of Robert I. Burns, S.J.*, ed. Larry Simon, Paul Chevedden, Donald Kagay, and Paul Padilla, 1:50–71. 2 vols. Leiden: E. J. Brill, 1995–1996.

Bono, José. *Historia del derecho notarial español.* 2 vols. to date. Madrid: Junta de Decanos de los Colegios Notariales de España, 1979–1982.

Bosom i Isern, Sebastià. "Arxiu històric comarcal de Puigcerdà." In *Guia dels arxius històrics de Catalunya,* 5:127–217. 5 vols. to date. Barcelona: Generalitat de Catalunya, 1982–1992.

———, and Oriol Mercadel i Fernández. "Puigcerdà." In *Catalunya romànica,* 7:216–220. 20 vols. to date. Barcelona: Enciclopèdia Catalana, 1984–.

———, and Salvador Galceran i Vigué. *Catàleg de protocols de Puigcerdà.* Inventaris d'arxius notarials de Catalunya 4. Barcelona: Fundació Noguera, 1983.

Boswell, John. *The Royal Treasure: Muslim Communities under the Crown of Aragon in the Fourteenth Century.* New Haven: Yale University Press, 1977.

Botet i Sisó, Joaquim. *Les monedes catalanes: Estudi y descripció de les monedes carolingies, comtals, senyorials, reyals, y locals propries de Catalunya.* 3 vols. Barcelona: Institut d'Estudis Catalans, [1908] 1976.

Brezzi, Paolo, and Egmont Lee, eds. *Sources of Social History: Private Acts of the Late Middle Ages.* Toronto: Pontifical Institute of Mediaeval Studies, 1984. Simultaneously published as *Gli atti privati nel tardo medioevo: Fonti per la storia sociale.* Rome: Istituto di Studi Romani, 1984.

Brocà, Guillem M. de. *Historia del derecho de Cataluña especialmente del civil y exposición de las instituciones del derecho civil del mismo territorio en relación con el código civil de España y la jurisprudencia.* 3 vols. Barcelona: Generalitat, [1918–1926] 1985–1987.

Burns, Robert I., S.J. "Anti-Semitism in Christian History: A Revisionist Thesis" (review article). *Catholic Historical Review* 70 (1984): 90–93.

———. "The Barcelona 'Disputation' of 1263: Conversionism and Talmud in Jewish-Christian Relations" (review article). *Catholic Historical Review* 79 (1993): 488–495.

———. "Canon Law and the Reconquista: Convergence and Symbiosis in the Kingdom of Valencia under Jaume the Conqueror (1213–1276)." *Fifth International Congress of Medieval Canon Law,* ed. Stephan Kuttner and Kenneth Pennington. Rome: Biblioteca Vaticana, 1980.

———. "Castle of Intellect, Castle of Force: The Worlds of Alfonso the Learned and James the Conqueror." In *The Worlds of Alfonso the Learned and James the Conqueror,* ed. Robert I. Burns, S.J., pp. 3–22. Princeton: Princeton University Press, 1985.

———. "Christian-Islamic Confrontation in the West: The Thirteenth-Century Dream of Conversion." *American Historical Review* 75 (1971): 1386–1434.

———. "Daughter of Abū Zayd, Last Almohad Ruler of Valencia: The Family and Christian Seigniory of Alda Ferrándis, 1236–1300." *Viator* 24 (1993): 143–187.

———. *Diplomatarium of the Crusader Kingdom of Valencia.* 2 vols. to date. Princeton: Princeton University Press, 1985–1991.
———. *Emperor of Culture: Alfonso the Learned of Castile and His Thirteenth-Century Renaissance.* Philadelphia: University of Pennsylvania Press, 1990.
———. *Foundations of Crusader Valencia: Revolt and Recovery.* In Robert I. Burns, *Diplomatarium of the Crusader Kingdom of Valencia,* vol. 2. (1991). 2 vols. to date. Princeton: Princeton University Press, 1985–1991.
———."The *Guidaticum* Safe-Conduct in Medieval Arago-Catalonia: A Mini-Institution for Muslims, Christians, and Jews". *Medieval Encounters: Jewish, Christian, and Muslim Cultures in Confluence and Dialogue* (Leiden) 1 (1995): 51–113.
———. *Islam under the Crusaders: Colonial Survival in the Thirteenth-Century Kingdom of Valencia.* Princeton: Princeton University Press, 1973.
———. "Jaume I and the Jews of the Kingdom of Valencia." *X Congrés d'història de la Corona d'Aragó,* 2:245–322. 2 vols. Zaragoza: CSIC, Institución Fernando el Católico, 1976.
———. *Medieval Colonialism: Postcrusade Exploitation of Islamic Valencia.* Princeton: Princeton University Press, 1975.
———. *Muslims, Christians, and Jews in the Crusader Kingdom of Valencia: Societies in Symbiosis.* Cambridge: Cambridge University, 1984.
———. "Muslims in the Thirteenth-Century Realms of Aragon: Interaction and Reaction." In James M. Powell, ed., *Muslims under Latin Rule, 1100–1300,* pp. 57–102. Princeton: Princeton University Press, 1990.
———. *Society and Documentation in Crusader Valencia.* In Robert I. Burns, *Diplomatarium of the Crusader Kingdom of Valencia,* vol. 1 (1985). 2 vols. to date. Princeton: Princeton University Press, 1985–1991.
———, and Paul Chevedden. "Al-Azraq's Surrender Treaty with Jaume I and Prince Alfonso in 1245: Arabic Text and Valencian Context." *Der Islam* 66 (1989): 1–37.
———. See also Epalza.
Cabanes Pecourt, M. D., ed. *Documentos de Jaime I de Aragón.* 5 vols. to date. Valencia: Anubar, 1976–. See also version by Huici Miranda.
Cabezudo Astrain, José. "Testamentos de judíos aragoneses." *Sefarad* 16 (1956): 136–147.
Canals i Ramon, Joana. *L'hereu—una institució en crisi?* Barcelona: Editorial Aedos, 1985.
Canellas López, Angel. "El documento notarial en la legislación foral del reino de Aragón." *Medievalia* 10 (1992): 65–81. [*Estudios dedicados al profesor Federico Udina i Martorell,* vol. 4.]
———. "El notariado en España hasta el siglo XIV: Estado de la cuestión." *Notariado público y documento privado: De los orígenes al siglo XIV* (VII Congreso Internacional de Diplomática), 1:99–139. 2 vols. Valencia: Generalitat, 1989.
———, ed. *Colección diplomática del consejo de Zaragoza.* 2 vols. and album. Zaragoza: Universidad de Zaragoza, 1972–1975.
Cantera Montenegro, Enrique. "Actividades socio-profesionales de la mujer judía en los reinos hispanocristianos de la baja edad media." In Muñoz Fer-

nández, Angela, and Cristina Segura Graiño, eds., *El trabajo de las mujeres en el edad media hispana,* pp. 321–345. Madrid: Asociación Cultural al-Mudayna, 1988.

———. *Los judíos en la edad media hispana.* Cuadernos de Investigación Medieval, Guía Crítica de Temas Históricos, 5. Madrid: A-Z Ediciones, 1986.

Cantera y Montenegro, Margarida. "Derecho y sociedad en la Rioja bajomedieval a través de los testamentos (siglos XIII–XV)." *Hispania* 165 (1987): 33–82.

Carreras i Candi, Francesc. "Desenrotllament de la institució notarial a Catalunya en lo segle XIII." In *I Congrés d'història de la Corona d'Aragó,* pp. 751–789. 2 vols. paginated as 1. Barcelona: F. Altés, 1909–1913. Also in his *Miscelanea histórica catalana,* 2:323–360. 2 vols. Barcelona: Casa Provincial de Caridad, 1905–1906.

Casas i Nadal, Montserrat. "Aspectes demogràfico-familiars de la vila de Cardona a mitjants del s. XIV (1342–1383)." *Cardener* 1 (1983): 53–68.

———. "Aspectes religioso-economics de la vila de Cardona segons els testaments del 1373 al 1383." *Cuadernos de historia económica de Cataluña* 19 (1978): 131–153.

———. "El 'Liber Iudeorum' de Cardona (1330–1334), edició i estudi." *Miscel·lània de textos medievals* 3 (1985): 121–350.

Cateura Bennasser, Pablo. *Sociedad, jerarquía, y poder en la Mallorca medieval.* Palma de Mallorca: Fontes Rerum Balearium, 1984.

Chalmeta, Pedro. See Ibn ʿal-ʿAṭṭār.

Charrin, Louis de. *Les testaments de la région de Montpellier au moyen âge.* Ambilly: Presses de Savoie, 1961.

Chazan, Robert. *Barcelona and Beyond: The Disputation of 1263 and Its Aftermath.* Berkeley, Los Angeles, London: University of California Press, 1992.

———. *Daggers of Faith: Thirteenth-Century Christian Missionizing and Jewish Response.* Berkeley, Los Angeles, London: University of California Press, 1989.

Chiffoleau, Jacques. *La comptabilité de l'au-delà: Les hommes, la mort, et la religion dans la région d'Avignon à la fin du moyen âge (vers 1320–vers 1480).* Rome: École Française de Rome, 1980.

———. "Les testaments provençaux et comtadins à la fin du moyen âge: Richesse documentaire et problèmes d'exploitation." In Paolo Brezzi and Egmont Lee, eds., *Sources of Social History: Private Acts of the Late Middle Ages,* pp. 132–152. Toronto: Pontifical Institute of Mediaeval Studies, 1984. See also Brezzi and Lee above.

Cohen, Jeremy. *The Friars and the Jews.* Ithaca, N.Y.: Cornell University Press, 1982.

Cohen, Mark R. *Under Crescent and Cross: The Jews in the Middle Ages.* Princeton: Princeton University Press, 1994.

Cohn, Samuel K. *Death and Property in Siena, 1205–1800: Strategies for the Afterlife.* Baltimore: Johns Hopkins University Press, 1988.

Colección diplomática de Jaime I. See Huici Miranda.

I Col·loqui d'història dels jueus a la Corona d'Aragó: Actes. Lérida: Institut d'Estudis Ilerdencs, 1991.

Conde, Rafael, and Francisco Gimeno. "Notarías y escribanías de concesión real en la Corona de Aragón." In *Notariado público y documento privado: De los orígenes al siglo XIV* (VII Congreso Internacional de Diplomática), 1:281–329. 2 vols. Valencia: Generalitat, 1989.

I Congrés d'història de la Corona d'Aragó. 2 vols. paginated as 1. Barcelona: F. Altés, 1909–1913.

Congreso Internacional de Diplomática. See *Notariado* below.

Corbella i Llobet, Ramon. *L'aljama de jueus de Vic.* Vich: Patronat d'Estudis Ausonencs, [1909] 1984.

Coria Colino, Jesús. "El testamento como fuente sobre mentalidades (s. XIII al XV)." *Miscelánea medieval murciana* 9 (1982): 193–219.

Crémieux, Adolphe. "Les juifs de Marseille au moyen âge." *Revue des études juives* 46 (1903): 1–47, 246–268 and 47 (1903): 62–86, 243–261.

Crusafont i Sabater, Miquel. *Numismática de la corona catalano-aragonesa medieval (785–1516).* Madrid: Editorial Vico, 1982.

Cubells i Llorens, Josefina, comp. *The Jews of Tortosa 1373–1492: Regesta of Documents from the Archivo Histórico de Protocols de Tarragona.* Jerusalem: Magnes Press/Hebrew University, 1991.

Cutler, Alan H., and Helen E. Cutler. *The Jew as Ally of the Muslim: Medieval Roots of Anti-Semitism.* Notre Dame: University of Notre Dame Press, 1986.

Delcor, Maties. "Els jueus de Puigcerdà al segle XIII." *Sefarad* 26 (1966): 19–46. Reprinted in his *Estudis històrics sobre la Cerdanya,* chap. 4. Barcelona: Editorial Barcino, 1977.

Denjean, Claude, et al. *Els jueus i els franciscans a Puigcerdà* (*segles XIII–XVI*). Col·lecciò Coneguem 3. Puigcerdà: Ajuntament/Arxiu Històric Comarcal, 1994.

———. "Vivre sa judéité a Puigcerdà du milieu du XIIIème siècle a la grande peste." *Mossé ben Nahman i el seu temps: Simposi commemoratiu del vuitè centenari del seu naixement 1194–1994,* 241–256. Gerona: Ajuntament, 1994.

De scriptis notariorum (s. XI–XV). Ed. Josefina Mateu Ibars. Rubrica 3. Barcelona: Universitat de Barcelona, 1989.

Díaz-Mas, Paloma. *Sephardim: The Jews from Spain.* Chicago: University of Chicago Press, 1992.

Documentos de Jaime I. See Cabanes Pecourt.

Documents dels jueus, Girona. See Escribà.

Doñate Sebastia, J., and J. R. Magdalena Nom de Déu. *Three Jewish Communities in Medieval Valencia: Castellón de la Plana, Burriana, Villarreal.* Hispania Judaica 8. Jerusalem: Magnes Press/Hebrew University, 1990.

Eire, Carlos M. N. *From Madrid to Purgatory: The Art and Craft of Dying in Sixteenth-Century Spain.* Cambridge, Cambridge University Press, 1995.

Emery, Richard W. *The Jews of Perpignan in the Thirteenth Century: An Economic Study Based on Notarial Records.* New York: Columbia University Press, 1959.

———. "Les juifs en Conflent et en Vallespir, 1250–1450." In *Conflent, Vallespir, et montagnes catalanes* (LIe Congrès de la Féderation Historique du Languedoc Meditérranéen et du Roussillon), pp. 85–91. Montpellier:

Congrès de la Féderation Historique du Languedoc Méditerranéen et du Roussillon, 1980.
———. "Les veuves juives de Perpignan." *Provence historique* 37 (1987): 559–569.
Encyclopaedia judaica. 16 vols. plus supplement. Jerusalem: Keter Publishing, 1971–1972.
Epalza, Míkel de. "Islamic Fidelity (*amān*) to Pacts (*ʿahd*) between Mudejar/ Morisco Muslims and Spanish Christian Authorities." In R. I. Burns, Paul E. Chevedden, and Míkel de Epalza, *Bilingual Surrender Treaties in Medieval Spain*. In preparation.
Epstein, Isidore. *The "Responsa" of Rabbi Solomon Ben Adreth of Barcelona (1235–1310) as a Source of the History of Spain*. New York: KTAV Publishing, [1925] 1968.
Epstein, Steven. *Wills and Wealth in Medieval Genoa 1150–1250*. Cambridge, Mass.: Harvard University, 1984.
Escribà i Bonastre, Gemma, and María Pilar Frago i Pérez, comps. *Documents dels jueus de Girona (1124–1595): Arxiu històric de la ciutat, Arxiu diocesà de Girona*. Gerona: Ajuntament, 1992.
———. See also Mañé, *The Jews in the Crown of Aragon*.
Estudis sobre història de la institució notarial a Catalunya en honor de Raimon Noguera. Ed. J. M. Sans i Travé. Barcelona: Fundació Noguera, 1988.
Ferrer i Mallol, M. T. *Les aljames sarraïnes de la governació d'Oriola en el segle XIV*. Barcelona: Consejo Superior de Investigaciones Científicas, 1988.
———, and Jaume Riera i Sans. "Miscel·lània de documents per a la història del notariat als estats de la corona catalano-aragonesa." *Estudios históricos y documentos de los archivos de protocolos [*or *Miscelánea en honor de Raimundo Noguera de Guzmán]* 4 (1974): 434–438, 444–445.
Fita, Fidel, and Gabriel Llabrés. "Privilegios de los hebreos mallorquines en el códice Pueyo." *Boletín de la Real academia de la historia* 36 (1900): 13–35, 121–148, 185–209, 273–306, 369–402, 458–494.
Fori antiqui Valentiae. Ed. Manuel Dualde Serrano. Madrid: Consejo Superior de Investigaciones Científicas, 1967.
Fueros de Aragón. See *Vidal Mayor*.
Furs de València. See *Fori*.
Galceran i Vigué. See Bosom.
Garbell, Irene. "The Pronunciation of Hebrew in Medieval Spain." In *Homenaje a Millás-Vallicrosa*, 1:647–696. 2 vols. Barcelona: Consejo Superior de Investigaciones Científicas, 1954–1956.
García, Angelina. *Els Vives: Una família de jueus valencians*. Valencia: Eliseu Climent, 1987.
García-Arenal, Mercedes, and Beátrice Leroy. *Moros y judíos en Navarra en la baja edad media*. Madrid: Hiperión, 1984.
Garcia Edo, Vicent. "Los primeros notarios valencianos: Aproximación a su estudio durante el reinado de Jaime I (1232–1276)." *Estudis castellonencs* 4 (1987–1988): 535–583.
García-Gallo, Alfonso. "Del testamento romano al medieval: Las lineas de su

evolución en España." *Anuario de historia del derecho español* 47 (1977): 425–497.

García Herrero, M. C. "La muerte y el cuidado del alma en los testamentos zaragozanos de la primera mitad del siglo XV." *Aragon en la edad media* 6 (1984): 209–245.

García Marco, F. J. "Tipología documental e investigación histórica: Las actas notariales como reflejo de la evolución de la sociedad aragonesa en la edad media." *Aragón en la edad media* 9 (1991): 31–53.

García Sanz, Arcadio. "El documento notarial en derecho valenciano hasta mediados del siglo XIV." In *Notariado público y documento privado: De los orígenes al siglo XIV,* 1:177–199. VII Congreso Internacional de Diplomática. 2 vols. Valencia: Generalitat, 1989.

Gerber, Jane S. *The Jews of Spain: A History of the Sephardic Experience.* New York: Free Press (Macmillan Inc.), 1992.

Giovanni Maiorana. See Sparti.

Girbal, Enrique Cláudio. "Beneficencia judáica en Gerona (documentos inéditos)." *Revista de Gerona* 18 (1894): 1–5. Also in David Romano Ventura, *Per a una història de la Girona jueva,* 2:543–547. 2 vols. Gerona: Ajuntament, 1988.

———. "Un testamento hebreo de la edad media [1470]." *Revista de Gerona* 5 (1881): 104–108. Also in David Romano Ventura, *Per a una història de la Girona jueva* 1:382–386. 2 vols. Gerona: Ajuntament, 1988.

Goitein, Shlomo D. *A Mediterranean Society: The Jewish Communities of the Arab World as Portrayed in the Documents of the Cairo Geniza.* 6 vols. Berkeley, Los Angeles, London: University of California Press, 1967–1993.

Grau Monserrat, Manuel. "Instrumenta Iudeorum (1327–1328)." *Amics de Besalú: V Assemblea d'estudis del seu comtat,* pp. 155–156. Olot: Assemblea, 1983.

Guilleré, Christian. *Girona al segle XIV.* 2 vols. Montserrat: Abadia, 1993.

———. "Juifs et chrétiens à Gérone au XIVème siècle." In *Jornades d'història dels jueus a Catalunya: Actes,* pp. 45–73. Gerona: Ajuntament, 1990.

Günzberg, Jordi. "Testamentos del siglo XIV y su aplicación a la demografía histórica: Estudio archivistico-metadológico." *Acta historica et archaeologica mediaevalia* 10 (1979): 89–98.

Gutwirth, Eleazar. "Muerte y mentalidad hispano-judía (siglos XIII–XV)." *El olivo* 13 (1989): 169–185.

Helmholtz, Richard H. "Married Women's Wills in Later Medieval England." In *Wife and Widow in Medieval England,* ed. Sue Sheridan Walker, pp. 165–182. Ann Arbor: University of Michigan Press, 1993.

Hillgarth, Jocelyn N. *Readers and Books in Majorca, 1229–1550.* 2 vols. Paris: Éditions du Centre National de la Recherche Scientifique, 1991.

———, and Giulio Silano, eds. *The Register Notule communium 14 of the Diocese of Barcelona (1345–1348): A Calendar with Selected Documents.* Toronto: Pontifical Institute of Mediaeval Studies, 1983.

Hinojosa Montalvo, José. "La comunidad hebrea en Valencia: Del esplendor a la nada (1377–1391)." *Saitabi* 31 (1981): 47–72.

———. *The Jews of the Kingdom of Valencia*. Hispania Judaica 9. Jerusalem: Magnes Press/Hebrew University, 1993.
———. "En torno a los judíos valencianos: La recuperación de una minoría olvidada." *Hispania* (Madrid) 50 (1990): 921–940.
Hoenerbach, Wilhelm. *Spanisch-islamische Urkunden aus der Zeit des Naṣriden und Moriscos*. Berkeley and Los Angeles: University of California Press, 1965.
Huici-Cabanes. See Cabanes Pecourt.
Huici Miranda, Ambrosio, ed. *Colección diplomática de Jaime I, el Conquistador*. 3 vols. in 6. Valencia: Hijo de F. Vives Mora, 1916–1922. See also version by Cabanes Pecourt.
Iancu, Carol. See *Les juifs à Montpellier*.
Iancu-Agou, Danièle. "Autour du testament d'une juive marseillaise (1480)." *Marseille: Revue municipale trimesterielle* 133–134 (1983): 30–35.
———. "L'Inventaire de la bibliothèque et du mobilier d'un médecin juif d'Aix-en- Provence au milieu du XVe siècle." *Revue des études juives* 134 (1975): 47–80.
———. "Juives et néophytes aixoises: Leurs testaments, 1467–1525." In *Eleventh World Congress of Jewish Studies,* division B, vol. 1, pp. 165–172. 9 vols. Jerusalem: Magnes Press/Hebrew University, 1994.
———. "Une vente de livres hébreux à Arles en 1434: Tableau de l'élite juive arlésienne au milieu du XVe siècle." *Revue des études juives* 146 (1987): 5–62.
Iberia and the Mediterranean World of the Middle Ages: Studies in Honor of Robert I. Burns, S.J. Ed. Larry Simon, Paul Chevedden, Donald Kagay, and Paul Padilla. 2 vols. Leiden: E. J. Brill, 1995–1996.
Ibn ʿAbdūn. *Séville musulmane au début du XIIe siècle: Le traité d'Ibn ʿAbdūn*. Ed. Évariste Lévi-Provençal. Paris: G. P. Maisonneuve, 1947.
Ibn al-ʿAṭṭār, Abū ʿAbd Allāh Muḥammad b. Aḥmad b. ʿUbayd Allāh. *Kitāb al-Wathāʾiq wa-siǧillāt*. Edited by Pedro Chalmeta and Federico Corriente as *Formulario notarial hispano-árabe por el alfaquí y notario cordobés Ibn al-ʿAṭṭar (s. X)*. Madrid: Academia Matritense del Notariado/Instituto Hispano-Arabe de Cultura, 1983.
Idel, Moshe. "Abraham Abulafia and the Pope: An Account of an Abortive Mission" (in Hebrew). *Association of Hebrew Studies Review* 7–8 (1982–1983): 1–17.
———. "Ramon Llull and Ecstatic Kabbalah, Preliminary Observation." *Journal of the Warburg and Courtauld Institutes* 61 (1988): 170–174.
———. *Studies in Ecstatic Kabbalah*. New York: State University of New York Press, 1988.
Jacobs, Joseph. *An Inquiry into the Sources of the History of the Jews in Spain*. London: David Nutt, 1894.
Jewish Women in Perspective. See Baskin.
Jews in Barcelona. See Mañé. Cf. Berner.
Johnston, Mark D. "Ramon Llull and the Compulsory Evangelization of Jews and Muslims." In *Iberia and the Mediterranean World of the Middle Ages:*

Studies in Honor of Robert I. Burns, S.J., ed. Larry Simon et al., 1:3–37. 2 vols. Leiden: E. J. Brill, 1995–1996.

Jordan, William Chester. *The French Monarchy and the Jews: From Philip Augustus to the Last of the Capetians.* Philadelphia: University of Pennsylvania Press, 1989.

Jornades d'història dels jueus a Catalunya: Actes (1987). Gerona: Ajuntament, 1990.

Judeolenguas marginales en Sefarad antes de 1492: Aljamía romance en los documentos hebraiconavarros (siglo XIV). Ed. Yom Tov Assis et al. Barcelona: Universitat de Barcelona, 1992.

Les juifs à Montpellier et dans le Languedoc à travers l'histoire du moyen âge à nos jours. Ed. Carol Iancu. Colloque International du Centre Régional d'Histoire des Mentalités, et du Centre de Recherches et d'Études Juives et Hébraïques, 1985. Montpellier: Centre de Recherches, 1988.

Kaganoff, Benzion C. *A Dictionary of Jewish Names and Their History.* New York: Schocken, 1977.

Katz, Jacob. *Exclusiveness and Tolerance: Jewish-Gentile Relations in Medieval and Modern Times.* New York: Schocken, 1975.

———. *Tradition and Crisis: Jewish Society at the End of the Middle Ages.* New translation by Bernard Dov Cooperman. New York: New York University Press, 1993.

Kedar, Benjamin Z. *Crusade and Mission: European Approaches toward the Muslims.* Princeton: Princeton University Press, 1984.

———. "The Genoese Notaries of 1382: The Anatomy of an Urban Occupational Group." In *The Medieval City*, ed. H. A. Miskimin, David Herlihy, A. L. Udovitch, pp. 73–94. New Haven: Yale University Press, 1977.

Kolatch, Alfred J. *The Complete Dictionary of English and Hebrew First Names.* Middle Village, N.Y.: Jonathan David, 1984.

———. *The New Name Dictionary: Modern English and Hebrew Names.* Middle Village, N.Y.: Jonathan David, 1984.

Kriegel, Maurice. *Les juifs à la fin du moyen âge dans l'Europe méditerranéenne.* Paris: Hachette, 1979.

Lacave Riaño, José L. "Pleito judío por una herencia en aragonés y caracteres hebreos: Notas acerca del procedimiento judicial en los tribunales judíos aragoneses." *Sefarad* 30 (1970): 325–337 and 31 (1971): 49–101.

———. "Un testamento hebraico fragmentario de Miranda del Ebro." *Sefarad* 46 (1986): 271–278.

Lalinde Abadia, Jesús. *Derecho histórico español.* Barcelona: Ariel, 1974.

Laredo, Abraham I. *Les noms des juifs du Maroc: Essai d'onomastique judeo-marocaine.* Madrid: Consejo Superior de Investigaciones Científicas, 1978.

León Tello, Pilar. *Judíos de Toledo.* 2 vols. Madrid: Consejo Superior de Investigaciones Científicas, 1979.

Lewis, Bernard. "Palimpsests of Jewish History: Christian, Muslim, and Secular Diaspora." *Jewish Studies: Forum of the World Union of Jewish Studies* 30 (1990): 7–13.

Llompart, Gabriel. "Documentos sueltos sobre judíos y conversos de Mallorca (siglos XIV y XV)." *Fontes rerum balearium* 2 (1978): 181–199.

———. "Testamentos de mercaderes mallorquines rogados entre musulmanes (1374–1388)." *Hispania* 44 (1984): 411–431.

Lourie, Elena. *Crusade and Colonisation: Muslims, Christians, and Jews in Medieval Aragon.* Aldershot: Variorum (Gower Pub.), 1990.

Madurell i Marimon, J. M. "Jueus gironins i la seva aljama (1349–1498), notes documentals." *Anales del Instituto de estudios gerundenses* [or *Homenaje a Santiago Sobrequés Vidal*] 22 (1974–1975):23–49 (interior pagination 1–27).

Magdalena Nom de Déu, J. R. "Les aljames catalanes segons les fonts hebraiques (aspectes de la vida i les institucions dels jueus catalans al segles XIII i XIV reflectits als '*respona*' rabínics)." *El debat intercultural als segles XIII i XIV* [or *I Jornades de filosofia catalana,* Estudi general, vol. 9 (1989)], pp. 201–214. Barcelona: Universitat de Barcelona, 1989.

———. "Etimologia no semítica de 'Call.' " *Calls* 2 (1987): 7–16.

———. See Doñate. See also Assis, Yom Tov.

Malkiel, David. See my introduction above.

Mañé, Maria Cinta, comp. *The Jews in Barcelona 1213–1291: Regesta of Documents from the Archivo Capitular.* Ed. Yom Tov Assis. Jerusalem: Hebrew University/Central Archives for the History of the Jewish People, 1988.

———, with Gemma Escribà, comps. *The Jews in the Crown of Aragón: Regesta of the Cartas reales in the Archivo de la Corona de Aragón.* Jerusalem: Magnes Press/Hebrew University, 1991.

Marcó i Dachs, Lluís. *Els jueus i nosaltres.* Barcelona: Editorial Pòrtic, 1977. Revised as *Los judíos en Cataluña.* Barcelona: Ediciones Destino, 1985.

Marín Padilla, Encarnación. "Ultimas voluntades judías: Testamentos de Duenya Falaquera, Reyna Abenardut y Davit Rodrich (siglo XV)." *Anuario de estudios medievales* 15 (1985): 497–512.

Mascaró Pasarius, Josep, ed. *Historia de Mallorca.* 10 vols. Palma de Mallorca: Esago Comercial, 1978.

Melammed, Renée Levine. "Sephardi Women in the Medieval and Early Modern Periods." In Judith R. Baskin, ed., *Jewish Women in Historical Perspective,* pp. 115–134. Detroit: Wayne State University, 1991.

Metzger, Thérèse, and Mendel Metzger. *Jewish Life in the Middle Ages: Illuminated Hebrew Manuscripts of the Thirteenth to the Sixteenth Centuries.* New York: Alpine Fine Arts, 1982.

Millàs i Vallicrosa, Josep M., ed. *Documents hebraics de jueus catalans.* In *Memòries* of the Institut d'Estudis Catalans, Secció Històrico-Arqueològica, vol. 1, fasc. 3, pp. 61–167. Barcelona: Institut d'Estudis Catalans, 1927.

———. "Esbozo histórico sobre los judíos en Barcelona." *Miscellanea barcinonensia* 12 (1966): 13–20.

Miret i Sans, Joaquim, and Moïse Schwab, eds. "Documents sur les juifs catalans aux XIe, XIIe, et XIIIe siècles." *Revue des études juives* 68 (1914): 49–83, 174–197.

Mirrer, Louise, ed. *Upon My Husband's Death: Widows in the Literature and Histories of Medieval Europe.* Ann Arbor: University of Michigan Press, 1992.

Molina Molina, A. L., and Amparo Bejarano Rubio. "Actitud del hombre ante la muerte: Los testamentos murcianos de finales del s. XV." *Misceldnea medieval murciana* 12 (1985): 185–202.

Moreshet Sepharad: The Sephardi Legacy. Ed. Haim Beinart. 2 vols. Jerusalem: Magnes Press, 1992.

Mossé ben Nahman i el seu temps: Simposi commemoratiu del vuité centenari del seu naixement 1194–1994. Gerona: Ajuntament, 1994.

Motis Dolader, Miguel Angel. "Disposiciones *mortis causa* de los judíos de Epila (Zaragoza) en el ultimo tercio del siglo XV." In *Homenaje al profesor emerito Antonio Ubieto Arteta,* pp. 475–498. Aragón en la Edad Media, vol. 8. Zaragoza: Universidad de Zaragoza, 1989.

———. "La documentación notarial como fuente para la historia de los judíos aragoneses en el siglo XV." In *El patrimonio documental aragonés y la historia,* ed. Guillermo Pérez Sarrión, pp. 249–260. Zaragoza: Diputación General de Aragón, 1986.

———. "Los judíos aragoneses en la baja edad media (1283–1479)." In *Historia de Aragón* 6 (1987): 149–184.

———. "Los notarios y la documentación judía a través de las Taqqanot otorgadas por el infante Alfonso V y la aljama zaragozana en 1415." In *El patrimonio documental aragonés y la historia,* ed. Guillermo Pérez Sarrión, pp. 261–271. Zaragoza: Diputación General de Aragón, 1986.

———, ed. *Documentos sobre los judíos de Borgia (Zaragoza): 1455–1500.* Textos medievales 79. Zaragoza: Anubar, 1988.

Muldoon, James. *Popes, Lawyers, and Infidels: The Church and the Non-Christian World, 1250–1550.* Philadelphia: University of Pennsylvania Press, 1979.

Mundy, John Hine. *Men and Women at Toulouse in the Age of the Cathars.* Toronto: Pontifical Institute of Mediaeval Studies, 1990.

Muñoz Fernández, Angela, and Cristina Segura Graiño, eds. *El trabajo de las mujeres en la edad media hispana.* Madrid: Asociación Cultural al-Mudayna, 1988.

Mutgé i Vives, Josefa. *L'aljama sarraïna de Lleida a l'edat mitjana: Aproximació a la seva història.* Barcelona: Consejo Superior de Investigaciones Científicas, 1992.

Myers, David N. *Re-inventing the Jewish Past: European Jewish Intellectuals and the Zionist Return to History.* New York: Oxford University Press, 1995.

Neuman, Abraham A. *The Jews in Spain: Their Social, Political and Cultural Life during the Middle Ages.* 2 vols. Philadelphia: Jewish Publication Society, 1948.

Nirenberg, David. *Communities of Violence: Minorities in Medieval Spain and France.* Princeton: Princeton University Press, 1996.

———. "A Female Rabbi in Fourteenth-Century Zaragoza?" *Sefarad* 51 (1991): 179–182.

———. "Muslim-Jewish Relations in the Fourteenth-Century Crown of Aragon." *Viator* 24 (1993): 249–268.

Notariado público y documento privado: De los orígenes al siglo XIV. VII Congreso Internacional de Diplomática. 2 vols. Valencia: Generalitat, 1989.

Oliver, Bienvenido. *Historia del derecho en Cataluña, Mallorca y Valencia: Código de las costumbres de Tortosa.* 4 vols. Madrid: Miguel Ginesta, 1876–1881.

Ollich i Castanyer, Immaculada. "Aspectes econòmics de l'activitat dels jueus de Vic, segons els 'Libri Iudeorum' (1266–1278)." *Miscel·lània de textos medievals* 3 (1985): 3–118.

———. "La història medieval i les noves tècniques d'anàlisis per ordinador: Els testaments de Vic del segle XIII." *Acta historica et archaeologica mediaevalia* 1 (1980): 11–27.

Pagarolas i Sabaté, Laureà. *El protocol del notari Bonanat Rimentol (1351): Capribrevium notularum, 13 de juliol–24 d'octubre, 1351.* Barcelona: Fundació Noguera, 1991.

Pérez de Benavides, Manuel M. *El testamento visigótico: Una contribución al estudio del derecho romano vulgar.* Granada: Instituto de Historia del Derecho, 1975.

Pita i Mercè, Roderic. "Cognoms que tenen origen en topònims francesos i que foren usats pels jueus medievals catalans." *Col·loqui d'història dels jueus a la Corona d'Aragó: Actes,* pp. 429–437. Lérida: Institut d'Estudis Ilerdencs, 1991.

Pons, Antonio. *Los judíos del reino de Mallorca durante los siglos XIII y XIV.* 2 vols. Palma de Mallorca: Miguel Font, [1958–1960] 1984.

Pons i Guri, Josep M. *Recull d'estudis d'història jurídica catalana.* 3 vols. Barcelona: Fundació Noguera, 1989.

———, et al., eds. "Manual d'Alcover (anys 1228–1229)." In *De scriptis notariorum (s. XI–XV),* ed. Josefina Mateu Ibars, pp. 161–294. Rubrica 3. Barcelona: Universitat de Barcelona, 1989.

Powell, James M., ed. *Muslims under Latin Rule, 1100–1300.* Princeton: Princeton University Press, 1990.

Powers, David S. *Studies in Qur'an and Ḥadīth: The Formation of the Islamic Law of Inheritance.* Berkeley, Los Angeles, London: University of California Press, 1986.

The Principles of Jewish Law. Ed. Menachem Elon. Jerusalem: Encyclopaedia Judaica, 1975.

Régné, Jean, comp. *History of the Jews in Aragon: Regesta and Documents, 1213–1327.* Ed. Yom Tov Assis. Hispania Judaica 1. Jerusalem: Magnes Press/Hebrew University, 1978. Indexed and improved reprint of French entries of Régné's "Catalogue des actes de Jaime I, Pedro III, et Alfonso III, rois d'Aragon, concernant les juifs (1213–1327)," *Revue des études juives* 60 (1910) to 70 (1920), and his supplementary "Catalogue" for Jaime II, *Revue des études juives* 73 (1923) to 78 (1925).

Riera Melis, Antoni. *La Corona de Aragón y el reino de Mallorca en el primer cuarto del siglo XIV.* 1 vol. to date (1298–1311). Barcelona: Consejo Superior de Investigaciones Científicas, 1986.

Riera i Sans, Jaume. "La conflictivitat de l'alimentació dels jueus medievals (segles XII-XV)." In *Alimentació i societat a la Catalunya medieval,* ed. M. T. Ferrer i Mallol, pp. 295–311. Barcelona: Consejo Superior de Investigaciones Científicas, 1988.

———. "Estudis sobre el judaisme català." *Calls* 1 (1986): 93–132, 2 (1987): 181–207, 3 (1988–1989): 103–134.

———. "Les llicències reials per predicar als jueus i als sarraïns (segles XIII–XIV)." *Calls* 2 (1987): 113–143.

———. "Notaris jueus i sarraïns." In M. T. Ferrer i Mallol and Jaume Riera i Sans, "Miscel·lània de documents per a la història del notariat als estats de la corona catalano-aragonesa." *Estudios históricos y documentos de los archivos de protocolos* 4 (1974): 434–438, 444–445.

———. See also Ferrer i Mallol.

Rimentol, Bonanat. See Pagarolas.

Romano Ventura, David. *De historia judía hispánica*. Col·lecció homenatges 1. Barcelona: Universitat de Barcelona, 1991.

———. "Fossars jueus catalans." *Acta historica et archaeologica mediaevalia* 14–15 (1993–1994): 291–315.

———. "Jafudà Alatzar, jueu de València (siglo XIV)." *Revista d'història medieval* [or *Jueus, conversos, i cristians*, ed. Ferran Garcia-Oliver] 4 (1993): 65–100.

———. *Judíos al servicio de Pedro el Grande de Aragón (1276–1285)*. Barcelona: Universitat de Barcelona, 1983.

———. "Els jueus en temps de Pere el Cerimoniós (1336–1387)." In *Pere el Cerimoniós i la seva època*, pp. 113–131. Barcelona: Consejo Superior de Investigaciones Científicas, 1989.

———. "Legado de un judío al rey Pedro el Grande." *Sefarad* 17 (1957): 144–149. Also in his *De historia judía hispánica* (*q.v.*), pp. 94–99.

———, ed. *Per a una història de la Girona jueva*. 2 vols. Gerona: Ajuntament, 1988.

Roth, Norman. "Bishops and Jews in the Middle Ages." *Catholic Historical Review* 80 (1994): 1–17.

———. "The Civic State of the Jew in Medieval Spain." In *Iberia and the Mediterranean World of the Middle Ages: Studies in Honor of Robert I. Burns, S.J.*, ed. Larry Simon et al. 2 vols. Leiden: E. J. Brill, 1995–1996.

———. "Dar 'una voz' a los judíos: Representación en la España medieval." *Anuario de historia del derecho español* 56 (1986): 943–952.

———. *Jews, Visigoths and Muslims in Medieval Spain: Cooperation and Conflict*. Medieval Iberian Peninsula, Texts and Studies 10. Leiden: E. J. Brill, 1994.

Rubio Vela, Agustín. *L'Escrivania municipal als segles XIV i XV: Burocràcia, política i cultura*. Valencia: Generalitat, 1995.

Rubió y Lluch, Antoni, ed. *Documents per l'historia de la cultura catalana mig-eval*. 2 vols. Barcelona: Institut d'Estudis Catalans, 1908–1921.

Russell, Josiah Cox. *Medieval Regions and Their Cities*. Bloomington: Indiana University Press, 1972.

Rutgers, Leonard Victor. *The Jews in Late Ancient Rome: Evidence of Cultural Interaction in the Roman Diaspora*. Cambridge: Cambridge University Press, 1995.

Santamaría Arández, Alvaro. *Ejecutoria del reino de Mallorca, 1230–1343*. Palma de Mallorca: Ajuntament, 1990.

———. "Mallorca en el siglo XIV." *Anuario de estudios medievales* 7(1970–1971): 164–238.

———. "Tensión corona de Aragón-Corona de Mallorca: La sucesión de Sancho de Mallorca (1318–1326)." *En la España medieval* [or *Estudios en memoria del Profesor D. Salvador de Moxó,* ed. M. A. Ladero Quesada, vol. 2] 3 (1982): 423–495.

Sarret i Arbós, Joaquim. "El testament d'un jueu, segle XIV." *Butlletí del Centre excursionista de la comarca de Bages* 25 (1929): 356–357.

Schwab. See Miret i Sans.

Schwarzfuchs, Simon. *A Concise History of the Rabbinate.* Oxford: Blackwell, 1993.

———. "L'image du chrétien dans les sources juives du Languedoc (XIIe–XIVe siècles)." In *Les Juifs à Montpellier et dans le Languedoc à travers l' histoire du moyen âge à nos jours,* ed. Carol Iancu, 113–127. Montpellier: Centre des Recherches, 1988.

Secall i Güell, Gabriel. *La comunitat hebrea de Santa Coloma de Queralt.* Tarragona: Diputació Provincial, 1986.

———. *Les jueries medievals tarragonines.* Valls: Institut d'Estudis Vallencs, 1983.

———. *Els jueus de Valls i la seva època.* Valls: Institut d'Estudis Vallencs, 1980.

———. "Mossé Cabrit, draper filantrop de Valls i de Santa Coloma de Queralt (siglos XIV–XV)." In *Aplec de treballs,* vol. 6, appendix. Centre d'Estudis de la Conca de Barbera, 1984.

Sefer ha-yovel li-khevod ha-Rav Dr. Avraham Vais: Ke-ot ha-aratsah be-ʿad terumato ha-kabirah, anu magishim lo kovets mehkarim mehaverav ve-talmidav. The Abraham Weiss Jubilee Volume. New York: Shulsinger Bros., 1964.

The Sephardi Legacy. See *Moreshet Sepharad.*

Septimus, Bernard. *Hispano-Jewish Culture in Transition: The Career and Controversies of Ramah.* Harvard Judaic Studies 4. Cambridge, Mass.: Harvard University Press, 1982.

———. "Piety and Power in Thirteenth-Century Catalonia." In *Studies in Medieval Jewish History and Literature,* ed. Isadore Twersky, 1:197–230. 2 vols. Cambridge, Mass.: Harvard University Press, 1979.

Seror, Simon. *Les noms des juifs de France au moyen âge.* Paris: Centre National de la Recherche Scientifique, 1989.

Serrano y Sanz, Manuel. *Orígenes de la dominación española en América: Estudios históricos.* Nueva Biblioteca de Autores Españoles 25. Madrid: Editorial Bailly-Bailliere, 1918.

Sevillano Colom, Francisco. "Gabriel de Vallseca, cartógrafo mallorquín del siglo XV." In *Homenaje al Dr. D. Juan Reglá Campistol,* 1:159–162. 2 vols. Valencia: Universidad de Valencia, 1975.

Shatzmiller, Joseph. "La 'collecta' de Perpignan (1412)." *Archives juives* 11 (1975): 20–24.

———. *Jews, Medicine, and Medieval Society.* Berkeley, Los Angeles, London: University of California Press, 1995.

———. *Recherches sur la communauté juive de Manosque au moyen âge, 1241–1329.* Paris: Mouton, 1973.

———. *Shylock Reconsidered: Jews, Moneylending, and Medieval Society.* Berkeley, Los Angeles, London: University of California Press, 1990.

Sheehan, Michael. *The Will in Medieval England from the Conversion of the Anglo-Saxons to the End of the Thirteenth Century.* Toronto: Pontifical Institute of Mediaeval Studies, 1963.

Shilo, Shmuel. "Wills." In *Encyclopaedia Judaica,* 16:519–530. 17 vols. Jerusalem: Keter, 1966–1981.

Simon, Larry James. "Society and Religion in the Kingdom of Majorca, 1229–c. 1300." Ph.D. dissertation, UCLA, 1989. Being revised and expanded for publication.

Simonsohn, Shlomo. *The Apostolic See and the Jews.* 8 vols. Toronto: Pontifical Institute of Mediaeval Studies, 1988–1991.

Sparti, Aldo, ed. *Il registro del notaio ericino Giovanni Maiorana (1297–1300).* 2 vols. (vol. 2, facsimile). Palermo: Accademia di Scienze, Lettere i Arti, 1982.

Tallan, Cheryl. "Opportunities for Medieval Northern European Jewish Widows in the Public and Domestic Spheres." In Louise Mirrer, ed., *Upon My Husband's Death: Widows in the Literature and Histories of Medieval Europe,* pp. 115–127. Ann Arbor: University of Michigan Press, 1992.

Taylor, Nathaniel L. "Medieval Catalonian Wills: Family Charter Evidence in the Archives." In *Discovery in the Archives of Spain and Portugal: Quincentenary Essays, 1492–1992,* ed. Lawrence J. McCrank, chap. 3. Binghamton, N.Y.: Haworth Press, 1994.

Toaff, Ariel, ed. *The Jews in Umbria.* 2 vols to date. Vol. 1: 1245–1435; vol. 2: 1435–1484. Leiden: E. J. Brill, 1993–1994.

Tyan, Émile. *Le notariat et le régime de la preuve par écrit dans la pratique du droit musulmane.* Beirut: Imp. St. Paul, 1959.

Udina i Abelló, A. M. *La successió testada a la Catalunya altomedieval.* Barcelona: Fundació Noguera, 1984.

———. "El testament català en el segle XIII: Supervivencies i innovacions." In XIIe Congrés d'Història de la Corona d'Aragó, or *Montpellier, la Couronne d'Aragon et les pays de langue d'oc (1204–1349)* [=Mémoires, Société Archéologique de Montpellier 15, 16, 17], 2:157–165. 3 vols. Montpellier: Société Archéologique de Montpellier, 1987–1989.

———. "Testament sacramental." In *Documents jurídics de la història de Catalunya,* ed. A. M. Bassols i Parés and Iago de Balanzó i Solà, pp. 43–50. Barcelona: Generalitat de Catalunya, 1992.

Utterback, Kristine T. *Pastoral Care and Administration in Mid-Fourteenth-Century Barcelona: Exercising the "Art of Arts."* Queenston, Canada: Edwin Mellen, 1993.

Vendrell Gallostra, Francisca. "Aportaciones documentales para el estudio de la familia Caballería." *Sefarad* 3 (1943): 115–154.

Ventura i Subirats, Jordi. "El coneixement de l'hebreu entre els conversos valencians de la fi del segle XV." *Revista de llengua i dret* (Generalitat de Catalunya) 20 (1993): 7–48.

Vicaire, M. H., and Bernhard Blumenkrantz, eds. *Juifs et judaisme de Languedoc, XIIIe siècle–début XIVe siècle.* Cahiers de Fanjeaux 12. Toulouse: Édouard Privat, 1977.

Vidal Mayor: Traducción aragonesa da le obra In excelsis dei thesauris de Vidal de Canellas. Ed. Gunnar Tilander. Leges Hispanicae Medii Aevi 4. 3 vols. Lund: Håkon Ohlsson, 1956.

Vidal, Pere. "Les juifs des anciens comtés de Roussillon et de Cerdagne." *Revue des études juives* 15 (1887): 19–55, 16 (1888): 1–23, 170–203. As book offprint, Paris: Revue, 1888. With translator's notes as "Els jueus dels antics comtats de Rosselló i Cerdanya," *Calls* 2 (1987): 26–112.

Vila, Pau. *La Cerdanya.* Barcelona: Editorial Empúries, 1984.

Villaronga, Leandre. *La moneda de Barcelona.* Barcelona: Editorial CYMYS, 1976.

Vovelle, Michel. *La mort et l'occident de 1300 à nos jours.* Paris: Gallimard, 1983.

Waley, Daniel. *The Italian City-Republics.* 3d ed., rev. New York: Longman, 1988.

Walker. See Helmholz.

Wernham, Monique. *La communauté juive de Salon-de-Provence d'après les actes notariés, 1391–1435.* Toronto: Pontifical Institute of Mediaeval Studies, 1987.

Yaron, Reuven. *Gifts in Contemplation of Death in Jewish and Roman Law.* Oxford: Clarendon Press, 1960.

Index

Abulafia, Abraham, 16
Abulafia, David, 43, 73
Adarra, Jahudà, 47–48
Africa, Jews leave, 12, 15
Alb, Mateu de, 100
Alfons III (the Liberal), 11, 40, 54; intervenes in wills, 59–60, 61–62, 64, 68
Alfons IV, 14
Alfonso X the Learned, 32
Andalusian tradition, 16
Anti-Semitism, 12, 19, 21
Arabic: Jews speak, 15, 41; medical texts, 15; names, 6, 7, 16, 77–78, 135; wills, 126–131
Aragon, realms (crown) of: anti-Semitism in, 12; Jews in, 12–16; language of, 12; Muslims in, 12, 33–38; parallel societies in, 17–22; upland Kingdom of, 11, 27–29 (*see also* Huesca; Zaragoza). *See also* Catalonia; individual cities by name
Arnau de Sagarra, 56
Asher de Lunel, 83–87
Asher Mossé Daví, 90–94
Ashkenazis, 14
Assimilation, 5, 6, 17
Assis, Yom Tov, 13, 14, 31, 119
Astruc Azarel, 40–41
Astruc de Porta de Penadès, 60
Astruc Jahudà des Cortal, 58
Azaria, Rabbi, 48
Baer, Yitzhak, 200 n.13
Barcelona: archives in, 1; Jews in, 16, 44, 45, 60; notaries and scribes in, 39, 40, 41–42, 44, 45; wills in, 56–57, 60
Barceló Torres, M. C., 35
Basañez Villaluenga, M. B., 34
Baskin, Judith, 114
Batlle, Carme, 99
Bedós, Mossé Eli, 97, 98–99
Bedós, Salamó, 104–106
Benedict XIII, Pope, 28
Bensch, Stephen, 39, 116
Benvenist de Porta, Vidal, 15
Benvenist family, 15, 55, 56, 57
Berner, Leila, 27, 70, 111
Blasco Martínez, Asunción, 28; on scribes, 36, 48–49
Bonisac will, 80–81
Bono, José, 45
Bonsenyor, Astruc, 15, 41, 58
Bonsenyor, Jahudà, 15, 41
Boswell, John, 35
Burial societies, 26
Business: Jewish-Christian relationships in, 41–42, 46, 72; will as document of, 127–129

Cabezudo Astrain, José, 27
Calatayud, 34, 35

Calendar, Jewish, 45
Calls, 3
Canellas López, Angel, 33
Cap family, 111
Carcassonne, will from, 122–124
Carreras i Candi, Francesc, 33
Castile, wills in, 32
Catalonia: burial societies in, 26; Jews in, 3, 16, 26; as maritime-commercial center, 11–12, 29–30; Muslims in, 18; Roman law in, 30; wills in, 29–30, 32. *See also* Aragon, realms (crown) of; individual cities by name
Charitable bequests, in wills, 24, 29, 83, 84, 87, 89–90, 101, 103, 107, 108, 111–112, 114, 119, 120, 121–122, 123, 133–134,138
Charles of Anjou, 124
Charrin, Louis de, 210–211 n.39
Chazan, Robert, 16
Chiffoleau, Jacques, 126, 137
Christians: in business with Jews, 19–20, 41–42, 46, 51–52, 72; conversion attempts by, 20–21, 29; as executors of Jewish wills, 93; names, 5–6, 7; as notary (*see* Notaries, Christian); as parallel society, 17–22; wills of, 32, 49–50, 116, 135–136; as witnesses to Jewish wills, 83, 87, 89, 94, 95, 99, 107, 108, 110, 114, 120, 122, 124, 133
Codicils, 122
Cohen, Jacob ibn Abraham, 97–98
Colomer, Pere de, 42
Conversionism, 20–21, 29, 199
Cooperman, Bernard Dov, 17
Copies, of wills, 52–53, 111, 132, 133

Death: duties, 28; gift in contemplation of, 23
Deathbed advice, 26
Dhimma model of autonomy, 17–21, 25, 51
Disposition, 28; partial, 24; last, 22, 23, 36, 127–131, 137
Disputation of Tortosa, 28
Disputation of 1263 (Barcelona), 21, 135
Double documents/wills, 29, 30–31, 46, 49, 69
Dowry, 9, 58; provided for in will, 80, 81, 82, 89, 97, 108, 111, 128, 133; recovered in will, 76, 80, 81, 83, 97, 100, 101, 104, 116, 121, 136, 137
Draguignan, will from, 2, 124–126

Egypt, wills from. *See* Geniza wills
Elias, Cresques, 14–15
Emery, Richard, 2, 9, 66; on documents, 78, 79, 81, 83, 86, 90, 93, 94; on names, 79
Epstein, Steven, 29
Exchange rates, 8–9, 61
Executor, 24, 26, 69, 79, 97, 98, 102, 112–113, 122; Christian, 93; discretion of, 70–71; duties of, 81–82, 89, 92, 130; king appoints, 65–66, 67; mismanagement by, 63–64; widow as, 75, 105, 115, 134
Exile/expulsion, 12, 14, 15, 22, 75, 79

Ferrer i Mallol, M. T., 36
Font Rius, J. M., 30
Fourth, Falcidian or Trebellianic, 2, 91, 237, 241
France: Jews emigrate from, 96; Jews expelled from, 12, 14, 75, 79
Fraud, in wills, 58–65
Funeral arrangements, 25–26; in wills, 24, 75, 127–128, 129, 130, 133, 138

Garbell, Irene, 80
García Arenal, Mercedes, 35
Geniza wills, 24, 25, 126–131, 137–138, 139; Latinate wills compared to, 130–131
Goitein, Shlomo, 5, 7, 115; on autonomous parallel states, 199 n.10; on burial practices, 25–26; on executors, 24, 26; on Geniza wills, 126–131, 137–138, 139; on inheritance laws, 38; on Islamic courts, 25; on Jewish scribes, 44; on names, 78; on wills as testamentary, 22, 23
Grau Montserrat, Manuel, 118
Gruny, Jaume, 56
Guardian, 80, 81, 82, 93, 134; widow as, 105, 116

Hebrew: marriage documents in, 43; as official language, 43–44; wills in,

22, 26–27, 29, 30–31, 46, 69, 126–131
Heir, universal, 2, 69, 80, 82, 83, 84, 89–90, 91, 97, 99, 102, 103, 104, 105, 107, 108, 112–113, 114, 116, 125, 130, 134, 242; wife as, 121
Hualart, Guillem, 97
Huesca, 34, 35

Iancu-Agou, Danièle, 126
Ibn 'Abdūn, 33
Ibn Adret, Solomon, 31, 44, 49, 50, 55–56, 211 n.44
Ibn Khaldūn, 36
Ibn Vives, Salamó, 62, 63
Immigration, Jewish: to Arago-Catalonia, 12–16; to Majorca, 75, 77, 79, 96
Inheritance laws, 2, 91; Jewish, 23–24, 38, 100, 114, 115, 116; Muslim, 24, 36–37, 38; Roman, 2, 23–24. *See also* Heir, universal
Islam. *See* Muslims
Italy, 3, 29, 39

Jacobs, Joseph, 71
Jahudà de la Cavalleria, 55
Jahudà of Limoux, 58–60
Jaume I (the Conqueror), 11, 18, 20, 21, 73, 74, 95, 96, 124; on autonomous community, 47; exchange rate established by, 8, 9, 61; intercedes for Muslim subjects, 37; intervenes in Jewish wills, 55, 56–57, 65, 66, 67, 68–70; on notaries and scribes, 34, 39, 41, 42–43; on Roman law, 30, 32; on validity of documents, 51–53
Jaume II of Arago–Catalonia (the Just), 11, 15, 34–35, 41, 47, 48, 49, 52, 62, 73, 74
Jaume II of Majorca, 52, 68, 73, 74, 102
Jaume III of Majorca, 73, 74, 102
Jews: Ashkenazic, 14; Arabic-speaking, 15, 41; aristocratic, 16; burial societies of, 26; in business, 41–42, 46, 72, 75, 78–79, 96; and Christians, 19–20, 30, 41–42, 46, 49–52, 72, 115–116; communities of, 17–22, 38, 46–48, 53, 111; converted, 20–21, 29; expelled or exiled, 12, 14, 15, 22, 75, 79; in Italy, 3; king's relationship with, 15, 18, 20, 21, 31, 47, 48, 51–52, 53–54, 55, 56–57, 58–65, 66, 67, 68–70, 74, 75, 91–93, 118–119, 132, 134–135; laws of, 23–24, 38, 51–52, 54, 68, 100, 114, 115, 116; literacy of, 44; in Majorca, 51, 74, 75–99; in medicine, 15; in Occitania, 13–14; parallel society of, 17–22, 38; in Perpignan, 74, 78–95; in Puigcerdá, 74, 95–99, 109; religious-intellectual clashes of, 16; Sephardic, 3, 80; sōfer (*see* Scribe, Jewish); in Valencia, 47–48; wills of (*see* Wills)
Joan I, 49
Jordan, William Chester, 14

Katz, Jacob, 201 n.21
Katz, Solomon, 17
King: as appeal court, 31, 37, 53; executors appointed by, 65–66, 67; intercedes in Jewish-Christian relationships, 51–54; intercedes in wills, 31, 54–72, 118–119, 134–135; Jews at court of, 15, 21; as legatee, 61, 62, 65, 91–93, 132; notaries and scribes appointed or validated by, 34–35, 36, 38, 39, 40, 41, 42–43, 46–47, 48; upholds Hebrew law, 51–52, 54, 68
Kolatch, Alfred, 7

Law, 91; Jewish, 23–24, 38, 51–52, 54, 68, 100, 114, 115, 116; Muslim, 24, 36–37, 38; Roman, 2, 23–24, 30, 32
Legitima, 2
Lérida: scribes in, 34, 35, 44–45, 48; wills in, 58–60
Lewis, Bernard, 31
Liber Iudeorum, 96, 98, 103, 111
Liber testamentorum, 100
Llull, Ramon, 12, 16

Magdalena Nom de Déu, J. R., 209–210 n.31
Majorca, Kingdom of, 73–99; Jews in, 51, 74, 75–99. *See also* Jaume II of Majorca; Occitania; Perpignan; Puigcerdá
Malkiel, David, 3

Marín Padilla, Encarnacíon, 28, 29
Marriage, documents for, 43, 51–52. *See also* Dowry
Massacre of 1391, 22, 27, 28, 111
Mauri, Bernat, 100
Melammed, Renée, 100, 116
Melechen, Nina, 7
Millás Vallicrosa, J. M., 101–102
Miret i Sans, Joaquim, 5, 70
Moneylenders, Jews as, 78–79, 96
Monopoly, notaries and scribes have, 41–42, 47, 49
Montpellier, 73, 81
Motis Dolader, M. A., 28
Muslims, 11; appeal to king, 37; in Aragon, 12, 33–38; in Catalonia, 18; conquered, 18; converted, 20–21; court of, 25; *dhimma* status of, 17–19; inheritance laws of, 24, 36–37, 38; Jews flee from, 15; scribes of (*see* Scribes, Muslim); toleration of, 18; use Christian or Jewish scribe, 35–36; in Valencia, 37; wills of, 36
Mutgé, Josefa, 35
Mysticism, 16

Nahmanides, 21, 60
Names, 4–8, 55, 62, 70, 98, 99, 112, 113, 118, 119–120, 121, 122, 123–124; Arabic, 6, 7; assimilation revealed by, 5, 6; Christian, 5–6, 7; courtesy titles in, 7; Jewish, 4–6, 7, 16, 77–78, 79, 135; Judeo-Arabic, 16, 77–78, 135; in Latinate wills, 135; in Perpignan, 84–85; in Puigcerdá, 103–104, 105–106, 109; Romance, 4–5; Sephardic, 80; women's, 5, 6, 7–8, 90
Neuman, Abraham, 31, 46, 49, 53
Nicholas III, Pope, 16
Nirenberg, David, 47
Notaries: in Barcelona, 39, 40, 41–42; Christian, 27–28, 30, 31, 38–43, 48–49, 71, 72, 131; crown-authorized, 39, 40, 41, 42–43; fee for, 132–133; functions of, 39–40; in Italy, 39; jurisdiction of, 38–39; monopolies by, 41–42, 49; for Muslim community, 35–36; numbers of, 39, 49; professionalize, 38; restrictions on, 40–41; rivals of, 48–49; special, 40–43, 46; wills by, 27–29, 30, 31, 33, 40, 45, 71, 72

Occitania, 11, 12; Jews in, 13–14, 79; wills in, 29, 122–126, 135
Oliana, Mateu de, 97

Palma de Mallorca, 73, 74–78
Penyafort, Ramon de, 12, 56
Pere I (II of Aragon), 55
Pere III (the Great), 9, 11, 21, 34, 58–59, 60–61, 68, 74
Pere IV (the Ceremonious), 35, 36, 52, 57–58, 64, 74, 118
Perpignan: as capital of Majorca, 73; Jews in, 74, 78–95; names in, 84–85; wills in, 57, 65–67
Pons i Guri, Josep, 45
Puigcerdá, 73; Jews in, 74, 95–99, 109; names in, 103–104, 105–106, 109; wills in, 32, 33, 100–117, 119–122

Rabbi, functions of, 31, 46–47, 211 n.44
Régné, Jean, 5, 118, 119
Romance: names, 4–5; wills, 23, 27–28
Romano, David, 61, 62
Roth, Norman, 18, 53

Salamó, Cresques, 58
Salamó of Tortosa, 69
Salamó Samiel, 65
Sanç I of Majorca, 73, 74, 75, 91, 93
Schwab, Moïse, 70
Scola, 101–102
Scribe, Jewish (sōfer), 40–42, 43–49, 131; in Barcelona, 44, 45; bilingual, 41; in Christian court, 51; Christian notary rivals, 48–49; functions of, 44–45, 46; hereditary position of, 47; king appoints, 46–47, 48; in Lérida, 44–45, 48; monopoly of, 47; for Muslim community, 35–36; validity of work of, 52; wills by, 28, 33; in Zaragoza, 48, 51–52
Scribes: Christian (*see* Notaries, Christian); as family-held positions, 34, 35, 47; Muslim, 33–38, 131; role of, 36, 48–49
Secall i Güell, Gabriel, 111, 118

Sephardic Jews, 3, 80
Septimus, Bernard, 15–16
Seror, Simon, 6, 8; on names, 90, 104, 112, 118, 120, 121
Shatzmiller, Joseph, 2, 124, 125
Sicily, 29
Slavery, 9, 129, 134
Sōfer. See Scribe, Jewish
Sunna, 52, 68, 241

Tallan, Cheryl, 100
Tarragona, 110, 111
Testament sacramental, 24–25
Toaff, Ariel, 29
Tomàs, Bartolomé, 43
Tourtoulon, Charles de, 30

Udina i Abelló, Antoni, 32

Valencia: Jews in, 47–48; Muslims in, 34, 35, 37; Roman law in, 32; scribes in, 34, 35; wills in, 32, 57, 62–63
Valls, 110–113
Vidal de Montpeller, 81–83
Vives family, 29

Waley, Daniel, 39
Webster, Jill, 118
Wernham, Monique, 126
Wills, 78–95, 102; archival use of, 1–2; in Barcelona, 60; as business document, 127–129; in Castile, 32; charity in (*see* Charitable bequests); Christian, 32, 49–50, 116, 135–136; codicils to, 122; conversionism affects, 29; copied, 111, 132, 133; cost of, 32–33; as disposition, 22, 23, 24, 28, 36, 127–131, 137; double, 29, 30–31, 46, 69; dowry in (*see* Dowry); ethical, 26; fraud in, 58–65; funeral arrangements in, 24, 75, 127–128, 129, 130, 133, 138; Geniza, 24, 25, 126–131, 137–138, 139; guardian appointed in, 80, 81, 82, 93, 105, 116, 134; king intercedes in, 31, 54–72, 118–119, 134–135; king as legatee in, 61, 62, 65, 91–93, 132; Latinate, 2, 3, 23–24, 29, 30–31, 46, 68–71, 113–114, 115, 116–117, 118, 122–126, 130–131, 135–136; law on (*see* Heir, universal; Inheritance laws); Muslim, 36; notarial, 27–29, 30, 31, 33, 45, 71, 72; Occitan, 29, 122–126, 135; oral, 45; in Perpignan, 57, 65–67; protested, 56–57; in Provence, 124–126; in Puigcerdá, 30, 33, 100–117, 119–122; requirements for, 45–46; in Sicily, 29; slaves in, 129, 134; as tapestry, 137; as testamentary, 22, 23, 36; in Valencia, 32, 57, 62–63; as window, 2, 3; witnessed (*see* Witness); women in, 100–117; women make, 28, 87–90, 95, 101–104, 106–107, 111–113, 114, 116, 119–121, 127, 129
Winer, Rebecca, 89, 90, 233
Witness, 45, 62–63, 77, 79–80, 81, 97–98, 102, 105, 113; Christian, 83, 87, 89, 94, 95, 99, 107, 108, 110, 114, 120, 122, 124, 133; function of, 24, 25, 26, 128, 129, 131; number of, 210–211 n.39; testimony by, 59, 60
Women: as executors, 75, 105, 115, 134; as guardians, 105, 116; names of, 5, 6, 7–8, 90; position/influence of, 100; as universal heir, 121; wills by, 28, 87–90, 95, 101–104, 106–109, 111–113, 114, 116, 119–121, 127, 129; in wills, 100–117

Yaron, Reuven, 23

Zaragoza, 27–28, 34, 58, 51–52

Designer:	U.C. Press Staff
Compositor:	The Maple-Vail Book Manufacturing Group
Text:	10/13 Galliard
Display:	Galliard
Printer & Binder:	The Maple-Vail Book Manufacturing Group